Felix Klos is a historian who has had access to unpublished Churchill papers and archives. He undertook his research at the Universities of Oxford and Cambridge and in archives throughout Europe.

'An exceptionally well crafted work of history. Politically, what is particularly important about it is the way that Churchill's argument was not about economics, but about the political need for collaboration between European states as a way of avoiding the return of small nation protectionism and the political antagonisms to which it gave rise.'

Professor Gareth Stedman Jones, King's College,
University of Cambridge

'A deeply researched and beautifully written exploration of a largely forgotten historical moment – Churchill's postwar campaign for a United Europe. This new study expertly brings together the political and the personal and conjures up the intrigue and passion of hobnobbing and negotiations above the rubble of destruction. This is a timely reminder of where the European dream came from and how, even at that time, it was derailed by short-sighted British politicians of both Right and Left.'

Professor Robert Gildea, University of Oxford,
winner of the Wolfson History Prize

'This accessible and thoroughly researched study explores Churchill's extraordinary contribution to the original emergence of the European "project", and will challenge muddled explanations of his thinking on Europe. An important book which could not have come at a better time.'

Dr Sue Onslow, Institute of Commonwealth Studies

'All historical writing speaks to the present through the past, but it is rare, very rare, to find a work of scholarship that is as decisively relevant as Felix Klos's portrait of Winston Churchill in his later career as a champion of Europeanism. This scrupulous, elegant book rejuvenates for the twenty-first century the prophetic vision of one of the towering figures of the twentieth.'

Vijay Seshadri, author, essayist and winner of the 2014 Pulitzer Prize

'All politicians suffer from having their words misquoted or taken out of context, but the posthumous conflicts over the precise nature of Churchill's views on European integration are probably in a class of their own. Timely, erudite and absorbing.'

Professor Peter Catterall, editor of *The Macmillan Diaries*

CHURCHILL'S LAST STAND

The Struggle to Unite Europe

FELIX KLOS

I.B. TAURIS
LONDON · NEW YORK

Published in 2018 by
I.B.Tauris & Co. Ltd
London • New York
www.ibtauris.com

ISBN: 978 1 78453 813 2
eISBN: 978 1 78672 292 8
ePDF: 978 1 78673 292 7

A full CIP record for this book is available from the British Library
A full CIP record is available from the Library of Congress

Library of Congress Catalog Card Number: available

Typeset in Stone Serif by OKS Prepress Services, Chennai, India
Printed and bound in Sweden by ScandBook AB

Why is it that you, Sir Winston, became the champion for the European ideal?
I believe this can be explained from two human qualities that also are the requisite
qualities for statesmanship: greatness of thought, depth of feeling.

(Konrad Adenauer addressing Churchill in 1956 at the occasion of the
awarding of the Charlemagne Prize, the highest honour for service to
European unity)

CONTENTS

LIST OF PLATES

PLATE 1 Prime Minister Winston Churchill in 1942. (US Library of Congress, Licensed by Wikimedia Commons)

PLATE 2 Winston Churchill, Harry Truman and Joseph Stalin at the Potsdam Conference in July 1945. The Leader of the Labour Party Clement Attlee was also in attendance, as the results of the 1945 General Election were not yet known in Britain. Churchill would learn during the conference that the Conservative Party he led had lost power in the United Kingdom. (US National Archives, Licensed by Wikimedia Commons)

PLATE 3 Count Richard Nikolaus Coudenhove-Kalergi (standing) at the welcome during the Pan-Europe Congress in Berlin, 1930. On the right sits his wife Ida Roland, actress. Count Coudenhove-Kalergi was one of the earliest driving forces behind greater European integration. (Photo by Imagno/Getty Images)

PLATE 4 A crowd gathered to hear Winston Churchill speak in Zurich, 1946. Churchill argued in the speech for 'a kind of United States of Europe' to preserve peace. (Photo by Hans Staub/Alinari Archives, Florence/Alinari via Getty Images)

PLATE 5 Commemorative plaque for the speech of Winston Churchill on 19 September 1946 at the University of Zurich. The final line translates into English as 'Let Europe arise!' (Wikimedia Commons)

PLATE 6 Duncan Sandys, British politician and Joint Secretary of the United Europe Movement, addressing a conference in the Ridderzaal at The Hague,

29 January 1948. Duncan Sandys (1908–87) was a key ally of Churchill's European project, as well as his son-in-law. (Original Publication: Picture Post – 4548 – Is Europe Nearer Union? Photo by Kurt Hutton/Picture Post/ Getty Images).

PLATE 7 United Europe poster. The official public inauguration of what ultimately came to be known as Churchill's United Europe Movement took place at the Royal Albert Hall on 14 May 1947. Five thousand United Europe posters were placed across London ahead of the meeting. At Churchill's instructions, a large red and white banner with the words 'EUROPE ARISE!' hung from the hall's ceiling. (Photo Credit: Historical Archives of the European Union, Florence. File 808.)

PLATE 8 Sir Winston Churchill speaks at the United Europe Movement at the Royal Albert Hall event on 14 May 1947. (Photo found in *Europe Unites: The Hague Conference and After*, published London 1949. Photographer unknown.)

PLATE 9 Churchill and Eden in London, 1954. Anthony Eden would successfully help discourage Churchill from pursuing his European plans. (Photo by Keystone-France/Gamma-Keystone via Getty Images)

ACKNOWLEDGEMENTS

For generously helping me set up the narrative of the book and sharpening my thinking, I am most grateful to my supervisor at Worcester College, Oxford, Robert Gildea; Anne Deighton at Wolfson College, Oxford; Sue Onslow at the Institute of Commonwealth Studies; Peter Catterall at the University of Westminster; Patricia Clavin at Jesus College, Oxford; Alan Packwood at Churchill College, Cambridge; Warren Dockter at Aberystwyth University; and Lord Watson of Richmond. For a stellar education and unwavering academic enthusiasm I am indebted to my tutors at Lincoln College, Oxford, Susan Brigden, Perry Gauci and Alana Harris; and my supervisors at Middlebury College, Michael Kraus and Allison Stanger.

For his patient, expert help in preparing a draft manuscript, my thanks are due to Mitchell Byrne. I am indebted to Stefan Curtress, Alexander Wilson, Matthijs Terhoeve and Oliver Baines for their invaluable assistance in my research travels.

I must also thank for their expertise and kind help the staffs at the Churchill Archives Centre (Cambridge), the Bodleian Library (Oxford), the National Archives (Kew), the British Library (London), the University of Zurich University Archives, the Zurich Cantonal Archives, the Dutch National Archives (The Hague), the Amsterdam Municipal Archives, the Strasbourg Municipal Archives, the University of Strasbourg Archives, and the Departmental Archives of the Bas-Rhin.

My greatest thanks are to my parents, Sven and Tina, and my brother and best friend, Caspar.

CHAPTER 1

'SOMETHING THAT WILL ASTONISH YOU'
ZURICH, 19 SEPTEMBER 1946

On Thursday 19 September 1946 Winston Spencer Churchill gave a speech at the University of Zurich that changed the world. The speech marked the beginning of the postwar process of European integration and prepared the ground for one of the most successful inventions of peaceful cooperation in human history: the European Union. For Churchill personally the speech was a pivotal point of his life and career. After a lifetime shaped by the devastation of two world wars it was his manifesto for what – at the age of 71 – he was determined would be his legacy: a permanent *Pax Europaea*.

A little over a year earlier, in July 1945, Churchill's political life had seemed all but finished. He had suffered a crushing defeat in the British general election and the magnitude of the loss was a painful humiliation for the prime minister who had been credited with saving Western civilisation in World War II. Churchill's Conservatives lost more than half of their seats – from 432 at the previous election they now had just 213. The rest of the world received the news with stupefaction. Joseph Stalin, who together with US President Truman was waiting for Churchill to return to the conference table at Potsdam after an election that looked like a formality, was mystified as to why Churchill had not been able to fix the results.[1]

To make matters worse, after tendering his resignation to the King at Buckingham Palace, Churchill had no home to return to. Chartwell, his beloved country house in Kent, was not yet habitable after the war; while the prime minister's official residence was turned over to Labour's Clement Attlee, and his London apartment near Victoria station had been sold in 1939. For some time the Churchills lived in the sixth-floor penthouse of the Claridge's Hotel, until Churchill's daughter Diana and her husband Duncan Sandys lent them their apartment in Westminster Gardens. There was a grim farewell Cabinet meeting on Friday 27 July, after which Churchill told his heir apparent and wartime foreign minister Anthony Eden: 'Thirty years of my life have been passed in this room. I shall never sit in it again. You will, but I shall not.'[2]

That weekend the family went to Chequers, the prime minister's official country home in Buckinghamshire, to collect their belongings and spend one last weekend in the place where they had lived through so much. It brought Churchill no happiness. There were the usual dinners and after-dinner movies, but none of the 'red boxes' containing secret information which Churchill thought of as oxygen for his restless mind. 'We saw with near desperation a cloud of black gloom descend,' recalled his daughter.[3] Before leaving Chequers everyone signed the Visitors' Book. Churchill went last and wrote beneath his signature a single word: 'Finis'.

A fortnight after the election his doctor found him sitting in his silk vest on his bed in his temporary home. 'It's no use pretending that I'm not hard hit,' he muttered. 'I can't school myself to do nothing for the rest of my life. It would have been better to have been killed in an aeroplane, or to have died like Roosevelt.'[4]

A few days later, perhaps conscious of his state of mind, he accepted an invitation from General Alexander, Supreme Allied Commander in the Mediterranean and a close friend, to go to his villa on Lake Como in Italy for a period of quiet rest. It was there and then, that painting, his lifelong source of solace, came to his rescue once again. As he picked up his brushes and opened his paintbox Churchill slowly began to heal from the wounds left by the election defeat, his harsh rejection by the British people.

Within three days of arriving at Alexander's villa, Churchill wrote to his wife that the holiday was doing him no end of good. 'This is the first time for very many years that I have been completely out of the world,' he told Clemmie. He had to concede that she might have been right about the election outcome: 'It may all indeed be a "blessing in disguise"'.[5]

In the months that passed between the Italian holiday and the day of his speech at the University of Zurich, Churchill found a new energy and resolve. He began to fully immerse himself in politics and the problems of the postwar world. Europe lay shattered, physically and morally defeated after two world wars, the second of which was the deadliest conflict in human history. As the world slowly learned the full extent of the atrocities perpetrated by the Nazi regime through the trials at Nuremberg, the alliance of victors – Great Britain, the United States and Russia – began to unravel. It became increasingly obvious to Churchill that Soviet Russia intended to extend its sphere of influence to the heart of Europe. On 5 March 1946 he warned the world in his famous 'Sinews of Peace' speech at Fulton, Missouri, that an 'iron curtain' had descended from Stettin in the Baltic to Trieste in the Adriatic.

It is often forgotten now that world opinion recoiled at the audacity of Churchill's Fulton address. Less than a year after the end of World War II no one wanted to face up to a new peril to world peace coming from the East. No one dared to challenge the Soviet Union after its armies so courageously wiped Nazi Germany out of eastern Europe. No one wanted to accept the division of Europe so soon after its liberation. The Russians, needless to say, expressed outrage at Churchill's words. US President Truman took more than two months to decide to publicly stand with Churchill. British dismay at the speech went so far that a motion of censure was proposed against Churchill in the House of Commons.

A largely ignored and now often forgotten aspect of the Iron Curtain speech was that it called for 'a new unity in Europe from which no nation should be permanently outcast'.[6] And yet it was this idea that would play a dominant role in Churchill's postwar political life. As he saw it, the only way to secure lasting peace after the devastation of the first half of the twentieth century was to build a European union. 'If I were 10 years younger,' he told his wife shortly after arriving back from Italy, 'I might be the first President of the United States of Europe.'[7]

Churchill's depression after being ousted from government in July 1945 was rooted in a deep sense of disappointment – he thought himself robbed of the chance to help build a lasting peace as Britain's prime minister. Now leader of the Opposition in the House of Commons, he held no executive power over British foreign policy. After five years of wartime government there was little glory, in his view, to be won in restructuring the Conservative Party or debating the ins and outs of the domestic economy in committee meetings.

Churchill, however, soon sensed that there was another way to make his mark on the postwar world. The publicity attracted by the Fulton speech taught him that his standing as Britain's indomitable wartime leader gave him free rein to speak on any topic that interested him. The mere mention of his name commanded the attention of audiences around the globe. If he picked his battles with care his influence would still be felt far and wide. As Churchill's son-in-law, Duncan Sandys, told him in a handwritten note on the eve of the Zurich speech:

> I am waiting impatiently to hear your Zurich speech. It is coming at a very good moment. The allied Governments have had plenty of time to hammer out some solution to the European problem and have quite obviously failed. I am sure that in the present circumstances the public in all countries is very much in the mood to listen to what the late pilot has got to say.[8]

On his way to deliver his address in Zurich, Churchill made a stop in the city of Bern. On 18 September 1946, the people of Bern packed the pavements four rows deep, piled out of every window and climbed onto their rooftops to catch a glimpse of this hero of the West. 'The enthusiasm evoked by Mr. Churchill's visit', wrote the British minister in Bern in his official report, 'eclipsed, so I was assured by those who should know, any reception received by any other figure in living memory.'[9]

Churchill sat in an open, gleaming, horse-driven carriage, with outriders in eighteenth-century costume. A friendly autumn wind swept up cigar ashes and strands of his thin grey hair as he waved his black John Bull hat at his admirers, clutching in his left hand a slim walking stick in anticipation of the end of the ride. With the assistance of his youngest daughter, Mary, Churchill dismounted the carriage right in front of the City Hall to deliver some remarks. The local authorities had made it clear that they expected no more of their 71-year-old visitor than stick to pleasantries and generalities.

Churchill's mind, however, was fully occupied with the address he was scheduled to deliver the next morning. He decided to give the people of Bern a foretaste of what he was planning to say. 'I hope', he said, looking out over the fully packed square before him, 'that we will see the day that Europe is as peacefully united and conscious of its fundamental values, as capable and prepared for future challenges, as is the happy, sunlit country that you have presented to me today.'[10]

During his visit to Bern he spent every spare minute preparing for the Zurich address.[11] Churchill, as was his habit of a lifetime, was working against a tight deadline to get his speech down to the finest of detail. He crafted and weighed every word and phrase with equal care. Though the ideas had been brewing in his mind for some time, he first dictated a draft to one of his travelling secretaries during the two-hour train ride from Bern to Zurich on the evening of Wednesday 18 September.

Churchill arrived just before 6 p.m. at the Zurich central train station to a welcoming committee headed by the British consul-general in Zurich, Eric Grant Cable. Cable was a thorn in Churchill's side. He had foolishly urged the Grand Old Man in a letter two days earlier to refrain from making any political statements in Zurich. 'What else would I speak of, if not politics?' Churchill exclaimed angrily when he first read Cable's warning.[12] Still fuming over the audacity of the letter, he refused to shake Cable's hand.

From the station Churchill was chauffeured to the Grand Dolder Hotel – a fairy-tale winter resort standing atop Zurich's highest hill – where he read parts of his draft speech to a small dinner party. The event lasted well into the night, giving the attending Swiss diplomats valuable insights into Churchill's thinking and intentions. He ended up leaving his company around 1 a.m. and working through dawn to nail down the last details of the speech.

Churchill went into the morning of Thursday 19 September with the same nervous energy that had carried him through the night. With the ruddiness gone from his face he looked frighteningly fragile.

Just before 10 a.m. Mary and her father motored down from the Dolder Hotel.[13] A stiff breeze blew through the crowns of lightly yellowed trees. In spite of a constant drizzle, the crowds were so great that the university gates had to be closed more than two hours before Churchill was scheduled to arrive.[14] After the official pre-lecture reception by the Zurich city government, Churchill and Mary walked towards the main entrance of the university through a student guard of honour.

Mary, wearing a fashionable bright red-velvet hat and holding a large bouquet of flowers, took her place in the front row. Anxiously bobbing her feet up and down, she worried her father was too old now to work through dawn and was pushing himself too hard. All rose as Churchill walked into the great hall. A male student choir burst into song. Churchill sat down in an armchair next to the podium waiting for the rector to finish a long-winded address of welcome.[15]

At 11.15 a.m. Churchill mounted the stage of the opulent, marble-clad hall. Usually the atmosphere under the cupola of the auditorium – an early twentieth-century addition to the ancient university – was rather cold. Now wreaths of yellow autumn flowers adorned the rostrum and galleries on either side of the auditorium. Twelve students in medieval costumes and feathered hats positioned themselves on both sides holding immense glittering standard-bearers representing various student societies.

Before Churchill the Zurich professors and their guests sat in expectant concentration. Behind him, in Paul Bodmer's vast naturalistic mural, a group of languid young women in long free-flowing dresses looked down in indifferent silence. Outside in the grass court flocks of students clustered round loud-speakers, which had been set up for the address, in hushed silence.

Churchill opened simply and quietly: 'I wish to speak to you today about the tragedy of Europe.'[16] He read his speech with plain, unaffected gestures, sometimes emphasising a word or a short sentence in a serene, undemonstrative tone.[17]

'This noble continent,' he said,

> comprising on the whole the fairest and the most cultivated regions of the earth, enjoying a temperate and equable climate, is the home of all the great parent races of the Western world. It is the foundation of Christian faith and ethics. It is the origin of most of the culture, arts, philosophy and science both of ancient and modern times. If Europe were once united in the sharing of its common inheritance there would be no limit to the happiness, prosperity and glory which its 300 million or 400 million people would enjoy.[18]

'Yet it is from Europe', Churchill went on, 'that have sprung that series of frightful nationalistic quarrels, originated by the Teutonic nations in their rise to power, which we have seen even in this twentieth century and in our own lifetime wreck the peace and mar the prospects of all mankind.'[19] He continued, diagnosing the European illness and preparing his audience for a bold cure:

> And what is this plight to which Europe has been reduced? Some of the smaller states have indeed made a good recovery, but over wide areas a vast, quivering mass of tormented, hungry, careworn and bewildered human beings gape at the ruins of their cities and homes, and scan the dark horizons for the approach of some new peril, tyranny or terror. Among the victors there is a babel of jarring voices; among the vanquished the sullen silence of despair. That is all that Europeans, grouped in so many ancient States and nations, that is all that the Germanic Powers have got by tearing each other to pieces and spreading havoc far and wide.[20]

Had the American military stayed at home after the Nazi invasion, Churchill told his audience, Europe would have fallen into a deep and potentially permanent darkness. As he put it: 'Indeed, but for the fact that the great Republic across the Atlantic Ocean has at length realised that the ruin or enslavement of Europe would involve their own fate as well, and stretched out hands of succour and guidance, the Dark Ages would have returned in all their cruelty and squalor.' And then, lifting his head with emphasis directly addressing his audience: 'Gentlemen; they may still return.'[21]

Having prepared his ground, Churchill turned to the heart of his message: 'Yet all the while there is a remedy, which, if it were generally and spontaneously adopted, would as if by a miracle transform the whole scene, and would in a few years make all Europe, or the greater part of it, as free and as happy as Switzerland is to-day.' 'What is this sovereign remedy?' he asked.

> It is to recreate the European Family, or as much of it as we can, and provide it with a structure under which it can dwell in peace, in safety and in freedom. We must build a kind of United States of Europe.[22]

Here was the key to securing lasting freedom, peace and prosperity for all of Europe. But how to get there? How to build a system as strong and stable as that of the United States of America out of the ruins of Europe? 'The process is simple,' he said. All that was needed to bring it about was 'the resolve of hundreds of millions of men and women to do right instead of wrong and gain as their reward blessing instead of cursing'.[23]

Churchill credited his predecessors in the interwar pan-European movement for their exertions, making it clear that his was a new course in the long history of the European ideal. He deliberately wrestled the idea out of the hands of dreamers and philosophers and placed it in the realm of the politically possible with a clever reference to President Truman's support for this 'great design'.[24] As he said so often in 1946, Churchill believed that the regional organisation of Europe would only serve to strengthen rather than undermine the work of the recently founded United Nations. 'Why', he asked, 'should there not be a European group which could give a sense of enlarged patriotism and common citizenship to the distracted peoples of this turbulent and mighty continent and why should it not take its rightful place with the other great groupings in shaping the destinies of man?'[25] Only 'an act of faith' could bring about this revolutionary transformation in world politics. Millions of families speaking many languages had to come to the table to make it possible, hence the Swiss example.

Now Churchill turned to one of the most delicate parts of his speech. The European Family that he wished to see united, by historical and geographical definition, included Germany, or, depending on one's viewpoint, the many German-speaking states and principalities of old. He left his audience in no doubt as to where the two world wars originated. They arose 'out of the vain passion of a newly-united Germany to play the dominating part in the world'. For the crimes and massacres that were committed by the Germans there was no equal at any time in human history. This deserved appropriate sanctioning: 'The guilty must be punished. Germany must be deprived of the power to rearm and make another aggressive war.'[26]

Dearly bought experience, however, had taught Churchill that if retribution and vengeance were allowed to break the fibre of German society yet another war could come sooner rather than later. And what to think of the new Soviet threat in the East? Churchill was anxious to keep Germany as a possible ally in case of Soviet incursion. He continued with a statement as striking in its strategic foresight as its fundamental humanity:

> But when all this has been done, as it will be done, as it is being done, there must be an end to retribution. There must be what Mr. Gladstone many years ago called 'a blessed act of oblivion'. We must all turn our backs upon the horrors of the past and look to the future.[27]

This was a stunning and for most Europeans premature offer of reconciliation to a country whose leaders little more than a year ago had fought tooth and nail to maintain their five-year-long occupation of Europe. Churchill looked ahead to a new Europe – a united Europe that urgently needed the goodwill and cooperation of all its peoples, including the Germans.

As if his listeners were not already sufficiently bewildered, Churchill warned that he was now going to say something that would 'astonish' them. It was six months since his Iron Curtain speech had sent shockwaves of disbelief through West and East alike, and his audience held its breath. He called upon France and Germany to enter into a partnership as the first step in building 'a kind of United States of Europe'. 'There can be no revival of Europe without a spiritually great France and a spiritually great Germany,' he declared, assuring the small states that the material strength of a single state would be made unimportant by the new European structure.[28]

The idea of a spiritually great Germany bound in power and ambition by France and the rest of Europe evoked, perhaps deliberately, the famous words of the French playwright Victor Hugo, spoken in the French National Assembly on 1 March 1871, right after the first of three consecutive Franco-German wars. Churchill kept an excerpt of Hugo's speech among his personal papers: 'And we shall hear France say "It is my turn. Germany here I am! Am I your enemy? No! I am your sister. Everything I have retaken I will return to you on one condition. It is that we shall in future act as one people, one family, one republic. I will destroy my fortresses if you destroy yours. My revenge is brotherhood."'[29] Within the broader idea of the United States of Europe, the specific method of

Franco-German reconciliation was the most controversial piece of thinking Churchill put before the world.

Churchill deliberately and with some emphasis left open the question of whether either the individual German states or a single federated Germany should be invited to join the new European structure. 'The ancient states and principalities of Germany,' he said, 'freely joined together for mutual convenience in a federal system, might each take their individual place among the United States of Europe.'[30] This idea was in accordance with US Secretary of State James Byrnes's recent speech at Stuttgart in favour of a federal Germany. It may also have been loosely based on Churchill's intimate knowledge of the foreign policy ambitions of postwar Germany's budding political leaders.

Months before the Zurich address, Konrad Adenauer, leader of the Christian Democrats in the British occupation zone and later the first chancellor of the German Federal Republic, became one of the first and foremost among them to back the idea of the United States of Europe. In the summer of 1946 Duncan Sandys went on a mission for his father-in-law, using his German network to get to Adenauer and take his temperature. In a long conversation in Cologne, Sandys learned that Adenauer hoped a federal Germany would be included in a federal Europe. Sandys was impressed by the former mayor of Cologne, just a year younger than Churchill but evidently in the springtime of his political career, and of all the Germans he met he thought him the most capable to govern a federal Germany one day.[31]

This was about as far as Churchill was willing to go into the scope and function of the United States of Europe. It became a recurring theme in the postwar years for him to warn against elaborate, precipitate constitution-making and detailed programmes for integration. It was essential first to build overwhelming enthusiasm for the idea in all corners of the continent. The 'act of faith' he spoke of involved millions of European citizens consciously taking part in the transformation of their continent and relied on a massive and urgent campaign of public education. There was no one better suited to lead that campaign than Churchill himself. His standing in the world right after the liberation of Europe is difficult to fully comprehend today. No man since has reached his heights of popularity and influence in the Western world. Churchill felt it was his role to light the torch; others would do the rest.[32]

In the spirit of the public campaign he was planning, Churchill issued a last urgent warning:

> Time may be short. At present there is a breathing-space. The cannons have ceased firing. The fighting has stopped; but the dangers have not stopped. If we are to

form a United States of Europe or whatever name or form it may take, we must begin now.[33]

In 1946 Europe and the West lived under 'the shield and protection of the atomic bomb'. The United States was the only nation to possess this weapon and it would, Churchill, thought, 'never use it except in the cause of right and freedom'. He foresaw that it would not be long until other nations would get a hold of the bomb. Its use by 'several warring nations', he cautioned, 'will not only bring to an end all that we call civilisation, but may possibly disintegrate the globe itself'.[34] Churchill was careful to offer peaceful cooperation with Soviet Russia, but his reference to the danger of the atomic bomb falling into the wrong hands was unmistakably directed at Stalin. The West, he thought, should conclude a postwar settlement from a position of strength – before the Soviets were able to develop their own bomb.

The speech closed with a summary of the propositions before Europe and the world. 'Our constant aim', he began, 'must be to build and fortify the United Nations Organisation. Under and within that world concept we must re-create the European family in a regional structure called, it may be, the United States of Europe.' Then, suddenly, came an altogether new piece of information. 'The first step', Churchill said, 'is to form a Council of Europe.'[35] The institution would function something like a Petri dish for a European Union: it was designed to cultivate the European spirit and provide a fertile base for organic union.

Finally, there were a few more words on the membership scope of United Europe. 'If at first all the States of Europe are not willing or able to join the Union, we must nevertheless proceed to assemble and combine those who will and those who can.'[36] This alluded directly to the nations behind the Iron Curtain. The communised belt of states near Russia's border were clearly unable at the time to join a political grouping of Western nations. While Churchill accepted the temporary division of Europe, he insisted on keeping the door open for all the free and democratic countries of Europe to join what he hoped would ultimately become a union of all of Europe.[37]

'In all this urgent work,' Churchill declared in the last sentences of the speech, 'France and Germany must take the lead together. Great Britain, the British Commonwealth of Nations, mighty America and, I trust, Soviet Russia – for then indeed all would be well – must be the friends and sponsors of the new Europe and must champion its right to live and shine. Therefore I say to you "Let Europe arise"'!"[38]

A great, prolonged burst of applause was Churchill's due from the academic congregation. The student choir closed the ceremony with a moving rendition of the Swiss national anthem. Churchill dismounted the podium and shuffled out of the auditorium to a standing ovation. On the way out of the hall he told one of the Swiss diplomats closest to him during the Switzerland visit, his eyes twinkling with mischief: 'You see, I didn't talk about the Russians.'[39] Only now did his nervousness dissipate. Only now did a sudden tiredness come over him.

There was no time to go back to bed. Next was a triumphal procession through Zurich's city centre. Churchill's reception from the locals after the speech was even more intense than that in Bern. White roses were scattered in his path as he gave the V-sign, the people of Zurich waving British flags and shouting messages of gratitude. At the very end of the parade, Churchill stepped onto a specially constructed rostrum on the Münsterhof where thousands were packed like sardines to hear him say a few words in public. He echoed that morning's speech, electrifying the crowd with a message of high hope. Europe as a whole, he told them, could be just as successful as the Swiss people in basing its unity on tolerance and overcoming cultural, ethnic and linguistic differences – for the political and economic benefit of all.

That night, the first telegram reaction to the speech arrived for Churchill in the Dolder Hotel. Swiss Foreign Minister Max Petitpierre congratulated Churchill on his 'profound and courageous' address. 'Like you, I am convinced that the health of Europe lies in the union of its people, not as a bloc but following the federalist formula of which my country has centuries-old experience.'[40] The next day, Friday 20 September, Churchill flew back to London. At the airport he asked the Swiss ambassador in Britain for the day's papers. He was waiting with bated breath for the world's reactions to his speech, telling the ambassador in his best 'franglais': 'je suis un peu anxieux about my intervention'.[41]

CHAPTER 2

'VAGUE AND PUZZLING IDEALISM'
1930–1940

Streaks of sunshine splashed on the largest lake in Switzerland and reflected back into the windows of the Palais Wilson, Geneva's waterfront *grande dame* and home to the Assembly Hall of the League of Nations. An Austrian-Japanese philosopher sat tense with excitement in the diplomatic gallery. Thursday 5 September 1929 had been marked in his calendar for months now. The Palais was filled to the brim with delegates, journalists, foreign ministers and prime ministers. Many of them stopped to shake hands and congratulate the philosopher and his wife in the gallery. He had been waiting for this day for nearly seven years. He was, in his own words, 'as happy as a small child under a Christmas tree'.[1]

Count Coudenhove-Kalergi, born the second son of an Austrian diplomat and a Japanese society beauty, grew up in a Bohemian castle in what is now the Czech Republic. He was exceedingly handsome and more than happy to be reminded of it. In his memoirs, the Count cited a passage from Thomas Mann's published diary, which vividly detailed his appearance. Mann wrote of Coudenhove-Kalergi ('one of the best-looking persons I have ever met'):

> Half Japanese, half mixed from the breed of Europe's international nobility, he really represents as one knows, a Eurasiatic type of noble cosmopolite, exceedingly fascinating and giving an average German the feeling of being somewhat provincial. Two folds between his orientally shaped eyes, under a pure, firm and proudly borne forehead, give to his smile the character of earnest determination.[2]

It was more than good looks that helped Coudenhove-Kalergi build a considerable reputation for himself. In 1923, after taking his philosophy doctorate in Vienna, he wrote the book that dominated his career and determined his legacy: *Pan-Europa*. The book was as much a manifesto for a popular advocacy group he had founded a year earlier as it was a philosophical treatment of the idea of European unification. 'The aim of this book', he wrote, 'is to awaken a great political ideal which at present lies dormant in the minds of almost all Europeans.'[3]

Three years later, in the autumn of 1926, Coudenhove-Kalergi's Pan-European Union organised its first large-scale conference. More than 2,000 delegates representing 24 countries attended the four-day Congress in Vienna. Among them were Albert Einstein, Sigmund Freud and Thomas Mann. The delegates unanimously adopted a seven-point programme that, among other things, called for the 'association of all European states which are willing and able to set up a political and economic union, based upon equal rights and peace'.[4] Aristide Briand, then near the height of his powers as foreign minister of France, decided to accept an invitation to become honorary president of Coudenhove-Kalergi's Union. This lent much-needed, practical credibility to a movement otherwise dominated by unrepresentative idealists and dreamers. Backed by one of Europe's most prominent statesmen, the first ever grassroots movement for the unification of Europe was gathering steam.

Briand, an angry-looking man with an iron-grey handlebar moustache, did not notice Coudenhove-Kalergi in the diplomatic gallery as he walked up to the rostrum of the Assembly Hall on Thursday 5 September 1929. Coudenhove-Kalergi admired him greatly as a gifted orator and France's apostle for peace. Briand's address was the much-anticipated high point of the tenth Assembly session of the League of Nations. He had announced two months in advance that he intended to address the question of European unification.

The League, founded after World War I as the world's primary instrument for maintaining peace through collective security and disarmament, was in dire need of the kind of positive attention Briand's revolutionary proposals would bring. Winston Churchill still saw the League as 'a priceless instrument of international comity'. 'If I am asked,' he told the House of Commons, '"How far will you go in support of the Covenant of the League of Nations?" I shall say we ought to go the whole way with the whole lot.'[5] But by 1929 the general public had lost considerable interest and faith in the organisation, mostly because of its failed attempts at postwar disarmament in Europe.

At a quarter to noon, Briand started to speak. He was heard all across Europe in a live broadcast relayed from Berlin. He started by greeting his close friend the German Foreign Minister Gustav Stresemann, who had arrived in Geneva that morning with the rest of the German delegation. There were some generic remarks about the progress of peace and a few words of praise for the British prime minister Ramsay MacDonald, who the previous day had called the extinction of war a moral issue. Briand spoke at length about the virtues of disarmament. Then, finally – just as Coudenhove-Kalergi had started to fear that Briand had had a last-minute change of heart – he turned to his topic:

> I have been associated with the propaganda of an idea which has been greatly canvassed during recent years [...] It has been in the minds of philosophers and poets for generations and now seems to have got a firmer grip on the minds of the people as a whole owing to the fact that it is seemingly a necessity [...] Where you have a group of peoples grouped together geographically, as in Europe, there ought to exist some sort of federal link among them.

That 'federal' link, Briand argued, should have economic, political and social dimensions and would largely keep intact the sovereign rights of the parties involved. He asked the foreign ministers of the European states in the Assembly to 'unofficially consider and study this question in order that later, perhaps at the next Assembly, we may be in a position possibly to translate it into reality'.[6]

Briand's words were received with a stormy applause. Coudenhove-Kalergi suppressed shrieks of excitement. As it stood, the plan for a federal Europe proposed to build on and expand the Locarno system with a view to preventing renewed war, kindling the spirit of solidarity and reconciliation, and burying political and economic hatchets in the whole of Europe. The Locarno Treaties of 1925 were based on a simple provision. As Churchill put it: 'if Germany attacked France we [Britain] should stand with the French, and if France attacked Germany we should stand with the Germans'.[7] It was a logical point of departure for Briand. In 1926, he and Stresemann had jointly received the Nobel Peace Prize for bringing the Locarno negotiations to a good end. Now, three years later, Briand's proposal for a kind of 'United States of Europe' would go much further in seeking a common political destiny.

Just a few months before Briand's dramatic speech in the Palais Wilson, Winston Churchill's political career suffered a serious blow. On 30 May 1929 the Conservative Party, which Churchill rejoined in 1924 after a two-decade stint with the Liberals, lost a general election. Stanley Baldwin, the Conservative prime minister, made way for Labour's Ramsay MacDonald. Churchill was narrowly re-elected in his own constituency, but had lost his prestigious Cabinet post of Chancellor of the Exchequer. One of Churchill's young Conservative friends, future prime minister Harold Macmillan, was out of Parliament altogether.

As the loss of political office meant a significant decrease in salary and political activity, Churchill – journalist and historian by profession – took up his pen to write the definitive biography of the First Duke of Marlborough, his famous forefather. On 2 August 1929 he decided to accept a handsome offer of £5,000 for the serial rights to the first volume of the Marlborough biography.[8] The next day, he left for a two-month speaking tour in Canada and his motherland America. There he would seek inspiration for a series of bi-weekly articles he promised to the *Daily Telegraph*.

As Churchill was busy saying his goodbyes to his hosts in Vancouver on 5 September he was unable to listen to the broadcast of Briand's address. But a few months after returning to Britain, having digested a manuscript of the speech, Churchill prepared a written response. In an article for the 15 February 1930 edition of the *Saturday Evening Post*, a widely circulated American weekly, Churchill declared himself entirely in agreement with Briand's plans for establishing federal links in Europe.[9]

He took much of his inspiration from what he saw in the United States, where he toured a state-of-the-art steel factory and was deeply impressed by the technological and scientific advances of American industry. Lamenting the dismal state of an 'impoverished' and 'disturbed' Europe, Churchill wrote:

> There is the economic and financial portent of the United States. Here is a region little larger than Europe and occupied by only a fraction of the population. Here, too, are regions of vast resources and educated inhabitants, but they are progressing, and prosper at a speed and in a degree never before witnessed, and still increasing.[10]

How did that stark contrast between American and European conditions come about? Churchill's answer was simple: Europe in 1930 was a 'rubbish heap', burdened by the losses of devastating war and terrorised by economic nationalism. Europe, Churchill observed, 'lay strained and impoverished by the greatest of all wars, disturbed by hatreds and jealousies which the conflict has only aggravated, hampered and burdened at every point by fetters and barriers they have themselves created and must spend a large part of their income to maintain'. The barriers Churchill referred to were the tariff barriers that restricted trade and production to specific areas. In his view, they were the distinct product of Europe's postwar settlement and hindered Europe's ability to build a vital economy. The United States, trading freely in a tariff-free federal system, made no such mistakes after World War I.

Despite the pain of the Great Recession, which followed the stock market crash of October 1929, the American economy was doing better than that of

Europe. Churchill was impressed by the dynamism of the American economy and the political stability that accompanied America's federal system of government. 'No European', he wrote, 'can gaze upon the astonishing spectacle of these internal tariff walls of Europe without being amazed at the embarrassment and difficulties in spite of which the peoples of Europe get their daily bread.' He continued:

> This lively impression is stimulated by a glance at the map of the United States and by observing that throughout the whole of that vast territory [...] there is no obstacle or barrier of any kind except those which Nature has raised and which science is overcoming. Certainly it would seem that the free interchange of goods and services over the widest possible area, or over very wide areas, is a dominating factor in the rapid accretion of material wealth.[11]

To Churchill's mind, Europe would do much better to adopt a similar approach to trade and untangle the complicated web of tariff barriers that had been growing steadily since the end of the Great War in 1919. How could it be that in order to travel between Paris and Stockholm in 1930, one required six different kinds of stamps and coins, crossed seven different borders, and used five different languages? Finding a solution to the problem of simultaneously wiping out the complicated 'rubbish heap' that Europe had become and saving what was underneath it – Europe's common historical, religious, legal and economic treasures – was an exceedingly difficult task.

Churchill believed that Briand provided most of the right answers in seeking to establish a type of federation akin to that of the United States. The most important aspect of Briand's federal link was economic, involving the removal of barriers restricting trade and production.[12] This spoke directly to Churchill's career-long commitment to the policy of free trade. He defected from the Conservative Party in 1904 to join the Liberal Party – known for its commitment to free trade – and was persuaded in 1923 to stand as a Liberal for the last time after the Tories renewed their hostility to free trade. In October 1930, having 're-ratted' to the Conservative Party in a quest for power, Churchill experienced severe difficulty in keeping his new Tory colleagues from again implementing anti-free-trade measures to combat unemployment.[13] It was completely in character for Churchill to approve of the economic grounding of Briand's proposal. He told his American audience:

> He [Briand] would like to see some 'federal link' established between all these different states. The most important component of that 'federal link' should be 'economic agreement' [...]'[14]

While Churchill endorsed Briand's emphasis on free trade in Europe, the essence of his support for some type of European federation relied on his mission to help avoid another devastating war at all cost. Though he was and still is often thought of as a warmonger in the public imagination, Churchill sincerely abhorred the atrocities of war. Having fought in a number of imperial wars as a young soldier, he reflected at the turn of the twentieth century: 'Ah horrible war, amazing medley of the glory and the squalid, the pitiful and the sublime, if modern men of light and learning saw your face closer simple folk would see it hardly ever.'[15] In 1901, then a 26-year-old Member of Parliament, Churchill was amazed to hear his colleagues in the Commons speak so shallowly of the possibility of war. He warned them that future European wars could only end 'in the ruin of the vanquished and the scarcely less fatal commercial dislocation and exhaustion of the conquerors'.[16]

Still before World War I, after attending German army manoeuvres at the invitation of Kaiser Wilhelm, Churchill wrote to his wife that war, though holding strange attractions, was a 'vile and wicked folly.'[17] If Churchill thought war against the general interest of all parties involved, he also saw more specific drawbacks for Britain. Writing in 1924 he suggested that Britain had 'no interest that would not be prejudiced by any war, great or small, near or remote, whether she were herself involved or not'.[18]

That same year, Churchill argued that it was some form of European understanding or cooperation that would root out the causes of war: 'There is only one hope for the revival of Europe. That is in the growth and cordial cooperation of Britain, France and Germany [...] it is only by a great renewed attempt to revive the concord and harmony of the European family that we and the world are to be saved from a continuous procession of privation and misfortune.'[19] After experiencing the shattering reality of the Great War (1914–19) as a government minister, it became Churchill's principal goal in life to help prevent a new European war. He seemed convinced that the Briand plan for a federal Europe was the right way to create the supreme deterrent power: political and economic unity.

In 1930, 'the monstrous absurdity' of Europe's precarious political situation was at the forefront of Churchill's mind. He pointed out that while the Romans had been able to secure more than 200 years of peace with the meagre sum of 800,000 armed men, Europe's tensely militarised situation held little promise of emulating a *Pax Augusta*. 'More than twenty million soldiers or trained reserves, armed with instruments of inconceivable destructiveness', he wrote, 'are required to guard the jigsaw frontiers of twenty-six jealous, impoverished and disunited states.' No intelligent observer could seriously think that this was a sustainable state of affairs.

The movement towards European solidarity, Churchill suggested, might prove to be 'the surest means of lifting the mind of European nations out of the ruck of old feuds and ghastly revenges. It may afford a rallying ground where Socialists and Capitalists, where Nationalists and Pacifists, where Idealists and Businessmen may stand together.' In short: 'It may be the surest guarantee against the renewal of great wars.' The main obstacle in the way of such a vision was the relatively new but strangely powerful ideology of nationalism. After the varying types of unity provided by the Holy Roman Empire, Christendom and later Napoleon, the post-World War I Treaty of Versailles was 'the fullest expression of national and racial feeling which Europe has ever known'.

Churchill thought of nationalism as 'an agent and not an end. It is a champion and not a breadwinner. It is a ladder and not a story; a process and not a result.' The result of Versailles was a fractured and weak Europe, divided by exaggerated particularisms and inward-looking national politics. France's relentless bullying and suppression of a morally and physically defeated Germany, he knew, would come at a frightful cost.

Europe's nationalism would find its victorious realisation at once unsatisfying and uncomfortable, Churchill warned. 'It is a religion whose field of proselytizing is strictly limited,' he wrote in a splendidly Churchillian passage, 'and when it has conquered its own narrow world, it is debarred, if it has no larger aim, by its own dogmas from seeking new worlds to conquer.' Hitler's National Socialists took just a few years after publication of Churchill's article to find their domestic victory as bitter as Churchill expected.

If the Great War should have taught ordinary Europeans just a single lesson, Churchill argued, it was that they should learn to reconcile their separate national identities and loyalties in a larger synthesis. 'Why', he asked, 'cannot the civilian realize himself as French, German, Spanish or Dutch, and simultaneously as a European and, finally, as a citizen of the world?' Only if Europeans utilised this wisdom so dearly bought in the war would they be able to avoid another large-scale conflict.

Here Churchill was building on an existing body of thought. He credited Coudenhove-Kalergi with resuscitating the ideal of Pan-Europe in the modern world. 'The form of Count Kalergi's theme may be crude, erroneous and impracticable,' he wrote, 'but the impulse and the inspiration are true.'

It helped Churchill's cause that Coudenhove-Kalergi's conception of Pan-Europe excluded Russia, which was overtaken by Vladimir Lenin's Bolsheviks (or Communists) in the Russian Revolution of 1917. Anti-Bolshevism nestled itself in the heart of Churchill's political philosophy in the years immediately after the Great War and remained there for the rest of his life. The core of his fear of the Russian Communists was his belief that their penchant for authoritarianism would destroy what he saw as the greatest democratic good of all: individual liberty. In April 1919 he wrote: 'Of all the tyrannies in history the Bolshevik tyranny is the worst, the most destructive and the most degrading.'[20]

After being appointed secretary of state for war and air by Prime Minister Lloyd George in January 1919, Churchill spent much of his time cajoling the Cabinet to provide unlimited support to the counter-revolutionary Russian 'White' forces in their protracted fight against the 'Red' Bolshevik forces. In one of his many strongly worded Cabinet memorandums on the Bolshevik threat, Churchill emphasised in May 1920 that the Soviet Union denied 'the most elementary rights of citizenship and freedom'.[21] He took his Cabinet campaign for the 'White' forces so far that the Prime Minister, a long-time Liberal ally and close friend, privately described him at the time as 'a dangerous man' with 'Bolshevism on the brain'.[22] It was only natural, then, for Churchill to suggest in his 1930 article: 'Let Russia slide back as Count Kalergi proposes, and is already so largely a fact, into Asia.'

While perhaps not for the Bolsheviks, the United States of Europe could only bring improvement for the rest of the world. Churchill wrote of the scope and design of his united Europe:

> For think how mighty Europe is, but for its divisions! [...] The mass of Europe, once united, once federalised or partially federalised, once continentally self-conscious Europe, with its African and Asiatic possessions and plantations, would constitute an organism beyond compare. It is evident that up to a certain point the developments now in actual progress will be wholly beneficial. In so far as the movement towards European unity expresses itself by the vast increase of wealth which would follow from it, by the ceaseless diminution of armies which would attend it, by ever increasing guarantees against the renewal of war, it bodes no ill to the rest of the world.[23]

It was not as clear from Coudenhove-Kalergi's books and pamphlets what was expected of Great Britain in the new Europe. Initially the Count propagated a purely continental federation 'co-operating on the basis of an entente cordiale with the British Empire'. In the course of the 1930s he seems to have adjusted the grand design to include Britain but not its Dominions. As he put it to

Churchill in the first of many carefully worded letters: 'Actually it seems impossible to organize any kind of European union without the participation and even leadership of Great Britain.' He warned Churchill, by now the voice of anti-appeasement Britain, that isolation from United Europe was a greater risk than participation. As in 1914, Britain would inevitably be dragged into the coming war. The only way to prevent this was to establish a Pan-European Union under British leadership. Coudenhove-Kalergi hoped to enlist Churchill's help as chairman of a British pan-Europe group, promising that together they might be able to prevent a European union under Nazi or Bolshevik hegemony.[24]

In 1930, Churchill could scarcely envisage British membership of a federated Europe. The backbone and starting point of his thinking about foreign policy was the continued prosperity of the British Empire and Commonwealth. From that perspective he believed that a new stability and prosperity on the European continent could only aid Britain's standing in the world. 'Every step that tends to make Europe more prosperous and more powerful', he wrote, 'is conducive to British interests.'

But even if a united Europe's progress, prosperity and peace would help Britain's path in the world, Churchill could not see how Britain could join a federal union as an ordinary member. He declared in 1930, as the British Empire was still the most powerful entity in global politics with by far the widest geographical reach: 'we have our own dream and our own task. We are with Europe, but not of it. We are linked, but not comprised. We are interested and associated, but not absorbed.'[25]

This might easily be interpreted as the whole underlying principle of Churchill's engagement with the idea of European unification in the 1930s. Britain would watch and aid the resurrection of Europe and 'without envy survey their sure and sound approach to mass wealth; being very conscious that every stride toward European cohesion which is beneficial to the general welfare will make us a partner in their good fortune, and that every sinister tendency will be restrained or corrected by our united strength'.[26] Rather than become an ordinary member of a federal union, Britain – as an outside sponsor – could simultaneously reap the benefits of peace and stability on the continent and maintain its place as a global power.

Here were the seeds of Churchill's famous three circles theory of British foreign policy. The first circle, the British Empire and Commonwealth, spanned Britain's colonial possessions and the family of nations that independently adhered to the British Crown – then still the 'white' Dominions: Canada, Australia, New Zealand and South-Africa. It extended to the Americas, Oceania, Asia and Africa. The second was the fraternal bond between the English-speaking peoples of the United States of America and Great Britain. The third was the collection of the ancient European states to which Britain belonged geographically and historically. In all three circles, Churchill thought, Britain ought to play a role. She should stand at the intersection of all three circles, guiding America in the ways of Old World diplomacy; remaining at the head of what he perceived to be the most successful empire in the history of mankind; and shepherding a flock of continental European states in their common pursuit of peace and material wealth.

Churchill's three circles theme was deeply rooted in his perception of Britain's exceptional position in the world:

> We belong to no single continent, but to all. Not to one hemisphere, but to both; as well to the New World as to the Old. The British Empire is a leading European power. It is a great and growing American power. It is the Australasian power. It is one of the greatest Asiatic powers. It is the leading African power. Great Britain herself has for centuries been the proved and accepted champion of European freedom. She is the centre and head of the British Commonwealth of Nations. She is an equal partner in the English-speaking world.[27]

Churchill's view of Britain's exceptional position is often seen as the first telltale sign of the disingenuousness of his later crusade for a United Europe. However, it was far more remarkable for Churchill, in 1930, to advocate the creation of a European federation than it was to place Britain outside the project. It is testament to his breadth of vision that he saw in economic and political union the preventative antidote to the real danger of renewed nationalistic aggression in Europe – a second Great War. How could Churchill seriously have contemplated full British participation in a European federation when the British Empire and Commonwealth he grew up with as a young soldier, journalist and politician was still at the height of its power?

In the latter half of the 1920s, when Churchill delivered four successful budgets as Chancellor of the Exchequer, the Empire faced no crises that demanded his attention. In fact, a new and happy era was on the horizon. The Imperial Conference of 1926 accepted that the Dominions would be seen as 'autonomous Communities within the British Empire' but refrained from granting them immediate control of defence and foreign policy.

Churchill warmly welcomed the recognition for heralding the 'the Age of Comprehension'. 'The Constitution of the British Empire', he said in a speech, 'depends now and henceforward solely upon good sense, good will, and loyalty to the Imperial Crown.'[28] In 1930 Britain was still the world's greatest trading nation and Europe's largest import market.[29] It was completely reasonable at the time for Churchill to expect Britain to wield continued influence over European trade policies even if it stood outside a European federation.

On 27 January 1931, almost a year after first writing about the United States of Europe, Churchill resigned from the Conservative Shadow Cabinet. While he managed to drum up the support of nearly a hundred Tory MPs in his crusade against Indian self-government, Churchill definitively fell from grace with the party establishment. This was the unofficial start of the 'Wilderness Years', the long and lonely period in the 1930s in which Churchill assumed little or no political responsibility as an estranged Conservative backbencher. He would have to wait until May 1940 to be called on to defend the British Isles and ultimately Western civilisation itself against Nazi tyranny.

Despite, or indeed because of, his preoccupation with the future of the British Empire, Churchill concluded his 1930 article in the *Saturday Evening Post* with a powerful expression of support for Briand's plans:

> The conception of a United States of Europe is right. Every step taken to that end which appeases the obsolete hatred and vanished oppressions, which makes easier the traffic and reciprocal services of Europe, which encourages its nations to lay aside their precautionary panoply is good in itself, is good for them and good for all.

Though no longer a Cabinet minister by this time, Churchill was still closely connected to the Tory leadership and was regarded as an important statesman in Britain and abroad. Amid a storm of cynical responses to Briand's plan in the British and continental European press, Churchill's endorsement of the 'United States of Europe' meant something big. Far from a gratuitous call from the political wilderness, it was an expression of a pioneering political faith.

Five months before publication of Churchill's article, on 9 September 1929, Briand followed up his address at the Palais Wilson by hosting a luncheon at Hôtel de Bergues, another historic landmark on Lake Geneva's waterfront. Briand gathered the heads of the European delegations to the League of Nations hoping to strangle at birth any possible objections to European federation. There were two main anxieties expressed at the table. First, German Foreign Minister Stresemann, who had welcomed the Briand plan that morning in his speech to the Assembly, wanted to ensure that a European federation would not undermine the broader functioning of the League of Nations. Briand countered that Article 21 of the League Covenant envisioned regional ententes and that surely Europe was such a region. Second, British Foreign Secretary Arthur Henderson warned of the danger that a European federation might be perceived as hostile to the United States and the Soviet Union. Briand told his lunch party that he had learned through diplomatic channels that the American government in fact welcomed his proposal, though no response from the Soviet Union was forthcoming. Satisfied with Briand's exposition, the European leaders invited him to produce a memorandum on European federal union for the consideration of their governments and prepare a report for the next year's Assembly meeting in Geneva.[30]

Briand's 'Memorandum on the Organization of a System for European Federal Union', when it was finally published on 17 May 1930, was a serious let-down for the leaders of the pan-European movement who gathered for a conference that day in Berlin. Count Coudenhove-Kalergi thought the memo 'patchwork, diluted and faded'.[31] Briand's written proposals seemed much less revolutionary than the rallying cry he had made in the Assembly, instead proposing to constitute a humbler European confederation within the framework of the League to establish some form of collective security. The memorandum did echo Churchill's article in lamenting the adverse consequences of the trade barriers that had been erected as a result of the Versailles peace settlement. Nevertheless, Briand called for the 'general subordination of the economic to the political problem' – a reversal in priorities from his speech in September.[32] As when Briand first presented his plan in Geneva, all major British news outlets poured cold water on the memorandum. The permanent officials at the British Foreign Office, conservative and cynical as ever, characterised Briand's proposals as 'hot air', 'clap-trap' and 'vague and puzzling idealism'.[33]

The British Labour government feared that a new independent European institution might undermine the authority of the League, that it would upset the balance of power, and that it would ultimately drive Britain away from its Empire and Commonwealth. Overwhelming British hostility towards the Briand memorandum had the crippling effect of tempering Briand's own enthusiasm for federation. In the following year's League of Nations Assembly meeting, when Briand proposed a brief resolution on European cooperation, he dropped references to 'federation' or 'union' altogether. The League's Commission of Inquiry into European Union died a slow death after its unproductive first session in January 1931. With the sudden passing of German Foreign Minister Stresemann, the onset of the Great Depression and the gathering storm of extreme nationalism, Briand's plan was by and large forgotten within a year.

What remained was Churchill's enthusiastic support for the idea. Such forward thinking on foreign policy proved to Leo Amery, Churchill's boarding school friend and long-time adversary within the Conservative Party, that he had been far off the mark in his recent private character assessment of Churchill. Amery wrote in his diary after a long heart-to-heart with Churchill in August 1929: 'the key to Winston is to realize that he is mid-Victorian, steeped in the politics of his father's period, and unable ever to get the modern point of view'.[34] Amery, who was a fervent supporter of Coudenhove-Kalergi's Union and had been one of the principal speakers at its recent conference in Berlin,[35] had to concede after the 'United States of Europe' article that Churchill was one of the very few to grasp the tide of modernity in foreign policy. This persuaded him in February 1938, just a few weeks before the fall of Austria, to set up an informal meeting between Churchill and Coudenhove-Kalergi.

The original plan was for Churchill to meet Coudenhove-Kalergi over lunch at Amery's London home. After some telegraphic misunderstanding Churchill decided to invite the count-philosopher to spend an afternoon at Chartwell, his cherished country home in rural Kent.[36] Upon meeting Churchill, Coudenhove-Kalergi later remembered, he was immediately reminded of Nietzsche's words from *The Dawn*: 'This is how I like man to be: honest towards himself and towards his friends; courageous in the face of the enemy; magnanimous in his treatment of the vanquished and at all times courteous.'[37]

Churchill reassured his guest that although he had neither written nor spoken publicly about European union for years, the idea still commanded his wholehearted support. The struggle against Hitler now seemed inevitable and all Churchill's energy went into preparing Britain for the fight. By 1935 Churchill reached the conclusion that European unity was no longer a viable option to prevent Hitler's war. The pressures of extreme nationalism simply became too great to effectively advocate the absorption of nation states into a larger whole. In a 1935 article Churchill prophesied that 'it would be many years until states and individuals learnt once more to reconcile the duties of patriotism with the claims of humanity, and find their personal and national wellbeing only in the general good'.[38]

Satisfied with Churchill's reassurances, Coudenhove-Kalergi prepared to return to London before dusk when Churchill suddenly demanded that he join him in his afternoon ritual and spend the night at Chartwell. Churchill had hot baths prepared and ordered his guest to take an hour-long pre-dinner nap. Churchill looked years younger, the Count thought, when he arrived at the dinner table in the glory of his pinkish rotundity.[39] He took delight in the sumptuous dinner put on by Chartwell's kitchen staff and remembered:

> One of Churchill's outstanding features is his capacity for enjoying life: there is nothing about him of the ascetic, of the saint or of the hypocrite. Goethe, if he were alive, would have said of him that he lived 'resolutely'. In him the stout heart of a hero is joined to the plastic imagination of the artist.

Coudenhove-Kalergi drove away the next morning with a signed copy of *Great Contemporaries*, Churchill's latest book. It was the start of a long if rocky political friendship.

Coincidence or not, just three months later, on 29 May 1938, Churchill's next article on the United States of Europe appeared in the *News of the World*, one of the world's best-selling newspapers. With Hitler's armies on the Czech border, he repeated almost verbatim many of his arguments from 1930. The ultimate purpose for the federation of Europe was still to prevent war. Aggressively marketed throughout Europe by Churchill's new literary agent, Emery Reves, the article reaffirmed the idea that Britain should take on the role of benevolent sponsor: 'We [Great Britain] are bound to further every honest and practical step which the nations of Europe may make to reduce the barriers which divide them and to nourish their common interests and their common welfare.'[40]

There were new proposals, too, some of them so forward-thinking that the modern-day European Union is still grappling with them. Churchill hoped governments would be wise enough to create European stamps, a single currency, a comprehensive tariff union and a common language.[41]

He went on to prophesy that Hitler's war would contribute to a new political unity in Europe. It would 'draw together the peace loving states and so contribute indirectly to the development of the Pan-European ideal'. This ideal would 'cement European forces, interests and sentiments in a single branch which, if it grew, would become the trunk itself, and thus acquire obvious pre-dominance.'[42] The European consciousness that would evolve from the common defeat of Communism and Fascism would be the breeding ground for a United Europe. It took just a few years for his prophecy to be borne out by the events of the darkest chapter of the twentieth century – in which Churchill himself moved centre stage.

CHAPTER 3

THREE DAYS IN JUNE
INDISSOLUBLE UNION, 1940

On the day Adolf Hitler began his invasion of western Europe, Winston Churchill became Prime Minister of Great Britain. 'I felt as if I were walking with destiny,' Churchill later wrote, 'and that all my past life had been but a preparation for this hour and for this trial.'[1]

One of the unexpected shocks of the early days of the war was the political and military vulnerability of France. The French defences crumbled quickly under the weight of German panzer divisions. On 14 June 1940, Hitler danced his 'jig of joy' in Paris.[2] The French prime minister Paul Reynaud, now operating from Bordeaux, was on the verge of yielding to the pressure of his ministers and his fascist mistress to give in to Nazi demands and negotiate an armistice.[3]

While Churchill was still busy forming his National government, some joint Anglo-French governmental infrastructure had already been put in place for the common direction of the war. In September 1939, the Supreme War Council came into being. In December of that year, the Anglo-French Coordinating Committee was established under the chairmanship of Jean Monnet, a French cognac salesman who worked his way up in the world to becoming an internationally connected financier and high-ranking civil servant. It was from Monnet's Coordinating Committee, which concerned itself with joint economic planning, that Churchill would first hear about a plan to turn the Anglo-French alliance into an indissoluble union: a single country with common citizenship and joint government.

On 28 March 1940, just a few months before Hitler's invasion of western Europe, the Supreme War Council issued a declaration that committed

France and Britain to never sign a separate peace with Germany. The two countries promised:

> that during the present war they will neither negotiate nor conclude an armistice or treaty of peace except by mutual agreement. They undertake not to discuss peace terms before reaching complete agreement on the conditions necessary to ensure to each of them an effective and lasting guarantee of their security.[4]

But on 11 June 1940, less than three months after this 'no separate peace' pledge, it became clear to Churchill and the British War Cabinet that the French army was already near collapse. France, with the second largest fleet in Europe and the second largest empire in the world, was close to succumbing to German pressure and failing to uphold its end of the bargain in the Anglo-French alliance. Some dramatic gesture was necessary to keep France in the war. If France stopped fighting Hitler's armies in continental Europe, Britain would face a German Europe bolstered by the strength of the French fleet.

Churchill also learned that day that Prime Minister Reynaud's ministers, Generals Weygand and Pétain most prominently among them, actively hoped to negotiate a separate armistice with Germany. Jock Colville, Churchill's private secretary, noted in his diary on 12 June: 'The French, although fighting with grim determination, are at the end of their tether, and although Reynaud wishes to fight to the end Pétain is willing to make peace.'[5] On Thursday 13 June, at a meeting of the Supreme War Council in Tours, Reynaud formally asked Churchill how the British government would react to a French request to be relieved of the responsibilities of the 'no separate peace' pledge. Churchill rejected the thought, saying that 'in no case would Britain [...] consent to action contrary to the recent agreement.'[6] Instead, he suggested, Reynaud should put the French situation to President Roosevelt and await his reply.

Joseph P. Kennedy, the American ambassador in London, arrived with a message from Roosevelt during a meeting of Churchill's War Cabinet on the night of 13 June. Though Roosevelt could not yet pledge that the US would enter the war – he needed Congress to authorise such a decision – he offered as much material support to the Franco-British alliance as he could at the time. Churchill was delighted with what he called the 'magnificent document' and wrote to Reynaud that night: 'We see before us a definite plan of campaign, and the light which you spoke of shines at the end of the tunnel.'[7]

That same day, 13 June, Churchill received from the leaders of the Anglo-French Coordinating Committee a stunningly forward-thinking memorandum. It proposed complete political and economic unity of France and Britain as a solution to the impending disintegration of the Anglo-French alliance.

Jean Monnet, the cognac salesman; his young French assistant René Pleven; and a junior minister in Churchill's government, Arthur Salter, were the chief architects of the document. It suggested to the Prime Minister that, in order to keep France in the war, 'there should be a dramatic declaration by the two Governments on the solidarity of the two countries' interests, and on their mutual commitment to restore the devastated areas, making clear also that the two Governments are to merge and form a single Cabinet and to unite the two Parliaments.'[8]

Churchill was unimpressed when first presented with the paper: 'I am fighting the war,' he told Monnet, 'and you come to talk about the future.'[9] Nonetheless, the idea of a complete union between France and Britain seems to have nestled in his mind that day. Around midnight on 13 June the Prime Minister sent a formal message to the French government in which he coined the phrase 'indissoluble union'. He wrote:

> In this solemn hour for the British and French nations and for the cause of Freedom and Democracy to which they have vowed themselves, His Majesty's Government desire to pay to the Government of the French Republic the tribute which is due to the heroic fortitude and constancy of the French armies in battle against enormous odds [...] We take this opportunity of proclaiming the indissoluble union of our two peoples and of our two Empires [...] We are sure that the ordeal by fire will only fuse them together into one unconquerable whole.[10]

On Friday 14 June, the defeatists in Reynaud's Cabinet who advocated political agreement with Germany were gaining strength by the hour. Reynaud felt he would be unable to hold on for much longer as prime minister. Desperate for a solution to France's plight, Churchill spent that night in conference with his most trusted advisers. Among this small circle was Duncan Sandys, a tall, exceedingly handsome, red-haired Conservative MP who was then just 32 years old. Sandys, who, according to his *New York Times* obituary, during his Oxford days established a reputation for being somewhat of a 'playboy', had been elected to the Commons and married Diana Churchill in 1935, giving him privileged access to Churchill.[11] The two men grew progressively closer in the late 1930s, when Sandys stood with Churchill in challenging Prime Minister Chamberlain's policy of appeasement.

Now that French-organised resistance had collapsed, the men discussed whether they should 'make the island [Britain] stiff with soldiers' by shipping the remaining French forces across the channel.[12] The reason and inspiration for this extraordinary plan was the visit René Pleven paid to Churchill earlier that night. Pleven, who ten years later would become the architect of a French plan to create a European army bearing his name, proposed to Churchill a slightly modified version of the Monnet–Salter memorandum of the day before. He wanted the Prime Minister to consider an indissoluble union of France and Britain while simultaneously evacuating the remaining French troops to Britain.

This was the first time Churchill was personally confronted with the urgency and zeal with which the plan for Franco-British Union was being prepared. Though perhaps not fully convinced of the institutional elements of the plan – Monnet's assistant was previously unknown to Churchill and could not claim to speak for the French government – the Prime Minister ordered Robert Vansittart, a published poet and the leading voice of anti-appeasement in the Foreign Office, to write up a draft of the plan for Franco-British Union for consideration at a later Cabinet meeting.

At about 2 a.m. another telegram arrived from President Roosevelt which was decidedly less positive than what Churchill first transmitted to the French. It now seemed that it would take the US much longer to commit to entering the war than it would take for France to collapse entirely. Disappointed but understanding of Roosevelt's position, Churchill predicted to his secretary of state for war, Anthony Eden, that 'France would crack internally in a day or two.'[13]

On the afternoon of Saturday 15 June, against all the odds, Reynaud proposed a constructive solution to the deteriorating military and political situation to the French Council of Ministers. Rather than sign a separate peace with the Germans, France would save its honour by staying in the war as a belligerent and operate from French North Africa. The French Empire, fleet and air force would be assets for the British war effort while the French army – completely overrun by the Germans in metropolitan France anyway – would capitulate.

The French Council reached an impasse, however, when General Weygand, commander-in-chief of the armed forces, refused to consider fighting on from North Africa. As Avi Shlaim concludes in his close analysis of the Anglo-French Union episode, 'Weygand was obviously determined to impose an armistice on the Government, force it to accept responsibility for the military defeat and prevent its departure to North Africa.'[14] That is to say, Weygand preferred a peace construction in which Prime Minister Reynaud assumed responsibility for a political armistice rather than accept the humiliation of military capitulation. The problem with this was that the Anglo-French 'no separate peace' pledge made one-sided armistice impossible without the approval of the British government. If the French government went down Weygand's route, it would either have to break the pledge or seek British approval.

The majority of the French Council eventually voted to go down the slippery slope of asking the British government for approval to discover the German terms of an armistice without directly asking for one. This was the compromise position suggested by Reynaud's vice-president, Chautemps, that broke the impasse in the Council. If the German terms proved too harsh, which Chautemps expected, there would be an excellent rationale to persuade the country and the defeatist elements of the French government to keep up the fight. Even better, if the British rejected the request to ascertain the terms of an armistice, the French would have no other choice than to stay in the war. But Reynaud sensed danger in the Chautemps compromise: if the British government approved the request, his whole diplomatic strategy would fall apart. British approval would give the defeatist ministers the momentum to seize control of the Council and start peace negotiations with Germany.[15]

Reynaud was defeated by a majority of ministers, 13:6, and in line with Chautemps's compromise formally put the French request before the British government. With its request to be relieved of the agreement of 28 March, the 'no separate peace' pledge, the French government was essentially asking to break up the Franco-British alliance. It was then – acutely aware of the adverse military consequences of the loss of the French Empire, air force and fleet – that Churchill and others in London started to think of the idea of Franco-British Union as a lifebuoy for Reynaud to keep the French in the war. Or, as Shlaim puts it, 'The British offer of union was essentially a response to the crisis in the alliance whose very existence was called into question by the French request for permission to negotiate a separate armistice.'[16]

Churchill needed France to offer continued resistance to Nazi Germany as much as Reynaud needed a dramatic statement from the British to keep his Cabinet in fighting spirit. In his war memoirs, Churchill wrote of the days in which the idea of Franco-British Union emerged:

> In these days the War Cabinet were in a state of unusual emotion. The fall and the fate of France dominated their minds. Our own plight, and what we should have to face and face alone, seemed to take a second place. Grief for our ally in her agony, and desire to do anything in human power to aid her, was the prevailing mood. There was also the overpowering importance of making sure of the French Fleet. It was in this spirit that a proposal for 'an indissoluble union' between France and Britain was conceived.[17]

A proclamation was necessary, it was felt, declaring the intention of both governments to direct the war with a joint cabinet, to share the postwar burden of repairing damages, and to organise mixed sessions of Parliaments. The draft of the plan, prepared by Vansittart as chief diplomatic adviser to the government, was well received in the British War Cabinet. Vansittart spent the morning at his country home with Monnet, Pleven and a few others, modifying the draft before delivering it to Foreign Minister Lord Halifax.

Churchill initially reacted with reserve, he later wrote, but when his War Cabinet almost unanimously embraced the proposal he came around: 'I was somewhat surprised to see these staid, stolid, experienced politicians of all parties engage themselves so passionately in an immense design whose implications and consequences were in no way thought out. I did not resist, but yielded easily to these generous surges which carried out resolves to a very high level of unselfish and undaunted action.'[18]

Afterwards he went to Chequers to dictate telegrams on the French situation to Roosevelt and to the leaders of the British Dominions. 'If words counted,' Churchill told his private secretary, 'we should win this war.'[19] Dinner was served at Chequers at 9.30 that night. Churchill's party consisted of regular guests: his daughter Diana and her husband Duncan Sandys; his close friend, teetotaller vegetarian and guru for all things scientific Professor Lindemann; and his private secretary Jock Colville. Colville wrote in the course of his diary account that night: 'it was the most dramatic and the most fantastic evening I have ever spent.'[20]

Before sitting down for dinner Colville heard via telephone that the position was deteriorating fast 'and the request to be allowed to make a separate peace was being put in a more brutal form'.[21] He continued in his diary:

> I imparted this to Winston who was immediately very depressed. Dinner began lugubriously, W. eating fast and greedily, his face almost in his plate [...] The Sandyses and I sat silent, because our spasmodic efforts at conversation were not well received. However champagne and brandy and cigars did their work and we soon became talkative, even garrulous.
>
> Winston and Duncan Sandys paced up and down the rose garden in the moonlight while, Diana, Lindemann and I walked on the other side of the house.[22]

Colville, by his own account, spent most of the time telephoning and listening among the roses to Churchill's comments to Sandys on the war. At one point he broke up the conversation to inform the Prime Minister that the French seemed to be slipping even further into chaos. Churchill burst out: 'Tell them that if they let us have their fleet we shall never forget, but that if they surrender without consulting us we shall never forgive. We shall blacken their name for a thousand years!' Only when it became obvious that Colville thought Churchill to be serious, the Prime Minister added: 'Don't, of course, do that just yet.'[23]

Despite the tragic developments Churchill seemed to be in high spirits later that evening, 'repeating poetry, dilating on the drama of the present situation, maintaining that he and Hitler only had one thing in common – a horror of whistling – offering everybody cigars, and spasmodically murmuring, "Bang, Bang, Bang, goes the farmer's gun, run rabbit, run rabbit, run, run, run."' Around 1 a.m. Churchill came back in from the garden and laid down on the sofa to tell 'one or two dirty stories'. At 1.30 a.m. he finally went upstairs.[24]

The whole tragedy of the Franco-British Union unfolded in a dazzling flurry of diplomacy on a single day, Sunday 16 June 1940. In the course of that morning's French Cabinet meeting, which started at 11 a.m. in Bordeaux, Prime Minister Reynaud's position became increasingly untenable. The octogenarian Marshal Pétain, a veteran of World War I who was nearly deaf, protested vehemently against the delays in seeking an armistice with Germany and threatened to resign. More and more of the ministers started supporting Pétain. Reynaud narrowly kept his Cabinet together by arguing that the French government should have the dignity to wait for its ally to reply to the request to be relieved of the Anglo-French Agreement. Whatever would come next from Churchill, it had to be good enough to keep Pétain and the rest of the defeatists in check.

At Chequers, Churchill awoke at 7.30 a.m. to a new batch of secret papers on the French situation. His private secretary found him lying in bed, 'looking just like a rather nice pig, clad in a silk vest'.[25] Churchill puzzled over what to do for some time that morning before calling a Cabinet meeting for 10.15 a.m. to consider Reynaud's request. After discussing the situation with Sandys in his bedroom, Churchill and his entourage hurried back to London in the pouring rain. The War Cabinet, it emerged, was prepared to relieve France of the 'no separate peace' pledge because it thought Reynaud, who sent the request, would otherwise see no other option than to resign. The Cabinet was terrified that with Pétain or Weygand at the head of the French government the Allies would be doomed. This meant the French strategy to keep the defeatists at bay, which relied on a British rejection of his request, failed spectacularly.

In a telegram at 12.35 p.m., drafted by Churchill, the British government consented to the French asking for the terms of armistice on the key condition that 'the French Fleet is sailed forthwith for British harbours pending negotiation'. At 3.10 p.m. a second telegram, this time drafted by the Foreign Office, re-emphasised Churchill's proviso about the French fleet and asked the French government to keep the British Cabinet up to date on any developments. Reynaud's plan had worked out in the exact opposite direction he hoped for. But an hour later, to Reynaud's profound relief, the telegrams were suspended on Churchill's orders. The British government changed its mind. What happened in London that afternoon to cause such diplomatic confusion?

On the morning of the 16th, a young French general, recently appointed under-secretary of state for national defence, landed in London to make contingency arrangements for the transportation of French government officials and troops to North Africa. On his arrival at dawn, he met with Jean Monnet and Ambassador Charles Corbin in his room in the swanky Hyde Park Hotel. Monnet and Corbin showed the junior minister the draft declaration of union between France and Britain. They said it was the only viable solution to avoid France's downfall. The young General was the only man in London, Monnet and Corbin argued, as a representative of Reynaud's government, who would be able to persuade Churchill of the necessity to publicise the declaration as soon as possible. His name was Charles de Gaulle.

On reading the draft put to him by two of its co-authors, de Gaulle remembered: 'I thought, like M. Corbin and Monnet, that the proposal could provide M. Paul Reynaud, in the supreme crisis in which he was plunged, with an element of comfort, an argument for tenacity to persuade his ministers. I agreed, therefore, to try and get Mr Churchill to adopt it.'[26]

The General met with the Prime Minister that Sunday morning to discuss the plan for Franco-British Union. Churchill recalled of this meeting that de Gaulle 'impressed on me that some dramatic move was essential to give M. Reynaud the support which he needed to keep his Government in the war, and suggested that a proclamation of the indissoluble union of the French and British peoples would serve the purpose.'[27] The General did exactly what Monnet and Corbin asked of him. Churchill was persuaded of the urgency with which the proclamation needed to be dispatched.

Encouraged by Churchill's backing, de Gaulle telephoned Reynaud with the good news at 12.30 p.m.:

> *De Gaulle*: I have just seen Churchill. There is something stupendous in preparation affecting the entirety of the two countries. Churchill proposed the

establishment of a single Franco-British Government, with you, perhaps, as head of a Franco-British War Cabinet.

Reynaud: It is the only possible solution for the future. But it must be done on a large scale and very quickly, above all very quickly. It is a question of minutes. I give you half an hour. It would be splendid.[28]

After his phone call to Reynaud, de Gaulle came to an agreement on a new draft of the declaration with Vansittart, Monnet and Pleven. The new draft included ideas for integration that seemed to come straight from the pamphlets of Count Coudenhove-Kalergi's Pan-European Union: common citizenship, a single currency, a customs union, joint financing of postwar reconstruction, a single War Cabinet and a joint supreme command. British Foreign Secretary Lord Halifax was the first to read it and was asked to put it before the Cabinet during its 3 p.m. meeting.

When the 10.15 a.m. Cabinet meeting finished, Churchill hastened to get to the Carlton Club in time for luncheon with General de Gaulle. Having spent most of the morning drafting a reply to Reynaud's request to be relieved from the Anglo-French Agreement, Churchill looked forward to discussing the situation with the representative (however junior) of the French government. General de Gaulle brought with him the new draft of the declaration for Franco-British Union and put it on the table for Churchill's inspection. 'But it is an enormous piece!' Churchill barked. He was expecting something far more concise. 'Yes,' answered de Gaulle, unfazed, 'and the implementation would involve a great deal of time. But the gesture can be immediate.'[29]

After lunch, the 3 p.m. meeting of the War Cabinet started with Churchill briefing his colleagues about his dealings with de Gaulle. The Prime Minister said he needed to suspend the telegrams that consented to Reynaud's separate peace request. The Prime Minister had given it a good deal of thought that day and came to the conclusion that the declaration for Franco-British Union would be a much better tool to keep France in the war. Churchill asked his War Cabinet to pass the draft proclamation round the table to be read and amended.

Monnet, de Gaulle and a few others sat waiting in an adjoining room. Anticipating the eventuality of a separate peace, de Gaulle was busy rerouting American arms from French to British ports. Monnet, for his part, made himself useful to Churchill by preparing to transfer French munitions contracts to Britain. Various British ministers came into their waiting room to suggest changes to the text, but in the end the essence of the declaration remained intact. Monnet remembered that Churchill 'behaved very fairly' in encouraging the Cabinet to adopt the declaration. 'At a grave time like this,' Churchill declared, cigar in mouth, wearing a grey suit with pink stripes, 'it shall not be said that we lack imagination.'[30]

Churchill's private secretary observed the afternoon's proceedings in continuous and growing disbelief.

> De Gaulle has been strutting about in the Cabinet, with Corbin too; the Cabinet meeting turned into a sort of promenade, Winston beginning a speech in the Cabinet room and finishing it in Morton's room [where de Gaulle and Monnet were waiting]; and everybody has been slapping de Gaulle on the back and telling him he shall be Commander in Chief (Winston muttering *"je l'arrangerai"* ["I will see to that"]).'[31]

Churchill was deeply impressed with de Gaulle in these last hours before the fall of France. De Gaulle, it seemed to Churchill, embodied all the fighting spirit that was left in the French. 'Under an impassive, imperturbable demeanour he seemed to me to have a remarkable capacity for feeling pain,' Churchill remembered. 'I preserved the impression, in contact with this very tall, phlegmatic man: "Here is the Constable of France."'[32]

At 4 p.m., General de Gaulle telephoned Reynaud with an update.

> *De Gaulle:* There is going to be a sensational declaration.
> *Reynaud:* Yes, but after five o'clock (17h.) it will be too late.
> *De Gaulle:* I will do my best to bring it to you at once by plane.
> *Reynaud:* Yes, but that will be too late. The situation has seriously deteriorated within the last few minutes. Unforeseen events have occurred.[33]

Reynaud felt he could hold his position if he heard positive news about the proposal before the next meeting of the French Council of Ministers, which was scheduled for 5 p.m. On hearing this, the draft proclamation was quickly polished, approved by the War Cabinet, and translated into French for de Gaulle, who read the final draft, Churchill noted, 'with an air of unwonted enthusiasm'.[34] De Gaulle again phoned Reynaud, this time to dictate the full text of the approved proclamation. On the other end of the line the French prime minister, armed with a pencil, took the text down word for word. 'On he wrote in a frightful scrawl, getting more excited as the message unfolded,' remembered Edward 'Louis' Spears, the British representative in Bordeaux, who was in Reynaud's room to suspend the earlier telegrams.[35]

When de Gaulle finished speaking on the phone, Reynaud asked, surprised to the point of incredulity: 'Does he agree to this? Did Churchill give it to you personally?' At this point, Churchill, who was listening to the conversation, picked up the phone and said: 'Hold on! De Gaulle's leaving now: he'll bring you the text [...] And now, we must meet quickly. Tomorrow morning at Concarneau [on the Brittany coast], I'll come with Attlee [Lord Privy Seal], the First Lord of the Admiralty, the Chief of Staff, and our best experts. And bring some good generals! *Au revoir!*'[36]

The Foreign Office immediately wrote to confirm the arrangements with Reynaud and informed the French prime minister that HMS *Berkeley* would be at his disposal to meet Churchill off the Brittany coast. At 8 p.m. the foreign secretary, Lord Halifax, instructed the British Ambassador in France: 'After consultation with General de Gaulle, P.M. has decided to meet M. Reynaud to-morrow in Brittany to make further attempt to dissuade the French government from asking for an armistice. For this purpose, on the advice of General de Gaulle, he will offer to M. Reynaud to join in issuing forthwith a declaration announcing immediate constitution of closest Anglo-French Union in all spheres in order to carry on the war.'[37]

The final draft proclamation of Franco-British Union which Churchill wanted to discuss with Reynaud face to face contained some undeniably Churchillian phrasing, including the very term 'indissoluble union'. It read in full:

DECLARATION OF UNION

At this most fateful moment in the history of the modern world the Governments of the United Kingdom and the French Republic make this declaration of indissoluble union and unyielding resolution in their common defence of justice and freedom against subjection to a system which reduces mankind to a life of robots and slaves.

The two Governments declare that France and Great Britain shall no longer be two nations, but one Franco-British Union.

The constitution of the Union will provide for joint organs of defence, foreign, financial, and economic policies.

Every citizen of France will enjoy immediately citizenship of Great Britain; every British subject will become a citizen of France.

Both countries will share responsibility for the repair of the devastation of war, wherever it occurs in their territories, and the resources of both shall be equally, and as one, applied to that purpose.

During the war there shall be a single War Cabinet, and all the forces of Britain and France, whether on land, sea, or in the air, will be placed under its direction. It will govern from wherever it best can. The two Parliaments will be formally associated. The nations of the British Empire are already forming new armies.

France will keep her available forces in the field, on the sea, and in the air. The Union appeals to the United States to fortify the economic resources of the Allies, and to bring her powerful material aid to the common cause.

The Union will concentrate its whole energy against the power of the enemy, no matter where the battle may be.

And thus we shall conquer.[38]

The Declaration of Union gave Reynaud the courage to fight his corner in the French Cabinet. Reynaud was delighted with the British government's proposal, for it allowed him to make an argument to his Council of Ministers 'to oppose, in the name of France's pledged word, any demand for an armistice'.[39] He felt that union with Britain meant independence for France exactly at a time 'when we had only the choice between union and certain slavery under the German jackboot'.[40]

The declaration turned out to be not enough to keep the French Council of Ministers together. What Reynaud did not know when he spoke to de Gaulle was that General Weygand had instructed army listeners to tap the Prime Minister's telephone. This ruined the surprise element of Reynaud's announcement of the offer of Franco-British Union. Even worse, in the little time between de Gaulle's phone call and the start of the French Cabinet meeting at 5 p.m., Weygand and Pétain found time to lobby the other ministers to reject the British proposal. Evidently, they were successful. The reaction from the Cabinet members after Reynaud read out the proclamation was incomprehensibly hostile.

Reynaud read the proclamation twice to his ministers and expressed his unqualified support for it. He told them that he agreed to meet Churchill in Concarneau the next day for face-to-face discussions. The ministers were torn by dissent and paralysed by defeatism. Under Pétain's influence they said they would rather seek armistice with Nazi Germany than continue fighting alongside the British. They were furious that the British government refused to reply to the French request to ascertain the terms of armistice and had sent over this radical offer instead. One minister said the union would demote France to British Dominion status; Pétain, who was convinced that Britain itself would fall prey to Hitler within three weeks, exclaimed that it was like 'fusion with a corpse'; and a third minister cried out: 'better be a Nazi province, at least we know what that means.'[41]

On the night of the 16th, Reynaud, no longer commanding the support of his Cabinet, resigned. In his fall he took with him any chance of the offer of Franco-British Union being considered seriously by his successors. Marshal

Pétain came to power. At 11.30 that night, in the first meeting of the new French Cabinet, it took Pétain ten minutes to come to agreement on armistice negotiations with Germany.

In London, meanwhile, Churchill got ready to travel to France, first by special train from Waterloo station to Southampton and then by destroyer to Concarneau. The destroyer would get the Prime Minister's party to the coast of Brittany at 12 noon the next day, just in time for his meeting with Reynaud. Clemmie came to see her husband off at Waterloo station.

There was a curious delay in the train starting. Churchill was already in his seat when a secretary arrived from Downing Street with a message from the British ambassador in Bordeaux: 'Ministerial crisis has opened [...] Hope to have news by midnight. Meanwhile meeting arranged for to-morrow impossible.' Churchill returned to Downing Street, he recalled, 'with a heavy heart'.[42] 'We knew then it was all over and Reynaud had lost,' Clement Attlee remembered of that moment. 'We got out of the train and drove back to Downing Street and went back to work.'[43] Later that night, the British ambassador phoned to confirm what Churchill and Attlee already expected to be true. Reynaud told the ambassador that forces in favour of ascertaining terms of armistice became too strong for him. Weygand and Pétain, according to a British representative in France, were 'living in another world and imagined they could sit round a green table discussing armistice terms in the old manner'. But their combined force proved too much for weak members of the French government, 'on whom they worked by waving the spectre of revolution'.[44] Churchill would not travel to France for another four years.[45]

Churchill heard of Pétain's request for an armistice on the radio at midday on Monday 17 June. Marshal Pétain formed a new French government with the objective of becoming a partner in the new Nazi Europe. He ignored Churchill's demand that the French fleet be sailed to British harbours. On the morning of the 18th, Churchill sent Jean Monnet to Bordeaux to take as many 'good' French government leaders to French North Africa as possible, putting a 30-seater seaplane, the *Claire*, at Monnet's disposal to complete the task. A group of figures of outstanding importance in French politics – and later in the movement for a united Europe – ended up boarding Monnet's plane. Among them were two great interwar prime ministers and long-time friends of Churchill's, Édouard Herriot and Léon Blum.[46]

The offer of indissoluble union materialised in an hour of crisis and was mainly meant to achieve the specific, short-term goal of keeping France as a belligerent allied force in the war against Germany.[47] In its essence, therefore, the project of Franco-British Union was a gigantic failure. The proposal collapsed in French indifference and hostility. 'Rarely has so generous a proposal', Churchill wrote, 'encountered such a hostile reception.'[48] Prime Minister Reynaud agreed, reflecting at the end of his account of the story: 'Such was the cavalier fashion in which was treated the proposal that Britain should unite with France to create the core of a new Europe.'[49]

The scheme had little to do with a doctrinaire federalist plan to create the nucleus of a postwar European Union. Churchill may have been a declared supporter of a kind of United States of Europe; but in 1940 he was certainly not ready to advocate the permanent submersion of the British state into a Franco-British superstate.

It was unclear at the time, even to many of the protagonists in the drama of June 1940, whether there were any long-term ambitions (federalist or not) tangled up with the drafting of the plan for Union. It is telling that the Prime Minister's private secretary, Jock Colville, who was involved at almost every turn, wrote in his diary on 16 June: 'It is a historic document and its effects will be more far-reaching than anything that has occurred this century – and more permanent?'[50]

The union of France and Britain, in Churchill's postwar telling, could have greatly helped the Allied cause in World War II. Churchill later speculated that if Reynaud had survived the 16th, the sheer persuasive force of the British presence at the proposed meeting in Concarneau on the 17th would have been enough to outmanoeuvre Pétain and the rest of the defeatists. The entire French government would have gone to North Africa, handed their fleet to the British, and fought the war side by side with the Allies. 'The Anglo-French Super-State or Working Committee, to which it probably in practice have reduced itself', Churchill thought, 'would have faced Hitler. The British and French Fleets from their harbours would have enjoyed complete mastery of the Mediterranean.'[51] From this position of power the Franco-British Union would have had it far easier attacking Fascist Italy in the Mediterranean and may have taken months off the war.

The 'Anglo-French Super-State' could then possibly have evolved into a permanent, full-fledged federal Europe on a London–Paris axis. It would have been impossible to disentangle the union after the war, especially because it was proposed to operate on the principle of joint reconstruction. The leaders of the union would have had a difficult time terminating its existence when, after perhaps a decade or more of joint reconstruction, the people of France and Britain had grown completely accustomed to common citizenship and joint organs of defence, foreign, financial and economic policies.

Prominent supporters of the European movement later saw in the project of Franco-British Union the high-water mark of opportunity for the unification of Europe. One of its main architects, Jean Monnet, wrote in 1978 that he did not think the plan a dogmatic one: 'for me, the plan had no federalist overtones.'[52] But in 1944, much closer to the actual event, he told *Fortune* magazine: 'Think what it would have meant if the political offer of union had succeeded. There would have been no way of going back on it. The course of the war, the course of the world might have been different. We should have had the true beginnings of a Union of Europe.'[53]

Whatever Monnet's opinion of the plan, the whole episode was of remarkable significance for his career. It is telling that he placed his account of those dramatic days in June 1940 in the opening chapter of his memoirs. Monnet, born in 1888, thought of the proposal as the starting point of the European period of his life – the one that proved to be by far the most important for his legacy. In June 1940 Monnet also came closest to Churchill. As the most senior Frenchman in London after the French Ambassador, Monnet had privileged access to all that pertained to the Anglo-French alliance. Because Monnet was an Allied appointee and a mere official, however, Churchill paid less attention to him than he did to de Gaulle.[54]

As a result Monnet had often to find ways of capturing Churchill's attention. 'My relations with Churchill were good,' he remembered, but 'my role [...] was not political.'[55] Churchill, likewise, viewed his interactions with Monnet moderately positively. In a confidential note to Foreign Secretary Anthony Eden on 16 January 1943 concerning Monnet's role as the civil head of the French National Liberation Committee, which defended France's honour in North Africa, he wrote: 'My own impressions of Monet [sic] in the crisis of June 1940 are not bad.'[56] That same year he told the British ambassador in Paris: 'Monnet, though on the make, is full of ability and sense.'[57]

Another ardent supporter of the postwar European movement, Paul Reynaud, also understood the immensity of the opportunity before the

French to create a new Europe from a Franco-British nucleus. On the day of his resignation, on 17 June 1940, he told Churchill that he was grateful for the imagination and audacity with which the Prime Minister had proposed the project for Franco-British unity. He was convinced even after the collapse of the plan that it would be 'the future for our two countries'.[58]

In his war memoirs Reynaud lamented postwar British aloofness from continental initiatives for European integration. 'From the reluctance which our neighbours today show to be integrated in one,' he wrote bitterly, 'it can be judged what a windfall for us was this offer of 1940. Let Weygand, who persists in justifying the treatment accorded to the proposal, go and beg Her Majesty's Government to repeat it today!'[59]

Count Coudenhove-Kalergi, the undisputed leader of the pre-war European movement, interpreted the offer of Franco-British Union as a 'generous Pan-European gesture' – a plan that should have had far-reaching long-term consequences. He thought that if Reynaud and de Gaulle had succeeded in persuading the defeatist faction in the French Cabinet to accept Churchill's offer, 16 June would have become the anniversary of United Europe: 'For the exiled Governments of Poland, Czechoslovakia, Belgium, the Netherlands, Luxembourg, and Norway,' he explained, 'would certainly have acceded to an Anglo-French Union.' He thought a single European Nation would have been born at the end of the war, with one Cabinet, one army, one economy and one Parliament.[60]

In Britain, too, some supporters of Franco-British Union had in mind the distant future of a United Europe. On Monday 17 June Jock Colville felt disappointed about the collapse of the union plan precisely on account of its long-term promise: 'There would have been great difficulties to surmount, but we had before us the bridge to a new world, the first elements of European or even World Federation.'[61]

After the war, Churchill himself looked back on the proposal for Franco-British Union in contradictory ways. Though he stressed in his memoirs that he was not the 'prime mover' in the project, he took part in drafting the proclamation as it was passed around the table and ultimately assumed full responsibility for dispatching it to the French prime minister.

On the evolution of Churchill's involvement with the scheme that weekend, Jock Colville wrote on Sunday 16 June: 'On Friday night [...] W. was bored and critical, but eventually went upstairs to discuss the matter with Chamberlain. Nothing more occurred here and certainly, last night [Saturday

15 June], the whole idea was far from Winston's mind and he was preoccupied with the necessity of saving the French fleet if France capitulated [...] presumably de Gaulle persuaded him to consider seriously this revolutionary project – on which, of course, Monnet, Amery, Salter, etc., had busily been working behind the scenes.'[62]

When asked in a 1980 BBC interview whether Churchill saw anything in the long-term implications of the plan, Colville said that 'the eventual effect was something that was fascinating, and he [Churchill] did say this is going to need a great deal of working out afterwards.'[63] In his own written account of the war, Churchill speculated at length about what the Anglo-French Union would have done to change the course of the war, but did not consider its long-term, postwar implications.[64] A British diplomat reports that when Churchill went to dinner at the British Embassy in Paris with Reynaud in January 1951, he asked: 'Perhaps you remember that offer of common citizenship I made to France in 1940 when you were Prime Minister. What did you think of it? I was never sure it was a good idea.'[65]

Even if the idea of the declaration of union was someone else's, and even if the Prime Minister had to be persuaded by his War Cabinet and General de Gaulle of its value, the offer of union remains forever associated with Churchill. Churchill was keenly aware of this directly after the war, when the offer was already become something of an embarrassment in the eyes of public opinion. Why would the Prime Minister have suggested the creation of a union from which, surely, there would have been no way back? Was it not better for Great Britain, which alone bore the brunt of the fight against Nazi Germany for a whole year after the quick fall and treason of France, to maintain its sovereignty and independence?

In light of this growing public scepticism, Churchill – after the general election defeat of July 1945 back to being a party politician – made sure to distance himself from the Franco-British Union. In a debate in the House of Commons on 16 August 1945, Churchill asked Attlee to clarify a number of astounding remarks made by the chairman of Labour's main policy apparatus, Professor Harold Laski. Laski had suggested that if the French voted Socialist in the upcoming elections, the British socialist government under Clement Attlee's leadership might renew the offer of June 1940. 'Much has happened in the five years that have passed,' Churchill said, 'and I am of the opinion that the idea of France and Britain becoming one single nation with common citizenship – alliance is another question – must, at the very least, be very carefully considered by the responsible Ministers before any such proposal is made to Parliament, still less to a foreign country.'[66] Attlee went no further in his response than to confirm for Churchill that 'Government policy is laid down by Ministers,' not by private individuals like Harold Laski, however powerful they were within the non-parliamentary Labour Party.[67]

Nowhere in their exchange, however, did it become clear that either the Prime Minister (Attlee) or the Leader of the Opposition (Churchill) fundamentally opposed the idea of ever discussing a similar offer of union. Of course Churchill would have abhorred the idea of the design for Franco-British Union being transformed into a narrowly Socialist European union. He loathed British socialism almost as much as he detested Bolshevism. Churchill committed a serious political gaffe that summer when he argued in a national radio broadcast that Attlee's Labour Party – always 'Socialist Party' in Churchill's vocabulary – would need a kind of Gestapo to maintain order if it were to win the elections. But the fundamental idea of union between France and Britain, even in the face of public scrutiny, Churchill could not quite rule out.

Churchill never advocated as strongly or consistently for an immediate and indissoluble Franco-British Union as he did for the gradual unification of all of Europe after the war. Perhaps Churchill's strongest reservation about the plan of June 1940 concerned how it might be perceived on the other side of the Channel: a great many Frenchmen might misinterpret it as a plan to subject France to British colonial rule. Vacationing in Italy in September 1945, Churchill told a visiting army doctor over dinner: 'Thank God also that the French didn't accept the offer to become citizens of Britain ... our offer, made in such good faith, would have been misinterpreted by some sections of French opinion as a desire to annex France as a Colony!'[68]

Nevertheless, the basic idea of creating a common citizenship in Europe stayed with Churchill. When the idea gained ground in the postwar movement for European unity, he explicitly embraced it with a view to what happened in June 1940. In May 1948, when Churchill prepared to give the keynote address at the famous Congress of Europe in The Hague, Duncan Sandys, by this time Churchill's trusted adjutant in the campaign for a United Europe, wrote in his speech notes: 'You should have no difficulty in expressing your support for the idea of the grant of a common citizenship without the loss of original nationality. (This is on a par with your offer to

France in 1940.)'[69] Churchill evidently agreed and told his audience on 9 May 1948:

> We hope to see a Europe where men of every country will think as much of being a European as of belonging to their native land, and that without losing any of their love and loyalty of their birthplace. We hope wherever they go in this wide domain, to which we set no limits in the European Continent, they will truly feel 'Here I am at home. I am a citizen of this country too.'[70]

CHAPTER 4

'A GOOD EUROPEAN'
FROM ADANA TO POTSDAM, 1940–1945

Notwithstanding the failure of Franco-British Union in June 1940, the rest of World War II saw Churchill at various points thinking about the unification of postwar Europe. Many of his plans focused on the far-reaching possibility of establishing an instrument of common European government. All of them included Germany and excluded Soviet Russia from the European family of nations.

As early as December 1940, when it was still unclear whether Britain would be able to withstand Hitler's relentless bombing campaign, Churchill developed a highly detailed idea of what Europe should look like after the Nazi defeat. On Friday the 13th, the Prime Minister divulged his plans for a Council of Europe in a dinnertime conversation at Chequers with Jock Colville and 'Prof' Lindemann, his German-born friend and scientific adviser.

'Germany', Churchill gently reminded his friends, 'existed before the Gestapo.' After final victory he hoped there would be five great European nations left standing: England, France, Spain, Italy, and Prussia, the Germanic state in the east under whose leadership the German Empire emerged in 1871. The rest of Europe would regroup in four confederations of smaller states. The Northern confederation would have its capital in The Hague; Mitteleuropa in Warsaw or Prague; the Danubian confederation in Vienna; and the Balkan confederation (led by Turkey) in Constantinople. Russia would have to withdraw back into Asia. The nine European powers would meet in a 'Council of Europe', which would be bolstered by a supreme judiciary and a Supreme Economic Council.

Churchill then added a military element to the Council of Europe, foreshadowing his later determination to push for a European army.

'Each power', he said, 'would contribute an air cohort – Prussia included – and boys of sixteen would be selected for it. Once enrolled they would be under no national jurisdiction, but they would never be obliged to co-operate in an attack on their own country.' All air forces would be internationalised, but every participating power, except Prussia for the duration of 100 years, would still be allowed its own militia. He ended his exposition by telling Colville and the Prof that 'all this is a thing of the distant future: we might have to give it one hundred years to work.'[1]

At a time when all of Britain and continental Europe was calling for German blood, it was near impossible for the British prime minister to publicly state this Grand Design for Europe. What made it even harder was that Churchill's new foreign secretary, Anthony Eden, along with leading civil servants in the Foreign Office, was vehemently opposed to Churchill's view of postwar Europe. After the United States and the Soviet Union formally entered the war against Nazi Germany, Churchill refused to yield on the idea that regional councils – including the Council of Europe – held the key to providing world security after the war. Foreign Secretary Eden and the Foreign Office, on the other hand, started arguing in 1942 that great power cooperation would be a better basis for world security.

That is, in Eden's conception, the United States, the Soviet Union, China and Great Britain would be the dominant forces in a new world organisation akin to the League of Nations. Eden was strongly supported by the Americans in his pursuit of great power cooperation and believed very early on that Stalin's postwar domination of eastern Europe was inevitable. He therefore preferred an organisation of western European states rather than one that would ultimately include all of Europe.[2]

By the autumn of 1942, events were finally moving in the direction of the Allied forces. Churchill experienced victory for the first time as prime minister when Alexander and Montgomery destroyed Rommel's army at El Alamein in the 'Battle of Egypt'. It gave the Prime Minister breathing space to further develop his thoughts about what Europe and the world might look like after the war.

On 21 October 1942, two days before Alexander and Montgomery opened their offensive in Egypt, Churchill sent a secret minute to Eden outlining his thinking. In many ways it was a response to the idea that was gaining such currency in the Foreign Office: great power cooperation. Churchill refused to accept its viability, arguing: 'we certainly do not wish to be shut up with the Russians and Chinese when Swedes, Norwegians, Danes, Dutch, Belgians,

Frenchmen, Spaniards, Poles, Czechs and Turks will have their burning
questions, their desire for our aid and their very great power of making their
voices heard.' Churchill wrote:

> I must admit that my thoughts rest primarily in Europe – the revival of the glory of
> Europe, the parent continent of the modern nations and of civilization. It would
> be a measureless disaster if Russian barbarism overlaid the culture and
> independence of the ancient states of Europe. Hard as it is to say now, I trust
> that the European family may act unitedly as one under a Council of Europe. I look
> forward to a United States of Europe in which the barriers between the nations will
> be greatly minimised and unrestricted travel will be possible. I hope to see the
> economy of Europe studied as a whole. Of course we shall have to work with the
> Americans in many ways, and in the greatest ways, but Europe is our prime care ...
> It would be easy to dilate upon these themes. Unhappily, the war has prior claims
> on our attention.[3]

The Prime Minister was somewhat ambiguous about Britain's role, but at
least included his country in the proposed Council of Europe: 'I hope to see a
Council consisting of perhaps ten units, including the former Great Powers.'[4]
This was in line with what he told the Prof and Colville over dinner at
Chequers two years previously. As before, communism was the big fear. Europe
would have to become Britain's 'prime care' after the war, at least in part
because Churchill could not bear to see the Soviet Union becoming the
dominant European power.

Two weeks after Churchill's minute, the Cabinet considered questions of
postwar settlement. This time Churchill contradicted his earlier statements
and suggested that the Russians, the Americans and even the British should
leave Europe to organise itself after the war. On 3 November 1942, Eden's
private secretary noted in his diary:

> Row in Cabinet today over post-war. There were two papers on the agenda, one
> about the Dutch and Norwegian proposals for establishing international bases in
> Europe, the other about relief in Europe after the war. These provoked the P.M. to
> the most obstreperous utterances. He said that the only way to run Europe after the
> war was for Great Britain and Russia to keep out and for Europe to be run by a
> Grand Council of 'the Great Powers including Prussia, Italy, Spain and the
> Scandinavian Confederacy'. He did not want America in Europe.[5]

By the time Churchill went to meet US President Franklin D. Roosevelt in
Casablanca in January 1943 to discuss the merits of 'unconditional surrender'
for the Axis forces, the Prime Minister started to think of postwar European
cooperation in slightly more radical terms. Shortly after the Casablanca
meeting, during which he still had the strategic upper hand, Churchill secretly

flew to Adana on the coast near the Turkish–Syrian border to attempt to persuade Turkey to join the Allied powers and to start organising postwar Europe in the East. It took a four-hour cross-continental flight in a small Commando bomber and an exceedingly difficult landing on a narrow airstrip in the Turkish mountains to get there.

From Churchill's discussions with President Inönü, held in railway carriages close to Adana's small airfield, it appeared that the Turks thought of Britain as the essential bulwark against Russia in Europe. During discussions on the afternoon of Churchill's arrival on 30 January 1943, Turkish leaders conveyed to Churchill their fear of a newly imperialistic Russia, to which the Prime Minister gave the reassuring reply that he 'would not be a friend of Russia if she imitated Germany'.[6] Early next morning, Churchill lay in bed in his private saloon carriage, where red silk hung from every wall, dictating a note on his views of global postwar security. He titled it 'Morning Thoughts'.[7]

In his note, dictated to Ian Jacob, who travelled to Turkey with the Prime Minister as the assistant military secretary to the War Cabinet, Churchill provided once more the rough sketch for a Council of Europe he first outlined in December 1940. He then took it one step further, writing:

> It is the intention of the Chiefs of the United Nations to create a world organisation for the preservation of peace, based upon the conceptions of freedom and justice and the revival of prosperity. As a part of this organisation an instrument of European government will be established which will embody the spirit but not be subject to the weaknesses of the former League of Nations.[8]

This was a note written with deep purpose – a statement of Churchill's deepest wishes for the postwar world. Alec Cadogan, one of the chief diplomats at the Foreign Office during the war, noted in his diary: 'He was awfully proud of it.'[9] With the radical notion of installing a type of European government going far beyond the limited remit of the League, Churchill was now completely out of tune with the conservative pragmatists of the Foreign Office. The response came from the pen of Gladwyn Jebb, head of the small policy-planning department in the Foreign Office, who was 'dumbfounded' that Churchill had confided to the Turks his innermost views about a postwar settlement. He circulated an alternative paper defiantly entitled 'Early Morning Thoughts'. Jebb, invariably referred to by Churchill as 'that pipsqueak', thought the Prime Minister's views were 'so impracticable as hardly to merit serious consideration'.[10] If it were up to Jebb's planning team, Britain would seek to involve the Russians in a world organisation rather than focus on creating a European bloc that could only anger and alienate them.

Eden, too, disliked Churchill's advocacy for the creation of an instrument of European government. The Foreign Secretary thought European unification would lead to the Americans reverting to isolationism and the Russians withdrawing from the larger structure of world security. In 1944, Eden most clearly articulated how he felt about Churchill's ideas on European unity: 'it is clear that the Soviet Union might regard any continental bloc as a threat to its own interests and it is extremely doubtful whether, especially in the postwar period, we would be able to work towards a United States of Europe in the face of Soviet opposition.'[11]

But the 'Morning Thoughts' note had already pre-empted such criticism. The regional councils the Prime Minister proposed would still be subordinate to the type of world organisation that Eden and the Foreign Office desired. The United States would be very closely linked to the Council of Europe. Nonetheless, Churchill warned that the future of Europe depended on the unpredictable attitudes of the Russians and the Americans. 'No one can predict with certainty', he wrote, 'that the victors will never quarrel among themselves, or that the United States may not once again retire from Europe.' It was for that reason that Churchill committed Britain – and hoped for American aid in this course – to doing her utmost to 'organise a coalition of resistance to any act of aggression committed by any Power'.[12] What better way to do this than to organise a European bloc?

It would become increasingly clear to Churchill during the course of the war that the Russians could not be counted on to become reliable political partners in the postwar settlement. Churchill had great regard for the courage of the Russian people but, when it came time to think about an occupation statute for Germany, the Soviet expansionist agenda was out in the open. The Russians wanted nothing less than to get as close to the heart of Europe as possible. That, of course, was unacceptable to Churchill, who told Jacob: 'we must stay as far east as we can get with our armies.'[13] Roosevelt, who used his last breaths of life to try to appease Stalin, prevented Churchill from setting such clear political war aims. The President's objective, to defeat Hitler and get out as quickly as possible, was irreconcilable with the European concern for the plight of a Soviet-dominated eastern Europe.

After Adana, Churchill took some time to recover from a severe bout of pneumonia, the nasty consequence of choosing to fly across Europe and North Africa in unheated bombers. When he came out of hospital, the Prime Minister decided to go public with what he had already told Eden, the Turkish President, President Roosevelt, and his War Cabinet. In one of his famous wartime BBC broadcasts, the Prime Minister turned his mind once again to the future of Britain, Europe and the world. On 21 March 1943 Churchill was heard in all corners of the Empire. The original broadcast, as well as translations into twenty-four languages – including German and Italian – was repeated throughout the night.[14] 'One can imagine', he began, 'that under a world institution embodying or representing the United Nations, and some day all nations, there should come into being a Council of Europe and a Council of Asia.' Churchill continued:

> As according to the forecast I am outlining the war against Japan will still be raging, it is upon the creation of the Council of Europe and the settlement of Europe that the first practical task will be centred. Now this is a stupendous business. In Europe lie most of the causes which have led to these two world wars. In Europe dwell the historic parent races from whom our Western civilization has been so largely derived. I believe myself to be what is called a good European and I should deem it a noble task to take part in reviving the fertile genius and in restoring the true greatness of Europe.[15]

Reserving some praise for the spirit of the League of Nations, Churchill provided a bare sketch of how the new Council might operate:

> We must try – I am speaking of course, only for ourselves – we must try to make the Council of Europe, or whatever it may be called, into a really effective league with all the strongest forces concerned woven into its texture with a high court to adjust disputes and with forces, armed forces, national or international or both, held ready to enforce these decisions and prevent renewed aggression and the preparation of future wars.[16]

Which European nations would belong to the Council of Europe? Churchill thought all of what geographically belonged to Europe could join the proposed instrument of common government. He left room for the possibility that some states would, for whatever reason, be unable to join at first. He was thinking primarily of the countries that might be robbed of their free will under possible Soviet domination. Churchill told the world: 'Any one can see that this Council, when created, must eventually embrace the whole of Europe and that all the main branches of the European family must some day be partners in it.'[17] Then came the most radical expression of support for long-term unification of Europe, based on the initial creation of the Council of Europe:

> It is my earnest hope, though I can hardly expect to see it fulfilled in my lifetime, that we shall achieve the largest common measure of the integrated life of Europe that is possible without destroying the individual characteristics and traditions of its many ancient and historic races.[18]

Note that Churchill did not say that his earnest hope was to see an integrated Europe without destroying the *sovereignty* of its many ancient nation states. That would have been a contradiction in terms. In an integrated political system, he argued, only the 'individual characteristics and traditions' of the European peoples would have to be protected. The Prime Minister was looking here to something far more meaningful than a short-term system of multilateral cooperation in which nation states retained their full remit of power. Instead, as he would argue persuasively after the war, he implicitly embraced the partial abrogation of national sovereignty as the primary prerequisite for unification.

There was just one ambiguity. Would Britain or even Russia become part of such an integrated European system? Churchill, conscious of the fact that the Americans and the Russians were listening intently to his broadcast, clouded the matter in rhetorical vagueness: 'All this will, I believe, be found to harmonize with the high permanent interests of Britain, the United States and Russia. It certainly cannot be accomplished without their cordial and concerted agreement and direct participation.' Perhaps the closest Churchill came to hinting at Britain's participatory role in Europe was when he said with regard to Britain and the British Commonwealth of Nations that 'it will not be given to any one nation to achieve the full satisfaction of its individual wishes'. Churchill's individual wish for Britain might have been to maintain its full influence in every corner of the globe but he keenly understood that the postwar settlement would be fraught with compromise. In 1943, no one could know definitively whether that might include compromising British sovereignty to lead a larger synthesis of European states.

Vagueness about the composition and workings of the proposed Council of Europe appears to be a deliberate Churchillian device. The Prime Minister believed that the character and constitution of postwar European institutions should be shaped by the citizens of Europe, not thrust upon them. 'Nothing could be more foolish at this stage', Churchill argued in his broadcast, 'than to plunge into details and try to prescribe the exact groupings of States or lay down precise machinery for their cooperation or still more to argue about frontiers' – at least while the war in the West was far from its conclusion, let alone in the Far East.[19]

It appears from the broadcast that Churchill was moved to support European unification by far more than the threat of communism alone. He thought of himself, in his own words, as 'a good European'. Still, much of Churchill's Council of Europe idea was based on the fear that the Soviet Union would attempt to subject large swaths of Europe to its will as its armies marched into the continent. As rational as that fear might appear to be with the benefit of hindsight, it was perplexing to many of the Prime Minister's closest allies.

Among them was Harold Macmillan, Churchill's resident minister at the Allied Headquarters in North Africa during the war and a younger Conservative MP who had supported him in the domestic fight against appeasement. Macmillan had been listening to Churchill's broadcast in General Alexander's camp, knowing that it would be for his generation to define more precisely Britain's role in Europe and the world after the war. In November 1943, during the Cairo conference, Macmillan and Churchill were in close company for a week. One night, after a meeting with President Roosevelt, Churchill came back in a bad mood, tired, and suddenly turned to Macmillan and said, 'Cromwell was a great man!' He replied, 'Yes, Prime Minister'. 'Aaah,' Churchill said, 'he made one fatal error. Born and bred as a child in the fear of the strength and power of Spain, he failed to see that Spain was finished and France was rising, hence the Marlborough wars, hence the century of war. Will that be said of me?' It took Macmillan some time to figure out what Churchill meant with his historical parallel before realising that the Prime Minister had lost interest in the Germans; they would be defeated in a few years. But *what would the Soviet Union be*; that was the big question for the postwar world. Churchill was always 'casting that strange, brooding mind forward', Macmillan later remembered.[20]

The issue of the organisation of postwar Europe first appeared on the official agenda of the Big Three (Britain, Russia and the United States) at the Yalta conference in February 1945. Churchill's personal position was clear. After the March 1943 world broadcast, during a visit to Washington, DC, in May 1943, the Prime Minister had reiterated his preference for the establishment of regional councils under the umbrella of a world organisation. He told American Vice-President Henry Wallace that each of the dozen or so countries that would make up the Council of Europe should 'appoint a representative to the European Regional Council, thus creating a form of United States of Europe'.[21] For inspiration, Churchill referred the Vice-President to the writings of Count Coudenhove-Kalergi.

By the time of the Yalta conference, however, Churchill, pragmatic as always, had accepted that his personal preference for the Council of Europe was not official British government policy.[22] The combined pressure from Eden, Foreign Office officials, the Americans, the Dominion leaders and the

Soviets forced the Prime Minister to let go of his proposal for regional councils. Instead, the 'Four Power Plan', which Eden and the Americans touted from the end of 1942, won the day. It proposed to root a system of world security in great power cooperation, creating a United Nations organisation based on the principal assumption that, in Eden's words, 'the great powers were in principle equally interested in maintaining the peace everywhere in the world, and that they would act together whenever and wherever it might be threatened.'[23]

This was far more palatable to Stalin than Churchill's regional plan because it allowed for Soviet influence in Europe. The plans also conformed to Roosevelt's hopes of being able to work with the Soviets to create a successful instrument of world government. In May 1944 Churchill ceased to push his regionalist Council of Europe approach and endorsed the Four Power Plan as official British policy.[24] A few months later, in August 1944, British representatives met their American, Russian and Chinese counterparts in the Dumbarton Oaks mansion in Georgetown, DC, where they agreed on the establishment of a postwar United Nations organisation.

At Yalta, in February 1945, official British policy remained unchanged. There was, however, an important sticking point for Churchill. Though it appeared inevitable that Stalin's military domination of eastern Europe was there to stay, the Prime Minister set out to curb Russian influence in Europe. Already in October 1944, this quest had led to a painful compromise between Churchill and Stalin on the division of influence in the Balkans. During their Moscow meeting on the evening of 9 October, Churchill scribbled on a half-sheet of paper his proposal for the postwar fate of the Balkan countries and pushed it towards Stalin. Taking just a few seconds to consider Churchill's proposal, Stalin grabbed a blue pencil and made large tick on the piece of paper. Stalin was delighted with the Prime Minister's recognition of Russian interests in the region. Churchill secured Western influence over Greece by signing away Romania and Bulgaria and dividing up fifty–fifty control over Yugoslavia and Hungary.[25]

At a quarter past four on 5 February 1945, Stalin, Roosevelt and Churchill opened discussions in the first plenary sessions of the Yalta conference. The men, together with their aides and interpreters, sat at a round table in the magnificent Lavidia Palace, home to the American delegation in Stalin's resort town on the Black Sea. Churchill and the British delegation stayed five miles away in a nineteenth-century villa, half Gothic and half Moorish, which, much to Churchill's delight, was especially renovated for the occasion. The topic under discussion was as complex as it was divisive: the future of Germany. It was just as important an issue to Churchill for the future of European peace as was the problem of postwar Russian ambitions in Europe.

A month before the Yalta conference, Churchill had sent Eden a note outlining his thoughts. The gist was that the Prime Minister supported a policy of getting Germany back on its feet to become a positive force in Europe. 'Obviously, when the German organised resistance has ceased,' he argued, 'the first stage will be one of severe military control.' But it was also much too early, he thought, for the Allies to reach final decisions on the question of German partition and the treatment of disputed regions like the Saar and the Ruhr. 'No one can foresee at the present moment what the state of Europe will be or what the relations of the Great Powers will be, or what the temper of their peoples will be,' Churchill wrote. 'There is therefore wisdom', he concluded, 'in reserving one's decisions as long as possible and until all the facts and forces that will be potent at the moment are revealed.'[26]

At Yalta, Stalin, who did not share Churchill's caution, asked his Big Three counterparts directly what to do about the dismemberment of Germany. With the Red Army just 40 miles from Berlin, Stalin was in a much stronger bargaining position than ever before. Two camps emerged. On the one side were Stalin and Roosevelt, who wanted to split Germany up into five parts. On the other was Churchill, who proposed to split Germany into two parts: Prussia – one of the big European powers in his Council design – and Austria-Bavaria. The rest of the German territories, Churchill proposed, would temporarily remain under international control. Stalin wanted a decision then and there, but Churchill succeeded in persuading Roosevelt to back his plan to study the full implications of Germany's partition in greater detail before taking a final decision.

Churchill could not prevent Roosevelt, however, from telling the conference that the Americans planned to withdraw from Europe within two years after final victory, which would leave Britain to occupy a large swath of Germany all on its own – a seemingly impossible task. Churchill's solution, partly conceived in response to strong demands from Charles de Gaulle, who had been excluded from participation in the conference, was to ensure the incorporation of a strong France in the postwar settlement.[27] Churchill was in no way enamoured of de Gaulle at this point, writing to Eden a month before Yalta: 'I cannot think of anything more unpleasant and impossible than having this menacing and hostile man in our midst, always trying to make himself a reputation in France by claiming a position far above what France occupies, and making faces at the Allies who are doing the work.'[28] Nevertheless, Churchill pushed Stalin and Roosevelt to agree that France could manage part of the American–British occupation zone in western Germany, giving the country a place among the victorious Allies. British self-interest in containing Germany was at stake here, for as Churchill argued at the negotiating table: 'We will need her [France's] defence against Germany. We have suffered badly from German robot guns and should Germany again get near to the Channel coast we would suffer again. After the Americans have gone home I must think seriously of the future.'[29]

The rest of the conference was devoted to working out the Dumbarton Oaks agreements on the United Nations organisation and settling a future for Poland. Here it seemed that Churchill won a victory when Stalin promised free elections in the part of Poland that had not been annexed by the Soviet Union in 1939. The final joint declaration on Poland, which accompanied the full Yalta communiqué, called for a free provisional government of national unity which would organise 'free and unfettered elections'. Despite the positive language, Churchill left Yalta with considerable anxiety about Soviet intentions in Poland and the rest of eastern Europe.

On Churchill's return to London, despite the many personal and political letters of congratulation and glowing reviews in the papers on his success at Yalta, he delicately expressed his doubts to the War Cabinet: 'if the terms of the communiqué agreed with Premier Stalin were carried out in good faith, all would be well. If, on the hand [sic], effective reality were not given to those undertakings, our engagement would be altered.'[30] And when Colville, who had stayed back in London, asked his boss how it went, Churchill shook his head from side to side, saying almost nothing, but then muttered, 'the President is a dying man.'[31]

President Roosevelt, in his quest to involve the Russians in the United Nations and the war against Japan, allowed Stalin to occupy Berlin, Prague and Budapest – the ancient European capitals that Churchill wanted so desperately to keep within a Western political settlement. Roosevelt had been inclined to give away even more than Churchill had been willing to in his October 1944 pact with Stalin which was designed to save Greece for the West. A few days later, after a day of parliamentary debate on Poland and dinner at Buckingham Palace, Churchill was informed of early Soviet intimidation in Romania. He told Colville there was nothing he could do about it because 'Russia had let us go our way in Greece; she would insist on imposing her will in Roumania and Bulgaria.'[32]

Churchill felt much differently about Poland. As the Prime Minister and his private secretary prepared to turn in around 2 a.m. that night, Churchill said: 'I have not the slightest intention of being cheated over Poland, not even if we go to the verge of war with Russia.'[33] Soon enough, however, Russia broke its promise of free elections. As the Americans contented themselves with Soviet membership of the United Nations, Poland fell into the claws of the Russian bear. It was a betrayal, tragedy and a deep personal embarrassment for Churchill. So shortly after its liberation from Nazism, Churchill was unable to protect Poland from a new type of tyranny.

Final victory arrived in Europe on 8 May 1945 with the unconditional surrender of Germany. While Churchill was immensely proud and relieved to have successfully defended Western civilisation against the Nazis, the challenges of the future still dominated his mind. In his victory address to the nation Churchill struck a remarkably sombre note. 'I could tell you tonight that all our toils and troubles were over,' he began. 'Then indeed I could end my five years' service happily, and if you thought that you had had enough of me and that I ought to be put out to grass I would take it with the best of grace.' Being put out of a job, however, was the last thing he wanted. Churchill wanted to be there for the postwar world, too. There was a new danger looming from the East and a new Europe to be constructed from the rubble heap.

It was Churchill's duty, he felt, to win the peace just as he had won the war. Having never actually been elected to the post of prime minister, his victory address was an overture to the British people. 'I must warn you,' he said, 'as I did when I began this five years' task – and no one knew then that it would last so long – that there is still a lot to do, and that you must be prepared for further efforts of mind and body and further sacrifices to great causes.' It became immediately clear what great cause Churchill had in mind: 'On the continent of Europe we have yet to make sure that the simple and honourable purposes for which we entered the war are not brushed aside or overlooked in the months following our success, and that the words "freedom", "democracy", and "liberation" are not distorted from their true meaning as we have understood them.'[34] For this purpose Churchill put himself at the disposal of the British people for another term of government. They would decide at the general election of 26 July 1945 if they wanted him.

Churchill had one more major diplomatic opportunity to put his stamp on the organisation of postwar Europe before the elections. He was due in Berlin on 17 July for the start of the Potsdam conference, the last of the major wartime conferences. It mattered little to the prospects of the Council of

Europe, which was already off the table. The Yalta conference, after all, reached a detailed state of negotiations on the workings of the United Nations Organisation.

The advent of a new American president after the death of Roosevelt on 12 April 1945 – the former Senator of Missouri Harry S. Truman – did little to change the apprehensive American attitude towards the Council of Europe. On Truman's first day in the Oval Office, the State Department put a special memorandum on his desk in anticipation of the Potsdam conference. Among its most important findings was this assessment of Churchill's Britain: 'The British long for security but are deeply conscious of their decline from a leading position to that of the junior partner of the Big Three and are anxious to buttress their position vis-à-vis the United States both through exerting leadership over the countries of Western Europe and through knitting the Commonwealth more closely together.'[35] Truman knew what he was getting.

The stately city of Potsdam, the old imperial seat of the Prussian monarchy at a short distance from Berlin, was in shambles when the leaders of the Big Three arrived. That was largely Churchill's own administration's doing. In the night of 14 April 1945, the Allies effectively destroyed the city with a 500-bomber raid. By the end of the war Churchill had lost control over the extensive and controversial air attacks that the Americans and the British used to break German resistance. Shocked by the images and stories of destruction, he asked his Cabinet in a terse one-sentence minute: 'What was the point of going and blowing down Potsdam?'[36]

In July 1945 he was able to see for himself for the first time what had been the fate of German civilians. It aroused mixed feelings in the Prime Minister. Though he was 'much moved [...] by their haggard looks and threadbare clothes', Churchill kept in the back of his mind that it could just as well have been London. 'If they had won the war, we would have been in the bunker,' he said.[37] The Prime Minister seemed absent-minded; not as beguiled by the awesome history of the place as everyone around him expected. His thoughts were on the upcoming election. Until the result of the election poll, Churchill said, 'I shall be only half a man.'[38]

President Truman and Churchill met for the first time in Berlin on 18 July. The Prime Minister remembered being impressed with Truman's 'gay, precise, sparkling manner and obvious power of decision'.[39] But if he held any genuine hope that Truman would make a volte-face in American policy and support a regional plan for European unification, he would have been disappointed.

Truman did not differ in any radical sense from his predecessor in his approach to the organisation of world security. Both men knew also that Britain now almost completely depended on America.

Over lunch on the 18th Churchill told Truman about Britain's dire financial position, having spent 'more than half her foreign investments for the common cause when we were alone, and now emerged from the war with a great external debt of three thousand million pounds'.[40] The Prime Minister understood why Britain was ever more likely to become a second-rate power after the war. As at Yalta, Britain would not be negotiating on an equal footing with Russia and America. Potsdam was bound to become a disappointing affair. Quite how disappointing it would turn out he could not predict.

On the day Churchill arrived in Berlin, he was told the stunning news that the Americans had tested the atomic bomb successfully in the New Mexican desert. This, above all else, defined the atmosphere of the conference. There was no doubt that the bomb would be used to end the war in Japan, meaning that the Allies had no need to persuade Stalin to send his troops to the Far East. The war might be won on British–American terms. The issues facing Europe, it was hoped, might be discussed on their own merits. President Truman only informed Stalin of the successful testing of the bomb on 24 July, a week into the conference. Though it is now widely thought that Stalin already knew everything about the nuclear programme through his intelligence network in America, it seemed to Churchill and Truman at Potsdam that Stalin was genuinely surprised by the announcement and had a limited understanding of the true destructive power of this new weapon.

While the war was still raging in the Pacific, the most important issue on the Potsdam agenda was the German problem and the related issue of Europe's postwar borders. On the night of the 18th Churchill dined with Stalin alone. Stalin, it appeared, had studied British politics in great detail and predicted a majority of 80 seats for Churchill's Conservatives. The main focus of their conversation was Europe. Over dinner the Prime Minister could express directly his concern about Russia's intentions in Europe. In his memoirs, Churchill recalled drawing 'a line from the North Cape to Albania, and named the capitals east of that line which were in Russian hands. It looked as if Russia were rolling on westwards.'[41] Stalin flat-out denied any expansionist intentions, telling Churchill that he was preparing to demobilise and withdraw. But it was clear then to Churchill that an iron curtain was descending over Europe. It took over two years for the global public to comprehend Stalin's ambitions.

It was agreed at Potsdam that Germany, demilitarised and disarmed, would be divided into four zones of Allied occupation. The country's greatest war criminals would be brought to justice at Nuremberg and 'denazification' became official policy, though no timeline was established to constitute a new national German government. Instead, the Allied Control Commission, composed of representatives from the United States, Britain, France and the Soviet Union, would run the country until it felt Germany was ready for domestic leadership. A Council of Foreign Ministers was established to draft peace treaties with Germany's former allies. Then there was a solution to the sensitive issue of German–Soviet–Polish border revisions. The Soviets insisted on holding on to the Polish territory they conquered in 1939 and giving Poland some German land in the west. As millions of Germans now in Poland were deported or fled to the western zones of occupation – those administered by the US, UK and France – it fell to the Western powers to take care of the flood of refugees from eastern Europe.

Many of the final negotiation results were already close to being concluded when Churchill flew to Britain with his daughter Mary on the afternoon of Wednesday the 25th to hear the election results. At a banquet given by the American delegation at Potsdam, Churchill had felt confident enough in the presence of his Labour opponent, Clement Attlee, that he proposed a toast to 'The Leader of the Opposition', adding 'whoever he may be'.[42] He expected to be back in Potsdam within 48 hours and predicted to King George VI that night in London, after a quiet dinner with his family, that the Conservatives would win a majority of between 30 and 80 seats. Conservative Central Office predicted a majority of a similar magnitude. Churchill's doctor, Lord Moran, even left half of his luggage in Potsdam on the assumption they would be back within 24 hours. The Prime Minister went to bed that night, he recalled, 'in the belief that the British people would wish me to continue my work'.[43]

The 26th of July was a black day for Churchill. He woke just before dawn, feeling almost physical pain at the sudden realisation that he might, in fact, lose the election. 'The power to shape the future', he feared, 'would be denied me'. Wearing his blue siren suit, the Prime Minister went into the Map Room set up for monitoring the election results as they came in. By noon it became clear that Attlee's Labour Party would have a landslide majority. Churchill's son Randolph and his son-in-law Duncan Sandys lost their seats in Parliament. At lunch, Churchill almost choking on his food in grief, his wife Clemmie told him, 'It may well be a blessing in disguise.' He replied, 'at the moment it seems quite effectively disguised.'[44]

At noon on 27 July Churchill held a farewell Cabinet meeting. 'It was a pretty grim affair,' Eden wrote in his diary. 'After it was over I was on my way to the front door when W. called me back and we had half an hour alone. He was pretty wretched, poor old boy. Said he didn't feel any more reconciled this morning, on the contrary it hurt more, like a wound which becomes more painful after first shock. He couldn't help feeling his treatment had been scurvy.'[45]

Churchill could scarcely come to terms with the thought that he would not be at the helm in the postwar world. On the afternoon of Friday 10 August, Churchill was chauffeured from London to Westerham, Kent, where he was to spend the weekend at Chartwell. One of his private secretaries, Miss Layton, was in the car with him. She wrote in a letter recalling that day:

> Victory over Japan was not yet an accomplished fact, but it hung in the air. And the streets of London, as we left Westminster, were already filling with rejoicing people. Not the same as at VE, but yet there was great relief. He looked at all this. We were somewhere in the neighbourhood of Tower Bridge when he said: 'You know, not a single decision has been taken since we left office to have brought this about.' I didn't know what to say in consolation, and only muttered something about wasn't it better for him now to have a rest. He looked from the car window, and after a while said 'No − I wanted − I wanted to do the Peace too.'[46]

CHAPTER 5

'LET EUROPE ARISE!'
SWITZERLAND, SEPTEMBER 1946

In September 1945, vacationing on Lake Como in Italy after five long years of war and six weeks of acute post-election depression, Churchill needed Charles Montag more than anyone else.

Montag was a man of quiet genius. Behind the unassuming appearance of a bank clerk was a gifted painter and one of the shrewdest European art dealers of the twentieth century. Born in the Swiss town of Winterthur in 1880, Montag left Switzerland at the age of 23 to pursue his artistic dreams in Paris, where he traded his earlier dark realism for neo-Impressionist, brightly coloured and rigidly constructed land- and seascapes. He quickly became acquainted with the stars of his time and place, including Monet, Matisse and Renoir. From the end of the 1910s onwards Montag started to focus exclusively on his art dealership and found his niche pushing works by his French friends with wealthy Swiss collectors.

In 1915, Montag and Churchill became acquainted in Cassis, a French town on the Mediterranean coast. Churchill was then a 41-year-old member of the British Cabinet and War Council. To his bitter disappointment, he had recently been relieved of his position at the Admiralty after the disastrous Dardanelles campaign – the military operation he designed which nearly destroyed his political career.[1] It was then, in the depths of his despair at being sidelined, that he discovered his love of painting.[2] Though he started out in the summer of 1915 under the artistic mentorship of the Irish painter Sir John Lavery, Churchill's meeting with Montag would lead to a long-term creative partnership.[3]

That Churchill was already a famous figure in British politics scarcely impressed Montag, who counted great French statesmen such as Georges Clemenceau and Aristide Briand as his friends. On their first encounter in Cassis, Churchill asked Montag outright what he thought of his painting. 'If your painting is as good as your politics,' Montag replied, 'Europe is lost.'[4] Churchill held still for a few seconds, his face frozen in a frown as he inspected Montag's, but then burst out in generous laughter. They became close friends and saw each other as often as time and convenience allowed. In August 1920, for instance, Montag travelled to Biarritz to help Churchill along while he was vacationing in southern France. 'Montag is vy [sic] anxious to teach me,' Churchill wrote to his wife on that occasion, '& most austere in all his methods. He was positively glad when the sun didn't shine yesterday because I was forced to give attention to the drawing, not having the brilliant light to play with.'[5] Montag became a regular correspondent, took his pupil round the galleries of Paris, and in 1921 even successfully entered Churchill's work in an exhibition at the prestigious Parisian Galerie Druet under the pseudonym Charles Morin where six of his works were sold.[6]

In September 1945, Churchill needed his paintbox, his brushes and Montag just as much as he had after the Dardanelles debacle. A fortnight after his electoral defeat, Moran found him sitting in his silk vest on his bed at the Sandyses' place in Westminster Gardens. Churchill admitted 'futile specu-lations' filled his mind and that he had to take sleeping pills to function. After lamenting the outcome of the Potsdam conference, which allowed Russia's western frontier to advance even further towards the heart Europe, he continued: 'I get fits of depression. You know how my days were filled; now it has all gone. I go to bed about twelve o'clock. There is nothing to sit up for [...] I don't mind if I never see England again.'[7]

Montag arrived in Italy on 13 September, as Churchill observed contentedly in a letter to his wife, with 'a magnificent outfit of colours and brushes'.[8] Though Montag was not a rich man, he brought a set of beautiful brushes and 20 small boxes of paint, which to his host's slight embarrassment would have cost him the hefty sum of about £50. Nonetheless, Churchill was as happy as a child with his new presents. His doctor, also present in Como, remembered him squeezing out the paint from the tubes one by one onto his fingertips, relishing the quality of the colour. That night at the dinner table Montag talked about how to predict the fall of nations by the state of their art. Churchill was polite enough to listen to his teacher, Moran noted in his diary, but much too seasoned a politician to attach value to this line of argument.[9]

It was now considerably cooler in Italy than when Churchill first arrived, clouds obscuring the sun, and autumn announcing itself in the wind. It did not keep Montag and his pupil from setting up their easels on the lake for four days straight. Montag's advice greatly helped Churchill, who was proud to report to his wife that of the nine paintings he did in Como the later ones were a 'remarkable advance' from his earlier painting. Churchill, while he thought Montag's own painting disappointingly deficient, was happy in the knowledge that 'one cannot paint in his presence without learning.'[10]

One of the most exciting elements of Montag's visit was the prospect he offered of a future painting expedition in the sunshine. Churchill wrote to Clementine on the morning of Montag's departure: 'He was very full of an invitation from "The Swiss family" for me to go on into Switzerland and paint for a few weeks there. On being pressed, he said it was the Federal Government & the Municipality of Zurich, where he lives.'[11] The only real obstacle for Churchill was how to finance the proposed holiday. 'This plan was too difficult altogether,' he told his wife, 'because as you realize one cannot take any money abroad, and it is absolutely necessary for one to know at whose cost one is living.'[12]

Whatever the administrative troubles surrounding the organisation of the Swiss vacation, Churchill wholeheartedly embraced the idea. During this well-deserved political siesta in Italy, he emptied his mind and cleansed his body of the poisonous stress that more than a few times led him to the brink of collapse during the war. He slowly came to terms with his harsh rejection by the British people at the end of the war. Just as he had done after the catastrophe of the Dardanelles campaign, he turned to his brushes and paints in a quest to heal his wounds. The prospect of perhaps being able to continue his recovery in Switzerland was highly alluring.

In Como, Churchill recuperated so successfully that he started imagining himself not being politically active at all in the aftermath of the war. By the end of the holiday his desire to keep up with the news had all but vanished. He now hardly missed the red dispatch boxes that his life had revolved around during the war. In exercising a different part of his brain Churchill found the peace and happiness that seemed impossibly distant from ever retuning after the general election. 'This is the first time for very many years that I have been completely out of the world,' he told Clemmie. 'I feel a great sense of relief which grows steadily, others having to face the hideous problems of the aftermath. On their shoulders and consciences weighs the responsibility for what is happening in Germany and Central Europe.' He had to concede that his wife might have been right about the election outcome: 'It may all indeed be a "blessing in disguise".'[13]

Charles Montag, meanwhile, set out to make it his personal business to overcome the financial and organisational difficulties that could bar Churchill from a painting holiday in Switzerland. His first port of call was the Swiss Anglophile banker Claus Vogel. Montag hoped that Vogel would be able to interest Swiss financiers and captains of industry in the project of getting Churchill to Switzerland for an extended vacation and, perhaps, an honorary doctorate.[14]

A problem was that Vogel had signed a petition – known as the 'Eingabe der Zweihundert' – initiated by 200 Swiss businessmen in November 1940. It asked the Swiss federal government to depose the editors-in-chief of Swiss newspapers critical of Nazi Germany. The idea was that this would prevent provocation and protect Switzerland from having to enter the war. As this information became public and, naturally, a serious source of embarrassment after the war, Vogel thought it best to form a consortium of businessmen and withdraw into the background.[15]

The group Vogel put together helped Montag secure most of the financial support for Churchill's visit. Huge Swiss conglomerates like Bally, Nestlé, Geigy and Sandoz as well as the prominent Bon hotelier family lined up to pay for Churchill's visit to their country.[16] Though there were some rumours that some of the companies financing the vacation had had shady dealings with Nazi Germany in the war, Thomas Maitland Snow, the British minister in Switzerland, told Churchill ahead of the visit that he thought all the companies involved were of fine standing and that Churchill 'need have no hesitation in accepting' them as his hosts.[17]

Anton Bon, the Swiss managing director of the Dorchester Hotel in London, was meant to play almost as important a role as Vogel in the realisation of the visit. Together with his hotelier brothers he set out to plan Churchill's transport and accommodation for the month-long visit. In May 1946, however, just when Churchill officially accepted his invitation to bring his family to Switzerland from late August to mid-September,[18] it surfaced in the British press that Anton had been involved in an illegal currency transaction. To save Churchill any embarrassment he quickly withdrew from the organising committee. In his stead, Charles Montag, Dr Jacques-Albert Cuttat, Legationsrat at the Swiss Foreign Service, and Oberstleutnant Hans Bracher, a high-ranking Swiss military officer, divided the scheduling work between them. Montag ended up bearing the brunt of the additional work, giving up a considerable portion of his time painting with Churchill to take care of all sorts of administrative tasks.

By way of preparation for the visit, the Swiss envoy in Paris, Carl Burckhardt, made an effort to meet Churchill for dinner while he was in Paris for the start of the post-World War II peace conference in July 1946. Joining them was the French Socialist ex-premier Léon Blum. 'I dined the other day with Winston Churchill,' Burckhardt reported to the Foreign Ministry in Bern on 27 July 1946, '[who] attacked the alcohol on hand in a pretty bold manner, with the result that I have to consider the second half of the conversation null and void. He was saying words, but it was hard to make out their precise meaning.'

During the first half of the evening, Churchill was lucid enough about the upcoming Swiss holiday. He told Burckhardt he wanted above all to swim – Lake Geneva, he thought, would be warmer in late August than the other lakes in the Swiss Alps. He took pleasure in the prospect of visiting the Swiss capital of Bern and hoped General Guisan, former commander of the Swiss army, would take him to see a military pageant. Despite these perfectly harmless intentions, Burckhardt had a feeling after the dinner that Churchill's vacation would end up in political controversy for the Swiss. 'There will be commentaries and certain repercussions in the press,' he predicted to his bosses at the Foreign Ministry.[19]

After the original idea of placing Churchill and family in a Bon family hotel in St-Moritz became politically untenable, the consortium settled on the lakeside town of Bursinel, halfway between Lausanne and Geneva. Churchill would stay in Villa Choisi, a magnificent eighteenth-century house on the shores of Lake Geneva surrounded by a leafy park, which once belonged to Colonel de Sacconay, a former military servant to Churchill's famous forebear the Duke of Marlborough.[20] Or as Churchill later described it: 'a lovely villa by the Lake of Geneva with Mont Blanc over the water in the background'.[21] The Swiss sponsors provided the staff in the house and the art to adorn it.[22]

Churchill's hosts initially budgeted the vacation at 20,000 Swiss francs.[23] In the end, the cost rose to an eye-popping 47,000 francs largely because the costs of the almost complete refurbishment of Choisi and the return charter flights were initially overlooked.[24] In today's money, the final cost of the month-long holiday would have been 1.5 million Swiss francs, or almost exactly a million pounds sterling. Churchill himself brought the 1946 equivalent of £90,000 in cash.[25]

With the finances settled, there remained a major political problem for the organisers. One of the ideas with which Montag enticed Churchill to accept his invitation to Switzerland was the prospect of receiving an honorary degree from one of the country's major universities. In December 1945 Montag and Vogel started to make soundings in the academic community of the University of Zurich.

To their frustration, it soon emerged that there was little to no chance the University of Zurich would be willing to confer the degree. The professors in the Law & Politics Faculty came up with a host of reasons as to why they were unable to confer the degree. Some believed that the right moment would have been straight after the war; others objected to the very principle of awarding politicians honorary doctorates, pointing to the shame that had come to the University of Lausanne for granting Italy's fascist leader Benito Mussolini one in 1937. It was for this reason that Lausanne flat-out refused to consider granting Churchill an honorary doctorate.[26] At the University of Zurich there was also the real procedural risk that if the rector put the idea to a motion some professors whose sympathies had been with Nazi Germany might choose to vote against it. According to protocol, just two negative votes would be enough to torpedo the motion's passing.

Of the few substantive scruples held by the Zurich professors the most important one was that the granting of an honorary doctorate might give the impression that the Swiss officially endorsed Churchill's famous 'Iron Curtain' speech, delivered just six months earlier in America. On 5 March 1946, speaking at President Truman's invitation at Westminster College in Fulton, Missouri, Churchill warned of Soviet expansionism and insisted that the division of Europe was a reality which had to be faced. 'From Stettin in the Baltic to Trieste in the Adriatic an iron curtain has descended across the Continent,' he said in the most famous passage of the speech. The image of the Iron Curtain, deriving from the nineteenth-century architectural design of safety curtains in theatres and first popularised in Nazi Germany by Hitler's propaganda chief Joseph Goebbels, was a particularly vivid way to capture the division of Europe.[27] The speech sent shock waves of disbelief through West and East alike.

If the Swiss were seen to support the Iron Curtain speech, the Zurich professors argued, there could be serious repercussions for Swiss–Russian diplomatic relations. They were clearly oblivious to the fact that Stalin felt no desire at all to maintain friendly ties with Switzerland. He despised the Swiss 'pigs' and had proposed to Churchill in 1944 to violate Swiss neutrality in order to attack Germany from the south. When Churchill told a Swiss diplomat about Stalin's proposal in 1946, he added: 'we, the English, don't do things like that. We don't invade a neutral country.'[28]

On 12 March 1946, less than a week after Churchill issued his clarion call at Fulton, the outgoing rector of the University of Zurich saw himself forced by his professors to abandon the idea of the honorary doctorate altogether. He wrote to Montag, the moving agent of the idea:

> Last Saturday another discussion regarding the honorary doctorate took place [...] this exchange of ideas was of course heavily influenced by the speech held in Fulton [...] The thought was expressed that after his [Churchill's] very firm positioning against Soviet Russia, a directly ensuing ceremony in Zurich would be interpreted as a willed and conscious protest. The notion was thus formed that at least during the current political turmoil, an honorary doctorate would arouse concerns. This way the highly qualified majority that is required is perhaps not achievable. A vote with negative outcome, however, must be avoided in all circumstances.[29]

Not yet defeated, Montag pushed on for a different solution and eventually persuaded the incoming rector of the university, Ernst Anderes, to invite Churchill to speak as a guest lecturer and present him with a framed 'Laudatio' – an academic thank you note featuring medieval calligraphy and lofty Latin phrasing. Churchill would deliver his address to the academic youth of the world in the Great Hall of the University of Zurich on Thursday 19 September, the last day of the visit.

If the Zurich professors had known what Churchill originally intended to say at Fulton, they might have been even more anxious about conferring an honorary degree. Even worse than suggesting that the English-speaking peoples form a fraternal bond to counter Soviet expansionism, Churchill had actually wanted to plead with the Americans for aid in forming a United States of Europe. Shortly before leaving for America, he spoke to Walter Graebner, the London Bureau chief of *Time* and *Life*, who was involved in buying the serialisation rights to Churchill's war memoirs. Churchill presented his plans for a long-term political and economic union of the states of Europe and asked: 'What do you think of that? Would something along those lines be suitable for my speech in America?'[30] Only after Churchill arrived in the United States to find that American opinion was even less ready for the idea of European unity than for his warnings about the Iron Curtain did he let go of the idea.[31]

And yet, it was a new unity in Europe that would become a core theme of Churchill's postwar political life. On 16 November 1945, in an address to a joint meeting of the Belgian Senate and Chamber, Churchill toyed publicly with the idea for the first time since being ousted from office. He told his Brussels audience in the closing sentences of his speech:

> I see no reason why, under the guardianship of the world organization, there should not ultimately arise the United States of Europe, both those of the East and those of the West, which will unify this Continent in a manner never known since the fall of the Roman Empire, and within which all its peoples may dwell together in prosperity, in justice and in peace.[32]

In the last weeks of 1945 and the early months of 1946, Churchill did not yet feel sufficiently confident about the message of the Brussels address to immediately follow it up with similar speeches. By the time he returned from Fulton in April 1946, however, the perfect occasion presented itself to retest the waters. Churchill was invited to spend a week in the royal lodgings of Amsterdam's Dam Square Palace by his wartime friend Queen Wilhelmina of the Netherlands. Frenzied crowds welcomed their liberator, who planned to revisit the Brussels message for his 9 May address to the Dutch States-General in the political capital of The Hague.

As he would time and again in his postwar speeches, Churchill presented a definition of free democracy to support his appeal for a European unity with sound constitutional principles. He designed, in his own words, 'simple, practical tests by which the virtue and reality of any political democracy may be measured'. The result was a masterful checklist of liberal democratic principles – the outcome of a lifelong study of and participation in British and European parliamentary democracy. Little was left to the imagination to understand that Soviet Russia failed the test. Seven separate points led to one concise question:

> Does the Government in any country rest upon a free, constitutional basis, assuring the people the right to vote according to their will, for whatever candidates they choose? Is there right the right of free expression of opinion, free support, free opposition, free advocacy and free criticism of the Government of the day?
>
> Are there Courts of Justice free from interference by the Executive or from threats of mob violence, and free from all association with particular political parties? Will these Courts administer public and well-established laws associated in the human mind with the broad principles of fair play and justice? Will there be fair play for the poor as well as for the rich? Will there be fair play for private persons as well as for Government officials? Will the rights of the individual, subject to his duties to the State, be maintained, asserted and exalted? *In short, do the Government own the people, or do the people own the Government?*

On the first item on the list – whether the people have the right to vote according to their will – Stalin and Churchill held wildly differing opinions.

Stalin could not comprehend Churchill's electoral defeat in July 1945, thinking that the Prime Minister should just have fixed the elections to ensure his continued reign. In Stalin's Russia, clearly, the government owned the people.

Further, Churchill paid enough tribute to the 'One World' ideal of the United Nations Organisation to justify an exposition of his idea of strengthening and establishing a number of 'special associations' – a throwback to his wartime ideas of establishing several regional councils to support a global structure. Rather than weakening the structure of the United Nations, Churchill believed that special associations such as the British Commonwealth or the fraternal bond between the English-speaking peoples would actually make the UN 'indivisible and invincible'.

Only in the very last sentence of the Hague address did Churchill make explicit what kind of special association he had in mind for Europe. It astonished the house that invited him to speak. 'I see no reason why,' he said, exactly as he had in Belgium six months previously, 'under the guardianship of the world organization, there should not ultimately arise the United States of Europe, both those of the East and those of the West, which will unify this Continent in a manner never known since the fall of the Roman Empire, and within which all its peoples may dwell together in prosperity, in justice and in peace.'[33]

While Churchill's appeal for the United States of Europe seemed to have anti-Soviet overtones, American opinion, coming around to the fact of the emerging Cold War, now reacted generally more favourably to the address than it had to the Fulton speech. Count Coudenhove-Kalergi, who was then living in the palatial Hotel Regina overlooking the Hudson River in New York City, wrote: 'Your magnificent speech before the Dutch Chamber raised new hopes for a free, united and prosperous Europe. Its echo in the United States was strong and favourable.'[34] The tide was turning in Churchill's favour. Coudenhove-Kalergi hoped that Churchill, who had already rejected a premature request to become honorary president of what the Count hoped would become a revived Pan-European Union, would preside over the Pan-European Conference that he was organising for the spring of 1947.[35]

Searching for an appropriate strategic position in the postwar battle for Europe in the early days of June 1946, Churchill asked an old friend and one of the Nobel Prize-winning architects of the League of Nations for advice. 'I have a feeling', he wrote, 'that an immense amount of pro-British sentiment, in Western Europe at any rate, could be evoked by my working in this association

[Pan-European Union], and also that I personally could save it from rivalry with the United States of America and might prevent its having at the outset a needlessly anti-Soviet bias.' The European movement, Churchill argued, 'might become very big indeed, and a potent factor for world peace.'[36]

Viscount Cecil of Chelwood warned Churchill against identifying himself with Coudenhove-Kalergi as long as possible to avoid the impression that the West was encircling Russia. Churchill agreed and wrote to Sandys: 'I think it would be a pity for me to join an organisation which had such a markedly anti-Russian bent, but I was not aware that this was Count C.K.'s conception.'[37] As Coudenhove-Kalergi would soon find out, Churchill had plans of his own to lead a movement towards European unity and was less than keen to share its leadership with a political amateur who had never held elected office.

Less than a month after the speech in the Netherlands, Churchill delivered a sweeping address on foreign affairs to the House of Commons. He spoke at length, for the first time, on Germany's position in postwar Europe. With 70 or 80 million Germans still living in the centre of Europe, Churchill hoped to arrive at a peaceful settlement as soon as possible with what now would inevitably become a divided country. No matter how grave and indescribable the crimes that had been committed under Nazi rule, it was time to put the past behind. 'Justice must take its course,' Churchill told the Commons, 'the guilty must be punished, but once that is over – and I trust it will soon be over – I fall back on the declaration of Edmund Burke, "I cannot frame an indictment against an entire people."'[38]

A new and safe Europe, Churchill thought, could not contain pariah nations. 'We must do our best for the German people,' he summarised, 'and after the guilty have been punished for their horrible crimes we must banish revenge against an entire race from our minds.' Germany was no longer the immediate danger to European peace; it was the chaos and degeneration engendered by the war and aggravated by the Soviet Union that threatened the continent. In order to save Europe from further damage it was necessary to offer resistance to the sovietisation of Europe. 'It is better to have a world united than a world divided; but is also better to have a world divided, than a world destroyed,' Churchill said, echoing the Fulton address. He closed with a foretaste of the creed of the lecture he was invited to give Zurich.[39] 'Let Germany live, let Europe arise again in glory, and by her strength and unity ensure the peace of the world.'[40]

On 14 July 1946 Churchill continued his tour of Europe in Metz, the capital of the Lorraine region in northeastern France, where a campaign for a revived

Germany was understandably a delicate proposition. He was disappointed that the British government refused to cover the full expenses of his chartered flight to France, meaning he had to contribute £200 of his own money. 'Rather shabby, wasn't it?' Churchill said, his face clouded as he told his doctor of the government's intransigence. 'Of course it couldn't be called a public duty,' he realised, 'though the Foreign Office said it would do good and are in favour of it.'[41] Churchill's status in continental Europe as the symbol of wartime achievement meant that his mere appearance could do more than years of patient diplomacy for British relations with the countries of continental Europe. He was an asset to Prime Minister Attlee and Foreign Secretary Bevin so long as he refrained from actively intervening in the foreign policy of the British government.

The Lorraine and its capital city held a special place in Churchill's heart. When he was eight years old, in the summer of 1883, little Winston went to Paris for the first time with his father. Noticing that one of the monuments on the Place de la Concorde was covered with flowers, the boy asked his father why this was. 'These are the monuments of the Provinces of France,' Randolph Churchill told him. 'Two of them, Alsace and Lorraine, have been taken from France by the Germans in the last war [the Franco-Prussian War of 1871]. The French are very unhappy about it and hope some day to get them back.'[42] Visiting Metz 63 years later Churchill was deeply moved by the fact that the Lorraine and the Alsace once again belonged to France.

Churchill's first visit to Paris was the start of a long love affair with the French Republic. In 1907, then a young minister, he attended French army manoeuvres and could not help but be moved by the sound of the Marseillaise and sight of the French bayonets that defended the liberties of Europe. Throughout his life, Churchill took every possible opportunity to vacation in the south of France, absorbing its culture and portraying its sunlit river beddings in his paintings. When he was called upon as prime minister to lead the fight against Nazi Germany, it was the plight of France that most concerned him after that of his native land. There was no greater place in 1946 to reconnect with France and its citizens than Metz, in the heart of what had been disputed territory for nearly a century. Nor was there a better time: 14 July was Bastille Day, the official French national holiday commemorating the start of the French Revolution and the annual pinnacle of national joy and democratic pride.

As he had done in Belgium and the Netherlands, Churchill wished to speak in Metz of the fate of postwar Europe. Speaking at a state dinner given in his honour, he shared with the French his worry that if Europe did not unite, there might arise 'a third and possibly a fatal holocaust'. 'Without the aid of a united Europe,' he said, 'the great new world organisation [the United Nations] may easily be rent asunder or evaporate in futility because of explosions which originate in Europe and may once again bring all mankind into strife and misery.'[43]

Churchill asked the French to do all in their power to urgently regain their national strength and work together with Britain in taking the leadership in uniting Europe. The address closed with an impassioned plea:

> Using my privilege as your old and faithful friend, I do not hesitate to urge upon all Frenchmen, worn or worried though they may be, to unite in the task of leading Europe back in peace and freedom to broader and better days. By saving yourselves you will save Europe and by saving Europe you will save yourselves.[44]

One man in particular, took in the speech with almost religious concentration. Robert Schuman, Churchill's host, was MP for the Moselle, part of the larger Lorraine region. That day had been one of unusual happiness for Churchill. Before the address, as it was a national holiday, a crowd of more than 50,000 turned out see him, wearing a grey top hat and a dark Victorian frock coat in the hot July sun, being guided through the city by Schuman.[45] Just 12 years Churchill's junior, Schuman looked like a Quentin Blake interpretation of the Big Friendly Giant with his twinkly eyes, long nose, disproportionately large ears and tiny, bald head on an abnormally tall and thin body.

Schuman grew up with the reality of European border disputes. Born in Luxembourg, he inherited the German nationality that his father received in 1871 after the Germans annexed the Lorraine. He did not a fight in World War I – the Germans excused him on health grounds – and then found himself a French citizen after the Lorraine was returned to France in 1919. He became active in French Christian Democratic politics between the wars and was a member of Paul Reynaud's wartime government with special responsibility for refugees. Schuman was a deeply devout Catholic and a lifelong bachelor who, due to his striking intelligence and commitment to European reconciliation, inspired trust and admiration in his British counterparts.

There is little evidence of Churchill's opinion of Schuman except that he liked his host enough after the Metz visit to send him a signed photograph. Harold Macmillan, however, a Churchill protégé in the Commons who first met Schuman through Churchill in 1949, thought him 'keen, amusing, deeply religious, and patriotic'.[46] A year later, Macmillan affectionately described Schuman in his diary as 'this strange, melancholy, quixotic figure, half

politician, half priest'.[47] When Churchill played half priest in Metz on Bastille
Day 1946 for the European cause, Schuman took his plea for France to save
Europe to heart. It took him just four years to catch up with Churchill and, as
French foreign minister, design the blueprint for the first direct institutional
predecessor of the European Union: the Schuman Plan for the European Coal
and Steel Community.

Churchill finally arrived in Switzerland on 23 August 1946, the first time he
had been there since 1913. Accompanied by Clemmie and his youngest
daughter Mary, he landed in a chartered gleaming-silver Swiss Air plane at the
small Geneva-Cointrin airfield. The Geneva privy councillor Perréard
welcomed the party with a short speech, which Churchill answered politely
before launching himself into the mass of people that had assembled at the
airfield.[48] He then set course for his Bursinel villa in a police-escorted open car.

Wearing a dark three-piece pinstripe suit and grey homburg hat, he looked
content to see Swiss youths run alongside the car. En route to Bursinel, Albert
Cuttat, the Swiss diplomat in charge of security during the visit, jokingly
told Churchill in the car that his arrival coincided with that of the Russians
with whom the Swiss government wanted to establish stronger diplomatic
relations. 'They refused your offer, did they?' Churchill responded, chuckling
at his comeback.

Vain enough to want to experience a bit more of the warm welcome given
to him by the Swiss people, he ordered his driver and the rest of the entourage
to make a slight detour through the centre of Geneva on the way to Bursinel.
This was a mistake. As the protocol team had published Churchill's route to
Bursinel beforehand, the unannounced detour made for the awkward event
that next to no one was in the city centre of Geneva to greet Churchill in his
open car. They were all waiting along the original route.

Churchill felt disappointed and repeatedly asked the chief of protocol,
Bracher, whether the people of Geneva even knew he was arriving on the
23rd.[49] It was, of course, not just vanity that moved Churchill to want to greet
as many of the Swiss commoners as possible. As he told Bracher, who wrote it
down in his diplomatic report of the visit, he was acutely aware that he was the
only political personality in the world other than Stalin who could attract
the grand masses. Churchill's immense popularity abroad was one of the
most important weapons in his arsenal against the westward march of
Soviet influence.

The most important instruction for the Swiss organisers was to not let the
press or anyone else interfere with Churchill's painting holiday. Villa Choisi

was so strictly guarded – 20 policemen attended Churchill on land while the Swiss navy brought a motor launch named *Unterwalden* from Lake Constance to guarantee his safety lakeside – that a Lausanne paper claimed the Swiss were calling him 'the prisoner of Choisi'.[50] Churchill would not accept outside invitations and was very reluctant to receive guests in Villa Choisi, especially those who were foolish enough, like the French Ambassador's wife, Madame Massigli, to arrive unannounced.

In the first week of his stay, Churchill spent quiet days in fine weather painting with Montag. He produced several sketches of a small island at a short distance from Choisi's tree-shaded lawns.[51] When the weather turned in the first week of September, Churchill spent more time painting under a military tent provided for him by General Guisan, the wartime commander of the Swiss army.[52] 'We have horrible weather here,' Churchill wrote to the British general Alanbrooke on 9 September, 'indeed they say it has never been so bad as this season. However the villa is very comfortable.'[53]

While resting and painting at Choisi, Churchill allowed a host of Swiss personalities to come by his villa. But the happier encounters for Churchill were those with his paintbox. On sunnier days, he would spend the whole afternoon painting from his villa garden. The vacation regime of the first three weeks followed the pattern of Churchill's home life. The morning, spent in bed amid cigar ashes and piles of paper, was devoted to maintaining his intensive, globe-spanning correspondence, preparing major upcoming speeches and writing the new Conservative electoral programme. From the comfort of his Bursinel bed, Churchill reached out to American Secretary of State James Byrnes, and the new president of the French Republic, Georges Bidault, who had just given a speech indicating his support for Franco-German reconciliation and United Europe.[54]

Churchill phoned and wrote to General de Gaulle, President Truman, Anthony Eden and countless others to keep up to date with the world, forgoing meaningful work on his war memoirs for which he had signed lucrative contracts in America and Britain. Lunch was usually served from 1 p.m. until 2.30 p.m., after which he would set up his easel on the lake and remain there, indefatigably, until sunset. Dinner – for which the men, as was Clemmie's rule, always appeared in full evening dress – was served until 9 p.m., after which there would be card games.

In the first week of September, Churchill began to focus his mind on current affairs and the upcoming speech at the University of Zurich. Writing to General Alanbrooke, Churchill observed: 'Things do not seem to be very good anywhere. Indeed I could easily find stronger terms in which to describe them.'[55] The speech at Zurich, confirmed for 19 September, gave Churchill the opportunity to do exactly that and, perhaps, offer his counsel for a solution. It was the future of Europe that increasingly dominated his thinking and his dinnertime conversations. One of the first things that struck a visiting army doctor after a dinner in Bursinel in early September was that 'he [Churchill] is a great European (he confesses – rather prides himself on this).'[56]

The immediate problem of the Soviet threat in Europe pointed Churchill in the direction of his long-held ideas for the unification of Europe. When General Guisan came down to Villa Choisi on 3 September, Churchill spent most of his time talking about Russia's intentions in Europe. Guisan came away with the distinct impression that Churchill had now fully reverted to his passionate anti-Bolshevism of the post-Great War period and seriously pondered the possibility of preventative war against the Soviet Union.[57]

Four days earlier, one of Churchill's most loyal friends, the South African prime minister Jan Smuts, came to Bursinel for a two-day visit. Smuts, a burly looking man with a well-kept, milk-white goatee and bright blue eyes, served with Churchill in both twentieth-century British War Cabinets and was the only person to have signed the peace treaties of both world wars. He was an utterly brilliant thinker. The master of his alma mater, Christ's College, Cambridge, once said: 'in 500 years of the College's history, of all its members, past and present, three had been truly outstanding: John Milton, Charles Darwin and Jan Smuts.'[58]

On 30 August 1946, at the age of 81, Smuts undertook to drive from Paris, where the peace conference was still going on, to Bursinel by himself. When he finally arrived a day later than announced – he ran out of petrol somewhere in rural France – the two men were kept inside Villa Choisi by pouring rain. They talked principally, Bracher wrote in his diplomatic report, about an outline for the upcoming Zurich address. Just two months earlier Smuts had told some Conservative MPs over lunch that, in order to revive the party, they must 'rid itself of its older men, perhaps even some of its older leaders, perhaps even the greatest leader himself'.[59] But here and now, in Switzerland, was a chance for Churchill to do what he did best. Smuts was a declared supporter of the idea of European unity and encouraged Churchill to speak on the future of Europe. After the weekend, Smuts drove back to Paris in solitude because the weather prevented him from boarding the plane Churchill chartered for his return journey.

Churchill expected a visit from one more distinguished guest at the Paris peace conference, James Byrnes. The Secretary of State's secret visit to Bursinel was arranged and planned for in the first week of September but he had to cancel at the last minute. He still played an important role in Churchill's preparations for the Zurich address with his landmark speech on postwar US policy in Germany delivered in Stuttgart on 6 September. Right after hearing of the address, Churchill demanded from Bracher that a full copy be brought to him. In the speech Byrnes promised something that Churchill had openly longed for: that the Americans would not retreat as quickly from Europe as they had after World War I. 'I want no misunderstanding,' Byrnes said at Stuttgart. 'We will not shirk our duty. We are not withdrawing. We are staying here.'

Even further, Byrnes held out the prospect of German membership of the United Nations as a reward for peaceful conduct and asserted that the economic unification of Germany was a principal objective of American policy. The speech read like a forceful critique of the Soviet insistence on exacting unrealistic reparations payments, blocking German economic recovery and, in effect, turning the Russian occupation zone into a satellite country. 'Germany is a part of Europe,' Byrnes said in a paragraph of special interest to Churchill, 'and recovery in Europe will be slow indeed if Germany with her great resources of iron and coal is turned into a poorhouse.'[60]

A necessary precondition for the true democratic revival of Germany, Byrnes said, was the return of internal governmental responsibility to democratic Germans. This, in turn, hinged on the drafting of a federal constitution for Germany by a national council consisting of the chief German officials within the several occupation zones. Byrnes closed his address with a summary of the newly defined direction of US policy: 'The American people want to help the German people to win their way back to an honorable place among the free and peace-loving nations of the world.'

This gave Churchill something to work with. Now that American opinion was shifting in his direction, he felt emboldened to put his own vision for Germany and Europe to the world. The only remaining sensitive point was Byrnes's assumption that the Germans would soon regroup in a united federal structure. During the war Churchill's idea had been to partition Germany into pre-existing states and principalities and perhaps involve them in European life on a detached or loosely connected basis. Before delivering the Zurich address, if he was to speak about postwar Europe, Churchill first needed to decide on his approach towards Germany.

For this particular pickle, Churchill needed Duncan Sandys, who, after having served in the British expedition in Norway in 1940 and as a junior minister in Churchill's wartime government, lost his seat in the House of Commons in the 1945 election. In June 1946 Churchill managed to interest him in his ideas for the unification of Europe.[61] Sandys was the only one in Churchill's direct entourage, Bracher observed when he and his wife Diana came to Bursinel to join the family for a week's holiday, who dared to challenge him in political discussions at the dinner table.

During the first weeks of the holiday in Bursinel the family noticed that the old man was becoming increasingly irascible. Finally, Sandys later recounted, he asked why his father-in-law was so crotchety. Churchill said Montag had arranged for him to speak at Zurich. 'On what subject?' Sandys asked. 'A comparison between the British parliamentary system and the Swiss cantonal system of government,' responded Churchill. 'But,' said Sandys, 'you know nothing about it.' 'That', Churchill flung back, 'is why I am so irritable.' Sandys suggested that the only right course was to forgo the original idea and prepare a speech on the issue they had been discussing passionately every night over dinner: the future of Europe.[62]

On Germany, conveniently, Sandys was considered something of a specialist. He had studied German at Oxford, where he had founded an Anglo-German Club, and spent the early part of his career with the British diplomatic mission in Berlin, leaving in 1933 after his superiors dismissed a critical memorandum he wrote about Hitlerism. It was only logical for Churchill to ask Sandys to help draft the passages on the German problem for the Zurich speech.[63]

On 6 September Churchill received a letter from Count Coudenhove-Kalergi, then living in the Swiss resort town of Gstaad, asking to be allowed to visit him 'while only a few miles separate us'.[64] After Churchill's speeches at Brussels, The Hague and Metz, Coudenhove-Kalergi had good hope that Churchill might want to coordinate European campaigns with him now that he was relieved of his governmental duties. In fact, three months earlier, on 15 June 1946, it was Churchill who reached out to Coudenhove-Kalergi first, asking in a radio telegram: 'What is the latest date you will be in Paris as I want my son-in-law Duncan Sandys to come and see you there?'

The telegram reached the Count while he was on a ten-day journey by ocean liner from New York, where he had spent the war years, to return home to Gstaad. He thought Churchill's telegram 'an excellent omen'. He reached the French coast on 18 of June at Le Havre, a city battered to ruins, from where he travelled to Gstaad by train. Here he found his house unscathed and neatly kept by a team of industrious and faithful servants. Resuming life as if nothing much had happened proved remarkably easy in neutral Switzerland. As Coudenhove-Kalergi recalled, Switzerland 'was a kind of museum displaying relics of a vanished world, a "national park" of pre-war culture'.[65]

In late August 1946 – Churchill had already arrived in Bursinel – Sandys finally called on Coudenhove-Kalergi at his home in Gstaad. Churchill had set up the meeting after careful consideration of how he might be able to use Coudenhove-Kalergi in the future. On 25 July 1946, Churchill told Leo Amery that his mind was fully occupied with pre-war pan-European ideas. 'I have thought a good deal about Coudenhove-Kalergi,' he wrote. 'His conceptions have a strong anti-Russian tendency, but I am still pondering upon the matter, and have interested Duncan Sandys in it.'[66] A day earlier, Amery, who spent the first three weeks of July hiking with his son Julian in the Swiss Alps, sent word to Churchill that he had met with Coudenhove-Kalergi and that the Count was 'busy reviving his pre-war Paneuropean organisation'.[67]

On 22 August, shortly before joining Churchill in Bursinel, Duncan Sandys came to lunch with Leo Amery. They had a long talk about Pan-Europe in preparation for Sandys's meeting with Coudenhove-Kalergi. 'He [Sandys] entirely shares my view', Amery wrote in his diary that day, 'that the only hope of keeping Germany with us is to hold out the prospect of playing a real part in a united Europe.' They agreed, too, that there was nothing better for Churchill to do with the rest of his life than to take the lead in the European movement.[68] When he finally arrived at Coudenhove-Kalergi's, Sandys told the Count what he was hoping to hear: that Churchill, as was already becoming obvious from the European speeches that year, was preparing an initiative for the unification of Europe. The added bonus for Coudenhove-Kalergi was that it now seemed that Churchill would seek his counsel and leadership collaboration in the initiative.

Not wanting to take on the role of honorary president of a revived Pan-European Union, a position which had been vacant since Briand's death in 1932, Churchill actually hoped to create an altogether new organisation in which he would take on the full duties of leadership. Coudenhove-Kalergi, thinking he might assume equal leadership responsibilities in the new initiative, handed Sandys a list of all the leading personalities who had been associated with his organisation before the war.

The Count, who was interested in Sandys as a conduit to Churchill, had been angling for another meeting with Churchill since the end of the war. Churchill, who, in turn, was interested in Coudenhove-Kalergi's existing base of support for the idea of European unity, decided to arrange for the Count to be driven to Villa Choisi on 14 September. In the meantime, on 11 September, Churchill first had Bracher and Cuttat, the Swiss diplomats, to lunch at Choisi. While Bracher discussed the achievements of the Red Cross with Clemmie, Cuttat questioned Churchill about Russian ambitions in Europe and the upcoming speech at Zurich. Cuttat wanted to know, specifically, if Churchill was planning to talk about Soviet Russia at Zurich as he had done at Fulton. 'I will not mention them,' was Churchill's answer, as Cuttat wrote it down in his report, 'but I will let the listeners conclude.' Clearly Churchill was preparing to give an address as controversial as that at Fulton:

> I know where I'm speaking. Switzerland is not like America, where everyone can say whatever comes into their minds, so that words lose their value. But President Truman applauded me at Fulton – you can verify this in the cinema. What I said there now almost everyone thinks in the West.[69]

Just five days before Churchill was due to speak at the University of Zurich, it was Coudenhove-Kalergi's turn to join Churchill for a luncheon at Villa Choisi. It was the first time they had met since 1938.

Churchill informed his guest that he intended to use his impending lecture at the University of Zurich to say something powerful on the unification of Europe. He would 'naturally give full credit' to what the pre-war Pan-European Union had already done for the European ideal. As Coudenhove-Kalergi later recalled in his memoirs, the idea of using the United States of Europe as the central theme of the Zurich speech gave Churchill back the excited, almost boyish vivacity that had disappeared so suddenly in the wake of electoral defeat. He wrote after seeing Churchill that day: 'He had hardly aged since I last saw him [in 1938] and was in a buoyant mood, full of energy and wit.'[70]

The first three weeks of Churchill's vacation were thus filled with painting, relaxing, memoir writing and, above all, preparing for the Zurich speech in Bursinel. Only in the last week of the visit did he and daughter Mary embark on an official tour of Switzerland, making public visits to Lausanne, Bern, Geneva and, ultimately, Zurich. As Churchill remembered in a short epilogue to his memoirs of World War II: 'When it became time to go I paid a very pleasant visit to Zurich University, and made them a speech about the tragedy of Europe and the plight to which she had been reduced, and I urged the foundation of a kind of United States of Europe, or as much of it as could be done.'[71] The programme in Zurich was so packed with activities that Churchill could hardly seriously consider accepting a pertinent invitation from the president of the Swiss group of European federalists *Europa-Union* to attend its conference that week. Nonetheless, the invitation was one of the few out of the hundreds addressed to Churchill during his stay that his secretaries, knowing what was on Churchill's mind, picked out for him to read.[72]

Clemmie was sadly unable to take part in the official part of the visit after having damaged a rib in a motorboat accident. Driving at full speed on the lake she lost her balance in a sharp turn and fell.[73] It was Clemmie, however, who persuaded her husband to start the tour by meeting with the president and committee of the Red Cross at their international headquarters in Geneva on 16 September. At the Red Cross's General Agency of War Prisoners Churchill heard for himself the plight of the quarter of a million German, Italian and Austrian prisoners of war that remained in Allied-controlled camps.

That afternoon Churchill and Mary travelled to the Swiss capital of Bern in a special train called *The Red Arrow*. The British minister in Switzerland, Mr Snow, together with a traditional choir and hundreds of cheering spectators, welcomed the high guests at a station especially constructed for the occasion outside the city centre. The British guests then drove in a low-wheeled carriage with a removable hood to the Château Lohn – the Swiss version of Chequers or Camp David. Arriving around 6 p.m. at Lohn, Karl Kobelt, president of the Swiss Confederation, and Max Petitpierre, foreign minister, were there to welcome Churchill to his temporary resting place.

Churchill and Petitpierre went into the salon on the ground floor. Churchill offered Petitpierre a cigar and asked Mary to bring them whisky. He suggested they would talk upstairs in the quietude of Churchill's bedroom in the chateau. The men ended up talking all night, Churchill telling stories of the war and the Potsdam conference that he would later recount in his memoirs. He told Petitpierre that Stalin despised the Swiss, knowing they would never convert to communism. Habitually more inclined to monologue than dialogue, Churchill launched into a sweeping assessment of the current state of affairs in the world. He talked at Petitpierre about the necessity of American aid for the reconstruction of Europe, the protective shield of the atom bomb, and the impossibility of the Big Three finding a common, peaceful solution to the German problem. Then, finally, before parting around midnight, he outlined his idea for the upcoming Zurich address. Churchill wanted to know just one thing from Petitpierre. Would the Swiss government be bothered or embarrassed by such a speech? To his satisfaction, the Swiss Foreign Minister said it would not.[76] 'He is a first-class man,' Churchill later said to Montag about Petitpierre.[77]

CHAPTER 6

'THE BIG THING IN A BIG WAY'
ZURICH, SEPTEMBER 1946

Churchill arrived at the Zurich central train station just before 6 p.m. on 18 September. Dinner was served for Churchill at 9 p.m. in a private dining room at the Grand Dolder Hotel. Churchill's company consisted of his daughter Mary, Legationsrat Albert Cuttat and Oberstleutnant Bracher.

Knowing that his speech the following day would be listened to, read and scrutinised all over the world, Churchill strutted excitedly round the dining room, faux moaning that he was 'forced' to give the speech and that its weight pressed so heavily on him that it 'ruined' what could have been a perfectly quiet holiday on the shores of Lake Geneva. The reality was that he could not have been more exhilarated by the prospect of stepping back into the limelight of world politics. Cuttat never saw him in finer form than that night: 'He bubbled over with spirit, delighted by his visit to Bern and filled with emotion by the idea that tomorrow he would address the world with an appeal of grand historical importance.'[1]

Churchill asked his dinner company if they would allow him to try out his unfinished draft on them. Without really awaiting an answer he launched into the first half of the speech at an agreeable pace, pausing every few sentences to comment on his intentions and phrasing. With just 12 hours to go until curtain time the rest of the text existed only in his head. Bracher's first impression was that the speech could not be compared in substance to the recent Iron Curtain address or the war speeches, but that it would have just as big an impact on the world.

'Churchill explained his painfully precise preparations and the consideration of every word and every sentence', Bracher wrote in his diplomatic report, 'with the argument that a speech that would be broadcast all over the world necessitated special preparation.'[2] Global attention, of course, was Churchill's own handiwork. In the second week of September he told his secretaries to approach the BBC, as well as the Columbia Broadcasting Co. and all the other major American broadcasting companies, to inform them that he intended to make a major speech at the University of Zurich on 19 September.[3]

'The French must understand', Churchill went on, explaining to his company the ideas at the core of the next day's speech, 'that their resentment towards Germany cannot compromise the rebuilding of a strong and liveable Europe. I love France and believe that she will raise herself up, while seeing that she is diminished, both morally and materially.' As for Germany, he thought its different constituent 'countries' should perhaps be asked to join the United States of Europe on an individual basis. 'The German people now have a last chance to make up for their past,' he said. 'If they do not seize their chance and let themselves be carried away by Communism as they let themselves be carried away by Nazism, that will be the end of our clemency and we will wipe them out.'

Cuttat then asked the most sensitive question of the evening. He wanted to know whether Great Britain, the only European country to emerge victorious from the war, would ever become a member state of the United States of Europe. 'I have preferred not to stress this point,' Churchill answered, 'so as to leave to the others the task of inviting us. One must not give the impression that we wish to control Europe, even though it is clear that only Great Britain is capable today of guiding her properly.' He added that Britain could hardly join at the same time as Russia: 'Or perhaps you invite Russia first, which will refuse, and in that case Britain will be able to join.'[4]

He predicted hostile reactions from the Soviet Union, reserved ones from France, and fairly favourable ones from the United States. Whatever the global response, Churchill was convinced the idea of European unity would take hold in the minds of man. Europe was ready for it. If governments reacted negatively he would use the instrument of public persuasion to win governmental agreement step by step. If the governments of Europe were unable or unwilling at first to form a European union, a popular movement of Europeans of all nations should bring it about. It would become an issue for networks of intellectuals, private organisations and parties to force reluctant governments to find unity of purpose. When Cuttat and Bracher uttered some scepticism about the likelihood of the new British Labour government playing along with his grand design, Churchill clarified he would never feel constrained by Socialist opinion.

He left his company with the promise that he intended to follow up the Zurich address with similar speeches at home. The ideas put forth on the morning of 19 September 1946 in Zurich were to be the heart of his last political cause. He would devote every last measure of his remaining strength to it.[5]

Late that night an anonymous source informed the *Manchester Guardian* that the Grand Old Man was still crafting his speech, describing it as 'a very weighty declaration indeed'.[6] At 1 a.m., when his company finally parted, Churchill determined that he was 'just' four hours away from finishing his preparatory work. In the end, he stayed up working until 7 a.m.[7]

The Zurich speech went down in history, as Churchill foresaw and intended, as a turning point – a Magna Carta of European unity. As Churchill intended, it raised the hopes of the general public for a solution to their woes. As Churchill foresaw, its plea to unite paid handsome dividends. The European ideal became a powerful ideological counterpoise to both nationalism and communism. As Lord Butler, the British statesman and celebrated Cambridge academic, said in the inaugural Churchill Memorial Lecture at the University of Zurich in 1967: 'the idea of a European family was not only a historical vision justified for its ends. In 1946, it was a political necessity.'[8]

The idea of the unification of all Europe, starting with western Europe, was not just a political necessity because it gave the European peoples hope for their future or because it held out the promise of permanent peace. Just as importantly, Churchill saw early on that Soviet Russia was pursuing the traditional tsarist imperialist foreign policy of gulping up as much of eastern Europe as possible. After the war Stalin felt it was only right to form a belt of sovietised states on its western border to fend off future threats from Germany or any of the other European states which had joined so enthusiastically in the Hitlerite assault on Russia.

In 1946, Europe lay paralysed and poverty-stricken in isolated impotence; Italy and France were in serious danger of succumbing to communism (the French elections of 11 November 1946 returned the Communists as the largest single party in the National Assembly); and Stalin kept an estimated 225 divisions, or about 2 million troops, on a war footing beyond Russian territory in eastern Europe, ready to march where the West allowed him. The Americans and the British, by comparison, kept a meagre 25 divisions in western Europe, some of which did not even have artillery.[9] In the autumn of 1946, it was not a wildly improbable thought, or at the very least it was an understandable fear, that the Soviets might break into western Europe and march all the way to the

North Sea and the Atlantic. It seemed that the only thing holding Stalin back was America's exclusive possession of the atomic bomb. But it was just a matter of time – Churchill estimated two to three years – until Stalin developed his own. The unification of Europe based on Franco-German rapprochement under British leadership and with American support was to Churchill a reasonable and urgently necessary solution to the postwar security conundrum. As he saw it, the life and liberty of the British Isles and Western civilisation depended on it.

For Churchill's Britain, as well as for continental Europe, the rise of the European family was also bitter economic necessity. The price of wartime victory was so steep that few dared face it in realistic terms. World War II cost Britain more than a quarter of its total wealth. From being the largest creditor in the world in the mid-1930s, Britain went to being its largest debtor after the war. Under the wartime Lend-Lease scheme, Churchill's government borrowed gigantic sums of money from the United States while selling overseas assets by the bulk just to keep the war effort going.

Deep financial crisis loomed in the summer of 1945 when the Americans abruptly brought the Lend-Lease agreement to an end. The new British Labour government found it difficult to provide for its own citizens and struggled even more to feed the displaced and impoverished Germans in the British occupation zone. Rationing in postwar Britain forced the British population to make do with 2,500 calories a day, while in western Germany people were kept alive on 1,100. The Chancellor of the Exchequer, Hugh Dalton, thought that the £80 million spent on aid to Germany amounted to 'us paying reparations to the Germans'.[10]

In April 1945, the celebrated economist John Maynard Keynes had warned Churchill's War Cabinet that without a lot of external help there would be no escaping complete financial collapse after final victory over Nazi Germany.[11] In the autumn of that year the Labour government sent Keynes to the United States to try to negotiate a new American loan. The American loan agreement he ultimately secured in Washington in December 1945 covered Britain's immediate postwar debts, but its terms were much harsher than anyone expected. Britain would have to pay $140 million a year in interest for the rest of the twentieth century, eventually eliminate its system of imperial preferences, accept a global system of multilateral free trade, and make its currency freely convertible, which ultimately led to a painful devaluation of the pound. Members on both sides of the House of Commons received news of the American loan agreement with horror.

Bob Boothby MP, who had been Churchill's private secretary before the war, was furious with the government for 'selling the British Empire for a packet of cigarettes' and with that threw a packet on the floor of the House.[12] Churchill himself, though he understood the need for a loan, complained that it would give the British government just two years to get its house in order.[13]

Contrary to popular perception of the 'special relationship', US–UK relations after the war soured quickly. The tension that developed was based on a fundamental conflict of interest in global politics. Britain hoped to remain a world power, holding on to its colonial possessions while it lacked the financial clout to do so, while the Americans were ideologically committed to dismantling the British Empire and possessed the financial resources to force their ally's hand. The Americans regretted that their money would be used, as one Democrat on the House Finance Committee put it, to promote 'too much damned socialism at home and too much damned imperialism abroad'.[14] The British were offended by American intransigence, thinking their moral standing in the world for having resisted Hitler in 1940 should have yielded a far more generous American attitude.

The Anglo-American alliance would only be mended in the autumn of 1947, when the UK and US finally concurred that they faced a common enemy in Europe and the world: Soviet Russia. More than a year after Churchill's Fulton speech the full extent of Soviet aggression was clear for most to see. As President Truman put it in a handwritten letter to Churchill on 14 October 1947: 'Our Russian "friends" seem most ungrateful for the contribution which your great country and mine made to save them [...] Your Fulton speech becomes more nearly a prophecy every day.'[15] In the meantime, the American loan agreement that Keynes had secured spoke volumes about Britain's postwar poverty and the painful postwar rift in the Anglo-American alliance. It was against this background that Churchill, impatient with Prime Minister Attlee's reluctance to look towards Europe for solutions, professed his belief at Zurich that unification would improve the economic fortunes of all European countries – including Britain. The most realistic solution of Europe's problem was also the most idealistic.

The all-important question left hanging in the speech was whether Britain would take part in the United States of Europe. Though the whole thrust of the address seemed to point in that direction, Churchill said in its last few sentences that the Big Three would stand outside the new structure and become its sponsors. Cheered on by the United States, the British

Commonwealth and Soviet Russia, United Europe would be built on the basis of Franco-German rather than Franco-British-German rapprochement.

But there were serious complications attached to Churchill's public stance at Zurich on the British role. The dangers of a purely, isolated Franco-German entente were far too great for Churchill to fully accept. First, as a trusted foreign policy adviser told Churchill at the time, it was far beyond the realm of the possible to establish a close and confidential working relationship between Britain and a purely continental union. United Europe would necessarily have to be built up to some extent in opposition to the other great groupings in the world and would certainly stir up suspicions in Britain. Most of the left-leaning British press, it was thought, would use its power to upset opinion and resuscitate wartime propaganda against Franco-German collaboration. Second, if the Franco-German union was not protected by some form of British participation, French moderate opinion would split, giving the Communists an ideal wedge to stick a hammer in, raise hell and seize power.[16]

So why did Churchill say at Zurich that Britain would restrict itself to sponsorship of the United States of Europe rather than openly seek participation in a European structure? Two explanations seemed as plausible then as they are to most historians now. The first was that Britain could not contemplate marrying its European neighbours only to divorce its Empire and Commonwealth. The second was that Churchill looked towards his motherland, America, rather than Europe to guarantee British security in the postwar world. Both considerations certainly played an important role in Churchill's postwar European policy and explain why he consistently believed that Britain could not become an ordinary member of a European federal union. But they still do not fully explain why he told the world at Zurich that Britain, the United States and Soviet Russia would function as the sponsors and champions of a continental union.

As he would make clear in the years after the Zurich speech, British participation in and leadership of a European union, or whichever name it would take, could be made compatible with imperial commitments and Anglo-American partnership. Britain would play a full and effective part in a union of European states, though the conditions of its membership would necessarily be of a different nature than that of the war-torn continental states. On account of its Big Three power status Great Britain would have to become an 'extraordinary' member of the United States of Europe, bringing with it the financial sponsorship and atomic protection of its mighty younger sibling America and the economic hinterland of the Empire and Commonwealth.

The only problem was that Churchill could not say anything as radical as that in September 1946. As he told Cuttat and Bracher on the eve of the address, he had to be extremely careful not to stress the point of British leadership in Europe. The British had to be invited by the continental countries to join a European union, and preferably only after the Soviet Union declined its invitation. This would show the world that Britain did not mean to provoke or encircle Stalin in any way by entering into and leading a bloc of European states while continuing a close partnership with the United States and heading the Commonwealth.

In September 1946 there was no way for Churchill to show all his European cards without incurring the wrath of global opinion for undermining the hope that Soviet Russia might become a peaceful and reliable partner in the United Nations. The situation appears to have left him with the option of playing a game of benign deception. Saying that 'Great Britain, the British Commonwealth of Nations, mighty America and, I trust, Soviet Russia – for then indeed all would be well – must be the friends and sponsors of the new Europe' really meant something like: 'mighty America and the Commonwealth of Nations must be the friends and sponsors of the new Europe while Great Britain leads Europe in the gradual realisation of political and economic union.' Soviet Russia would have to be content looking eastward. It certainly did not mean that Churchill sought British entry into a rigid federal union; it appears he was hoping for a construction in which Britain could maintain its global power status.

The Zurich speech made headlines in all the European papers that could express themselves freely. It was so far beyond anything considered 'normal' foreign policy, however, that journalists initially struggled to offer insightful analysis or even just to grasp Churchill's bold ideas. Most newspapers just printed the speech verbatim on the front page without further comment. In Britain, while the courage of his message was understood, none of the main newspapers fully embraced Churchill's conception of the United States of Europe. The *Daily Express*, Lord Beaverbrook's sensationalist newspaper with a circulation of 3.5 million, suggested Churchill might now 'live with a double glory', remembered by posterity as 'the contriver of victory and as the visionary of peace'.[17] Like almost all other papers, however, it failed to comprehend the full significance of Churchill's position.[18]

The *Manchester Guardian* criticised the timing of the speech, questioned the feasibility of its proposals, and focused on the confusion it aroused among world leaders who were convened in Paris at the time for negotiations on a postwar peace settlement. 'Even the representatives of the Western democracies are wondering', the paper said, 'whether Mr. Churchill has prophetically described a vision of the world to be or whether he has not rather reiterated the familiar Pan-European aspirations so laboriously expounded by Count Coudenhove-Kalergi.'[19] The Liberal *News Chronicle* had similar concerns about the impact of Churchill's speech on the Paris talks. 'There is a widely expressed view', the paper wrote, 'that Mr. Churchill has picked a curious time to advocate a policy which was certain, as he must have known, to embarrass the hard and uphill effort which 21 nations are now making in Paris to hold together the victorious war alliance.'[20]

The Observer, then still reliably Tory in its outlook, took more kindly to the new ideas for Europe. 'In our judgment,' it wrote in an editorial contrasting the Zurich speech to a Soviet-friendly speech given by the US secretary of commerce a week earlier, 'the recently evolved Churchill ideas, which are both older and newer, correspond more nearly to the needs of to-day and to-morrow.'[21] The Australian *Weekly Review* was the only outlet to consider in detail what Churchill meant by the notion of British sponsorship of the Franco-German partnership. It came to the conclusion that – although he might have better addressed French fears of the Reich by stating explicitly that Britain would come in as a founder member – 'it would be ridiculous to suppose that he intended his own country to be withdrawn from Europe.'[22]

The Times wrote in its leader the next morning that there was 'imagination ready to overleap caution and convention' and that Churchill showed once again that he was 'not afraid to startle the world with new and even, as many must find them, outrageous propositions'.[23] But would Europeans submit themselves to the organisation Churchill proposed? *The Times* thought not. 'It must be admitted that there are few signs of it. Even in western Europe there is little to suggest that the unity so much spoken of, and indeed so much desired, is on the way.' The division Churchill assumed between East and West was seen as 'the peril of his argument and of its enunciation at this moment'.[24]

But, the leader conceded, if hopes of maintaining the unity of all Europe proved 'ultimately and unmistakably vain', there would no doubt be a return to Churchill's idea for the initial unity of western Europe alone. *The Times* thought 'the inclusion of Germany within the unity [Churchill] postulates', so unacceptable to European opinion at the time, the most problematic turn of the speech. It suggested instead that something more modest than a Council of Europe could lead towards the European unity that Churchill desired.[25] The poetic justice and supreme irony of this argument was that its author,

Con O'Neill, later went back to work for the Foreign Office and in 1972 conducted the negotiations for British membership of the European Economic Community – now known as the European Union – under Prime Minister Edward Heath.

As Churchill foresaw, Stalin despised the idea of a European union and in particular the suggestion that it would be sponsored by Great Britain. Churchill had tried to mollify Stalin with his suggestion – added at the very last moment to the final draft of the speech – that Soviet Russia might also become a friend and sponsor of the United States of Europe ('for then all would be well').[26] Nonetheless, *Pravda*, the Moscow communist mouthpiece, had a field day with the speech. 'The conception of the United States of Europe has a special meaning,' it wrote. 'Not for nothing did Churchill lovingly recall Aristide Briand, who saw in the plan for a United States of Europe an advancement of the anti-Russian Treaties of Locarno. Friendship between France and Germany is what Churchill speaks of now. But that was also the method of which Laval and Ribbentrop spoke in their time.'[27] Stalin himself was drawn to echo this hostility in two interviews given five days after the Zurich speech. He believed Churchill was a dangerous political adventurer for talking of the possibility of a new war and 'accusing' the Soviet Union of expansionism. Stalin declared that the Soviet Union sought to maintain healthy ties to the Western democracies and the rest of the world and praised the British Labour government for taking a far less hostile stance.[28]

The American press was not quite persuaded of the necessity to look beyond US–Soviet cooperation to build a system of world security. The general attitude towards the speech was one of admiration for its prose and scepticism of its anti-Russian slant. The *St. Louis Post Dispatch* took the typical view that 'actually it was a bid for the establishment of a European bloc of nations under the aegis of Britain.' Another St Louis paper, the *Star Times*, was more outspokenly critical: 'If Mister Churchill wants to make his regional bloc so big why does he not let peacemakers rearrange Europe as best they can, and appeal for deeper confidence and broader support of the United Nations.' Further in the Midwest, the *Chicago Times* questioned the originality of the speech, saying: 'Mister Churchill is simply proposing on a grander scale what secretary of State Byrnes proposed at Stuttgart recently: a revived but disarmed Germany joined in a federal system. To this Churchill would add France and other European nations as a regional organisation within the United Nations.'[29]

Though the leading New York papers placed no editorial comments on the Saturday morning after the speech, the *New York Herald Tribune* found fault with the idea of forgiving Germany and reserving it a place at the heart of the European family so soon after the war. Walter Lippmann, however, the famous columnist writing for the *Washington Post*, had something positive to say. He zoomed in on Churchill's idea of having the old German states and principalities join in a federation. Churchill did not express himself definitively on this difficult issue, but Lippmann enthusiastically embraced the idea of conditioning German participation in the United States of Europe on the country's partitioning into many less powerful entities. 'Mr. Churchill is, and always has been, a great European,' he concluded, 'and he is voicing, and proposing to guide to constructive ends, the deep concern of civilized men across the Atlantic at the prospect that Europe might become the battlefield between America and Russia.'[30]

Continental Europe's main newspapers were divided on the speech. The first newspaper in which Churchill read his own address on the front page, the Swiss moderate, quality paper *Neue Zurcher Zeitung*, thought it was an important speech but that it held the danger of aggravating tensions between East and West.[31] In Berlin, the Russian-controlled newspaper *Nachts Express* followed Moscow's line in writing that Churchill was merely 'strengthening his front for a third World War'.[32] This belied the well of local enthusiasm stirred up by the European idea in occupied Germany. Lord Beveridge, the civil servant and architect of the postwar British welfare state, reported on his visit to the German occupation zones in 1946: 'everywhere I was asked with a wistful hopefulness about Mr. Churchill's speech at Zurich in which he proposed a United States of Europe. What were the prospects for getting this plan adopted? It seemed the one positive hope that had come their way.'[33]

In France, where reconciliation with the Germans was the most difficult proposition of all, the conservative and moderate papers were sceptical and even hostile towards the idea of Franco-German rapprochement. The French largely thought Germany did not quite deserve to be raised to its feet yet. Even the progressive Catholic paper *L'Aube* said that 'France must first obtain in the east the guarantees for which she is asking. Then we can speak, like Gladstone and Churchill, of the "blessed act of oblivion"'.[34]

Le Monde pointed out that it was far more difficult for the French to forget the cruelties of the war than Churchill seemed to think: 'the psychological conditions for reconciliation are lacking. French opinion [...] is far more vicious than ever before. National socialism, the Occupation with its hardships, and the horror of deportations have truly separated France from Germany.'[35] The French prime minister, Georges Bidault, a Christian democrat, said ambiguously: 'Mr. Churchill's genius is of a special kind. That is all I can say.'[36] The French Communist outlets, of course, were outwardly livid. As such, *L'Humanité* wrote: 'British policy aims to make us into a more and more "spiritual" people, in the sense that Hitler wanted to transform France into a vegetable garden and a "Luna Park" for his German overlords.'[37]

The French ambassador in London, Alain Roché, went so far as to encourage the British Labour government to distance itself from Churchill's speech, calling the Foreign Office on the morning of the 20th to say that 'the French people would be quite incapable of responding to Mr. Churchill's call for a 'blessed act of oblivion towards Germany'''.[38] The Foreign Office duly published an official reaction in *The Times* stating that the foreign secretary, Ernest Bevin, was not consulted about the Zurich speech and did not know Churchill intended to articulate a vision for European unity. As neutral as that sounded, Foreign Office opinion on the Zurich speech was sharply sceptical, even among those who before the war envisaged a federal Europe. The permanent under-secretary of state, Sir Orme Sargent, who in 1938 circulated a paper on Anglo-French union as the first step to European federation, now told the Swiss ambassador in London on 23 September:

> I don't know under which influences and impressions Churchill spoke at Zurich. Perhaps it was what he saw in your country: the co-existence of different races and languages. But Mr. Churchill must know very well that it is not the same thing on the international plane – everything is far more complex and difficult, everything requires such prudence.[39]

The ambassador came away with the impression that the Foreign Office adopted the exact same attitude as *The Times*: appreciative of the courage and boldness of Churchill's vision but depreciative of its practicability.

In a press conference that day Prime Minister Clement Attlee made sure to remind the world in his rather more colourless cadence that Churchill spoke at Zurich as a private person and did not in any way represent government opinion abroad. Moderate, pencil-moustached Attlee, 'a modest man with a lot to be modest about' as Churchill once called him, thought fondly of his predecessor but was not given to his kind of sweeping foreign policy visions. Though a long-time supporter of the idea of European federation, Attlee now felt resentment towards Churchill for launching the idea of integration into the realm of practical politics. Perennially underestimated, prosaic and self-effacing, Attlee was a quietly brilliant politician who focused on building the foundations of the British welfare state while Churchill focused on the future of Western civilisation. Churchill's became the voice above the babel, putting realism at the service of an age-old ideal. As Churchill put it in a deleted passage from the Zurich speech: 'I therefore declare for the United States of Europe, and in such years as may be left me I will do what I can to further that sacred cause.'[40]

Personal letters of admiration, astonishment and encouragement started pouring in from all over the world. Leo Amery praised the address to the heavens:

> You have indeed lit a torch to give its message of hope to shattered Europe. The French are startled, as they were bound to be, but the idea will sink in all the same. As for the Germans your speech may have been just in time to save them from going Bolshevist. You have done few bigger things, even in the great years behind us.[41]

On the same day, Amery told Sandys, 'Winston has indeed done the big thing in a big way,'[42] while in his diary he focused more cynically on the intellectual authorship of the British idea of the United States of Europe, taking satisfaction in his perception of reality that the whole line of Churchill's argument was 'obviously' based on his recent London University address which he had sent to Churchill at the time. 'It would be interesting in this last chapter,' he noted, 'if Winston and I who have so consistently differed, even when in the same government, now at least see eye to eye and work together.'[43]

For Count Coudenhove-Kalergi it was an unbelievable blessing to have the world's leading international statesman behind the idea of Pan-Europe. He was beside himself with joy. 'God bless you for your glorious speech promising decisive victory in your second battle for Europe,' he cabled to the Dolder Hotel on the 19th. And four days later, in a longer handwritten letter: 'Your speech made me one of the happiest men on earth – I cannot express my feelings of gratitude for all it meant for Europe, for the Pan European Movement and for me! Your help is incalculable in its tremendous consequences: now that *you* have raised the European question the Governments can no longer ignore it.'

In a brief note of criticism, Coudenhove-Kalergi touched on a fundamental difference of opinion that would never be resolved. He agreed with Churchill's basic idea that the French and German people must enter into a partnership, but felt that 'this reconciliation will be the consequence, not the condition of European Union.'[44] Coudenhove-Kalergi hoped for a similar succession of events in Europe to the one that had transpired in America after the Civil War, where reconciliation and cultural integration slowly followed federation rather than the other way around.

Churchill insisted in Zurich, as before, on the gradual approach to union. Reconciliation, short-term governmental cooperation and a mass campaign of public education, he thought, should come before definitive constitution-making. The metaphors that Churchill liked best to describe his conception of the United States of Europe were that of the living plant and that of lighting a fire. The plant would grow organically; the fire would slowly turn into an all-consuming blaze.[45] Here was the essence of the divide between the radical federalist thinking that prevailed among many on the Continent and the long-term pragmatism that dominated British thinking. The radical federalists were building a machine; Churchill was growing a living organism. Before too long the divergence in approach would lead to heated conflict between Churchill and Coudenhove-Kalergi, who came to see Duncan Sandys as a 'distinguished adversary [and] my most dangerous opponent, determined to supplant me in the leadership of the movement.'[46]

From within the existing federalist movement in Great Britain there came criticism of Churchill's specific conception of the United States of Europe but overwhelming gratitude for his general support for the cause. Frances Josephy, Chairman of the British Federal Union, an organisation that started advocating for European federation in 1938, wrote a letter to the editor of *The Times* in which she defended Churchill's call to focus on the nations who were willing and able to join – that is, the democratic Western states – a possible United States of Europe.

Not having been privy to Churchill's conversation with the Swiss diplomats on the eve of the speech, Miss Josephy criticised his stance on Britain's role. British exclusion from the project, she thought, 'would be a major calamity'. She explained it would be harmful from all points of view. Without British initiative and participation the union would never come about. 'From the point of view of Britain, nothing could be more dangerous than to find herself precariously perched on the perimeter of a united Europe potentially united against her.'[47]

German pro-Europeans like Konrad Adenauer – nicknamed *Der Alte* ('the old man') because, at the age of 73, he was one of the oldest democratically elected national leaders in world history – welcomed the general message of Zurich but disagreed with some of its features. The Swiss consul-general in Cologne, Franz von Weiss, a good friend of Adenauer's, reported to his bosses from the British occupation zone on 22 September: 'Winston Churchill's Zurich speech has caused the biggest stir here in the Rhineland, because it is in full accordance with the ideas of the leader of the

Christian Democratic Party in the British zone, the former mayor of the city of Cologne, Konrad Adenauer.' Weiss, perhaps unfamiliar with Churchill's long personal history with the European ideal, thought Churchill appropriated Adenauer's ideas about the United States of Europe through Sandys.[48]

If he did, Sandys would have been careless in explaining to Churchill some of the main elements of Adenauer's conception. Unlike Churchill, Adenauer did not want to leave the option open of giving the separate German states sovereign rights within a federal Europe. He wished only for a single, federal Germany with the right of self-determination to enter into a federal Europe.[49] But whatever their differences, it is remarkable that Churchill sent Sandys to the British occupation zone in Germany ahead of the speech to measure German opinion on the idea of a European union. The outcome of Sandys's reconnaissance mission plausibly encouraged Churchill further to draw a 'spiritually great Germany' into his conception the United States of Europe.

Churchill looked back on his speech and the whole Swiss visit with a sense of satisfaction. The public reception had been overwhelming, even for Churchill, who later remembered: 'I have not been welcomed, I have been worshipped.'[50] Gratitude went out to Charles Montag, who was instrumental in the realisation and organisation of the whole visit. Right before his flight home to London, Churchill wrote Montag a few lines of thanks from his plush room in the Dolder. 'At the moment of leaving Switzerland,' he told his friend and teacher, 'I must thank you for all you have done in setting on foot the plans which have given me such a truly delightful holiday in your beautiful country. I was greatly touched at my receptions by the Swiss people everywhere, and the welcome given me in your native city of Zurich will long remain in my mind.'[51] Churchill's European campaign was about to begin.

CHAPTER 7

'THE IDEAL SHOULD BE EUROPE'
CAMPAIGNING IN BRITAIN I, 1946–1947

There was little time to sit back and enjoy the victorious fruits of the Swiss holiday if Churchill was serious about building a European union. It was essential to exploit the momentum the Zurich speech generated. In necessary contrast to the magniloquent rhetoric with which Churchill attempted to persuade the world of the rightness of the European ideal, he and his closest associates were ruthlessly pragmatic in trying to ensure British (read: Churchillian) leadership of the emerging European movement.

A day after the speech, Leo Amery told Sandys, 'the great thing is that he should now follow up Zurich and not let the torch die down,' suggesting that this was a foreign policy vision that would woo British voters and should be developed at the forthcoming party conference in Blackpool.[1] Sandys was encouraged to join the campaign by the letters he started receiving for his father-in-law immediately after the Zurich speech. He kept 16 special files in his office, all for different European countries, containing thousands and thousands of pleas from ordinary European citizens asking for Churchill to hold onto the torch of European unity.[2]

Churchill's political inner circle made an effort to encourage him further. Leo Amery, for instance, wrote to him on 20 September, 'you cannot leave the matter with one speech. This morning's silly leader in *The Times* shows how much more is needed in the way of follow up and amplification.' Amery believed that Churchill could rouse Conservative voters with the idea of the United States of Europe and with a world vision that swapped the 'mere black and white ideological fight between American mid-Victorian individualism and Russian State slavery' for a world organised in partner groups of nations as Churchill had originally proposed as wartime prime minister.[3]

Churchill needed little prodding to start his post-Zurich campaign. Before making his first moves, he needed to fully understand the lie of the land in the existing European movement. On 23 September, he sent Count Coudenhove-Kalergi – first port of call in all matters relating to European unity – a short and unceremonious telegram from his new London home in Hyde Park Gate demanding information: 'Please send urgently full particulars of work and organisation of your Union.'[4] Churchill was planning an informal strategy luncheon at Chartwell and hoped to have a clearer idea of Coudenhove-Kalergi's activities before then.

Invited to Chartwell to talk over the post-Zurich plans were three Conservative politicians of differing distinction: Leo Amery, Duncan Sandys and Bob Boothby. Amery had served in Churchill's War Cabinet and, at the age of 72, was one of the wise old men of the Conservative Party. His chief value, in that respect, was his lifelong commitment to strengthening British ties with the Empire and Commonwealth. After World War II, Amery, now a backbencher, vociferously represented the imperial wing of the Conservative Party. Sandys, as we have seen, was a junior minister in the war who rapidly became one of Churchill's closest advisers. Boothby completed the initial nucleus of Churchill's post-Zurich strategy team. A former private secretary to Churchill in the late 1920s, he was a supremely gifted but enigmatic, irascible and rakish Conservative MP. After embroiling himself in a scandal involving Czech gold in 1940, he never quite recovered his one-time status of potential future prime minister. It did not help either that he started a semi-public, lifelong affair in the mid-1930s with Lady Dorothy, wife of his close colleague and fellow Conservative MP, Harold Macmillan. No wonder, then, that it was whispered in the corridors of Westminster that at his christening the good fairies had given Boothby every gift, except the ability to distinguish right from wrong.[5]

Whatever his shortcomings, Boothby was a known supporter of European unity. In February 1946 he started putting forward constructive proposals for Britain to take the lead in an integrated western Europe. He was one of the few politicians to see, with Churchill, the painful truth that Britain emerged from the war little better off than its neighbours across the Channel. 'The smaller nations of Western Europe, of which we are one,' he told the Commons in February, 'cannot hope to survive politically or economically in isolation.'[6]

Little over half a year later, the Zurich speech gave Boothby a chance to rekindle his pre-war partnership with Churchill. On 22 September, he caught

Churchill's attention with an animated article in the *News of the World* entitled 'Britain Must Take Lead in Building New Europe'. Boothby underlined the historical importance of Zurich and urged broader acceptance of the temporary division of Europe into an eastern and a western sphere of influence. He sounded just one note of criticism: he was unhappy with the ambiguous silence about the part Great Britain was to play. 'There can be no doubt,' Boothby wrote. 'Not only must we be in it [the United States of Europe], we must take the lead.' He estimated Churchill essentially agreed with him. 'Mr. Churchill can hardly mean that we should confine our support of a Western European Federation to applause from the side-lines. On a memorable occasion he himself offered complete union with Britain to France.'[7]

What held Amery, Sandys and Boothby together was that they had stood with Churchill long before he was adored around the globe as the Nazi-crushing, cigar-chomping hero of the West. In the 1930s, when Churchill's was a voice in the wilderness, they had backed him. Then Churchill was campaigning against the government's appeasement of Nazi Germany; now he proposed to 'rouse the fervour of a crusade' for the United States of Europe in which a newly federated Germany would play a full part.[8]

In fact, almost all of Churchill's closest associates in the postwar campaign for a United Europe were drawn from the ranks of his pre-war supporters, who had met in an informal, semi-secret group calling itself 'the Focus'. The Focus, in the words of one of its more prominent members, was intended 'for discussion and for the exercise of indirect influence through the political Parties and newspaper Editors and proprietors'.[9] The group, whose central goal was to warn the government and the public of the dangers of Nazism, gave Churchill a platform. It had started to come together in June 1935 and held its first public meeting on 3 December 1935 in the Albert Hall.[10] At that meeting, Churchill later wrote, '[...] gathered many of the leading men from all parties [...] We had the feeling that we were upon the threshold of not only gaining respect for our views but of making them dominant.'[11]

After reactivating the more intimate nucleus of Conservatives, Churchill instructed Sandys, who quickly became the principal moving agent in the postwar campaign, to get in touch with the rest of the Focus to invite them, as he put it, to 'meet again to discuss the present international situation'. They were informed that the 'Handling Group' that Churchill was mounting for a United Europe was differently conceived than the Focus in that its agenda was 'bold, public and sustained action' in the international sphere; not subtle, domestic influence.[12]

Reactions were mixed among the old Focus members. Dr Mallon, a former governor of the BBC, was highly enthused, while Lady Violet Bonham Carter, formerly Violet Asquith, Churchill's closest female friend and a governor of the BBC, was a 'trifle sulky' after falling out with Churchill in the final years of the war. In the end, Churchill told Sandys to let the matter drop and start the campaign for European unity without the wider circle of the Focus, retaining the tight inner circle instead.[13] Other Focus stalwarts like Harold Macmillan and Lady Violet would actively join the campaign a few months later. Soon after they did, Eugen Spier, a German-Jewish refugee from Nazism who helped fund the activities of the Focus in the mid- and late 1930s, met with Churchill to discuss United Europe and, as he later recalled, declared himself 'fully prepared to co-operate with Churchill once again in the same way as I had done over the work of the Focus'.[14] On the condition of anonymity, he promised to raise a fund of between £5,000 and £10,000 to cover the immediate expenses of the new United Europe group.[15] The old group found a new cause.

On 24 September, a day after Churchill cabled Coudenhove-Kalergi for information on his Union, Duncan Sandys and Leo Amery talked for more than an hour in the latter's huge Victorian home in London's Embankment Gardens. Sandys told his host that he was quite prepared to make the European campaign his life's work for the immediate future. Amery replied that he would be equally willing to spend a large portion of his time as an elder statesman sitting on any sort of committee. After a brief discussion of possible membership of the larger British Committee they hoped to build around their nucleus, Sandys and Amery considered the delicate question of what position Coudenhove-Kalergi might take in the movement. They neither wanted to sidetrack him nor to continue fighting the Churchill campaign under the banner of a philosopher's pre-war movement. It would be for them, in coordination with Churchill, to think of a solution as soon as time and circumstances permitted.

That same day, Julian Amery, Leo's 26-year-old son and soon to be Harold Macmillan's son-in-law through his marriage to Catherine Macmillan, went to see Coudenhove-Kalergi and his wife in Gstaad. Over mushroom soup and eggs, Coudenhove-Kalergi gave him an overview of his thoughts on European politics. He proudly showed Julian his correspondence with General de Gaulle, seemingly undisturbed by the fact that de Gaulle, like Churchill, more often than not merely tendered polite acknowledgements by way of response. Coudenhove-Kalergi told Julian that he sincerely hoped that Sandys would organise a British group for European union to match the groups he was building in Switzerland and France. Self-assertively arrogant as always, he believed that his lunchtime meeting with Churchill on 14 September had inspired Churchill to speak on Europe at Zurich. In actual fact, the Foreign Office had already issued a statement to the press on the morning of the 14th saying that Churchill intended to deliver at Zurich 'a considered statement on the present state and future of Europe'.[16]

Coudenhove-Kalergi won support from the youngest Amery scion for his view that federation should precede European reconciliation, rather than the other way around as Churchill proposed it. When Churchill's telegram arrived the next morning, he asked his guest to personally deliver a response. On leaving Gstaad it was plain to Julian that 'he [Coudenhove-Kalergi] has no organisation worth mentioning, and his chief value must lie in his gifts as a propagandist and his untiring enthusiasm for the European idea.'[17]

On Julian's return to London, he sat down with his father to discuss plans for the post-Zurich campaign. The Amerys cared deeply for their Bohemian friend but were sceptical of some of the more controversial elements of his thinking about European union. His conception was clearly pro-American and anti-Russian, but on both counts he took it in an uncomfortably radical direction. During his conversations with Julian, Coudenhove-Kalergi confessed that he believed that Pan-Europe would be something close to a function of American policy. This convinced Julian, who feared that Coudenhove-Kalergi's 'panic terror of Russia and Communism overshadowed his plan of Pan-Europe', that his was a deeply flawed conception.

Fear of radicalised Russophobia hit painfully close to the heart of the Amery family drama. Julian's older brother, John Amery, was a troublesome and unpredictable young man who ran away from Harrow – the same boarding school where Leo Amery and Churchill met for the first time – at the age of 16. During World War II, John developed an obsession with the idea that communism, not German fascism was the greatest threat to world peace. While Julian was on active service in the Balkans and father Leo served in Churchill's War Cabinet, John Amery tried raising an army of British prisoners of war held in Germany to fight alongside the Nazis, supposedly to save Europe from Bolshevik Russia. In December 1945, after pleading guilty on eight counts of treason, John became one of the last men to be hanged at Wandsworth Prison in London. Neither Leo nor Julian ever quite recovered from the shock.

On the 26th, Leo told Julian that 'Winston was very keen' about the European campaign and that he, Sandys and Boothby were going to

Chartwell in a few days for a strategy lunch. He would suggest to Churchill that Julian should go too. Like his son, Leo thought that Coudenhove-Kalergi's role should be confined to that of 'propagandist and theorist rather than as organizer and leader of the movement'. Julian's opinions on European union, however, were different from his father's in one important aspect. Julian believed, he wrote, that 'Pan-Europe will never work unless England goes into it wholeheartedly,' while his father still showed reserve on that point out of loyalty to the British Commonwealth of Nations. By September 1946, however, Leo had come round a good deal and, Julian noted in his diary, 'since the union of Europe will inevitably be very very loose for many years to come, the problem is probably only theoretical.'[18]

The next morning, on the 27th, Sandys went to see Julian Amery. They found themselves in full agreement in their assessment of Coudenhove-Kalergi's personality and organisation and on the problem of Britain's role in a European union. Britain would have to come in as a full member from the beginning. Julian wrote to Churchill that afternoon enclosing Coudenhove-Kalergi's extensive reply. The letter persuaded Churchill to summon Julian on Monday morning to come down to his country home in Westerham, Kent, for the luncheon that day.[19]

On Monday 30 September, Leo Amery was first to arrive at Chartwell. He found Churchill busy cleaning out one of the artificial pools he had built on his property and fixing a small toy waterfall. There was something 'delightfully boyish', Amery thought, about Churchill's love of beautifying his house before it would be given to the National Trust and turned into a museum.

Sandys, Boothby and Julian Amery soon joined the elder Conservative leaders. During the drive down to Chartwell both Sandys and Boothby were very irritated with Eden, a conspicuous absentee from the post-Zurich plotting team. Eden, graced with thick iron-grey locks, became under-secretary of state at the Foreign Office in 1931 and rose spectacularly fast in the House of Commons. In 1934, at the age of 38, he got his first major appointment as Lord Privy Seal. He became foreign secretary to Churchill in December 1940, staying in post for the rest of the war and opposing the Prime Minister's plans for the postwar creation of a Council of Europe. Thwarted in his quiet hopes of succeeding Churchill as party leader after the painful election defeat of July 1945, Eden remained the crown prince and foreign policy expert of the Conservative Party.

It was a serious blow to Conservative Europeanists that Eden made no meaningful moves towards supporting Churchill's design. Eden's major foreign policy speech that week at Watford did not mention the Zurich speech once, let alone defend it. Julian noted in his diary that Randolph Churchill said his father, too, was furious about Eden's speech and was hoping for someone to answer it.[20] For the time being, it seemed Eden was more in tune with the cautious, Euro-agnostic approach of his close friend the Labour foreign secretary, Ernest Bevin, than he was with that of the leader of his own party.

Arriving at Chartwell, the younger men greeted Leo Amery and Churchill, dressed in his blue siren suit, working away on the toy waterfall. A substantial lunch was served, lubricated with plenty of Pol Roger champagne. 'At my time of life,' Churchill told his guests, 'I have decided to simplify the problem of midday drinks, and now indulge only in this harmless sparkling beverage.' After lunch, however, Churchill saw himself forced to break his champagne rule when there appeared an old Drambuie and port. Julian thought Churchill in great form, speaking with enthusiasm and sincerity on the European question and describing the new foreign secretary, Ernest Bevin, as 'that deflated Boanerges' (a Greek term for thunder).

The lunchtime talk boiled down to Churchill telling his guests that he meant to bring together leading continental statesman in a conference in London to start a European movement which he intended to lead personally. He thought Europe, including Germany, ripe for such a movement to 'sweep right through and dominate every party'. Before the international meeting of leading European statesmen, he planned to constitute a committee and organisation in Britain, perhaps under the administrative direction of Leo Amery, which would be all-party, non-party and above-party.

'Churchill was quite emphatic on the point of European unity,' Julian wrote in his diary that day, as distinct from the strategic conception of a West European bloc. From Churchill's brief remarks on the role of the Russians in the new Europe that day – 'they must go back' – it was evident that he embraced both the political ideal and the strategic conception. The Russian menace strengthened Churchill's support for the European ideal; it was not the conditioning element.

Churchill closed by saying he believed that the plan for the United States of Europe was the only way of preventing another European war, and that the United States of America, to which European quarrels had been a constant liability in the first half of the century, would eventually welcome and embrace his plans. He grew progressively keener and instructed his guests towards the end of the lunch to organise a public meeting in the Royal Albert Hall in the autumn of 1946 to inaugurate the European movement in England – a timeline which eventually proved a bit too ambitious.[21]

Amery the elder set out the next day to inform potential members on the British committee of leading public figures about Churchill's intentions. 'Churchill is by no means minded to let the matter rest with a single speech, but is really anxious to follow it up,' he told Sir Walter Layton, the wealthy Liberal Party politician and newspaper proprietor who was deemed 'most useful in view of his connection with the *News Chronicle* and the *Economist*'.[22]

A few days later, Churchill was due to speak at the concluding session of the Conservative Party conference in Blackpool. Addressing a mass meeting in Blackpool's Winter Gardens, Churchill kept his promise of continuing the Zurich message. Though traditional annual political. mud-slinging was at the centre of his speech, Churchill also struck a more conciliatory note: 'We wish to be happy and prosperous, and will only give our support to the political parties, whatever they may be called, who will vote for a United States of Europe.' He pledged to give his last measure of devotion to creating a European union and take on a leading role in propagating the idea in Britain and abroad.[23]

Wholly satisfied with the Blackpool address, Leo Amery wrote to suggest to Churchill possible continental allies for the European campaign. 'I think you will find the M.R.P. in France [Robert Schuman's Christian democratic political party], and the Catholics generally in Europe, the most helpful element in the campaign for a united Europe.'[24] The Catholics were certainly attracted by Churchill's historical and spiritual conception of Europe as essentially representing Christendom, the medieval and early modern Catholic geopolitical power bloc covering most of geographic Europe. From the ranks of the Christian democrats eventually emerged the men now considered to be the founding fathers of the European Union: Konrad Adenauer of Germany, Robert Schuman of France, and Alcide De Gasperi of Italy. While all of them had long personal histories of support for the idea of European unity, none of them would have been able to do anything meaningful about it had Churchill not launched his campaign at Zurich.

Well before the onset of winter in 1946, Churchill started to think about a statement of purpose and to round up prospective members for what would become known as the British United Europe Committee. On Thursday 10 October, he invited Sandys, Leo Amery and Boothby for a meeting in his room in the House of Commons. He told them that he was especially keen to secure good Labour representation on the committee so as to avoid any impression of a party stunt in the foreign policy arena. The Amerys prepared a draft definition of purposes for the committee, which was then amended and added to by Boothby and Sandys before Churchill could take it home for the weekend for further consideration.[25] A week later, during another hour-long meeting in his room in the Commons, Churchill presented his definitive conclusion that the British movement should start with a small handling committee of eight or so members.

David Maxwell Fyfe, a somewhat dull, Scottish-born barrister who had already cemented his place in history by serving as one of the chief British prosecutors at the Nuremberg trials, was chosen as second-string adminis-trative leader of the committee behind Amery. In his own words, Maxwell Fyfe had knocked 'fat boy' Hermann Göring 'off his perch' in one of the best-known cross-examinations of the twentieth century.[26] His success at Nuremberg had not been down to fiery charisma, but merciless determination. The *Daily Sketch* wrote in August 1946: 'Fyfe, according to his steady Northern lights, mistrusts brilliance and inspiration, believes in application and preparation.'[27]

Exclusively and mockingly known as 'Sir Donald' to Churchill, Maxwell Fyfe was a small, square man whose olive skin and thick black eyebrows gave him a distinctly Mediterranean appearance.[28] Despite having supported Chamberlain's policy of appeasement before the war, he had received his first government appointment under Churchill in 1942 as solicitor-general. He joined the United Europe group in December 1946 as one of its senior patrons. Being the only member of Churchill's post-war 'European' inner circle who was on the wrong side of the appeasement debate, some in the Commons viewed his commitment with suspicion, believing he was compensating for not backing Churchill before the war.[29]

Churchill promised to write to potential Labour supporters and further reported to the inner circle that day that he had failed to secure the backing of his friend the influential, uncompromising imperialist Conservative Viscount Cranborne – nicknamed 'Bobbety' – who was later known as the Marquess of Salisbury while serving as a senior member of Churchill's peacetime government (1951–5). In his letter rejecting membership of the committee, Bobbety said he thought that the movement should focus on western Europe exclusively. This either misunderstood or ignored Churchill's basic idea that, as Amery put it in his diary, 'it is by preaching a united Europe that Western Europe will come into being as the first step.'[30] Churchill wrote to Bobbety confidentially, elaborating on his long-term ideal and short-term strategic considerations for Europe:

I am not attracted to a Western bloc as a final solution. The ideal should be EUROPE. The Western bloc as an instalment of the United States of Europe would be an important step, but the case should be put on the broadest lines of a unity of Europe and Christendom as a whole [...] Moreover, without Germany, however sub-divided or expressed, there is no force of nationhood in the West which could hold the balance with the Soviet power.[31]

That weekend, Sandys brought Count Coudenhove-Kalergi to Chartwell for another strategy luncheon. It had been eight years since they first met at Chartwell and sixteen years since Churchill first wrote on the United States of Europe. Churchill put his cards on the table as he did in his letter to Bobbety. The ideal, he argued, was to ultimately unite all of Europe – not just a western bloc – in which Germany would play a central part.

Churchill was hoping Coudenhove-Kalergi would accept a non-executive role in the coming international campaign, devoting his unsurpassed enthusiasm and pledging his existing base of support without becoming a dominant force. Sandys warned his father-in-law on the telephone the night before the lunch that Coudenhove-Kalergi had something very different in mind. 'Leo, Bob and I have had various talks with Coudenhove during the past week [...] it would seem that he has hopes of getting the new movement entirely into his own hands,' he said. 'His idea appears to be that you will be Honorary President and that he with the title of General Secretary would run the organisation, direct the propaganda, and everything else.'[32] This was an unacceptable scenario to Churchill and the inner circle, who all agreed that complete control of the movement should be firmly kept in Churchill's hands. Perhaps Coudenhove-Kalergi, with his literary talents and grasp of the cause, could then serve as a director of publicity.

On a grey Sunday afternoon, Churchill sat down at the lunch table across from Coudenhove-Kalergi in Chartwell's dining room. He listened politely to the Count's proposal to reorganise the old pan-European movement in the way which Sandys warned of the night before. Then, politely disregarding anything Coudenhove-Kalergi just said, he launched into a monologue outlining his own plan, foreshadowing much of what would eventually happen in the coming year.

Churchill said he wanted to start that winter by forming an all-party British committee to popularise the idea of a United Europe at home. He reassured his guest that the committee would inevitably consist of many of the British members of the pre-war Pan-European Union – Leo Amery being a prime example. In the early spring of 1947 there would be a meeting to constitute the international movement between the United Europe Committee and a host of leading statesmen involved with the different national councils working towards European unity on the Continent. The international council would be charged with making the necessary arrangements for a conference 'somewhere on the Continent'.[33] He planned to use his friendly relations with the new prime minister, Clement Attlee, to convert the British Labour Party to his cause.

As Count Coudenhove-Kalergi said his goodbyes, Churchill looked him in the eyes and said:

> You may be sure that a man like me, upon whom life has bestowed an abundance of success, does not wish to use the United Europe movement to further any personal ambitions. You have created this movement. It could therefore be conducted without my assistance – but hardly without yours! You may rest assured that I will always deal fairly with you.[34]

But the new postwar movement for European unity could easily do without the direction of the pre-war philosopher who first popularised the idea. It could not do without a figure of Churchill's calibre. Churchill planned to deal fairly with Coudenhove-Kalergi because he knew it was essential to maximise support for the common goal of European union. It was still highly uncertain what form that union would take, however, and it would take just a few years for matters to come to a head with Coudenhove-Kalergi on this point.

By the end of October, Churchill's nucleus had drawn up a draft statement of aims that equally appealed to Sir Walter Layton, the Liberal newspaper man, and Kenneth Lindsay, the Labour politician and master of Balliol College, Oxford, who won a parliamentary seat for the Combined English Universities in 1945.[35] 'Our sacrifices give us [the British people] the right,' the draft statement read in part, 'our victory imposes on us the duty and our interests confirm the wisdom of giving a lead to the European nations.' On the practical side of things the statement proposed to form a small British handling group under Churchill's aegis to make the necessary arrangements for a larger international campaign.[36]

Churchill was preparing to issue the statement to the public and the press on the United Europe nucleus on 14 November. When the big day came around, however, Layton called Amery to say that he thought it silly to make an announcement without any sort of explanation. Victor Gollancz, the left-wing publishing tycoon who joined the handling group at Churchill's urging, was in agreement with Layton, and the announcement was postponed until after the first formal meeting of the provisional United Europe group on 3 December in Churchill's room in the House of Commons.

Meanwhile Churchill sought the support of a Frenchman he imagined would be just as worried about the Soviet threat in the East and just as disposed to seek a common European solution as he had been in June 1940: General de Gaulle. He relied on Duncan Sandys, whose tenacity was the perfect complement to Churchill's visionary eloquence, to go on a reconnaissance mission. In 1941, a year after helping Churchill navigate the Franco-British Union episode, Sandys had incurred a serious leg injury in an automobile accident. Having decided against amputation, he underwent a series of operations that saved his feet but left him in constant pain and with a pronounced limp for the rest of his life. The pain affected Sandys considerably, who could be as short-tempered as he was tough. 'The man was a steamroller,' one contemporary in the House of Lords remembered. 'He would grind away in first gear and nothing could stand in his path.'[37]

Appreciative of Sandys's talents, on 23 November Churchill sent his son-in-law a cheque for $4,000 (nearly $50,000 today, adjusted for inflation) 'in connection with the expenses of the British Handling Group of the United States of Europe'.[38] This would allow Sandys to travel around the Continent on Churchill's behalf garnering support for the Zurich speech until more elaborate fundraising machinery was set up.

'I should like to know', Churchill asked de Gaulle in a letter, 'whether you would agree to send some trusted friend of yours to meet my son-in-law, Duncan Sandys [...] It seems to me that an interchange of views in strict privacy might be advantageous to both our countries.'[39] To Churchill's delight, de Gaulle agreed to meet Sandys himself.

Sandys set off on 29 November for a lunchtime meeting with de Gaulle in his quiet home town of Colombey-les-Deux-Églises, three hours east of Paris. The proud, chain-smoking general used his house, La Boiserie, as his home base of political exile. The place was as grim in November as it was lush in the summer. Having been ousted from government in January 1946, de Gaulle quietly prepared his memoirs surrounded by his collection of swords.[40] He would remain isolated there until 1958, doomed by his fickle rigidity, waiting to be recalled to power in a moment of national crisis. Nevertheless, Churchill felt that de Gaulle was the only man up to the job of restoring the honour of France. He thought the General impossible to deal with, a prima donna, but his support for the United States of Europe was a desirable prize.

On his way to Colombey, Sandys carried with him a note containing the vital question of his visit. 'You will have seen my speech at Zurich,' Churchill wrote, 'and it is my conviction that if France could take Germany by the hand

and, with full English cooperation, rally her to the West and to European civilization, this would indeed be a glorious victory and make amends for all we have gone through and perhaps save us having to go through a lot more.'[41] What would de Gaulle make of this?

Sandys arrived around midday and stayed with the General for luncheon. He found him a kind and welcoming host, though it was immediately evident that de Gaulle would forever hold it in his elephantine memory that the Big Three, as he, perhaps rightly, saw it, snubbed France in the war by treating it as a lesser power. '*À Yalta et à Potsdam on nous a mis à la porte*' (We were dismissed at Yalta and Potsdam) was a remark he threw into the conversation repeatedly throughout the afternoon.

Before lunch the men had an hour's talk about Russia's intentions in Europe. Sandys showed de Gaulle a secret British report on Soviet troop dispositions in eastern Europe suggesting that Stalin kept more than 200 divisions on a war footing, waiting to march to the North Sea. Basing his judgement on instinct rather than fact, de Gaulle was sure that the Russians were not as strong as Churchill seemed to think and, in any case, were not yet ready for war. Taking the long view, however, he told Sandys that 'war between the Western Democracies and Soviet Russia is sooner or later a virtual certainty.'

After lunch de Gaulle took Sandys for a walk around his property for about an hour before retiring to his study. They now turned to the idea of European union. De Gaulle said he believed firmly in the project but thought France should make its support 'conditional upon the settlement of outstanding differences between herself and Britain'. The General wanted guarantees for long-term French military occupation in Germany and, perhaps, enlargement of the French occupation zone; permanent allocation of coal from the mighty German Ruhr by way of reparations; international control of the Ruhr industries; and Anglo-French agreement on the colonial future of the Arab countries. '*Voilà mes conditions*,' he said laconically, a hard glint coming into his eyes.

Sandys could not believe his ears. How could the French ever make European union a subject for bargaining when it was so clearly an idea from which they had even more to gain than the British? How could de Gaulle ask for this much from a position of complete and utter weakness? The French, Churchill would later recount, paid with their lifeblood to be able to fly the Tricolour over Strasbourg.[42] They lost their honour – though not their pride – after Marshal Pétain's deal with the devil. In the autumn of 1946 the country was on the verge of monetary collapse. To make matters worse, the French Communists were the second largest party in the National Assembly and were poised to grow stronger by the day. But de Gaulle stuck to his point. Britain would have to satisfy every single French demand in order to establish a trusting Franco-British partnership at the heart of Europe. *Quel courage!*

It emerged that de Gaulle disagreed with one of the main themes of the Zurich speech. He saw the revival of a 'spiritually great Germany' as a dangerous development for Europe and abhorred the idea that United Europe would have to start with Franco-German rapprochement. Sandys reported from Paris:

> He [de Gaulle] said that the reference in Mr Churchill's Zurich speech to a Franco-German partnership had been badly received in France. Germany, as a state, no longer existed. All Frenchmen were violently opposed to recreating any kind of unified, centralised Reich, and were gravely suspicious of the policy of the American and British Governments. Unless steps were taken to prevent a resuscitation of German power, there was the danger that United Europe would become nothing else than an enlarged Germany. He stressed that if French support was to be won for the idea of European union, France must come in as a founder partner with Britain.[43]

With a view to the subsequent history of European integration, it was ironic for de Gaulle to insist on immediate British membership. The 1960s saw successive British governments – though not Churchill's in the early 1950s – begging for entry into the European Union (then called the European Economic Community), only to be denied by President de Gaulle's loud and clear '*Non*'.

For the time being, however, de Gaulle's scepticism did little harm to the progress of Churchill's European movement. At the end of the afternoon the General even promised Sandys he would from time to time express his qualified agreement with the idea of the United States of Europe. More than that Sandys could not get out of him. 'He is far too much of an individualist', Sandys told Churchill, 'to consider working together with any group of people, either in France or abroad, on any project which he had not himself initiated.'[44] Pride and jealousy were as much of an obstacle to de Gaulle as were his substantive concerns about Churchill's design for a European union.

Before Sandys's report of the meeting even reached Chartwell, Churchill set out to secure support for United Europe at the highest governmental level in Britain. On 27 November 1946 he sent a lengthy letter marked 'Private' to his former War Cabinet colleague Clement Attlee. 'My dear Prime Minister,' he began, 'this is about the United States of Europe.' Using Attlee's own publicly stated convictions – 'Europe must federate or perish!' – Churchill pleaded for clarity and support from the Labour Party for the formation of his all-party group. He was dismayed that 'the project has been bruited about in Reynolds News,' a Labour paper, after Churchill contacted a few potential Labour members at Attlee's suggestion. He feared that the Prime Minister might prevent Labour MPs from taking part in the movement altogether. 'I should be very much obliged if you would let me know how the matter stands,' he wrote, 'because if there were to be a veto on Socialist members joining this organisation, I should have to make another plan.' Churchill was hoping his movement would stand on the same basis as the New Commonwealth Society, another all-party organisation of which he was still British honorary president. 'If this is not to be, pray let me know,' he told Attlee.[45]

Joining Churchill for an exploratory meeting on the afternoon of 3 December 1946 were the inner circle and a few additions from different political parties. Leo Amery, Sandys, Boothby, Layton, Ernest Brown, the wartime leader of the National Liberals, George Gibson, a Labour member of high standing in the trade union world as a former chairman of the nation's largest federation of trade unions, and Juliet Rhys Williams, a prominent Liberal politician who was predominantly interested in economic integration. The left-wing publisher Gollancz was unable to come at the last minute.

Churchill opened with a general outline of the idea of the United States of Europe and explained that he had resolved to devote a considerable part of his time and energies to advancing the cause. He tactfully assured the Labour attendees of Prime Minister Attlee's general sympathy with their cause. It made Leo Amery 'smile inwardly', he wrote in his diary that day, that Churchill continued by professing his belief that the movement would be entirely subordinate to the United Nations. Though Amery believed in the sincerity of his words, he knew it would be difficult for Churchill to persuade friends and foes alike that the regional conception of a United Europe was wholly compatible with the One World ideal of the United Nations. Churchill wrapped up his opening remarks by presenting his plan of action: he would form a small handling group to determine a programme for the larger committee and organise a campaign of mass meetings in Britain and on the Continent.

The attendees, led by Amery and Layton, talked around the table in Churchill's room as if it were the introductory session of a small college seminar. By the very nature of the occasion, they made little progress except to agree on the general principle that, as one of them put it in his summary notes, 'there are cultural, spiritual, political and economic reasons favourable to a progressive pooling of sovereignties in Europe at this time.'[46] The provisional committee would come before the public with non-political, religious and academic elements and three or four more members would reinforce the next meeting on 18 December.[47] It was in this spirit that Churchill approached Bertrand Russell, the famous mathematician and philosopher, to join the United Europe Committee, or what one of his private secretaries then still called the 'provisional group of the United States of Europe'.[48] Russell immediately accepted.

On 4 December, Churchill received from Attlee a polite but decidedly discouraging response to his initiative. 'In respect of joining your organisation,' Attlee wrote, 'it has been suggested that the objects aimed at by the organisation would be better achieved through the United Nations Association rather than through a separate society, the aims of which might be misunderstood and misrepresented.'[49] This was an unexpected setback. The result was that Churchill started to approach his committee more as a non-political organisation than an all-party one. It was to stimulate the pre-existing federalist organisations and provoke a response, as Churchill put it, 'from the war-wrecked millions of the Continent of which we form a part'.[50]

The second United Europe meeting on 18 December 1946 welcomed four new members: Gollancz; the Rev. Gordon Lang, a Labour MP; and Miss Josephy and Colonel King, the leaders of a group of British federalists which had existed since 1938. The difficulty in producing a final manifesto for the group was that Josephy and King brought with them a far more impatient and radical position than most were willing to accept. 'These federalists are so set on federalism as a system,' Amery complained in his diary, 'that they not only want to drag England into a European federation but also want to include Russia and anything they can lay hold of.'[51] He thought that King and Josephy were plotting a real alternative to the United Nations – with a federal Europe growing into world government as soon as possible – instead of the regional reinforcement to the UN that Churchill had in mind.

For Churchill, it was unthinkable to allow Russian membership of a United Europe. The whole point was that Europe would be led by Great Britain, however that would be achieved. It was also much too early to think of Britain as an ordinary member of a European federal union. It would have to join later on, as he told the Swiss diplomats on the eve of the Zurich speech, perhaps at the invitation of the other countries or after Russia declined its invitation. Preferably, Britain would be one of the founder members of a much looser

Council of Europe, which would create a European public opinion and provide the basis for further initiatives.

Churchill eventually appeased Colonel King and Miss Josephy with a few amendments to the existing draft text of the founding manifesto. He handled the issue of Europe's relationship to the United Nations by deft analogy. Analogy was a much-favoured weapon in his rhetorical arsenal. As he had argued in his unpublished essay on oratory written at the age of 23, 'the influence exercised over the human mind by apt analogies is and has always been immense [...] the effect upon the most cultivated audience is electrical.'[52] In this specific case, Churchill deployed his weapon with maximum effect.

He spoke in military terminology – easy to follow for an audience which had just come through half a century of wars. A great army, he explained, has General Headquarters (the UN). The headquarters cannot be expected to deal directly with divisions and brigades (the individual nations of the world), for this arrangement would quickly degenerate into chaos. Everyone knew that within the Army one must have Groups of Armies (like United Europe) by which alone the will of the Supreme Command (the UN) can be made effective.

CHAPTER 8

'WE SHALL HAVE DONE OUR BEST'
CAMPAIGNING IN BRITAIN II, 1947–1948

On the last two days of 1946, Churchill followed up his organisational efforts on the United Europe Committee by contributing two consecutive pieces to the *Daily Telegraph*. The medium of writing afforded him the opportunity to elaborate on his Zurich address with a detailed consideration of some of the practical elements of his idea. The timing of the articles, published on 30 and 31 December 1946 – right in the middle of negotiations on the founding manifesto of the United Europe Committee with representatives from all political parties and outside organisations – suggests that they were meant to some extent to woo the different strands of opinion within the existing British movement for European unity. They were of such importance to the movement that a well-to-do supporter, the newspaper mogul and owner of the *Telegraph* Lord Camrose, decided to pay for the printing of 10,000 copies of the combined articles in pamphlet form.

In the first article, entitled 'United Europe: One Way to Stop a New War', Churchill compared the European situation in the autumn of 1946 with that of 1938. In order to step out of the dark immorality which once again prevailed over the greater part of Europe, he asked for 'an act of the sublime'. He selected France 'as the land from which the signal should come', prodding them to take Germany by the hand 'and lead them back into the brotherhood of man and the family of nations'.

Because the article also appeared in the American magazine *Collier's* that week, Churchill spent some sentences attempting to persuade the United States to endorse the idea of United Europe. 'Would it not be reasonable prudence to use the power which has come to the New World to sterilise the infection-centres of the old?' he asked. The creation of a United States of Europe, he argued, would buy the Americans permanent peace and security at home. Churchill then tried to convince the Americans, patrons and guardians of the United Nations, that the regional grouping of Europe would be fully in accordance with the founding UN Charter.

His was a defensible reading of chapter VIII of the Charter, which provides the constitutional basis for the involvement of regional organisations in maintaining international peace and security. But Churchill wanted to stretch the provision a bit further, declaring the 'fundamental practical truth' that the central structure of the UN could not stand or function without regional organisations. Regional groupings already existed in the Americas, the British Commonwealth of Nations and the Russia-led brotherhood of Slavonic countries. Perhaps an Asiatic bloc would also come into being under China's leadership. 'Why', Churchill asked, 'should there not be a place, and perhaps the first place – if she can win it by her merits – for Europe, the Mother Continent and fountain source not only of the woes but of most of the glories of modern civilisation?'

In Churchill's conception Britain's role was not confined to any single one of these circles or 'pillars of world peace'. It was a partner in the English-speaking world, the head of the British Empire and Commonwealth, and 'a part of Europe and intimately and inseparably mingled with its fortunes'.[1] This was Churchill's expansive, almost megalomaniac postwar vision of Britain's role in the world. He sincerely believed Britain was and would always be an equal partner in the 'special relationship' with America, and the leading power in Europe. He hoped Britain would be able to hold on to its imperial possessions in every corner of the world and expected that the self-governing Dominions would continue to adhere to the British Crown.

There were, of course, severe difficulties holding Britain back in the realisation of this worldview. A debilitated domestic economy, surging independence movements in the colonies, and increasing financial and political dependence on the United States were the primary pains of postwar Britain. The country had neither the political clout nor the financial resources to play the role it felt entitled to after defending Western civilisation against Nazism. An acute awareness of these problems only strengthened Churchill in envisaging for his country a position of power at the heart of three great overlapping circles. Britain, with all its wisdom and experience, would teach America the ways of the Old World, walk with Europe on the path to unification and permanent peace, and continue to bring the fruits of civilisation to its overseas territories. The important thing was the issue of compatibility: standing at the intersection of three circles, Churchill thought, Britain would be able to do everything at once.

Having set up the broad themes of his narrative in the first article, Churchill turned toward his 'Grand Design of a United Europe' in the second, published the day after. It ranks among Churchill's most detailed descriptions of what a United Europe might ultimately look like. The first and most important precondition of unification, Churchill argued, was for Europeans to think of themselves as such. 'All the people living in the continent called Europe have to learn to call themselves Europeans, and act as such so far as they have political power, influence or freedom,' he opened.

As he proposed at Zurich, the creation of the Council of Europe, comprising as many countries as were able and willing to join, would be the first step. Aside from its general function of providing a platform for European consultation and further integration, the Council would have four main tasks. First, it would have to work steadily towards 'the abolition or at least the diminution of tariff and customs barriers.' Second, it would 'strive for economic harmony as a stepping-stone to economic unity'. Third, it would have to 'reach some common form of defence'. And fourth, inseparably woven with all of the above, it would have to establish a common currency. 'Luckily,' Churchill added, predicting exactly what the euro would look like when it was first issued in 2002, 'coins have two sides, so that one can bear the national and the other the European superscription.' European postage stamps, passports, and trading facilities would all flow out naturally from the 'main channel' of the Council.

He then launched the idea of forming societies and organisations to promote the idea throughout Europe, preparing his readership for the impending announcement of the constitution of his own United Europe Committee. Though Churchill was optimistic about the attitudes towards United Europe of government leaders around the world, he stressed that he could not afford to rely on governmental action alone. It might well be, he argued, that not every willing country would actually be able to join the European club at first. 'The nucleus must be formed in relation to the structure as a whole,' he wrote, 'so that others can easily join as soon as they feel inclined or feel able. The ideal is so commanding that it can afford gradual realisation.' Clearly, he was casting his mind forward over many decades, realising that it would take the countries behind the Iron Curtain a long time to be free of Soviet domination.

Churchill did the rare honour of citing another writer to illustrate his main point, namely Mr Sewell of the *Southern Daily Echo*, a local paper he read on his return from Zurich.[2] He was enchanted by Mr Sewell's spiritual conception of Europe, seeing it as wholly in line with his own:

> Geographers point out that the Continent of Europe is really the peninsula of the Asiatic land mass. The real demarcation between Europe and Asia is no chain of mountains, no natural frontier, but a system of beliefs and ideas which we call Western Civilisation
>
> 'In the rich pattern of this culture there are many strands: the Hebrew belief in God; the Christian message of compassion and redemption; the Greek love of truth, beauty and goodness; the Roman genius for law. Europe is a spiritual conception, but if men cease to hold that conception in their minds, cease to feel its worth in their hearts, it will die.[3]

The spiritual conception of Europe inevitably seeped through in the final draft of the manifesto of Churchill's United Europe Committee. Unanimously approved under Churchill's chairmanship and published in the Friday morning papers of 16 January 1947, the Declaration of Principles of the 22-member United Europe Committee was nothing short of remarkable.[4] It was a masterpiece of compromise, presenting in careful language some of the most sensitive elements of the idea of a European union: whether the ultimate objective was world government, whether it would encompass western Europe or all Europe, and whether Britain would be involved:[5]

(1) The final elimination of war can only be assured by the eventual creation of a system of World Government.
(2) The aim must be to unite all the peoples of Europe.
(3) Britain is an integral part of Europe and must be prepared to make her full contribution to European unity.[6]

Miss Josephy and Colonel King of the Federal Union turned out to be realistic negotiators. They understood that it was much more helpful to influence Churchill in their more radical direction than stay away from the Committee altogether. Miss Josephy told the National Council of the Federal Union on 26 January, defending the Declaration of Principles: 'Mr Churchill's Committee would have issued a statement with or without the co-operation of the four federalists on it, but because of their co-operation the statement was very much more federal and in line with the policy of FU than it would otherwise have been.'[7] Churchill was simply too important a person to ignore when his policy corresponded in such large part with that of the established federalists.

A day after the announcement, one of the signatories of the Declaration of Principles, Commander Stephen King-Hall, a naval officer who built up a considerable reputation as a writer and broadcaster before the Second World War, elucidated the manifesto in a BBC news talk. One of the obvious questions on everyone's mind was what sort of role Britain would play in a European union. The manifesto's points that Britain was 'an integral part of Europe' and that it 'must be prepared to make her full contribution to European unity' still seemed to be open to differing interpretations. Did it mean that Britain would seek to be a founding member of a new governmental institution for Europe? Would that cut across ties with the other nations of the British Commonwealth?

King-Hall explained the movement had to start in Britain because 'we are part of Europe even though we are also part of our British Commonwealth' and called on the people of Britain to take up the work of the movement: 'Discuss this with your friends. Hold meetings. Preach the gospel. Organise yourselves as seems best to you to further this cause, so that generations to come may say: "It was in 1947 that there began the great movement which at long last led to the unity of the European peoples."'[8]

Similarly, in a BBC radio discussion, David Maxwell Fyfe explained that the Churchill movement intended to spur individual action. It hoped to include all nations 'in the stream of European Civilisation of which the citizens could say "I want to be a good European."' Though Churchill questioned the wisdom of going on a programme with two 'crypto-Communists' (the other guests), he approved wholeheartedly of Maxwell Fyfe's performance, writing to Sandys: 'I think he did very well considering [...] [he] had these two swine biting at him all the time.'[9] Given Churchill's approval of Maxwell Fyfe's words, and his own continuous and passionate talk of being a good European, he certainly hoped Britain would take its place in United Europe. The crucial issue that remained was how to structure United Europe so that British responsibilities and ambitions as a global power broker could remain intact.

At the Foreign Office, most were clear on Churchill's intention to include Britain in his conception of European unity. To Bevin, who wrote a Foreign Office circular on the government's attitude towards Churchill's committee, it was clear what Churchill meant: 'It will be seen that this proposal is for the formation of regional grouping under the Charter of the United Nations, in which Great Britain would participate but the Soviet Union would not.'[10] The ensuing hostility from the government, on account of the perceived anti-Soviet, pro-German character of the movement and the apparent misunderstanding that Churchill was proposing British membership of a federal union, was also clear. On 3 February 1947, the Foreign Office declared in an official reaction: 'His Majesty's Government are definitely opposed to this movement for a United States of Europe.'[11]

Writing from Chartwell for the opening contribution of the first issue of *United Europe*, the widely distributed newsletter of Churchill's United Europe group (80,000 copies), Churchill elaborated on his intentions for his campaign in Britain:

> When the Nazi power was broken, I asked myself what was the best advice I could give to my fellow citizens here in this island and across the channel in our ravaged continent. There was no difficulty in answering the question. My counsel to Europe can be given in a single word: 'Unite!'
>
> It might have been hoped that with victory won, there would have been formed a European union as one of those regional associations for which provision was made in the Charter of the United Nations Organisation; but nothing of the kind has taken place.
>
> We decided to launch a popular movement to which all could rally who believed in Europe and wished to work together for her salvation and revival [...] We must spread the knowledge that this thing is really possible, so that the conviction of the people may be converted into the conduct of the nation. We must create a climate of opinion. We must set a strong, fresh wind to blow, not only through the Chancelleries of Europe, but in all places where Europeans meet together to discuss their affairs. Once the sense of being Europeans permeates the minds of ordinary people in every country you will see that practical action by governments will swiftly follow.
>
> It is for the Government to execute policy: it is for unofficial movements such as ours to inform, inspire and mobilise public opinion.

Notwithstanding the high-flown ambitions of the United Europe Committee and its call for non-partisanship, the National Executive Committee of the Labour Party reacted with hostility. Within days the Executive forbade Labour members to back Churchill's committee, citing its anti-Soviet slant as the main source of embarrassment to the government.[12]

Labour's position, best summed up by Hugh Dalton at a party conference, was narrowly partisan: 'It is much better that we should have a permanent association with democratic Socialists in Western Europe than that we should go whoring after false gods all over Europe and the known world.'[13] Despite the hostility, all eight Labour members of the United Europe Committee ended up defying the Executive's 'diktat' saying they must disassociate from the Churchill movement. Nevertheless, Labour's stubborn stance remained a major handicap to the movement.

The general public was much more willing to embrace Churchill's initiative than was Labour officialdom. Sympathetic letters and small-time donations from all over Britain started to stream in to support the committee directly after its press communiqué of 17 January. On 23 January, Sandys's secretary was able to start paying in the cheques when Churchill opened an account for the committee. This was the start of a more formal approach to fundraising.

A few months later, Lord McGowan of the British chemicals company ICI and Sir Walter Layton of the *News Chronicle* formed a consortium of British businessmen to support the movement, giving it a secure financial base for its activities. Within a few months they raised close to £30,000 (the 2017 equivalent of a little over £1 million) in donations. Prominent British financial tycoons and leading conglomerates, seeing benefits to the elimination of trade barriers and the creation of economic stability in Europe, stepped up to foot United Europe's bills and fund its campaign. Among them were Edward Beddington-Behrens, a close friend of Harold Macmillan's, Rothschild, General Electric, Vickers, Lever Brothers, Marks and Spencer, and Boots.[14]

Lord McGowan presided over periodic lunches in London, often with Churchill in attendance, during which British captains of industry were kept up to date with the progress of the movement and were invited to contribute financially. As McGowan put it in one of his invitations, playing into a sense of enlightened self-interest: 'Europe's recovery is so necessary to our own economy that I submit we should do all we can to help in furthering Mr. Churchill's plan.' After the first lunch alone, for which Churchill arranged Jamaican cigars and provided the opening remarks,[15] the industrialists coughed up a casual £21,000.[16] Major benefactors were Austin Motors, Ford Motors, Rolls-Royce, Monsanto Chemicals, Lancashire Steel Corporation and United Steel.[17] When McGowan and Churchill repeated the recipe a year later, they raised another £32,582 – bringing the total from the two lunches to something close to £2 million in today's money.[18] In the years after that, Churchill was quite shameless in using his name and prestige to talk considerable amounts of money out of McGowan's pockets. As he put it in a letter to McGowan in July 1949: 'I have no hesitation in commanding this cause again to you and your friends and in asking you, to the utmost of your ability, to help our Movement to continue its campaign at full pressure.'[19]

In July 1948 Sandys and Beddington-Behrens travelled to the United States to expand the movement's financial base of support and to meet the leaders of the American Committee for a United Europe. John Foster Dulles, the Republican foreign policy expert and later secretary of state under President Eisenhower, and his brother Allen Welsh Dulles, the first civilian director of the

CIA, had registered the American Committee as a philanthropic organisation and set up its executive committee. Any financial assistance which the American group decided to give, Sandys told Churchill before leaving for America, would be 'devoted entirely to the international campaign on the Continent'.[20]

On his return to London, Beddington-Behrens reported to Churchill that they had met with the Dulles brothers, who 'spoke in the strongest terms about the necessity of a United Europe'. The Rockefeller family promised they would assist financially and suggested the cause, if properly organised, would perhaps require as much as $25 million.[21] Between 1948 and 1960 the American Committee ended up backing the European movement with around $3 million – the equivalent of nearly $30 million in 2015.[22] In all this Churchill played a central role. After setting up the first transatlantic contacts, he travelled to New York with Boothby in March 1949 to solicit funds for the movement himself. Three months later the European movement received a cheque from the American Committee to the tune of $25,000 (a quarter million dollars in today's prices).[23]

On 18 March 1947, Churchill added two more important allies to the United Europe Committee. Over luncheon in the Gilbert & Sullivan Room at the Savoy, Lady Violet Bonham Carter and Harold Macmillan participated for the first time in the discussions of what Lady Violet thought 'an extraordinary assortment' of people: Bertrand Russell, Sandys, Boothby, Gollancz, Lady Rhys Williams, Walter Matthews the dean of St Paul's Cathedral in London, Maxwell Fyfe and, of course, Churchill himself were all there.

Lady Violet earned the rare Churchillian honour of an affectionate nickname, 'Bloody Duck', and served as the unimpeachably loyal president of the Liberal Party. Macmillan, Churchill's resident minister in the Mediterranean during World War II, was a respected MP who, since co-authoring a 1927 book on the integration of Europe's heavy industries with Bob Boothby, was warmly sympathetic to the idea of European union.

Both new recruits were in the small circle that had stood with Churchill against appeasement in the 1930s. Both went on lecture tours in Germany in January 1947, meeting each other in Bonn and finding overwhelming German support for the message of the Zurich speech. Both were affectionately welcomed by Churchill, who invited them to cocktails and potatoes before sitting down for the main lunch. Churchill was discursive when it came to business that day, laying out as usual a spiritual conception of Europe and focusing on the plight of ordinary Europeans: 'why shouldn't the people live, poor things – & enjoy a little happiness & food & family & simple things.'[24] 'He is of course terribly gloomy about the country, which he feels is sliding to ruin,' Bonham Carter wrote in her diary that day, justifying Churchill's long passages of purple prose.

Nonetheless, she and Macmillan came away with the message of high hope that the United Europe Committee planned to spread around Britain and continental Europe. The most productive deed of the afternoon was the amendment and approval of answers to a questionnaire put to the committee by a group called the United Nations Association. Among other things it wanted to know what countries the committee included in the term 'United Europe'. 'The position of Britain and Russia, whilst in many respects similar, is not identical,' Churchill et al. wrote.

Russia was seen as 'the leading Asiatic power' and therefore unlikely to play a full part in the European system. Great Britain's homeland territory, on the other hand, was in Europe. With the official loss of Pakistan and India in 1947 and rapid decolonisation elsewhere – Ceylon (Sri Lanka) and Burma (Myanmar) were ceded in 1948 and the government was confronted with insurgency in Malaya beginning in June 1948 – came a reconsideration of Britain's place in the world. It was more than just imperial trouble that forced new solutions and attitudes. In February 1947 the British government declared it 'wished to transfer the costly task of defending Greece from communist subversion to the Americans', indicating the extent to which Britain was unable to carry the burden of the Cold War in Europe.[25] While Empire and Commonwealth still figured at the top of Churchill's agenda, his committee statement continued with this assessment of Britain's European role:

> The question as to whether Britain can become a full member of the European family, to which she both historically and culturally belongs, will depend upon her being able to reconcile her European with her imperial responsibilities. But this should not be difficult. Within a single generation the Dominions have twice been drawn into war on account of European quarrels. They could, therefore, hardly fail to approve the participation of Britain in a common effort to eliminate the sources of future war in this continent.[26]

Churchill enjoyed the luncheon meeting immensely and was so impressed with the waiters and staff, working away valiantly while there was a strike on, that he ordered his secretaries to double the tip. Lady Violet enjoyed herself equally as much, writing to Churchill that night: 'It was such a deep joy [...] to feel that we were once more going forward together, side by side, on a great new adventure [...] Our first task should be to teach men to *hope* once more. My constant love. Ever yr B.D. – Violet.'[27] Whatever the limitations of Churchill's committee, it brought together those in Britain with a genuine wish to heal the wounds of the twentieth century with the antidote of voluntary economic and political cooperation.

Polling evidence from that month, March 1948, reveals the extent to which the British public had become both aware and supportive of plans for European unity. Churchill's campaign was not the only contributor: the announcement of Marshall Aid in June 1947, as well as the launch in January 1948 of Bevin's plans for a western European defence alliance, brought the United Europe campaign further into view. Research Services Limited conducted a wide-ranging survey probing the attitudes of Britons towards specific elements of European unity, focusing on western European states.

To the question of freedom of movement – 'People could travel freely from country to country, so that they could go and work wherever they liked, and people who wanted to, could come here and work' – 27 per cent said they were against while 66 per cent were in favour. On plans for a customs union – 'Our products could go to every country in the Union without paying duty and the products of other countries in the Union could come in here without paying duty' – just 14 per cent were against and 76 per cent were in favour. There was less overwhelming support for Churchill's long-term plans for a single European currency (42 per cent for vs 39 per cent against) and the least enthusiasm for a defence union (35 per cent for vs 53 per cent against) in which British troops might serve under a foreign commander.[28]

The official public inauguration of what ultimately came to be known as Churchill's United Europe Movement was celebrated at the Royal Albert Hall on 14 May 1947. Five thousand United States of Europe posters dominated the London streetscape ahead of the meeting. At Churchill's instructions, a large red and white banner with the words 'EUROPE ARISE!' hung from the hall's famous dome.[29]

The great platform of the Albert Hall was filled with about 2,000 prominent supporters of the movement, including leaders from all spheres of British public life. Just a month earlier Churchill had stood on the same platform extolling the cause of United Europe before the Primrose League, an organisation founded by his father in 1883 to spread Conservative values. Sandys warned Churchill the day before the Primrose meeting that some Conservative backbenchers were in danger of becoming hostile to his campaign if he did not take them into his confidence about his plans. Churchill thus asked his assembled colleagues 'to give the whole question their earnest consideration, so that all of us may join in the invocation and indeed in the prayer 'Let Europe Arise'.[30]

Now, a month later, ambassadors and diplomats from all across Europe crowded the Albert Hall's royal boxes. A delegation of eager French federalists and members of the French National Assembly took their seats in a hall filled to capacity with more than 10,000 enthusiasts. The members of the United Europe Committee took their places on the platform after a festive luncheon at the Savoy Hotel with a few visiting French federalists. In the chair, personifying the spiritual approach to Europe was the archbishop of Canterbury, Geoffrey Fisher, who introduced the meeting and its speakers.

Sandys decided that the ceremony would not open, as Churchill had proposed, with a performance of 'When wilt thou save the people?', a hymn he remembered being sung in his Liberal days. The hall's grand organ, hand-picked by Prime Minister Gladstone and filling the stage with its nearly 10,000 pipes, might have offered a splendid accompaniment to an apt spiritual text:

> When wilt thou save the people? O God of mercy, when? The people, Lord, the people, not thrones and crowns, but men! God save the people; thine they are, thy children, as thy angels fair; from vice, oppression, and despair, God save the people![31]

Sandys, on paper just the general secretary of the United Europe Committee, had become so powerful and independent a voice that he felt able to overrule Churchill on such matters. In the days leading up to 14 May, he concentrated on the focal point of the inauguration: Churchill's keynote address.

Julian Amery later remembered that, a few days before the event, Churchill sent his draft speech to Sandys for inspection and improvement. Sandys disliked large parts of it and decided to take it upon himself to rewrite the draft completely. Churchill, in turn, disapproved of much of what Sandys sent back to him. He rang up Sandys's home to ask for the original speech. Sandys said he was very sorry but he had torn it up. As there was no common copy, Churchill ended up having to exhaust himself on very short notice to make the speech his own again.[32] Through no fault of his own, it was the Zurich situation all over again.

The Archbishop of Canterbury welcomed Churchill onto the stage for the opening address at 7.45 p.m. He delivered his speech, broadcast by the BBC on its Home and European services for the millions who listened in on the wireless, with a clear depth of feeling. He was in a conciliatory mood towards the Soviet Union and warned that if Europe could not see its way to some form of common government, the world would certainly not be able to either. As at Zurich, he painted a picture of the darkness out of which Europe had to emerge after the wars of the first half of the twentieth century. In what was probably his most dramatic statement on the plight of Europe, Churchill captured the music of people's thinking. 'But what is Europe now?' he asked:

> It is a rubble-heap, a charnel-house, a breeding-ground of pestilence and hate. Ancient nationalistic feuds and modern ideological factions distract and infuriate the unhappy, hungry populations. Evil teachers urge the paying-off of old scores with mathematical precision, and false guides point to unsparing retribution as the pathway to posterity. Is there then to be no respite? [...] Are the States of Europe to continue for ever to squander the first fruits of their toil upon the erection of new barriers, military fortifications and tariff walls and passport networks against one another?

The way to answer these difficult questions was to ask his audience and all of Europe's citizens to resolve to come together and seize the supreme opportunity before them to unite and forget the miseries of past and present. Churchill had proof, in the form of the results of a parliamentary poll on European federation conducted by Count Coudenhove-Kalergi in the early months of 1947, that the opportunity was supreme indeed. To the question 'Are you in favour of a European federation within the framework of the United Nations organisation?' the overwhelming majority of respondents (all of them holding seats in their country's upper or lower chambers) answered yes. In France, where more than half of the National Assembly filled out Coudenhove-Kalergi's questionnaire, 98.2 per cent were in favour of federation. In Britain, where a third of MPs replied, 98.3 per cent answered yes. Numbers from the rest of the 13 (predominantly western) European countries that were polled amounted to an average positive response of 97.1 per cent.[33]

The sheer magnitude of the task before Europe was reason for Churchill to refrain from drawing up a specific programme for its realisation. His role was that of pulling the idea of United Europe out of the realm of philosophy and into the realm of practical politics – not of writing detailed constitutions. 'Far off, on the skyline,' he said, 'we can see the peaks of the Delectable Mountains. But we cannot tell what lies between us and them.' He ultimately hoped for 'the federation of the European States and for the creation of a Federal Constitution for Europe', but thought it would be far better to get there gradually than to put into effect counterproductive, over-hasty plans.

So far the speech echoed much of what had already been said in Brussels, The Hague, Metz and Zurich. By the very nature of the occasion, however, Churchill also ventured into new territory. His thinking about Europe had evolved far since first talking about the 'United States of Europe' in the 1930s, with the most dramatic development being that he now envisaged a leading role for Britain.

'We ourselves are content,' he said in the name of the United Europe Movement, 'in the first instance, to present the idea of United Europe, in which our country will play a decisive part, as a moral, cultural and spiritual conception to which all can rally without being disturbed by divergences about structure.' The immediate task of the meeting was to inaugurate an organisation to promote the cause of United Europe in Great Britain, giving the idea 'the prominence and vitality necessary for it to lay hold of the minds of our fellow countrymen, to such an extent that it will affect their actions and influence the course of national policy'. This time, also, Churchill said of the Franco-German partnership at the heart of Europe: 'the prime duty and opportunity of bringing about this essential reunion belongs to us [Britain] and to our French friends across the Channel.' Of France and Britain, Churchill added: 'They must go forward hand in hand. They must in fact be founder-partners in this movement.'

It is hard to avoid the conclusion on reading these lines that Churchill hoped for his country to play a decisive role in the new United Europe. If the project were meant only for the continentals, there would have been little point in setting up a pressure group for the unification of Europe in Britain. What Britain's 'decisive part' would look like was unclear – only a trip to the Delectable Mountains would yield solid answers.

The speech made the familiar references to the supreme position of the United Nations, American responsibility in Europe, the necessity of reviving France and Germany, and the Soviet-friendly conception of United Europe. 'Looking out from the ruins of some of their most famous cities and from amid the cruel devastation of their fairest lands,' Churchill said, 'the Russian people should surely realize how much they stand to gain by the elimination of the causes of war and the fear of war on the European Continent.'

A group of Communist demonstrators, parading near the entrance of the Albert Hall throughout the session with placards bearing slogans such as 'Save Europe Now – From Churchill', evidently disagreed.[34] It is likely that they were unaware that Churchill's advocacy for a United Europe long antedated the postwar rise of Russia as a European power – though the urgency Churchill manifested at Zurich and the Albert Hall was undoubtedly heightened by the westward march of Soviet influence.

For the first time in the campaign Churchill spoke of Italy, Germany's fascist ally in the war. He hoped that the act of blessed oblivion that was necessary for Germany would also apply to Italy and looked back to the glories of the Roman age as a model for modern Europe. He asserted: 'We hope to reach again a Europe purged of the slavery of ancient days in which men will be as proud to "I am a European" as once they were to say "Civis Romanus sum"'.

Then came an answer to the question on everyone's lips: which countries were in and which were out? The aim was to bring about the unity of all the nations of Europe, but, as before, Churchill showed himself a realist in the assumption that there would be countries unwilling or unable to join at the start. 'Some countries will feel able to come into our circle,' he said, 'and others later, according to the circumstances in which they are placed.' In private, Churchill would shortly tell the former Liberal leader Archibald Sinclair that the distribution of Marshall Aid through the Organisation for European Economic Cooperation (OEEC) had at least temporarily defined the borders of United Europe: 'The difficulties about defining the frontiers of United Europe have, for the time being, been settled by the sixteen nations pact [OEEC], although of course any of the ones inside the Iron Curtain are free to join the club as and when they please or dare.'[35] Any country that played by the rules of liberal democracy and individual freedom would always be welcome at what he called the 'European Council table'. This flexibility of timing was essential for the nations already forced into the Soviet orbit of influence, where people were arguably less free than they were in 1939.

Though Churchill did not make it explicit, it seems reasonable to surmise that he hoped for that flexibility to apply to Britain, too. It was as clear to Churchill in 1947 as it was in 1930 that Britain could not join a federal union as an ordinary member while it clung to its world power status and straddled his three intersecting circles. The British Empire and Commonwealth were too powerful a demand on the country for it to turn into a mere member state of a federally united Europe, subject to the whims of a central government it did not control.

In the spring of 1947 Churchill felt more comfortable talking about a leading British role in Europe quite simply because the world was coming to terms with the division of Europe. This was the most radical development since the Zurich speech. Then, in September 1946, Churchill would have been harshly criticised for threatening the Soviets with establishing a British-led European bloc. Now, in May 1947, the situation was different. Churchill could hardly be condemned for 'provoking Russia' when it was clear to the world that it was Stalin who was pursuing an aggressively expansionist policy in Europe.

For proponents of British leadership of a European union there remained the problem of how to reconcile Britain's position at the head of a vast Empire and Commonwealth with the privileges and responsibilities of common European government. If Britain were invited by the others to join a European union, as Churchill hoped, it would at the very least have to become an 'extraordinary' member, bringing with it the economic hinterland of the overseas territories and the self-governing Dominions – Canada, Australia, South Africa and New Zealand.

In the United Europe campaign Churchill fought equally for the advancement of Western civilisation and the interests of the British Isles. He understood better than most of his contemporaries that the rapid disintegration of Empire implied closer British dependence on and integration into the European continent.

'If Europe united is to be a living force,' he said at the Albert Hall, 'Britain will have to play her full part as a member of the European family.' It was a message of high courage and stunning generosity. After the disintegration of their lands in and after the war, the continental European countries had little to lose by European integration. Great Britain, on the other hand, emerged from the war victorious and still one of the Big Three powers in the world. Its national sovereignty had not been violated. It stood alone in 1940 and put the geographic advantage of the Channel to full use.

While it can be seen with the benefit of hindsight that to propose a merging of sovereignties was a sensible act of enlightened self-interest, it would have been much more difficult at the time to get past serious psychological barriers. Churchill and those closest to him in the movement may have argued at the time that Britain would benefit economically from easy access to European markets and politically from peace and stability on the continent; to many sceptics it felt like an act of madness. Why would one of the great world powers attach itself to the beleaguered corpse that was continental Europe? How could that ever be compatible with Britain's interests and global responsibilities?

Because Churchill was speaking at the Albert Hall to an almost entirely British audience, advocating the cause of United Europe in the name of his newly minted organisation comprising leaders from every sphere of British public life, he addressed the role of the Empire and Commonwealth in the proposed European union. He hoped Britain would seek to lead Europe with the approval of the Dominions:

> It is necessary that any policy this island may adopt towards Europe and in Europe should enjoy the full sympathy and approval of the peoples of the Dominions.

> But why should we suppose that they will be with us in this cause? They feel with
> us that Britain is geographically and historically a part of Europe, and that they
> also have their inheritance in Europe [...] We may be sure that the cause of United
> Europe, in which the mother country must be a prime mover, will in no way be
> contrary to the sentiments which join us all together with our Dominions in the
> august circle of the British Crown.

Being part of a European structure would thus be compatible with Britain's role
at the centre of the Empire and Commonwealth. There was no principled
objection to British membership, just the implied and understandable
sentiment that Britain could not at present or in any foreseeable future
become an ordinary member of a rigid federal union. That did not prevent
Churchill and the United Europe Movement from proposing a solution in
which Britain would be at the centre of a looser, organic union, starting with a
distinctly non-federal Council of Europe.[36]

This was a clever insurance policy for a post-colonial world in which Britain
would become less politically bound to Empire and Commonwealth and less
relevant as a junior partner in the Anglo-American alliance. The loss of
significant influence in Asia with the granting of independence to India in
1947, for instance, may well have further encouraged Churchill's courting of
Europe. This was then also intertwined with the rise of the Soviet Union as a
global power, for, as Churchill later reflected on the disintegration of Empire:
'Certainly Russia rejoiced at every sign of the diminution of our influence in
the world and sought by all the means in her power to expedite and bedevil the
birth of the new nations.'[37]

Churchill felt comfortable pursuing the grand strategy of placing Britain at
the centre of global power, performing a precarious balancing act between his
three circles, and saying preciously little about the precise shape of British
involvement in the proposed union of European states. The campaign for a
United Europe, after all, would last longer than the span of a human life. The
idea, Churchill thought, was so commanding that it would long outlive him and
his younger Europeanist deputies. The campaign would be marked by giant
leaps and serious setbacks. 'If our purpose is delayed,' Churchill declared in the
last sentence of his Albert Hall address, 'if we are confronted by obstacles
and inertia, we may still be of good cheer, because in a cause, the righteousness
of which will be proclaimed by the march of future events and the judgment of
happier ages, we shall have done our duty, we shall have done our best.'[38]

At the end of the afternoon the Albert Hall congregation, ecstatic after
Churchill's address, adopted a final resolution which professed the belief that:

the peoples of Europe must create unity among themselves and together make a positive European contribution to the progress of civilization and world order; and, recognizing that Britain must play her full part, pledges its support in the forthcoming campaign for a United Europe.[39]

The public inauguration was a resounding success, giving the movement for European unity national cachet and energising both its founders and its supporters. Churchill's sweeping speech naturally stood at the centre of the whole affair. Juliet Rhys Williams wrote to Churchill a day after the gathering to say 'how superb I thought your speech last night, and how proud I felt to have been associated with you, even in a small way, in this great effort to sustain the European ideals & ways of life'.[40] A sense of almost childish excitement was palpable in Churchill's inner circle. As in the 1930s, they were ready to fight the myopia of sitting governments.

The Economist, already pro-European in outlook, devoted two full pages of analysis to the Albert Hall meeting and its speeches, noting with delight that Churchill had done it once again. Like Churchill, the magazine was sceptical of the feasibility of the short-term union of all of Europe, pointing out that even within western Europe powerful communist elements would work against federation. Notwithstanding the many difficulties accompanying the idea, Great Britain would have to be the prime mover in the new movement: 'quite obviously the lead in this matter lies with the British and not – this time – with the French.' Criticism was reserved for Churchill's proposed methods: creating a public mood in favour of European unity was thought to be dangerous 'because the practical difficulties are immense and beyond public control'.[41] Representing the opposite of this view, Con O'Neill of *The Times* approved of the Churchill method of public persuasion but questioned the basic idea of uniting western Europe against Russia's will.

The speech was powerful enough, in combination with earlier grassroots work from Count Coudenhove-Kalergi in the US, to persuade the American Congressman Boggs and Senator Fulbright to move a resolution in the United States Congress. With the unanimous approval of the American press, it stated: 'That the Congress hereby favours the creation of the United States of Europe within the framework of the United Nations.'[42] It was already clear in the spring of 1947 that American opinion was turning round in Churchill's favour, but the passing of this unambiguously worded resolution confirmed and solidified American support for European unity.

The basic outlook of the United Europe Movement in May 1947 was a more developed version of what Churchill proclaimed at Zurich. The movement avoided advocating a specific constitutional form for United Europe; hoped for the United States of Europe to become one of the main pillars of world security (and perhaps much later world government); and invited the responsible governments to make use of the public mood generated by the movement. The most remarkable turn since Zurich was that Churchill now felt able to talk openly about the decisive part he wished Britain to play at the heart of the European family. Blatant Soviet hostility allowed him the breathing space that was lacking at Zurich to talk about British leadership of Europe. Just as importantly, he expressed more elaborately and openly than before his belief that British membership of a European union would be equally beneficial for Europe and the British Commonwealth of Nations.

After its inaugural celebration at the Albert Hall, the United Europe Movement continued to hold mass public meetings as well as smaller meetings. In the first four months of 1948 the town halls of Birmingham, Manchester and Leeds and the Guildhall in London filled to capacity for speakers like Macmillan, Maxwell Fyfe, Leo Amery and Boothby. Even Eden, who declined two consecutive invitations to serve on the Executive of the movement and to lend his support on the Albert Hall platform, was eventually persuaded to deliver a few speeches on behalf of the movement.[43]

During the summer and autumn of 1948, small meetings in all corners of the country largely replaced the far more costly mass meetings. The movement set up a Speakers Department, which maintained a qualified panel of about 130 speakers, many of whom were MPs from different sides of the political aisle. In 1948, requests for United Europe speakers for local events averaged 14 a week. The movement became exceedingly popular among the student populations of Cambridge and Oxford, where the United Europe Movement became the second largest society.[44]

A popular national poster design competition gave the movement much of the material for a United Europe Exhibition at the London Tea Centre on Lower Regent Street. At the exhibition's opening ceremony on 17 November 1948, including several ambassadors and ministers of European countries, Churchill appeared in order to give some remarks on the progress of the movement and the purpose of the exhibition, which presented the national traditions of European states. It is one of the rare moments in the United Europe campaign of which there exists film footage of Churchill speaking. Up until that point, film newsreels had failed to cover the major speeches at Zurich (September 1946) and the Albert Hall (May 1947).

Rising to speak after the Dean of St Paul's, Churchill read from a single sheet of paper his warning against prematurely deciding on the constitutional form of a United Europe. 'There are those who advocate the immediate creation of a European customs union and a complete political federation,' he said. 'There are others who consider that close consultation between Governments is the most that can be hoped for, and who regard any form of constitutional or organic union as utterly impractical.' Churchill belonged to a group that favoured organic union, holding the middle between both extremes. 'To imagine that Europe today is ripe for either a political federation or a customs union', he said, 'would be wholly unrealistic but who can say what may or may not be possible in the future.'[45]

CHAPTER 9

'HERE I AM AT HOME'
THE CONGRESS OF EUROPE, MAY 1948

A high and a solemn responsibility rests upon us here this afternoon in this Congress of Europe striving to be reborn. If we allow ourselves to be rent and disordered by pettiness and small disputes, if we fail in clarity of view or courage in action, a priceless occasion may be cast away for ever. But if we all pull together and pool the luck and the comradeship – and we shall need all the comradeship and not a little luck if we are to move together in this way – and firmly grasp the large hopes of humanity, then it may be that we shall move into a happier sunlit age, when all the little children who are now growing up in this tormented world may find themselves not the victors nor the vanquished in the fleeting triumphs of one country over another in the bloody turmoil of destructive war, but the heirs of all the treasures of the past and the masters of all the science, the abundance and the glories of the future.

(Winston S. Churchill, The Hague, 7 May 1948)

On a sparkling spring day in 1948, Winston Churchill restlessly awaited the arrival of 20-odd political allies in his room in the House of Commons. He wore his beloved dotted navy blue bow tie, and dark Harris Tweed suit lightened only by a white pocket square. Today would be the first time Churchill entered No. 10 Downing Street, the official residence and office of the prime minister, since losing the general election in July 1945.

The party that spilled into his room was nothing if not motley. There was Lady Violet Bonham Carter, Churchill's Liberal confidante, looking prim and serious in white gloves and a hat decorated with three large white roses. Next to her was Kenneth Lindsay, a square-jawed idealist who sat in Parliament for the Combined Universities. And just a little farther behind was the kind and familiar face of Harold Macmillan, a loyal Churchillian Conservative MP who bore a remarkable resemblance to Lewis Carroll's walrus – impeccably dressed in high stiff collar but with the bushiest moustache of the lot.[1] Churchill looked around the assembly and roared with contagious enthusiasm, 'Have we a flag?', and then for the order of the day: 'Let us march on Downing Street!'[2]

Churchill, sporting his precious John Bull hat, walking stick and cigar, led the group as it proceeded solemnly from the House of Commons, through New Palace Yard, across Parliament Square, and up Whitehall, passing through the marble-clad splendour of British power. Churchill, all V-signs and broad smiles, visibly enjoyed the growing interest of the crowds along the less than half-mile route to No. 10. Policemen on duty were caught off guard by the unusual spectacle and hurriedly stopped traffic to accommodate the safe passage of Britain's wartime hero and the strange school-crocodile of politicians in his wake.

After the party of 20 settled into the Prime Minister's office, Churchill finally unfurled the papers he had clutched in his hand during the entire procession. They were the resolutions adopted a month earlier at the great 'Congress of Europe' in The Hague calling for immediate governmental action on European unity.

A year earlier, in late August 1947, the idea for the Congress of Europe arose when Duncan Sandys met Joseph Retinger in the Swiss lakeside town of Montreux. Though almost 20 years Sandys's senior, Retinger, a Polish writer and political adviser, cut a similarly fine figure. His friendly round rimless glasses provided a pleasant contrast with his square face and dark, brooding eyes. Before involving himself in the European movement, Retinger, became the youngest person ever, at the age of 20, to receive a doctorate from the Sorbonne. After moving to Britain in 1911, he grew close with fellow countryman Joseph Conrad. In World War II, Retinger became a close adviser to the exiled Polish leader General Sikorski. Aged 56, he parachuted into occupied Poland to strengthen its underground resistance network. Like Sandys, Retinger came out of the war with a permanent limp. Retinger became involved in the postwar movement for a United Europe when he helped Paul van Zeeland, the former Belgian prime minister, found an influential private pressure group for the economic integration of Europe. It was the only one of the major movements working towards European unity that came into being before Churchill even spoke at Zurich.

In Montreux, both Retinger and Sandys attended a large-scale conference of European federalists as observers. Sandys was sent by Churchill; Retinger by Van Zeeland. Energised by a day of conference manifestations and under the spell of their hotel view of Lake Geneva, the two men stayed up 'the whole of one night' to discuss the idea of joining forces and organising a similar conference of their own.[3]

The conference Sandys and Retinger resolved to organise would have to be different from the Montreux meeting of European federalists in one crucial aspect: it would have to be blessed, respected and organised by leading European statesmen. It would bear the stamp of approval of a generation of older, battle-scarred politicians who led Allied Europe to victory in World War II, without losing the energetic support of the younger federalists. The federalist organisation gathered at Montreux seemed powerful enough, with 100,000 paid-up members all across Europe, but its strength did not rise to the level where it could hope to influence the upper echelons of governmental policy-making. Sandys and Retinger agreed that the grassroots European federalist movement consisted of idealists and dreamers who lacked the credibility or experience to ever have a realistic shot at moulding the political future of Europe.

In Winston Churchill, though he was not committed to their methods, the federalists had their only high-powered ally. With the European campaign in full swing, Eden claimed that Churchill told him privately: 'Nothing will induce me to be a federalist.'[4] Whatever his methodical preference, in the broader pursuit of European unity, Sandys and Retinger could not have wished for a better figurehead for the movement than Europe's liberator himself. If anyone could rouse and bind together the many private organisations and initiatives for a United Europe that emerged after the war it would be Churchill.

Earlier that summer, Sandys started to do Churchill's bidding in pursuit of the international coordination of the many private groups working towards European unity. After persuading the United Europe Movement at home that it was necessary to create more effective machinery for the international coordination of activities of the various European movements, Sandys succeeded in establishing an international Liaison Committee, which held its first official meeting on 10–11 November 1947 in Paris.[5] The meeting agreed that the member groups of the Liaison Committee would organise 'a Conference of representative Europeans to be held at The Hague in the spring of 1948'.[6] When the committee met again on 13–14 December, it ratified the November agreement and renamed itself the 'Joint International Committee of the Movements for European Unity'. Retinger became the International Committee's secretary-general. Sandys became its chairman and ensured Churchill's views prevailed as to the scope and organisation of what he decided would be called the Hague 'Congress of Europe'.[7]

The agreed aims for the Hague Congress were adopted on the occasion of the December meeting in Paris:

(1) to demonstrate in striking fashion the powerful and widespread support which already exists for the European idea;
(2) to produce material for discussion, propaganda and technical studies; and
(3) to provide a strong new impetus to the campaign in all countries.

Sandys was exceedingly happy with the organisational power the new International Committee afforded him: 'The fact that we have now created an effective instrument for joint actions will considerably strengthen our appeal to the public and lend greater weight to our efforts.'[8] He was right. With representative Europeans and leading statesmen from almost every European country calling for a United Europe at the occasion of a grand international gathering under Churchill's auspices, neither public opinion nor governments could possibly ignore the issue. The date for the Congress was set for 7–10 May 1948. Churchill was its honorary president.

In the offices of the British Labour Party, news of the impending Hague Congress was received with horror. The Labour Party was deeply suspicious of Churchill's motives and feared that the conference would function as a thinly disguised platform for Churchill to embarrass the government. Though Churchill's organised advocacy for a United Europe was meant to be all-party, non-party and above party, the reality was also that Churchill was the leader of the Opposition in the House of Commons. His interference in the Labour government's foreign policy – his unrelenting pressure to push it towards European unity – was seen by Attlee and Bevin as an unwelcome distraction. With public opinion on the side of Churchill, sceptics saw the campaign as little more than a calculated party stunt.

Though perhaps expected after Labour's scepticism towards the United Europe Movement, Churchill first heard of Labour's doubts about the Hague Congress in January 1948. Renowned continental Socialists such as Léon Blum, Paul Ramadier and Paul-Henri Spaak accepted their invitations and started making soundings among their Socialist colleagues in London. They came away with the impression that the Labour Party intended to boycott the Congress. Churchill saw the looming danger of a Europe-wide Socialist boycott of the conference: it was plausible that the continentals might reconsider their initial positive response and acceptances if British Labour held firm. Sandys was equally alarmed: 'It is bad enough to have Europe divided into east and west. If the west is to be divided further into Socialists and non-Socialists, that will be the end of all our hopes. Everything turns on the attitude which will be adopted in the next two or three weeks by the British Labour Party.'[9]

Accordingly, Churchill made it his personal business to persuade Labour to give the Congress its stamp of approval. He started his campaign in the House of Commons – the arena in which Churchill still thought himself the cleverest, quickest and sharpest matador. The truth was that he seemed to have lost some of his debating sparkle after the war. His pronouncements appeared to gain in wooliness what they lost in wit.

On 23 January 1948, however, Churchill found his old form. In the course of the foreign affairs debate Churchill pressed Prime Minister Attlee for a positive statement on his, Churchill's, private efforts towards a United Europe. He expressed the hope that Labour would be able 'to keep the idea of a united Europe above the party divisions which are inevitable, permissible and even tolerable in all free countries. Let us try on a basis above party to bring the collective personalities of the anxious States and nations as a whole into the larger harmony on which their future prosperity – aye, and indeed their life – may well depend.'

Yielding to the pressure of Churchill's rhetoric, Attlee responded agitatedly: 'I have already said that we welcome the fullest support for the united Europe idea.' He was quick to add a caveat: 'As regards any particular organisation, it would not be right for the Government to pronounce an opinion on it.'[10]

Far from satisfied, Churchill sat down on 1 February to write to the Prime Minister urging him to give explicit support for the Hague Congress. He asked Attlee 'to make it clear that the efforts of the promoters of this conference, which in no way conflicts with the policy of his Majesty's Government, enjoy your good will and that members of the Labour Party need have no hesitation in attending'. Churchill pointed to the overwhelming political support for the Congress (support came from all political denominations except the Communists), and the many invitations already taken up by Attlee's Socialist peers abroad. In response, Attlee deflected responsibility for the endorsement Churchill sought. Labour's main policy apparatus, the National Executive Committee, would have to make a pronouncement on the matter. 'I think you realise', Attlee wrote, 'it would be undesirable for the Government to take any official action in regard to this conference.'[11]

On the day Churchill received Attlee's disappointing response, Churchill's United Europe Committee met for a short sitting in his room in the Commons at

4 p.m. A thorny issue on the agenda was the friction that had been building regarding the Labour attitude to the Hague conference. Gordon Lang MP, honorary secretary of Churchill's committee, and a number of other Labour members were in revolt against Sandys. Churchill tried to reason with them, but after the attacks on Sandys – when Sandys said he was ready to 'fade out' – Churchill blazed forth: 'I am not going to "fade out" whatever happens. I shall go to The Hague – if need be alone – & make a speech which will be read & heard all over the world. I can make Bevin a laughing stock. I can gain great credit for the Conservative Party. That is not my object however. My aim is to build a United Europe.'[12]

In the wake of this outburst Churchill immediately contacted Emanuel Shinwell, Labour Party chairman and minister of war, to seek endorsement for the Congress from the Labour Executive. Here he had no luck. Shinwell's reaction after his meeting with Churchill was so openly hostile that Churchill decided to send the press the full correspondence that had passed between himself, Attlee and Shinwell. Shinwell did not give an inch, deriding the value of the Congress and reaffirming the Executive's decision to discourage Labour members from attending. He wrote:

> It is felt that the subject of European unity is much too important to be entrusted to unrepresentative interests and the proposed composition of the congress seems to us open to objection, in particular because the number of private individuals selected by an unknown process robs the congress of any real representative character. My executive feel that such a congress can scarcely hope to make any practical contribution towards the furtherance of European unity and may, on the contrary, discredit the idea.[13]

Churchill, hurt and displeased with the partisan tension over what he hoped would be an all-party effort, forwarded Shinwell's letter to Attlee, commenting:

> I can only hope that this is not the last word the British Labour Party and yourself, as its leader and the Prime Minister of Great Britain, have to say on this issue. Whatever your decision the international organizing committee will, I am sure, go forward with the conference, and we hope that party differences in various countries will not be allowed to impede the policy to which Mr. Bevin, in the name of your administration, has so rightly committed himself.[14]

Notwithstanding this plea, Attlee certainly intended to say no more on the issue. Churchill, as figurehead and principal driving power behind the Congress, could not afford to let it rest. Four days after receiving Shinwell's rejection, he used a party political broadcast to vent his frustration with a characteristic splash of cheek: 'As this is Valentine's Day, I had better make it clear that I am not making any proposal for a coalition government.' Speaking of the Hague Congress, Churchill warned, 'if they [Labour] succeed in sabotaging this conference at The Hague it will involve them in the lasting discredit of having, by their narrowness and bitterness, inflicted injury upon the whole free and civilised world and its future.' How, Churchill asked angrily, could European unity possibly come about if the British were 'unable to lay aside even for the sake of such a cause, even for the sake of such a cause on which we are all agreed, party strife and party prejudices'?[15]

On 21 February 1948, a week after his Valentine's Day outburst, Churchill first heard the news of a Communist coup in Czechoslovakia. President Beneš capitulated to the Czech Communist leader Klement Gottwald and was forced to endorse a new cabinet dominated by the Communists. The new regime immediately shut down the free press and closed the country's borders. The world looked on in silence and disbelief as the Czech bastion fell for the second time in less than ten years, this time not by a threat from without as when Hitler mounted his invasion but by an assault from within. To make matters worse, Jan Masaryk, Churchill's old friend who stayed on as foreign minister in the Communist-controlled Cabinet, was found dead outside his residence a few weeks after the coup. It is unknown to this day whether Masaryk committed suicide or was murdered by the Communists.[16]

Between the Czech crisis and his immersion in the business of the naval estimates in late February and early March there was precious little time for Churchill to spend on changing Labour's mind on the issue of the Hague Congress. It fell to Retinger, the secretary-general of the organising International Committee, to exhaust whatever channels remained to turn around the British Labour executive. In what was meant to be a conciliatory letter, he addressed Labour's main concerns, of which the fear and expectation that Churchill's would be the dominating presence at The Hague clearly topped the list. On this issue, Retinger, right though he may have been, did much to hurt the chances of actually persuading the Labour Executive: 'On the Continent,' he reminded them matter-of-factly, 'Mr. Churchill is universally regarded as the liberator of Europe and the great champion of European unity. The support and encouragement which his presence at The Hague would provide is regarded by men of all parties as not only welcome but absolutely essential to the success of the Congress.'[17]

The letter, predictably, did nothing to mollify the Labour Executive. Three weeks later, on 22 March, the International Socialist Conference in London adopted a forceful resolution to announce their official boycott of the

Hague Congress: 'The ideal of European unity can only be saved from corruption by reactionary politicians if the Socialists place themselves at the head of the movement for its realisation.'[18] Bob Boothby immediately wrote to assuage Churchill's fears that the Hague Congress might fall apart on account of partisan strife: 'I have had a word with [Ronald] Mackay [Labour MP and ardent federalist], and he quite agrees that the best thing to do now is to go right ahead with the Hague Conference, on the date as originally planned. He will come himself, with quite a large Labour contingent.'[19]

Among that contingent was Gordon Lang, who intended to defy 'Labour's Diktat' and described the attitude of the National Executive at a public meeting in Manchester as 'unhelpful and unfair, and quite contrary to the current of opinion in the Labour Movement in this country and on the Continent'.[20] Lang was proven right when it appeared that the number of Labour MPs who applied for invitations to the Congress greatly exceeded the number of places originally allotted to them, moving the organisers to enlarge the total British delegation to The Hague from 100 to 130.[21]

In early April the tragedy of the coup in Prague was still at the forefront of Churchill's mind, giving a powerful impulse to his United Europe efforts. Much of the European campaign, of course, developed in line with Cold War politics and the emergence of a new bipolar world.[22] Churchill needed to find a way to counter the undermining effect of the Socialist boycott of the Hague Congress in order to have a shot at effectively unifying western Europe against the Soviet threat. To broaden support for the Congress he wrote and widely disseminated a passionate six-page open letter to the Socialist ex-prime minister of France Léon Blum. Blum, an owlish-looking man with a waterfall of thin grey moustache hair draped around his mouth, had paid a few backhanded compliments to Churchill in an opinion piece in *Le Populaire*. Blum argued that Churchill's overwhelming influence in the United Europe movement amounted to an embarrassment to international socialism and that 'the Federalist movement would have great difficulty in emerging from the shadow of a too illustrious name'.

In response Churchill reminded Blum and his friends of the basic fact that it had been he who provided the impetus for the movement for a United Europe and the Hague Congress: 'When at Zurich in September 1946 I revived the ancient and glorious conception a United Europe,' he began, 'I had no idea it would become a Party question.' In a bid to lead by bipartisan example, Churchill continued with praise for Bevin's work towards European unity:

The position of a Minister, holding the high executive Office of Foreign Secretary, is quite different from that of a private person, even if he has the misfortune to be, to quote your flattering words, 'too illustrious'. The Minister has executive responsibility and has to act as well as to speak. There will be great credit for Mr. Bevin, and indeed for all, if a good result is gained and Europe stands erect once more in her fertility and splendour. Those will be unworthy of the occasion and fall below the level of events, who allow Party feelings or personal likes and dislikes to stand in the way of the main result.[23]

The *pièce de résistance* of Churchill's defence came when he deftly pointed out that it had been his call for European unity that prompted American support in the shape of the Marshall Plan: 'I cannot feel that my own initiative has been harmful [...] You must remember that Mr. Marshall [US secretary of state] at his News Conference on June 12, 1947, disclosed that my advocacy of the United States of Europe had influenced his development of the idea that Europeans should work out their own economic recovery and that the United States should extend financial help.' Marshall Aid ended up being a decisive stimulus to western European unification if only because it forced the Soviet Union to reveal its true colours. Stalin refused to accept badly needed financial aid on behalf of Moscow and the countries behind the Iron Curtain, dividing the continent even more clearly than before. Proud as he was of having been a link in setting in train the Marshall Plan, Churchill copied into his letter to Blum the exact text of General Marshall's press conference.[24]

After his long exposition, he finally asked Blum to make 'plain in a manner conducive to the dignity and independence of all Parties' that French Socialist Party members would be permitted to attend The Hague in full freedom.[25]

Socialists from across Europe, despite the official party boycott, eventually published their intention to come to The Hague in their private capacities, including Léon Blum. In Britain, more than 40 Labour MPs decided to ignore their party's official stance. Not to be denied, the Labour Executive launched a last-ditch offensive to keep party members from attending. On 21 April, at a time when most travel and accommodation arrangements had already been made, an astonishingly hostile letter was sent to all Labour members who were known to want to follow Churchill to The Hague:

> The National Executive Committee strongly disapproves of members taking part in the Hague Congress, whether as individuals or as representatives of organisation. The National Executive Committee is unconditionally opposed to any action which might appear to associate the prestige of the governing majority party in Great Britain, however indirectly, with an organization calculated to serve the interests of the British Conservative Party.

I trust that you will therefore reconsider your published intention of attending the Hague Congress and I shall be glad to hear of your decision.

In the end, though numbers dwindled more quickly than Churchill hoped in the last few weeks before the Congress, a healthy contingent of 23 Labour MPs chose to ignore the Labour leadership. On the eve of the Congress, a French cartoon thus pictured Bevin telling Attlee, 'A pity we've abolished the death penalty', as a group of runaway Labour MPs sneaked off with their bags saying 'The Hague'. Many more Labour members and sympathisers from outside the House of Commons ended up joining Churchill and the Labour MPs in The Hague. With that result, Mackay, the ever-optimistic federalist leader of the British delegation, lost a bet to Duncan Sandys. Being the gentleman Australian-born solicitor that he was, Mackay congratulated his friend Sandys warmly after the Congress and sent him a £5 cheque with an accompanying note that read: 'The bet was for 25 Labour MPs and in the long run only 23 went.'[26]

On Wednesday 3 March 1948, with the Hague Congress still in the offing, Churchill invited the Executive of his United Europe Committee for a luncheon in the Gondoliers Room at the Savoy. The Savoy Hotel and Theatre were favourite haunts of Churchill's: he first attended an opening night at the Savoy at the age of 12 and became a regular on account of his lifetime love for Gilbert & Sullivan operettas. In May 1911, he founded his own private dining club, 'The Other Club', in the Savoy's Pinafore Room – a marvel of wooden panelling with views of the Thames – where it has met exclusively and regularly since then. At Churchill's invitation, Sandys became a lifelong member.

Churchill was battling a cold but, Violet Bonham Carter thought, looked 'fairly well though he coughed a little & blew his nose from time to time'. After the chairman's remarks, in which he urged the movement to add a little more precision to the message of European unity in view of the upcoming Hague Congress, Churchill looked on approvingly as Boothby presented a memorandum with characteristic frankness on the movement's political policy. 'There is no need to become involved, at this stage', Boothby said, 'in theoretical discussions about federation.' The movement wanted to build a European union 'from the bottom upwards', achieving political unification and economic integration gradually rather than in one fell swoop. It was essential, Boothby argued, to create an International Authority to coordinate the heavy industries of the Ruhr if the movement seriously hoped to 'make Western Europe an economic unity capable of standing up to the Soviet Union or the United States in the modern world'.[27]

Boothby's recommendations were accepted in Britain and presented to the Joint International Committee, which gathered in Paris that month to produce a draft political report for the Hague Congress that month. It ended up advocating for the establishment of a Council of Europe with the capacity to secure further integration, and, no less importantly, involved a direct reference to Britain:

> No scheme for European union would have any practical value without the full participation of Great Britain. The United Kingdom is an integral part of Europe. At the same time she is the centre of a world wide Commonwealth. But Britain's dual position need raise no insurmountable difficulties. Economically, Europe and the Commonwealth would be greatly strengthened by being associated together. Politically, the Dominions have as much to gain as the peoples of Europe. Twice in a generation, they have had to send their young men to die in wars which started in Europe.[28]

At the Savoy, Churchill had talked at length to Mr Pieter Kerstens, an amiable Dutch senator who travelled to London to attend the meeting as a guest of Churchill's committee. Kerstens, a keen-eyed, bespectacled gentleman who sported a fashionable sideburn-less centre part hairstyle, was the former minister of commerce of the Netherlands government exiled in London during the war. He was well known and liked among European political elites and, as chairman of the Dutch Reception Committee, was responsible for the organisational and hospitality arrangements for the Hague Congress. With Churchill putting his political capital on the line in The Hague, Kerstens made it his business to treat Churchill and the other likely members of the British delegation with special care and attention. He made sure to travel frequently to London to keep them updated on the organisational proceedings.

Kerstens returned to the Netherlands from his meeting with Churchill with renewed resolve to create all preconditions for the success of what could become a momentous event in the history of Europe. The local organisation of the Hague Congress really got off the ground around this time. Kerstens quickly assembled a small organisational committee and left planning for the accommodation of the expected number of 800 delegates to the *Dames-comité*, or Ladies Committee.

The first and most important challenge was to find funding. Kerstens was mounting a conference costing about 200,000 Dutch guilders – the equivalent of close to a million euros in 2017 – and knew that the organising International Committee had little to no money to contribute. Nonetheless, it was decided that the delegates to the Congress would have to pay no more than their own transport costs. The cash-strapped Dutch government was of little help. It put the ancient Ridderzaal (Knight's Hall) at the disposal of the Congress for its plenary sessions and footed the bill for the huge security operation the Congress required but was unable to provide further financial support.

Kerstens therefore discreetly sought to engage private financial backing. In early March, he started writing to the CEOs of large Dutch multinationals. He struck gold with Philips, the electronics manufacturer, which made one of the largest single contributions, of 25,000 guilders, and agreed to supply the necessary equipment for the conference. Philips also put Kerstens in touch with other potential corporate contributors. At a lunch organised by Philips CEO H.F. Van Walsem, Kerstens secured further handsome contributions from Lever Brothers, the Amsterdam and Rotterdam banks, and the Dutch Brenninkmeyer family – owners of C&A, the international chain of retail clothing outlets. Incredibly, Kerstens matched Philips's contribution of 25,000 guilders from his own personal wealth. Even so, the final accounts for the conference showed a loss of 17,800 guilders.[29] It is unclear who ended up making up for the shortage.

The money was spent on staff, hotels, daily luncheons in four separate restaurants, and nightly sit-down dinners at the swanky Kurhaus for the whole Congress. Kerstens was anxious to welcome the visitors in a dignified manner and succeeded beyond expectations. Macmillan later remembered finding The Hague a breath of fresh air in the midst of severe austerity in Britain:

> It was agreeable to escape for a few days from the restrictions and hardships of our somewhat arid regime at home into the easier conditions of Continental life. Of course, we had no money, or very little – there was an economic crisis 'on' at the time. So we had a very meagre allowance of currency. But we were given food tickets by some of our European friends and hospitably entertained by others. Such are the fruits of victory.[30]

Violet Bonham Carter shared Macmillan's satisfaction with the Dutch arrangements, writing to Kerstens after the Congress: 'I was so deeply impressed by the neatness, tidiness, cleanliness and order of everything (after our poor batter, dirty England!) and by the infinite kindness shown to us by all your people.'[31]

Kindness emanated mostly from the Ladies Committee, which faced the formidable task of housing all delegates after it received a full list of participants less than two weeks before the start of the Congress. The Hague area still bore deep scars of the war and was having to cope with a massive housing and hotel shortage. The citizens of the seaside town of Scheveningen had been evacuated in 1942 for the building of the Atlantik Wall and returned after the war only to find scattered fragments of their wrecked homes. To make matters worse, the Allies mistakenly bombed The Hague's city centre in 1945, leaving 8,373 houses flattened and another 19,703 damaged to the point of inhabitability.[32]

Even more problematically for the Ladies Committee, close to half of the hotel capacity in the Hague area lay in ruins after the war. The popular Oranje Hotel in Scheveningen was left demolished, while the Palace Hotel lost its northern wing to two misdirected bombs, and the monumental Savoy and the Rauch both fell into serious decay. In the face of such adversity, the ladies succeeded in securing bulk reservations with 22 hotels in the Hague area (some especially renovated for the occasion) and arranged for private lodging of at least 300 leftover delegates with volunteer members of female groups.[33] Sitting behind long tables at Schiphol airport in Amsterdam as the delegates arrived for the Congress on Thursday 6 May 1948, the Dutch ladies trilingually dealt with any questions as to where the guests would spend the night. The French delegation ended up retiring to the Twee Steden, right in the city centre, while the British delegation set up camp by the dunes of nearby Scheveningen.

While Churchill delegated almost all of the Congress's organisational aspects to Sandys, Retinger and Kerstens, he made sure to personally intervene whenever a difficult issue of critical importance to the success of the Congress came up. At home, in the Palace of Westminster, the upcoming conference generated much broader interest in and support for the United Europe campaign than ever before. Churchill sensed this was a golden opportunity to bring the subject before the House of Commons and show that the United Europe campaign was more than a one-man foreign policy stunt. He decided to give his personal backing and that of the United Europe Movement to Boothby and Mackay in asking Prime Minister Attlee to grant parliamentary time for a debate on their motion on Western Union.[34] Only in this way would MPs get a chance to debate European integration before the Hague Congress.

The motion, commanding the support of approximately 200 MPs of all parties, called for the creation of a political union in western Europe 'strong enough to save European democracy and the values of Western civilization'. It concluded by calling for a constituent assembly for a democratic federation of Europe with defined powers in 'external affairs, defence, currency, customs, and the planning and production, trade power and transport'. Unsurprisingly, many of the Conservative signatories were staunch Churchill supporters.[35]

The government, reluctant to give time to anything that obtained broad Tory support, ultimately bowed to all-party pressure and allowed discussion on the motion during the foreign affairs debate of 5 May – two days before the opening session of the Hague Congress.

Another issue close to Churchill's heart was the presence of a German delegation in The Hague, the first to materialise in European society after the war. To his mind, there could be no United Europe without a spiritually great Germany. The organising International Committee made contacts in Germany a month before the Congress and ensured that the 60 or so invited German individuals had military exit permits to leave the country.

The next step was to obtain visas for the Germans from the Dutch government. As Prime Minister Beel of the Netherlands planned to host all the delegates at a cocktail party on the opening night of the Congress, the German delegation would enjoy official sanction. This was a delicate matter for the government of a country liberated from German occupation less than three years previously, meriting discussion in an emergency Dutch Cabinet meeting of 3 May 1948. After a heated debate, the ministers were only persuaded that they should grant the Germans visas when Foreign Minister Baron van Boetzelaer van Oosterhout informed his colleagues that Churchill threatened to interfere personally if the Dutch government refused to cooperate.[36]

Churchill made the most of his chance to meet some of postwar Germany's budding political leaders. On 21 May 1948, less than two weeks after the Congress, the leader of the German Christian Democrats, Konrad Adenauer, reported on his meeting with Churchill at The Hague:

> We had a get-together with Churchill with about seven of us where we spoke a few words to him. He answered very politely and declared that he did not carry in his heart any hatred or hostility towards Germans, that we must work together for federalism and that a European federation is the only salvation for Europe and for Germany. In that he is completely right.[37]

Churchill never learned German at school and Adenauer – dubbed by Churchill 'the wisest German statesman since the days of Bismarck' – barely spoke English. The language barrier posed somewhat of a challenge for their subsequent political friendship,[38] but a friendship it was. To the dismay of much of the British public, Adenauer appeared in public with Churchill in London after he was returned as prime minister in October 1951. And in 1954, when Adenauer gave Churchill a silver goblet for his 80th birthday, Churchill wrote to say that he was 'high on the list of your admirers'.[39] The shared cause of European union brought them together. In 1949, in a warm message for his birthday, Adenauer addressed Churchill as 'the champion of European unity'.[40] Churchill, in turn, wrote to Adenauer to say in September 1950 that regarding the unification of Europe 'many things are moving in the way that you and I desire.'[41]

Less politically significant, but firmly speaking to Churchill's sensitivity for symbolism, was the controversy over the design of a European flag. Sandys came up with a large red 'E' on a white background, the white part of which, according to the *New Yorker*, looked a good deal like 'a pair of gentlemen's long underpants hung out to dry'.[42] When the Dutch announced they were ready to produce hundreds of these flags in March 1948, Churchill told his United Europe Committee that it was too early to adopt a European flag and that there might later be an international competition to come up with a design.[43] He had Lady Rhys Williams, another honorary secretary, write to Kerstens: 'We showed him [Churchill] the flag which was proposed. He quite agreed that this would not do, and considered that the time was too early yet to adopt any form of flag and insignia [...] I hope Mr Sandys will not be disappointed.'[44] Sandys, naturally, was chagrined and determined to use his red 'E' anyway. He succeeded in appeasing Churchill with his suggestion to adopt the flag not as that of Europe but as that of the Congress of Europe.[45]

Before Churchill agreed to this diplomatic solution, Sandys had first to fend off formidable competition for his design. The self-centred and impatient Count Coudenhove-Kalergi insisted on adopting his own 'croix-soleil' as the flag and symbol of Europe. He was shocked to hear from Sandys that the red 'E', not the flag the Count had used since the 1920s, would flap over The Hague's government buildings in May. Sandys refused to consider adopting the Count's flag mostly because he thought it 'a lousy flag – almost entirely dark blue, relieved only by a yellow ball with a small red cross in it.'[46] Incidentally, dark blue and yellow were the Coudenhove-Kalergi family colours.

Coudenhove-Kalergi, near hysteria, wrote to Churchill on 14 April:

> I am sure you will understand my feelings: for me this is as if someone would suggest to you to replace the Union Jack with the letter 'B'! Nobody would understand why this beautiful flag should suddenly be dropped at the Congress for Europe and replaced by a prosaic letter of the alphabet. I am also sure that this change of symbols would be interpreted by all those who fear a British hegemony, as 'E' meaning 'England' as well as 'Europe'.

By way of reconciliation, the Count's old friend Leo Amery – who had received copies of his pleas about the flag to Churchill and Sandys – suggested to Sandys the hoisting of both flags at the conference and settling the question at

The Hague for the future.[47] Churchill was in no such conciliatory mood and instructed Sandys to deal with Coudenhove-Kalergi's outburst. Sandys wrote: 'I believe I explained to you in a previous letter that the 'E' sign is simply being used as a propaganda symbol for the Congress and that we make no claims for it as a future flag of Europe.'[48] A propaganda symbol it certainly became, for upon arrival in The Hague the delegates were all handed specially designed packets of cigarettes with the letter 'E'. Sandys's put-down letter settled the issue for Churchill and the International Committee. Churchill could finally focus on his most important contribution to the Congress: his opening address.

The four-day Congress of Europe officially got underway on Friday 7 May 1948. Delegates from all over Europe started trickling into the leafy Hague the previous day to obtain their Congress papers and information at the enquiry office in the Dierentuin (the botanical gardens which were also a zoo until the Nazis confiscated the animals). Among them were many of the protagonists of the story of twentieth-century European integration. From Britain came a cast of distinguished characters that included two future prime ministers, Anthony Eden and his nemesis and successor Harold Macmillan. From France arrived former prime ministers Daladier, Ramadier and Reynaud and future prime minister François Mitterrand. From Germany came Konrad Adenauer, later West Germany's first chancellor, and Walter Hallstein, a professor from Frankfurt who would later become the first president of the European Commission.

In the early days of May The Hague flaunted itself like a bridesmaid. As Thursday 6 May was *Hemelvaartsdag* in Holland, a public holiday, streams of families blissfully cycled through town. Red, white and blue azaleas and Sandys's Congress flag adorned the ancient Ridderzaal, where Churchill was scheduled to open and close the Congress. In between the opening and closing sessions, committee work (divided between economic, political and cultural committees) took place in the zoo and in rooms adjacent to the Knight's Hall.[49]

At 6 p.m. on Thursday, Churchill descended from the skies 'like a beaming cherub'.[50] He was a few hours late, but the British ambassador's wife, the commander-in-chief of the Dutch royal navy, a representative from the American Embassy and an honorary guard of marines waiting for him at Valkenburg military airport did not mind much.[51] After dutifully inspecting the guard Churchill drove to the British Embassy, where the police strained to keep exuberant crowds at a safe distance.[52] It was clear that the local holidaymakers thought of the impending gathering as Churchill's Congress more than anything else.

Accompanied by Anthony Eden, his wife Clemmie, his son Randolph, and his son-in-law and personal assistant Christopher Soames, Churchill arrived at the embassy in time for a small dinner party and a good night's rest before Friday's opening ceremony. In the absence of Sandys, who had the entire organisation of the Congress on his plate, Captain Soames was a natural choice to assist Churchill. In 1944, Prime Minister Churchill asked Soames to write a paper on the supposition that postwar Europe would be divided into two blocs and that West–East relations would be hostile. The paper, titled 'A European Democratic Union', argued that there was 'a crying need' for a union of all European countries as a positive alternative to international communism. Churchill revisited the paper sometime in 1947 and its central ideas drove much of what he planned to say at The Hague.[53] On the night of his arrival, he showed the text of his keynote speech to Philip Nichols, the ambassador in The Hague, who suggested just one slight amendment which Churchill accepted.[54]

It was expected that Churchill, the honorary president of the Congress, would infuse the delegates from all over Europe with the spirit of hope and defiance that he had kindled in the war. After the celebrated speeches at Fulton and Zurich in 1946, anticipation was through the roof for what looked like the perfect occasion to deliver another one of his great postwar orations. Churchill started thinking seriously about his speech on 24 April – a good two weeks before the conference – when he invited Bill Deakin to dine with him at Chartwell. Deakin, a renowned Oxford historian and Churchill's loyal literary assistant, had stayed the night at Chartwell just five days earlier, when the men celebrated the publication of the first instalment of the serialisation of Churchill's war memoirs in *Life* magazine.

Churchill intended to include a short tribute to the history of the idea of European unity, but what he wanted to know from Deakin he could not provide that night. Instead, the following day, Deakin sent Churchill a short memo on the 'Grand Design' of Henry IV of France. Churchill, though proud of having revived the idea for a United States of Europe at Zurich, happily yielded his claim of authorship of the idea to King Henry, who, between 1600 and 1607, worked on a plan to set up a permanent committee representing the 15 leading Christian states of Europe. 'After this long passage of time,' Churchill wrote in the final draft of the speech, 'we are the servants of the Grand Design.' *The Grand Design*, with Churchill's wholehearted approval, later became the title of the published version of his opening address.

A few days after Deakin's memo provided Churchill with the material for a full paragraph of his 30-minute address, Sandys sent Churchill a 13-page memo containing highly specific suggestions and an idea for a general outline. Churchill, grateful for the preparatory work, adhered to Sandys's outline in places and adopted one or two of his more elegant phrases. But the final draft was completely and unmistakably Churchill's: he dictated and manually corrected at least seven drafts of the speech before mounting the stage in the Knight's Hall.

Sandys's speech notes were perhaps most valuable for their cautionary value and strategic guidance. Sandys was anxious for Churchill to avoid serious gaffes like party political retribution for the Socialist boycott. 'You will, I hope,' wrote Sandys, 'avoid any attack upon the Socialists which would embarrass the many Socialists from all countries who are attending the Congress in defiance of their Party Leaders.' Churchill obliged and afterwards received praise in the European press for keeping his speech non-political.

Sandys took three pages to describe the purpose and proposed functioning of a European Deliberative Assembly, the creation of which became the ultimate objective of the Congress. He presented it to Churchill as having 'none of the Constitutional snags of other similar proposals' and yet satisfying 'the strongly felt desire for the immediate creation of some European institution'. Churchill agreed and decided to pen a short but forceful appeal for the European Assembly in his final draft: 'The task before us at this Congress is not only to raise the voice of United Europe during these few days we are together. We must here and now resolve that in one form or another a European Assembly shall be constituted which will enable that voice to make itself continuously heard and we trust with ever-growing acceptance through all the free countries of this Continent.'

The final page of Sandys's memo suggested how Churchill might want to tackle painting a picture for the distant prospects of European unity in the closing paragraphs of his speech. The recommendations provide striking insight into that which was reasonably expected of Churchill and what Sandys understood him to support at this stage. He wrote:

You should have no difficulty in expressing your support for the idea of:

(a) The grant of a common citizenship without the loss of original nationality (This is on a par with your offer to France in 1940.)

(b) The creation of a single European Defence Force (This is in line with your advocacy of an International Police Force.)

(c) The development of a unified Economic system (This is an innocuous phrase which commits you to nothing precise.)

You will not wish to commit yourself to the adoption of a Federal Constitution. Paragraph 26(d) [of the prepared Political Report] refers to the eventual conclusion of a Federation with an elected European Parliament. I suggest that you should confine yourself to pointing out that if we are in earnest, we must be ready to make some sacrifice of our separate sovereignties (Whilst not committing yourself to Federation, I hope you will be equally careful not to commit yourself against it, since this would alienate a very large section of those who are most prominently identified with the European Movement.)[55]

On 30 April, a few days after Sandys issued his suggestions, Violet Bonham Carter chimed in with a somewhat distressed note on the most radical idea floated in the preparatory work for the Congress: the establishment of a political federation. 'I gathered from you,' she wrote to Churchill after speaking to him at a dinner party, 'that you did not think we should be *asked* at The Hague to enter into any such hard-and-fast, cut-and-dried, long-range undertakings.' She thought, as Churchill did, that haggling over paper constitutions would only aggravate divisions and hurt immediate progress. What was left to agree on was radical enough: 'If we get a mutual defence arrangement, economic integration, and a Charter of Human Rights, enforceable by law, we shall have gone a long way towards unity.'[56]

At 2.15 p.m. on a splendid summery Friday, Churchill entered the Ridderzaal, a hall of great dignity with a raised rostrum and a crimson canopy. Bonham Carter, sitting with the British delegates, thought Churchill looked 'benign and Pickwickian' in a Victorian frock coat that might have been his father's. He took a seat behind a table on the dais, where he was sandwiched between the Hague burgomaster and the presiding chairman of the opening plenary session, Paul Ramadier, easily recognised by his goatee. Not much farther to his right sat Prince Bernhard – the young, handsome German-born aristocrat who shared Churchill's penchant for Cuban cigars and midday champagne – and his wife Princess Juliana of the Netherlands, wearing a short off-white fur coat and a red beret-like hat tilted on her head.[57] As the government kindly suspended the smoking ban in the Knight's Hall for Churchill's comfort, his first act was to light a cigar and let the curled smoke slowly fill the air.

After a few welcoming words by the burgomaster, Senator Pieter Kerstens stood up to pay tribute to Europe's liberator: 'To no single man in Europe do we owe so much as to him. But for him there would not be a Congress of Europe.'[58] This was Churchill's cue to rise to the lectern himself. He calmly arranged his notes and allowed his round, horn-rimmed glasses to descend to his nostrils. He began:

Since I spoke on this subject at Zürich in 1946, and since our British United Europe Movement was launched in January 1947, events have carried our affairs beyond our expectations. This cause was obviously either vital or merely academic. If it was academic, it would wither by the wayside; but if it was the vital need of Europe and the world in this dark hour, then the spark would start a fire which would grow brighter and stronger in the hearts and the minds of men and women in many lands. This is what actually happened.

Churchill recounted the official achievements of European governments in pursuit of European unity and expressed his hope that the rest of Europe, including the eastern states, would be able to join the nucleus of Britain, France and the Benelux in due course. He had reason to call what he saw before him now the 'Voice of Europe'. A number of former prime ministers, 29 former foreign ministers and many ministers in office attended the Congress. All political parties, except for the Communists, were represented. Religious figures, writers and artists, captains of industry and prominent trade unionists packed the Knight's Hall to the brim in a hemicycle arrangement.

Addressing all of these different shades of European opinion, Churchill's speech wisely avoided the explosive issue of political federation. But what he said instead was no less radical: he announced his willingness to sacrifice at least some degree of national sovereignty for the purpose of European unity. This had come at the advice of Duncan Sandys, who wrote in his speech notes: 'Some merging or joint exercise of sovereign powers is ultimately essential, and it is well that at the outset we should make it clear that we understand this, and, when the time comes, will be ready to accept it.'[59]

A mere three years after the liberation of his host country of the Netherlands, Churchill expressed his readiness to intertwine Britain's fate to some extent with its war-torn neighbours on the continent. He paused for breath before giving the Congress a prescription of his political wishes: 'It is impossible to separate economics and defence from the general political structure. Mutual aid in the economic field and joint military defence must inevitably be accompanied step by step with a parallel policy of closer political unity.' Here was the rub:

It is said with truth that this involves some sacrifice or merger of national sovereignty. But it is also possible and not less agreeable to regard it as the gradual assumption by all the nations concerned of that larger sovereignty which can alone protect their diverse and distinctive customs and characteristics and their national traditions all of which under totalitarian systems, whether Nazi, Fascist, or Communist, would certainly be blotted out for ever.[60]

Sharing a degree of sovereignty in Europe seemed like the only way forward to enduring peace after Europe's national enmities had caused devastating war twice in the lifetime of a single generation. One of the most powerful achievements of the present Congress was that it brought together a younger generation of Europeans, who had witnessed World War II, and an older generation – Churchill's generation –who had lived through both world wars and understood more clearly that Europe's national hatred brought fundamental instability to Europe and the rest of the world. Churchill felt it his duty and destiny to impress on his audience the most fundamental insight of his lifetime of war experience: 'I have the feeling that after the second Thirty Years' War, for that is what it is, through which we have just passed, mankind needs and seeks a period of rest.' A United Europe was the indispensable vehicle to secure that rest.

But what of Britain's Empire and Commonwealth? If Britain were to 'gradually assume a larger sovereignty' with its European neighbours, what would happen to the ties of blood that bound countries like Australia, Canada, New Zealand and South Africa?

Leo Amery's expertise and interests rendered him uniquely qualified to devise a solution to the problem of Britain's double position as head of the Commonwealth and full member of the European family. Hence he was given the task to get to work on what Sandys called 'the Empire side of our campaign'.[61] On the eve of the Hague Congress, after extensive consultation with Commonwealth leaders, Amery had persuaded the economic sub-committee of the United Europe Movement to put forth a document outlining the compatibility of the Commonwealth and European union for Britain. The memorandum stated:

> Great Britain has an important role to play as a member of the European Union; she has another role as a member of the British Commonwealth. There is nothing inconsistent or incongruous in this. The Commonwealth and the Western European Union have complementary needs, and in close co-operation of Commonwealth and Union Britain would be a vital hinge [...] Britain is not faced with a choice of Commonwealth or European Union; Britain needs both.[62]

Sandys appreciated the salience of Amery's thinking and sent Churchill, as source material for his opening address at The Hague, a speech delivered by Amery in Leeds on 4 March. 'How', Amery had asked his audience, 'is this idea of European unity to be reconciled with the fact that we are also the heart and centre of a Commonwealth with world wide responsibilities spread over all seven seas?' The difficulties, he argued, though many, were not insuperable.

European markets would be profitable for Britain as well as the Dominions, and, perhaps more importantly, 'a free and friendly Europe' would be the best guarantee for the security of the whole Commonwealth.[63]

Churchill gratefully adopted Amery's line of argument, including its focus on the principle of compatibility rather than the details of how such a position might work. Now, in the Ridderzaal, he touched briefly on the point of European unity and Commonwealth cohesion. He ultimately wished to see a form of world government in which the 'Council of Europe, including Great Britain linked with her Empire and Commonwealth', would be an important supporting pillar. And later in the speech, Churchill said: 'We in Britain must move in harmony with our great partners in the Commonwealth, who, I do not doubt, though separated from us by the ocean spaces, share our aspiration and follow with deep attention our trend of thought.'

Towards the end of his speech, Churchill returned to his exhortation that the delegates did not come to The Hague to draw up elaborate constitutional schemes. He said:

> I take a proud view of this Congress. We cannot rest upon benevolent platitudes and generalities. Our powers may be limited but we know and we must affirm what we mean and what we want. On the other hand it would not be wise in this critical time to be drawn into laboured attempts to draw rigid structures of constitutions. That is a later stage, and it is one in which the leadership must be taken by the ruling governments in response no doubt to our impulse, and in many cases to their own conceptions.
>
> We are here to lay the foundations upon which the statesmen of the western democracies may stand, and to create an atmosphere favourable to the decisions to which they may be led [...] But undue precipitancy, like too much refinement, would hinder and not help the immediate mission we have to fulfil.[64]

The positive step forward that Churchill wanted to take here and now was the planting of a European Assembly as the seed for what he liked to call 'an organic union'. This way, Churchill's mission of a United Europe would not be confounded by an ill-conceived and premature federal constitution. It would grow gradually, guided by the possibilities and limitations of the future. The speech, already punctuated by rounds of loud applause from the delegates, ended with a thunderous, minutes-long standing ovation that was heard far outside the Ridderzaal. Churchill, moved to tears, could do no more than sit down in his chair and take in the overwhelming praise that was his due.

After Friday's friendly overture, ending in a reception hosted by the Netherlands government in the gardens of Kasteel Oud-Wassenaar,

Saturday's committee meetings seemed incomprehensibly chaotic. The three committees – political, economic and cultural – met to discuss prepared reports and propose amendments to resolutions that would be presented in the final plenary sessions on Monday. If that sounded civilised enough on paper, the reality of 800 delegates and more than 200 journalists jockeying to be closest to the action was a heavy burden on the committee chairmen. As one British delegate observed in his diary, the proceedings seemed 'not far removed from a bear garden'.[65] It was telling enough that Paul Ramadier, the chairman of the political committee, exclusively spoke in front of a chalkboard that said 'quiet please, *also during translations*'.

Churchill gleefully took no part in the difficult business of formulating tidy resolutions. His presence loomed so large that the committees simply could not have functioned with him in the room. Equally, as is evident from his speeches, he was unconcerned with the detailed practicalities of the vision for European unity he had set out. Instead, on Saturday morning he and Mrs Churchill motored to Soestdijk Palace at Queen Wilhelmina's invitation to meet with her, Prince Bernhard and Princess Juliana. After lunch and a leisurely stroll with the young couple's three children, Churchill quietly left for Paleis 't Loo, the Queen's residence in Apeldoorn, for high tea and dinner. Joined by Eden, who drove straight from The Hague in time for dinner, Churchill was offered and gladly accepted royal lodgings in the Queen's palace.

Hundreds of people flocked to 't Loo on Sunday morning to catch a glimpse of Churchill with the Queen. They only succeeded when Churchill left the palace after lunch, the timing of which had been announced in a national radio broadcast. At 1.30 p.m. sharp a fleet of black cars with British licence plates appeared in front of the palace. Shortly thereafter the heavy doors of 't Loo's main entrance opened and out came Queen Wilhelmina with her guests. Churchill said his goodbyes with a deep bow to the Queen and kissed his wife, who returned to The Hague in a separate car while Churchill and Eden travelled to Amsterdam for the public high point of the Congress of Europe. Churchill would be the main speaker and star attraction during a mass open-air rally in Amsterdam's main square. Hundreds more greeted Churchill as he drove over the Paleislaan and towards a close-by monument. He answered the cheers with V-signs while the Queen remained on the palace steps until Churchill was out of sight.[66]

Around 3 p.m., en route to Amsterdam, Churchill suddenly ordered his chauffeur to stop the car when he spotted an agreeable-looking roadside tavern near the town of Bussum. The police cars in front of Churchill failed to notice this and drove on. 'I want to have a nice cool drink,' Churchill told a bewildered waiter on the packed terrace of De Gooische Boer. Within minutes, Churchill and Eden were enjoying a cold beer in Bussum's spring greenery. When the police cars returned to see where they had lost the Grand Old Man, Churchill acted as paymaster and left his waiter with a strong, jovial handshake and a generous tip.[67]

In the May sunshine, accompanied by music from a municipal brass band and an amalgamated choir of 500, Amsterdam appeared to be just as much *en fête* as The Hague. A specially chartered train brought the rest of the Congress delegates to Amsterdam central station, and the historic Dam Square started filling up with upwards of 40,000 people waiting to hear Churchill speak. The streets were lined with people, one delegate wrote, 'as tho' for a King'.[68] The delegates, arriving 30 minutes late, marched to the main square of Amsterdam where they took seats in the centre of the square. The warmest welcome was for Churchill, who received a deafening ovation when he stepped out of his car and onto the purpose-built stage in front of the Royal Palace.

The rostrum was festively festooned with a sea of white, blue and orange flowers, Dutch flags and, naturally, the Congress's own red 'E'. There was accommodation on the platform for perhaps some 25 people and velvet chairs reserved for the principals. Churchill, Count Coudenhove-Kalergi and the chief organisers of the Congress were among the dignitaries on the platform. Mayor d'Ailly opened the meeting and welcomed the Congress delegates to the historical heart of Amsterdam. Churchill, who wore a red rose in his lapel, took in the sun rays and listened to the 500 singers perform the hymn 'Europe unite' (in four languages) that had been composed for the occasion. He gave polite attention to an hour's worth of other speeches before delivering his second and last major address of the weekend.

The atmosphere and impact of Churchill's Amsterdam open-air address can best be described by comparison to John F. Kennedy's 1963 'Ich bin ein Berliner' speech. In Berlin, Kennedy unmistakably echoed his hero's Amsterdam speech. Looking out over the great concourse of the people of Amsterdam, Churchill's message was one of hope for a united European future. Like Kennedy after him, he identified himself directly with the people standing before him. Like Kennedy after him, he promised protection against communist Russia:

> This is the Europe which we wish to see arise in so great a strength as to be safe from internal disruption or foreign inroads. We hope to reach again a Europe

united but purged of the slavery of ancient, classical times, a Europe in which men
will be proud to say, '*I am a European*'.

We hope to see a Europe where men of every country will think as much of
being a European as of belonging to their native land, and that without losing any
of their love and loyalty of their birthplace. We hope wherever they go in this wide
domain, to which we set no limits in the European Continent, they will truly feel
'*Here I am at home. I am a citizen of this country too*'.

A popular Dutch Catholic priest closed the Amsterdam meeting by asking
Churchill to show the thousands of people, crammed into the square below,
his famous V-sign, only this time not signifying victory but peace in Europe.
Churchill at first did not understand the priest, but when Senator Kerstens
hastened to clarify what was asked of him, he stood up, relocated his cigar from
his right hand to his mouth, took a step forward and proudly formed his V to
thunderous applause. According to a British delegate in the audience, he
looked 'like a Giant Panda with a bamboo shoot'.[69] All delegates and onlookers
then rose with Churchill to hear the choir of 500 angelic voices sing Felix
Mendelssohn's sacred hymn *Beauti Mortui*.[70]

Churchill spent Sunday night, the third night of the Congress, with the
British ambassador and prepared quietly for the final plenary sessions of the
Congress on Monday. On Sunday morning, when Churchill breakfasted with
the Queen, the plenary session of the cultural committee had already produced
a unanimous resolution calling for a European Charter of Human Rights.
Monday's focus was on the discussions of the political and economic
committees.

The plenary session of the political committee was held in the morning. The
political resolution was unanimously approved with no serious disagreements
and constituted a considerable victory for Churchill's line of thinking against
the viewpoint of the more impatient federalists. Rather than calling for the
immediate establishment of a political federation, the resolution found that
what would ultimately be called 'the European Union or Federation' should start
with the immediate calling of a European Consultative Assembly whose
members were to be nominated by the parliaments of the participating
nations.[71] That was exactly what Churchill had asked for in his opening address.

The economic committee had been in session until 6 a.m. that morning.

A fierce debate ensued, punctuated by a violent thunderstorm that raged
outside the Ridderzaal and at one point plunged the room into complete
darkness. Just as the storm abated, Churchill arrived and felt moved to
intervene before the final economic resolution was put to a vote. 'I think we

PLATE 1 Prime Minister Winston Churchill in 1942.

PLATE 2 Winston Churchill, Harry Truman and Joseph Stalin at the Potsdam Conference in July 1945. The Leader of the Labour Party Clement Attlee was also in attendance, as the results of the 1945 General Election were not yet known in Britain. Churchill would learn during the conference that the Conservative Party he led had lost power in the United Kingdom.

PLATE 3 Count Richard Nikolaus Coudenhove-Kalergi (standing) at the welcome during the Pan-Europe Congress in Berlin, 1930. On the right sits his wife Ida Roland, actress. Count Coudenhove-Kalergi was one of the earliest driving forces behind greater European integration.

PLATE 4 A crowd gathered to hear Winston Churchill speak in Zurich, 1946. Churchill argued in the speech for 'a kind of United States of Europe' to preserve peace.

PLATE 5 Commemorative plaque for the speech of Winston Churchill on 19 September 1946 at the University of Zurich. The final line translates into English as 'Let Europe arise!'

PLATE 6   Duncan Sandys, British politician and Joint Secretary of the United Europe Movement, addressing a conference in the Ridderzaal at The Hague, 29 January 1948. Duncan Sandys (1908–87) was a key ally of Churchill's European project, as well as his son-in-law.

UNITED EUROPE

PUBLIC MEETING
(arranged by the United Europe Committee)
AT THE

ROYAL ALBERT HALL
(Manager: C. S. Taylor)

ON

WEDNESDAY, MAY 14th 1947
at 7.30 p.m.

CHAIRMAN:

His Grace The ARCHBISHOP OF CANTERBURY

SPEAKERS WILL INCLUDE :

Rt. Hon. WINSTON CHURCHILL, M.P.,
Mr. GEORGE GIBSON, C.H.
LADY VIOLET BONHAM-CARTER.
Mr. VICTOR GOLLANCZ.
Rt. Hon. OLIVER STANLEY, M.P.

Tickets from : Royal Albert Hall (KENsington 8212) and usual Agents.

Reserved and Numbered Seats - - 1/6; 2/6; 5/-; 10/-
Unreserved Seats: Admission free by ticket.

The Modern Press, Oakfield Road, West Croydon.   H2403

PLATE 7 United Europe poster. The official public inauguration of what ultimately came to be known as Churchill's United Europe Movement took place at the Royal Albert Hall on 14 May 1947. Five thousand United Europe posters were placed across London ahead of the meeting. At Churchill's instructions, a large red and white banner with the words 'EUROPE ARISE!' hung from the hall's ceiling.

PLATE 8   Sir Winston Churchill speaks at the United Europe Movement at the
Royal Albert Hall event on 14 May 1947.

PLATE 9 Churchill and Eden in London, 1954. Anthony Eden would successfully help discourage Churchill from pursuing his European plans.

may congratulate ourselves upon the success of our remarkable adventure,' he began, turning to explain his absence in the regular sessions of the Congress. 'I have been told by my Socialist friends and opponents in England [...] that I should dominate the Congress.' Generous laughter broke from the assembled delegates. 'So I thought it right to keep away and I have kept away from what I believe have been most animated and virile discussions.'

In what Harold Macmillan remembered as 'a somewhat Wagnerian atmosphere', Churchill saw an opening to tailor his impromptu remarks to the dramatic effects of the weather:

> We heard the thunder – it almost silenced your discussions. One of the objects which has brought us all together here to-day is to prevent the thunder of war and terrorism and regimentation from silencing the free discussions of decent people met together to find the best way out of the difficulties of the human race.

Churchill's purpose was to move the economists to unanimously accept the resolution before them. Without agreement on the economic resolution, indeed, without agreement on the essentials, the Congress would be deemed a failure. How could Churchill force the governments of Europe to seriously consider and implement the Hague Congress resolutions if there was no united European opinion to speak of?

'I am only speaking as President *en titre* of this meeting,' Churchill continued, 'and I say to you without hesitation that it may be famous in the history of Europe if you all unite to make it as in the next hour or hour and a half [...] We must be united. I urge you not to fail at this juncture.' His speech had a great effect on the audience and the resolution passed.[72] That evening Churchill spoke freely and at length to Prince Bernhard and the Dutch prime minister and minister for foreign affairs during a dinner party at the British Embassy. 'All three were much interested in his views,' the British ambassador wrote in his official report of the Netherlands visit, 'especially in the confidence he expressed that with the help of the United States of America the nations of Europe would together certainly find a way of preserving their civilization and their way of life.'[73]

The next morning, Tuesday 11 May, Churchill left The Hague for Oslo in a privately chartered jet. He looked back on the Congress knowing that its main achievement was to give the movement for European unity a decisive impulse. Hundreds of European leaders returned to their native countries bearing a message of hope and an urgent cause to rally around: the constitution of a European Assembly. As Churchill put it to Lord Layton two weeks after the Congress: 'The unanimous conclusions arrived at by this influential and representative gathering will give a powerful new impetus to the campaign in all countries.'[74] Paul-Henri Spaak perhaps captured best this sense of accomplishment when he reflected that the Hague Congress 'meant that the unity of European countries was no longer a dream that was supposed to happen in a hundred years, but a problem of the day, the solution of which was urgent'.[75]

Even the radical federalists, the 'cranks of Europe' as *The Economist* dubbed them, disappointed that the Hague Congress did not yield a federal constitution, ultimately came to realise the significance of the momentous occasion they witnessed.[76] The Swiss writer Denis de Rougemont, though openly critical of Churchill's unwillingness to commit to the federal approach, later conceded: 'Everything else flowed from the Congress [...] from each of the three committees of which it was made up, there emanated three great series of institutions.'[77] It greatly satisfied Churchill that there was no doubt about his central contribution. As Count Coudenhove-Kalergi remembered generously: 'the whole Congress revolved round the outstanding personality of Winston Churchill.'[78]

Having just completed the march on Downing Street, the drama and solemnity of which was carefully pitched to match that of the Hague Congress of Europe, Churchill now found himself in the Prime Minister's office. It was just large enough to hold the entire party of United Europe loyalists that accompanied Churchill. As he unfurled the paper he had clutched in his hand during the walk over, he looked across the table at Attlee, Bevin and several other senior ministers.[79]

Attlee, who according to Churchill combined 'a limited outlook with strong qualities of resistance', found himself in a pickle.[80] He was on record as saying 'Europe must federate or perish' – a fact of which Churchill never tired of reminding him – but had grown increasingly sceptical of Churchill's high-profile campaign for a United Europe. Though himself in a friendly mood, he was counting on Ernie Bevin, whom he regarded as 'an exceptionally good dog', to do the barking for him and reject the demands Churchill was about to make.[81]

Then Churchill spoke. He began by reiterating that the whole movement for European unity was 'non-party, all-party and above-party' and that he wished to contribute to, not obstruct, the government's foreign policy. Speaking with the zest and precision of someone who knows his cause and understands his audience, Churchill distilled the entire outcome of the Congress into a single demand:

The immediate constitution of a European Consultative Assembly.

CHAPTER 10

'WHERE ARE THE GERMANS?'
THE COUNCIL OF EUROPE, AUGUST 1949–1951

As soon as Churchill finished speaking, Ernie Bevin, a short, stout and sickly man with a thick Somerset accent, launched a series of rather specious arguments against the European Assembly. Generally Churchill felt great respect for Bevin, whose work as minister of labour in Churchill's wartime coalition helped defeat Nazi Germany. After the war Churchill admired Bevin's steadfast resistance to communism and his unwavering commitment to strengthening Britain's ties with the United States. When Bevin died in April 1951 Churchill felt like he had lost a dear friend and meant it with all his heart when he said in a statement to the press: 'I am deeply grieved at the death of my wartime comrade. A valiant spirit has passed from us. He has his place in history.'[1]

But this meeting in Attlee's room was not about Bevin's war record or Atlantic relations. It was not even principally about resisting the Soviet Union. The European Assembly was to give a voice to European opinion and to serve as the starting point for possible further integration initiatives. On this issue Bevin and Churchill fundamentally disagreed. Indeed, Stephen King-Hall, who took part in the march on Downing Street, had forewarned Churchill that the British government was planning to turn down participation in the European Consultative Assembly. That, he said, would be 'like a slap across the face with a wet fish'.[2]

Bevin accepted, and even appreciated, the need for consultation between European governments in the emerging Cold War. For this reason he engineered a Franco-British mutual defence pact in 1947, with the Treaty of Dunkirk, and subsequently the Brussels Pact of March 1948, providing a platform for intergovernmental cooperation in social, economic and military matters between Britain, France and the Benelux. He was also a helpful factor in distributing Marshall Aid through the OEEC and would become instrumental that year in committing the United States to a Western system of collective defence called the North Atlantic Treaty Organisation, better known today by its acronym, NATO. Clearly the Foreign Secretary deserved his place in history. Churchill acknowledged in 1957 that the British government, 'much inspired by the stout-hearted and wise Mr. Ernest Bevin, took the lead in rebuilding something of the Concert of Europe, at least in what was left of Europe'.[3]

The problem for Churchill in the late 1940s was that Bevin saw no reason to go beyond traditional treaty-making between nation states. Bevin tolerated and encouraged consultation between governments; he was deeply suspicious of any attempt at merging sovereignty in Europe. One of Bevin's closest advisers remembered hearing the Foreign Secretary say about Churchill's idea for an embryonic European Parliament: 'If you open that Pandora's box, you never know what Trojan horses will jump out.'[4] While appreciative of what the proposed Council of Europe with a European Assembly might do to bring the French and the Germans closer together, Bevin feared a large European body of parliamentarians would become an unwelcome, loud and insistent influence on the policy of national governments.

Looking at Churchill and the deputation of United Europe supporters behind him, Bevin was groping for steady ground on which to reject the demands of the Hague Congress. It looked like Attlee was open to be pushed in Churchill's direction, but Bevin was clearly determined not to let him move. He wanted to avoid, he said, 'any reference to the surrender of sovereign rights' and said that any alternative to governmental negotiations would more likely be harmful than helpful to the cause of European unity.[5] Churchill offered a semantic compromise, saying he liked to speak instead of 'countries acquiring an enlarged or enriched sovereignty through membership of a European Union'.[6] Bevin seemed unconvinced and went on suggesting that he had had intimations from other European governments that they were alarmed at the prospect of a European Assembly and said that it would be in real danger of Communist exploitation – a somewhat absurd line of reasoning seeing as the participating governments would never appoint Communist representatives to begin with. Ambassadors, officials and professional diplomats, Bevin concluded, would do a much better job working towards European unity than a transnational group of parliamentarians could ever wish to do.[7] Judging by this unhappy encounter it seemed unlikely indeed that the British government would ever consent to creating the European Assembly.

Churchill decided to keep the pressure of public opinion on Attlee and Bevin until they finally yielded to his demands. On 27 July, a little over a month after the march on Downing Street, Churchill sent more detailed information – prepared by the British delegates to The Hague and the International Committee – to Prime Minister Attlee on the convening of a European Assembly. 'The creation of a European Assembly would represent an important practical step in the advance towards a United Europe,' Churchill reminded Attlee, 'and would greatly help to create a sense of solidarity among the European peoples in the face of increasing dangers which beset them. In this the lead should be taken by Britain.'[8]

Attlee was curt and dismissive in his response. He operated under clear instructions from Bevin when he wrote that the governments – not parliaments or independent organisations – should take the lead. Then again, he thought 'it was not the right time for Governments to take this major initiative when their hands are so full already with urgent and difficult problems.' He strongly discouraged Churchill from moving a resolution in the House of Commons on the European Assembly, warning that it would not have the support of the government or the Labour Party.[9] Three weeks later, on 21 August, just when Attlee returned from his holiday and after the French and Belgian governments went public with their support for the Assembly, Churchill urged Attlee and his government once more to 'place themselves more in line with Western European opinion'.[10] That same day, Churchill told Attlee that he had decided he would give their correspondence on the issue to the press. He felt the public needed to know that it was the British government that was dragging its feet.

This turned out to be a tactical masterstroke and a clear example of how Churchill was benefiting as opposition leader from his European campaign. The BBC led the evening news with a full analysis of the correspondence, and most of the printed press condemned Attlee for not taking a more constructive stance. The *Daily Telegraph* thought it difficult 'to see why they [members of the British government] should persist in withholding their collective support' after the French and the Belgians officially endorsed the Hague resolutions. That month, French Foreign Minister Robert Schuman and Belgian Foreign Minister Paul-Henri Spaak had published their intention to organise a conference 'which would pave the way for the establishment of a European Assembly'.[11]

'Surely Mr. Attlee's answer is unwarrantably dusty,' the paper concluded. The *Manchester Guardian* noted that Attlee was not, in principle, against the idea, but, seeing as public opinion in all western Europe was now ready and eager for a first European institution, he would really have to act urgently: 'it would be a pity not to get some kind of machinery established while the iron is hot.'[12] In the meantime, Churchill grew increasingly impatient and angry over the government's attitude towards the European Assembly, writing confidentially to Eden on the subject: 'Conceit, jealousy, stupidity are all apparent in the behaviour of Bevin and other Socialist leaders concerned.'[13]

After the initial stand-off between Churchill and Attlee the most important, intense and consistent channel of pressure on Attlee and Bevin was applied through the European Movement. The European Movement came into being in October 1948 as the rebranded and better-organised version of the earlier International Committee. It held together Churchill's coalition of groups proposing different methods to bring about the unity of Europe. Churchill reflected in 1957 that the movement was:

> launched to devote itself to the propagation of the theme of European unity and the examination of ways in which it could gradually be put into effect. I say gradually. There were many different opinions among those concerned, and some wanted to go faster than others. In large enterprises it is a mistake to try to settle everything at once [...] It was of importance that when the inevitable lulls, delays and obstacles occurred we should not be considered to have abandoned our ultimate goal.[14]

Led by Duncan Sandys as executive director, assisted by the indefatigable Joseph Retinger as secretary-general and with the inspiration of Churchill as one of its honorary presidents, the European Movement prepared memorandum after memorandum to push the governments of the Brussels Pact – Britain, France and the Benelux – towards establishing the Assembly. Schuman's plan for a governmental conference on the Assembly, for instance, came verbatim from one of the memorandums written by the European Movement.

The pressure seemed to have its desired effect on the British public, too: on 8 September 1948 the *Daily Express* published an opinion poll which showed the majority disappointed with the government for not doing enough to establish a European union.[15] Of a broad spectrum of voters identifying with the Conservatives, Labour or the Liberals, 68 per cent supported economic union,

65 per cent wanted military union, and 58 per cent favoured political union 'providing for a European Supreme Court'.[16]

There was little room left to resist for Bevin after the French and Belgians officially adopted the proposals of the Hague Congress. The organised power of the European Movement, growing American support for some form of European unification, Franco-Belgian insistence on creating a European Assembly, and public opinion at home combined to push the British government to let Churchill have his Council of Europe. One British diplomat remembered Bevin telling him shortly before making up his mind about assenting to the creation of the Assembly: 'We've got to give them something and I think we'll give them this talking shop in Strasbourg, the Council of Europe, we'll give them this talking shop.'[17] Little did he know that this innocuous-sounding 'talking shop' would be the breeding ground for some of the early milestones in the history of European unification.

As a result of a British counter-proposal to establish a Committee of Ministers responsible to national governments, the Council of Europe came into being on 5 May 1949 with two principal organs: a purely deliberative, non-executive Assembly of parliamentarians and an executive Committee of Ministers. The Consultative Assembly, the product of Churchill's campaign, would meet for its debates for about a month a year in a public setting in the city of Strasbourg. The Committee of Ministers, the product of Bevin's will, would come together whenever necessary to make decisions based on unanimity. It was only logical that Strasbourg became the seat of the Council of Europe. Its geographical position in the centre of western Europe was charged with emotion: by 1949 the French and the Germans had fought thrice in a century over the Alsace-Lorraine, the region in the north-east of France of which Strasbourg is the capital and largest city.

All resolutions adopted in the Assembly would have to go to the Committee of Ministers for final agreement and approval. This meant in practice that the British government retained the option of blocking any policy towards the further unification of Europe that went against its interests. Notwithstanding this compromise formula, Britain, France, Belgium, the Netherlands, Luxembourg, Italy, Ireland, Norway, Denmark and Sweden took the historic step of creating the first European political institution. Eighty-seven members of an embryonic European parliament would come together for their first full session in August 1949 to see eye to eye on the difficulties surrounding the progressive breakdown of national barriers.

FIRST SESSION: AUGUST 1949, STRASBOURG

Churchill arrived at Strasbourg on 9 August, on a warm Tuesday night, with high expectations and 'the usual court' of family, typists and secretaries. Also joining him that day was Bob Boothby, who happened to be vacationing near Churchill in Italy in the weeks immediately preceding the opening of the European Assembly. Despite having supported Churchill in the campaign since Zurich, Boothby was the only controversial choice on Churchill's team of Tories in Strasbourg.

The government divided Britain's 18 member spots for the first session of the European Assembly according to party strength in Parliament. This meant that there were eleven Labour representatives, six Conservatives, and one Liberal. Labour sent a strong team of MPs including three government ministers: Herbert Morrison, Hugh Dalton and William Whiteley. The reason was, as Denis Healey, one of the Labour delegates, wrote in his report on the first session, 'that a strong and experienced Delegation was necessary, particularly in order to stand up to Churchill and other Tory ex-Ministers'.[18]

As leader of the Opposition, Churchill was given the freedom to decide on the make-up of the Conservative delegation. He chose to become its leader and surround himself with an alliance of younger members including such mainstays of the United Europe Movement as Maxwell Fyfe and Macmillan. Sandys would be pulling the strings from behind the scenes on behalf of the European Movement. They were nicknamed collectively the 'Strasbourg Tories'.

Boothby's appointment initially hung in the balance because of his own tarnished reputation and his semi-public affair with Macmillan's wife, Lady Dorothy.[19] As it was clear that Macmillan would be the deputy leader of the Strasbourg Tories, Churchill worried that these two would be unable to work together. Realising this to be the case and fearing that he would miss out, Boothby wrote a long letter to Sandys months before the first session, begging him to put in a good word with Churchill. 'This is your show and we all know it,' Boothby wrote. 'I cannot help but think that, if I could be appointed to this Assembly, we could work very closely together.'[20] Churchill cared deeply for Boothby but seemed to find it difficult to decide on his inclusion.[21] The balance finally tipped in Boothby's favour when Sandys telephoned to tell Churchill that 'it would only be for matrimonial and personal reasons that Mr. Macmillan and Mr. Boothby would not get on,' and that Boothby should be included on the grounds that he knew more about the whole issue of European union than any other Conservative MP.[22]

On 9 August 1949, long after the dust of the Assembly appointments had settled, Churchill invited Boothby to accompany him for luncheon and the usual champagne on the day-long train ride from the town of Chiasso, on the Swiss–Italian border, to Strasbourg. It proved to be an eventful ride. When they reached the Franco-Swiss border control station at Basel, a group of photographers who had been tipped off swarmed onto the train and encircled Churchill in his carriage like gnats. Boothby later wrote that he was much impressed by Churchill's stoic indifference to what seemed like a dangerous mass invading his personal space.[23]

As the train cut through the mountainous Swiss countryside and approached the vast plains of the Franco-German borderlands, Boothby and Churchill thought about the days ahead, talking first about the economic plight of Europe and then more generally about the course of the campaign for European union. Boothby ventured to ask Churchill 'what he really meant by his Zurich call for a "a kind of United States of Europe"'. Churchill declined to delve into detail, telling Boothby instead: 'We are not making a machine, we are growing a living plant.' And then, changing the metaphor: 'We have lit a fire which will either blaze or go out; or perhaps the embers will die down and then, after a while, begin to glow again.'[24] The Council of Europe was the seed of Churchill's living plant. It was for the parliamentarians in the Assembly to water and breathe life into it, pushing national governments to integrate where it served the common cause.

The first order of business after arrival that Tuesday night in Strasbourg was a 9 p.m. dinner with the attending Conservative MPs. They met in Villa Levy at 7 Rue Brahms, a stately home on the outskirts of town that the Municipality of Strasbourg provided for Churchill in gratitude for his services in rescuing the city from German occupation. Churchill's villa became the headquarters for the Strasbourg Tories, and dinners like this one gave them the chance to coordinate policy in the Assembly. The villa also became a hub of social activity for everyone in the Assembly who was important enough for Churchill to entertain. Macmillan and the rest of the Tories went out there most days for luncheon, dinner and drinks. 'How he [Churchill] can stand it, I cannot imagine,' Macmillan wrote home a few days into his stay. 'He is entertaining very freely – Americans, French, Belgians, Dutch, Italians – all who can in any way be flattered or cajoled.'[25]

Some of the guests that arrived at Churchill's villa that first night did not experience as smooth a journey to Strasbourg as they had hoped. With the International Sleeping Car Company employees on strike, Maxwell Fyfe,

Macmillan and Walter Layton, the lone Liberal, were forced to sit up in their coach seats from their 2 p.m. Victoria station departure on 8 August until arrival in Strasbourg at 6 a.m. on the 9th.

The rough ride did nothing to diminish the spirit of deep-felt excitement and anticipation in which they met. The Strasbourg Tories hoped and sincerely believed they had a unique opportunity, Macmillan wrote, to 'found a new order in the Old World – democratic, free, progressive, destined to restore prosperity and preserve peace'.[26] Rebuilding Europe would involve a lasting change in the structure of European politics, one which most attending representatives in Strasbourg accepted: that the member countries would gradually and voluntarily hand over parts of their sovereignty to a common instrument of European government. Some members, a minority of radical federalists, were hoping for immediate surrender of all sovereignty. Another minority, a handful of Scandinavians and the British socialists most prominently among them, rejected Churchill's idea of gradual union. How those competing visions evolved could only be seen starting the next morning, when Churchill and his trusted adjutants would set foot in the auditorium of the University of Strasbourg to meet their European colleagues for the first sitting.

The gathering of the first European parliament in the Palais Universitaire was an historic event, particularly for the people of Strasbourg. It was a German leader, Kaiser Wilhelm I, who opened the iconic buildings of the university after the brutal Prussian invasion of Strasbourg in 1870. Seventy years later, the Nazis morphed the university into a study centre for the superiority of the Germanic races and used its laboratories to conduct gruesome experiments on human beings. Now, in August 1949, leaders from all over Europe walked over the Avenue de la Liberté – not the Kaiser-Wilhelm-Strasse, as it was previously known – to reach a hall ready for European parliamentary debate. The only problem was that the Germans were not there to share in the triumph of reconciliation.

The plan and rules of the Consultative Assembly were a compromise between British and continental parliamentary traditions. As was continental tradition, plenary sessions took place in a semicircular hall. As in the British Parliament, members spoke from their place rather than from a podium. And then there was a new custom: members were seated alphabetically rather than by party or country. 'This was to have a salutary effect upon our debates,' Macmillan later remembered, 'by adding to the spontaneity and tending to depress a purely partisan or national approach to the emerging problems.'[27]

Throughout the first session Churchill sat happily between the president of the Belgian House of Representatives, Mr Van Cauwelaert, and a Mr Cingolani of Italy, conversing loudly and enthusiastically in his rugged French. The bars and backrooms, as was the case in Westminster, quickly became the heart and centre of political wheeling and dealing.

The Assembly established six committees to do the preparatory work before discussion in the plenary sittings. The Strasbourg Tories were well placed in each of them. Churchill sat on the committee on scientific and cultural questions; Macmillan served on the political committee; David Eccles on the economic committee; Maxwell Fyfe on the legal committee; and Boothby on the committee of general affairs.

The first day immediately embroiled Churchill in a fight with the Labour representatives over the election of the Assembly's leadership, which would consist of a president and four vice-presidents. The first president, elected unanimously, was a stocky, Socialist former Belgian prime minister and president of the United Nations General Assembly, of towering personality and influence in European politics: Paul-Henri Spaak. Spaak had played a big part in persuading Bevin during the discussions of the five Brussels powers to create the Council of Europe and was a bona fide Anglophile after having spent the war years in exile in London.

The first elected vice-presidents were lesser-known men from Italy, Denmark, France and, after a somewhat embarrassing partisan struggle for the last remaining post, Walter Layton from Britain. Churchill and the Strasbourg Tories found the Labour nominee for vice-president, William Whiteley, unacceptable for the job, mostly because he was said to have no understanding of continental Europe whatsoever. As Macmillan wrote to his wife from Strasbourg: 'It was freely rumoured that Whiteley (in spite of two wars in his lifetime) had never till today crossed the Channel. It was said that on arrival at Calais he had been heard to exclaim: "By Jove, they're white. I thought they were niggers!"'[28] Churchill felt strongly that the Liberal press baron Layton should take up the position instead. 'We put up Layton; and canvassed freely for him,' Macmillan reported home. 'L. was terrified and wanted to withdraw.'[29] Then Churchill seized the quivering Layton during an interval and thundered at him 'If you retire now, I will never speak to you again. You will have betrayed me. You will have betrayed the whole Liberal Party!'[30] Layton had little choice but to carry on.

Most in the Assembly were inclined to follow Churchill's preference for Layton and pledged their votes for him. But the elections became a tighter squeeze than expected when the leader of the British representatives, the Labour minister Herbert Morrison, went so far as to bid for French Socialist votes for Whiteley by signing away the chairmanship of the international Socialist movement to a French rival. After all was said and done, the members of the Assembly cast secret ballot papers. 'The excitement and the heat were intense,' Macmillan remembered. In a turn of fortune that served to heighten the partisan drama even further, Churchill was chosen to read out the result of the voting. Every time Churchill spoke the lights were lowered, one French delegate remembered, to pay 'homage to one whom every free man owes so deep a debt'.[31] To his relief and satisfaction Layton won by 52 to 47 votes. 'All this was perhaps rather reprehensible,' Macmillan realised, 'but it was very enjoyable.' Hearing of Churchill's antics a week after his arrival in Strasbourg, Prime Minister Attlee was scathing: 'my impression is that Winston decided that the stage [the Council Assembly] was suitable for a prima donna act.'[32]

After this opening day spectacle, the Assembly adjourned. This gave Macmillan a chance to bring Churchill back to his villa for a nap. 'This is the most fun I've had for years and years,' he kept repeating to Macmillan as he lay down on his bed fully dressed. 'This is splendid. This is really fun.'[33]

While Churchill stayed at Strasbourg, the fun continued well into the nights. He entertained royally in Villa Levy, serving his guests champagne, lobster, roebuck stuffed with foie gras and more champagne. Apologising to his wife for not writing home earlier, Macmillan explained two weeks after the Assembly's formal opening that he was unable to get a spare minute to write anything down while Churchill was in town. 'Churchill's arrival', he wrote, not unkindly, 'meant the usual hours – no sleep till 2:30 a.m. or so – and the whole pressure of that tireless and inexorable man.'[34]

A few hours later Churchill and Macmillan braved the August heat to return to the Palais Universitaire in the city centre for the afternoon session of the Assembly. On the agenda was the scope of the Assembly's future discussions. The British government had tried and succeeded in the negotiations on the Statute of the Council of Europe to formally limit the Consultative Assembly to debates on cultural and legal issues, leaving all that mattered most to national governments – the political, economic and military issues – to private discussions between foreign ministers in the Committee of Ministers.

Churchill was keenly aware that a deliberative body like the Assembly was meant to advise and, for the time being at least, could not have any executive power. He had no intention, however, of accepting a restrictive debate regime and asked Macmillan to 'raise this broad question as a matter of urgency'.[35]

The right of the Assembly to discuss whatever it elected to discuss became the first defining issue of the 1949 session. The chief questions Churchill and most others in the Assembly wanted to bring up were the large political ones. As Macmillan defined them in a letter home, '(a) the declaration and system of enforcement of human rights (b) the whole political problem – federation, or union or what?'[36] These were the broad themes that sooner rather than later needed be developed in Strasbourg. The ability of a transnational assembly to do so was the whole *raison d'être* of the Council of Europe.

After a long debate on Friday 12 August on the scope of the Assembly's agenda, the Assembly decided to ask the Committee of Ministers to grant permission to widen its scope of discussion. As Macmillan wrote to his wife: 'Churchill more or less "led" the Assembly in all this – much to Morrison's discomfiture.'[37] The Assembly was informed the next afternoon that the ministers acceded to their demands: a new subject could now always be proposed and within five days the Assembly would hear a decision from the ministers. By all means, this was a meaningful victory for the Assembly. But Churchill wanted more and was reluctant to accept the compromise. Macmillan remembered having to 'keep moving from [his] seat to try to press [his] moderating views upon [Churchill] by whispering in his ear'.[38]

That Friday evening, more than 20,000 people assembled for a mass public meeting in Place Kléber, Strasbourg's main square. Sandys was behind the effort, organising the demonstration on behalf of the European Movement. French flags and the European Movement's 'E' flew atop every building. The line-up of speakers was extraordinary: Reynaud, Spaak and, finally, Churchill all appeared on a balcony overlooking the square to inspire the crowds with the spirit of unity. Churchill started his speech with a fair warning, booming in bumpy French: 'Mesdames et Messieurs les Strasbourgeois, prenez garde! Je parlerai en français!' [Ladies and Gentlemen of Strasbourg, beware! I'm going to speak French!]. He spoke kindly and effectively and as Macmillan observed patronisingly, 'with a better accent than usual'.[39]

All but one of the balconies and windows overlooking the square were jam-packed with people; the exception was Ernie Bevin's, who was in Strasbourg to attend the Committee of Ministers. Bevin's grand study in the Maison Rouge Hotel afforded a panoramic view of the whole spectacle. The sight of Europe's unofficial leaders rousing a fully packed square to the cause of United Europe may have been too much to stomach. 'It must have been a painful experience for that vain and inflated egotist,' wrote Macmillan that night.[40] The reflections of the diplomat Evelyn Shuckburgh, later to become Eden's principal private secretary, give a view from the other side: 'Twice I remember sitting in a hotel room on the main square in Strasbourg, helping first Bevin and then Morrison to determine coolly how much British sovereignty they would be justified in giving away, while outside on the square the great Winston Churchill and the popular but less great Duncan Sandys were promising Union Now to applauding multitudes.'[41] The Place Kléber celebrations, Macmillan thought, seemed to make a positive impact on the degree of respect with which the professional policy wonks at the Foreign Office treated the European Movement, its ideas, and its patrons. Even the king of all cynics, Gladwyn Jebb, began 'to watch his step.'[42] Shortly after the first session, a minute circulated in the Foreign Office declaring a change in policy from a tendency to boycott the European Movement to an attitude of 'benevolent neutrality'.[43]

After settling some essential procedural questions, the second defining issue of the first session was one of special importance to Churchill: the future of Germany in Europe. Under the rules of the Council of Europe the Assembly debate on Germany would have to wait on approval from the ministers to discuss the issue. Just as importantly, it had to wait on the momentous event of the first democratic elections in Germany since before Adolf Hitler came to power in 1933, which were scheduled in the new Federal Republic of Germany – otherwise known as West Germany – on Monday 15 August 1949.[44] The Federal Republic's constitution, the Basic Law, stipulated a commitment to participation in the development of political union in Europe.[45]

Monday 15 August was also a public holiday in Strasbourg for the Catholic Feast of the Annunciation. On that day, too, Churchill was honoured with the freedom of Strasbourg in a grand public display. As he drove around the streets in an open car, he was under the impression that all of the day's exuberant festivities in the city were in his honour. When Macmillan clarified to Churchill that they were for the public holiday and not for him, he was visibly disappointed.[46] 'It took a lot of explaining,' Macmillan later told the BBC.[47]

Then, on Tuesday and Wednesday, the Assembly finally gathered for a big plenary debate on the political future of Europe. This was Churchill's chance to address the German situation. Macmillan suddenly realised that Churchill had been meticulously preparing for this moment for an entire week. He wrote in his diary:

> This extraordinary man, during the early sittings, seemed to come down almost too rapidly to the level of normal political agitation. His intervention in the

Layton-Whitely incident and his several short speeches on the question of the powers of the Assembly to fix its own agenda were all calculated – perhaps intentionally – to reveal him as a Parliamentarian, rather than as a great international figure. You can imagine that we were all a little alarmed at this. For our pains, we were treated with a firm and even harsh refusal to accept our advice. He certainly took more trouble to listen to the debates than I have ever known him do in the House of Commons. He walked about, chatted to each representative, went into the smoking-room, and generally took a lot of trouble to win the sympathetic affection of his new Parliamentary colleagues. This was done with much assiduity. He used his villa for entertaining the more important to luncheon and dinner; and he took much trouble over all this determination to charm them as well as impress them.[48]

On the afternoon of Tuesday 16 August, all of that 'normal' parliamentary activity was deliberately suspended. When Churchill rose to speak to the Assembly he at once reclaimed his status of great international statesman. Rather than congratulate himself and his movement on the institution of the Council of Europe, he looked forward to what the Assembly might achieve next. In 1949, he was occupied both with the Soviet threat and, increasingly, with the fear that some part of Germany, if it was not raised to its feet by the West, might rise remilitarised, vengeful and in the hands of the Communists. The German question was the central theme of his speech and set the tone for the rest of the Assembly session.

'He shocked some; he almost bullied others,' Macmillan wrote in an article on the first sitting for *The Spectator*. Looking around the hall Churchill's eyes rested on the ten seats that were kept empty as a symbol of the Assembly's intention to unite *all* Europe, not just the states that were at liberty to join in 1949. His glasses almost sliding off the tip of a nose shiny with sweat, Churchill blazed forth: 'Where are the Germans?'[49]

He pushed for an immediate invitation to be sent to the new West German government to join the Council of Europe, knowing it was the key to true European reconciliation and the only way to contain the menace in the heart of Europe. 'We cannot part at the end of this month on the basis that we do nothing more to bring Germany into our circle until a year has passed,' Churchill said. 'That year is too precious to lose. If lost, it might be lost for ever. It might not be *a* year. It might be *the* year.'[50]

Confident that he had set the Assembly on course to achieve his goals, Churchill left Strasbourg the day after the speech to go for a short holiday in Monte Carlo. He put Macmillan in charge of boosting the German membership agenda with the help of Sandys and the rest of the Strasbourg Tories. He intended to come back in a week's time to help push a resolution through the

Assembly, demanding that the Committee of Ministers take steps to invite West Germany directly or call a special meeting to consider it. In the meantime, he asked for Macmillan to cable him daily reports of the proceedings in Strasbourg. Nearly every day of his absence Churchill would then telephone Macmillan late at night to discuss the details of his report.[51]

The task of pushing West German membership was made more difficult by the fact that even the most enthusiastic Europeans, like the Assembly president Paul-Henri Spaak, thought the inclusion of West Germany in the Council of Europe far too difficult a task for the Assembly to accomplish in the short term. For almost all Frenchmen, inviting 18 German delegates into the Assembly was still much too sensitive a prospect to fight for in earnest.

The solution Macmillan and Churchill devised in their correspondence was to couch the whole question in terms more general and therefore more palatable to the French. They would ask the Committee of Ministers for permission to discuss 'the position of the German Federal Republic and the Saar Territory in relation to the Council of Europe'.[52] While the leading Labour representatives pushed to keep the question of West German membership off the agenda, Churchill let Macmillan know he would be back in on 24 August to personally persuade the leaders of the Assembly to proceed with his plans.

On the day Churchill was supposed to return to his Strasbourg villa, a doctor in Monte Carlo telephoned Churchill's doctor in London, Charles Moran: 'I think Mr Churchill has had a stroke. I would urge you to see him as soon as you can.'[53] As Churchill's host in Monte Carlo explained to Moran on his arrival that day, Churchill was playing cards at 2 a.m. in the morning when he lost some of his balance and felt a strange, cramp-like sensation in his right arm and leg. He continued playing, but when he awoke in the morning the feeling was still there. 'What has gone wrong, Charles?' Churchill asked with a tremble when Moran reached his bedroom. 'Have I had a stroke?' Moran reassured him it was a small one – 'a very small clot has blocked a very small artery' – but, indeed, a stroke nonetheless.[54]

A day later, word reached Strasbourg that Churchill was severely ill. Rumours had started to spread when the assembled press in Monte Carlo saw Moran arrive and leave without further comment on Churchill's health. His minor stroke, the first in a series that were to plague him until the end of his life, was deliberately concealed from the public everywhere.[55] Meanwhile, Sandys, who was apparently informed by the doctors or Churchill himself, reassured the Assembly that his father-in-law was in no serious danger. Churchill would, however, not be able to return to Strasbourg.

The moment he recovered, Churchill flew back home and started to telephone Macmillan from Chartwell with increasingly pressing messages and demands. It was the second time in their relationship – the first having occurred in World War II when Macmillan was Churchill's resident minister in the Mediterranean – they had to solve a delicate problem over the phone. Things had not become easier in the intervening six years. Churchill was still an impatient, fiery, obstinate old man. 'Once more it was difficult to explain to him, at a distance, the changing complication of the scene,' Macmillan remembered with a keen sense of understatement. He wanted desperately for Churchill to come and help him in Strasbourg and use his prestige to bulldoze French resistance against West German membership.[56]

The changing scene forced Macmillan to abandon the idea of raising the German question as a stand-alone issue. Instead, he decided to pursue a strategy of embedding the German question in the report of the political committee, which came before the Assembly for debate, amendment and approval on Monday 5 September. He made sure that the political report included a resolution that called for an emergency session of the Assembly in the early months of 1950 to discuss potential new member states. When the moment came in the Assembly to discuss the resolution, Macmillan would speak on it with Churchill's explicit support.

On the morning of 5 September, Macmillan awoke feeling 'conscious that a heavy responsibility lay upon me.'[57] At 4 p.m., when the resolution on new members finally came up for discussion, he rose to his feet to speak. He had changed from his flannel suit into a more formal black suit and a stiff white collar. As the Assembly's attention started to focus on him, he looked affable but more nervous than usual.[58] Those who did not understand English plugged in their headsets for simultaneous interpretation.

Macmillan started by reminding the Assembly of Churchill's speech on 14 August, linking the resolution on new members to what Churchill had demanded three weeks earlier: 'Where are the Germans?' He then told his listeners something they may not have known: that Churchill, as wartime prime minister of Great Britain, had written a secret minute to his foreign secretary concerning a Council of Europe in October 1942. 'I ask the Assembly to note the date: October 1942,' Macmillan said for added emphasis.

A few nights before, Churchill had given Macmillan the text of the minute over the telephone, with permission to quote from it. Churchill himself did not bother in the circumstances to ask Eden or the British government, to which the document formally belonged, for authorisation.[59] The first crop of European parliamentarians were about to hear a remarkable few sentences that had never been published before:

> I must admit that my thoughts rest primarily in Europe – the revival of the glory of Europe, the parent continent of the modern nations and of civilisation. It would be a measureless disaster if Russian barbarism overlaid the culture and independence of the ancient States of Europe. Hard as it is to say now, I trust that the European family may act unitedly as one under a Council of Europe.
>
> I look forward to a United States of Europe in which the barriers between the nations will be greatly minimised and unrestricted travel will be possible. I hope to see the economy of Europe studied as a whole.[60]

Churchill's minute caused an intense stir of excitement in the hall, moving the representatives and helping to accomplish what he hoped it would.[61] It dispelled any notion that Churchill's campaign for a United Europe was a partisan stunt designed to embarrass Attlee and Bevin and, more importantly, led to the unanimous adoption of the political resolutions before the Assembly.[62] That night, when Macmillan was having a bath at his hotel in preparation for a big party organised by the European Movement, Churchill called from Chartwell to congratulate and thank him for pulling it off so admirably. In spite of repeated attempts by senior Labour members to thwart Churchill's plans the Committee of Ministers would now be forced to make a decision on the Assembly's recommendation to admit West Germany.[63]

Just before the first session closed, a standing committee was brought into being to liaise with the ministers on the specific issue of German membership, making an emergency session of the Assembly unnecessary. Ernie Bevin, coming round to the idea that it was geopolitically advantageous to contain West Germany in a larger European structure, cooperated admirably with his European colleagues.

On 30 March 1950, after a session of the Committee of Ministers in Strasbourg, the German Federal Republic received a formal invitation to become a member state of the Council of Europe. Konrad Adenauer, who was elected West Germany's first chancellor that summer, accepted the invitation on behalf of his newly minted country. Less than five years after the end of the war, West Germany formally entered the circle of European states which declared itself intent on unification.

If there was to be a path towards more cooperation and integration, considerable changes to the structure and statute of the Council of Europe were required. As it stood, the Committee of Ministers had far too much control over the Assembly to allow the Council of Europe to develop into anything more than the purely collaborative institution it was. The Committee of Ministers itself was still so closely bound to national interests that it was hardly possible to make any autonomous European decisions in Strasbourg. Everything still depended on national governments.

Churchill, Boothby and Sandys, talking about this very problem in a meeting of the executive of the United Europe Movement, agreed that the reason the Council of Europe was making such slow progress was that the Committee of Ministers voted by unanimity. If only that difficult voting system could be abolished and the voting behaviour of the ministers be made public, there would be fewer delays and more action.[64] Churchill commented on this problem in the House of Commons after the first session: 'the contrast between the activities of the Assembly and the apparent inaction of the Committee of Ministers has created the impression that the Ministers are not wholehearted in their intention to promote the Union of Europe.'[65]

The solution backed by Sandys and Churchill in the political debate of the first session – largely based on the work of the European Movement – was to create within the framework of the Council of Europe a European Political Authority 'with limited functions but real powers'.[66] The principle of merging sovereignties for common political and economic action, they argued, was already unanimously accepted at the Hague Congress of Europe. The European Political Authority would democratically decide on a common policy for human rights, foreign policy and economic affairs. With the Committee of Ministers functioning as a kind of embryonic Cabinet and the Assembly as an embryonic Parliament, the Political Authority would oversee and create 'functional' institutions dealing with a vast range of areas of European integration.

The member states of the Council of Europe would still be able to choose to stay out of some of those institutions but would have to stay under the larger umbrella of a gradually deepening and widening European union – what Sandys liked to call integration à la carte. A year later the European Movement, led in its discussions by Sandys, Amery and Boothby, further developed that multi-speed idea. The movement's executive recommended that states that wanted to establish closer links between themselves should be encouraged to do so. They might create a federal organisation if they so desired, as long as its structure and scope would be decided on by all member states of the looser European union. The federal organisation would then also remain open to the other member states to join when and if they felt ready.[67] It was a perfect compromise for Britain, which, on account of its global ambitions and responsibilities, was still wholly unlikely to commit to federation.

The ultimate failure of the plan for a European Political Authority, which stranded with the hostility of the ministers, spelled doom for the power of the Council of Europe and Churchill's leadership of the European Movement. As we will see, frustrated with the inability of the Assembly to forge real change in the political structure of Europe, the French started proposing independent 'functional' authorities like the Schuman Plan and the Pleven Plan with the explicit aim of bringing about short-term federation in western Europe. Churchill saw no reason for Britain to join the French authorities as long as they made it impossible for Britain to hold on to a position of influence in the world through political leadership of the British Commonwealth and a close partnership with the United States.

At varying points throughout the first session the Strasbourg Tories, including Churchill in his speeches from the floor, sought to establish the whole basis of European union with an enforceable charter of human rights for Europe. The idea was this: in order to prevent totalitarianism and the oppression of the individual from ever returning in European politics, individual citizens had to be given the right to take the violation of their basic rights to a court more powerful than a national equivalent. Never before in human history had individual citizens been able to take a state to an international court.

The incentives for Churchill and the Assembly to back such a radical innovation in international law were clear. On the one hand, the Western powers truly believed that they had a shot at crafting a new world order in which the cruelties of World War II would never return. On the other hand, a European human rights convention held the promise of protecting the integrity of liberal democracy in western Europe against Communist disruption or the kind of Soviet interference that had been the downfall of Czechoslovakia. It could usefully serve as a litmus test for membership of the Council of Europe: only if a country accepted the jurisdiction of a European court to enforce basic human rights could it be eligible to join.[68]

While the idea of a supranational European court would be of momentous consequence for the European legal order, the global precedent of the UN Declaration of Human Rights and the real threat of Communist subversion in western Europe seemed to render it more or less uncontroversial territory. Or did it? On a closer look, Churchill went against the express advice of moderate press opinion at home, and one of his closest friends.

The Times was most apprehensive about the idea that freedom from discrimination on account of political or other opinion on a European scale would enable Communists in France or Germany to haul Britain before a European court. The *Scotsman* newspaper had a different problem, reporting in August 1949 that the European Court of Human Rights 'theoretically would enable any condemned collaborator to demand a rehearing of his case by the Court'.[69]

Frederick 'Prof' Lindemann, who was then drafting a chapter on the atomic bomb for Churchill's war memoirs, generally took *The Times*'s line and said that 'it may well one day become necessary to lay down that a party like the Communists, which does not accept the democratic premise of rule by the majority, cannot claim the democratic privileges of freedom of association, of expression of opinion and so on.'[70] The Charter of Human Rights, he argued, might make such a course impossible. The widely shared British fear was therefore that the Charter would be open to exploitation against British interests.

Churchill seemed not to be thwarted too much by the criticisms of his plans. Since the Communist coup in Prague in February 1948, much of his European campaign had revolved around the idea of being able to enforce human rights in (western) Europe. Shortly after he first heard about the coup, Churchill wrote to ask the General Purposes Committee of the United Europe Movement to 'turn its attention to the need for a statement on Human Rights'.[71]

'In the centre of our movement,' he told the delegates of the Hague Congress in May 1948, 'stands the idea of a Charter of Human Rights, guarded by freedom and sustained by law.'[72] The *Message to Europeans*, adopted at the end of the Congress as a summary of its resolutions, existed in five articles, two of which were concerned with the Charter.[73] At the next major conference of the European Movement in Brussels, meeting to discuss specifically social and cultural issues on 26 February 1949, Churchill once more stated his support for the plans being drawn up for a European court. 'We have the Charter of Human Rights,' he said, 'and we must have a European means of defending and enforcing it.'[74]

On 12 July 1949 the European Movement submitted a draft convention on human rights for the consideration of the Strasbourg Committee of Ministers, with a request that it be placed on the agenda of the Assembly in August. A week later, in a preparatory meeting of the United Kingdom representatives to the Council of Europe in the Prime Minister's room, Churchill made two important points on behalf of the Conservative part of the delegation. When asked by representatives of the government what the delegates would specifically like to discuss in the Assembly, he said that, aside from German membership, he was strongly of the opinion that 'the Assembly should consider the question of a European Court on Human Rights.'[75]

Churchill's front man for Human Rights in Strasbourg was David Maxwell Fyfe, who spent the better part of his time after the Hague Congress, where he had sat on the cultural committee 'to say something on human rights', using his legal background and connections to prepare a draft European Convention of Human Rights for the International Judicial Section of the European Movement.[76] The meeting of the European Movement at Brussels in February 1949 gave him a first chance to present his work and measure his progress. As with Churchill, he later wrote, the key for him was to establish a European Court to enforce the 'basic decencies of life'.[77]

In the first session of the Assembly, Maxwell Fyfe won an important victory when he brought a concrete proposal to create a European court out of the Assembly's standing committee for legal affairs. He teamed up with Pierre-Henri Teitgen, the French minister of justice, to submit his draft Charter to the Assembly on 19 August 1949. The resolution was passed convincingly.

The Committee of Ministers responded by appointing a committee of experts to give further advice on the proposed Convention. Here some of the more specific trouble started. The experts left out of their own version of a draft Convention some of the key rights identified by Maxwell-Fyfe in the Assembly's legal committee. Instead they limited themselves to ten basic rights on the lines of the UN Declaration.

A year later, the Assembly compromised on legal definitions but essentially reinserted all the rights that Maxwell Fyfe wanted. The ministers eventually conceded to the Assembly's demands and signed the European Convention on Human Rights in Rome in October 1950. Whatever the extent of compromise on the catalogue of rights – the Convention notably lacked the social and economic rights so desirable for social democrats – the signing of the Convention was one of the most important achievements of the Council of Europe.[78] The French foreign minister, Robert Schuman, called it 'the first concrete result achieved at Strasbourg'.[79] The British government was so pleased that it even applied the Convention to its colonies, though it was not until 50 years later that 'New' Labour introduced the Human Rights Act, incorporating the Convention into English law. The cases submitted under the Convention since have been a driving value to the protection of democratic rights in Europe as well as to the further integration of the continent.[80]

SECOND SESSION: STRASBOURG, 1950

After the first session of the Consultative Assembly, Churchill and his deputies still seemed to be in full control of the movement towards European unity. Despite the unmistakable tension between the federalists, who wanted to write a federal constitution there and then, and the still open-minded gradualists, Churchill felt that the inclusion of West Germany was just a first step in what the Council of Europe could achieve. All he needed to do to keep Britain involved in the process was to dominate the Assembly with a central position between the 'constitution makers' and the 'do-nothings'.[81] It was Harold Macmillan who best summed up the pragmatic Tory position on how to get Churchill's organic union: 'I believe we shall reach our purpose by practical experience and experiment – trial and error.'[82]

Both in public and in private, Churchill continued to express the idea that Britain somehow would have to play a key role in a European union. This would at once satisfy the Cold War need to contain the Soviets in Europe, honour American pleas for European unity, and strengthen and justify the Empire–Commonwealth in the postwar world through Europe. After a concise analysis of Churchill's thinking on European unity between 1904 and 1948, Allen Packwood, the historian and guardian of Churchill's personal and political papers at Cambridge, thus concluded: 'My view is that by 1948, faced with a Labour government that was retreating from Empire, a strong external Soviet threat, and an American ally that wanted a stronger Western alliance, Churchill had accepted that Britain's immediate future lay not just with Europe but in Europe.'[83]

In private, Count Coudenhove-Kalergi impatiently demanded Churchill's full views on Britain's role in Europe. He understood, he wrote to Churchill, that Britain wished to promote a European union in which it could play a full role but prevent immediate federation, which was thought to be too radical a commitment for a country straddling three great circles of power. The Count got it in his head that it would be best to form a European federation without Britain. He warned Churchill that the movement for European unification had reached 'a dangerous impasse' because of the British reluctance to embrace the idea of immediate federation and tried to tease out an affirmative reply from Churchill – pointing to the 1930 *Saturday Evening Post* article in which Churchill placed Britain outside a European federation – so as to give him cause to direct the European Movement towards the idea of a purely continental federation.[84]

This Churchill declined to accept after Sandys warned him that Coudenhove-Kalergi was abusing the European Movement and, he told his father-in-law, 'you as its leader'.[85] More importantly, Churchill's views had evolved since 1930, largely because of the devastation of World War II, the rise of an expansionist Soviet Union in the emerging Cold War, rapid decolonisation and the weakening of Britain's standing in the world as a result of its financial dependence on the United States. On 8 May 1949, three days after the creation of the Council of Europe, Churchill told Coudenhove-Kalergi that countries like Britain and Switzerland had, on account of their geography, history and external connections, 'special problems of their own'. For Switzerland this concerned its traditional policy of neutrality; for Britain it was its close ties to the nations of the British Commonwealth.

Without giving clear policy prescriptions, Churchill declared himself convinced that workable solutions could be found. 'You should certainly not imagine', he told Coudenhove-Kalergi, 'that Britain will not be willing and able to play a full and worthy part in bringing the great conception of United Europe to fruition.'[86] The Count was not quite mollified and wrote back insisting that it was British reluctance to accept federalist prescriptions that was holding the movement towards European unity hostage. 'The impression is growing on the Continent', he wrote, 'that it [Great Britain] wishes to promote Union, but to prevent Federation.'[87] While the Count thought federation was the only way to reconcile French and German interests, Britain needed a less rigid type of union to simultaneously maintain its leadership in Europe and in the Empire and Commonwealth.

In a further letter to Coudenhove-Kalergi written in December 1949, Churchill made his point about Britain's role in Europe more emphatically, though again he left open what kind of European union Britain might ultimately be a part of:

> I do not agree that the solution to our problem is to create a Europe excluding Britain. As M. Schuman said in the French Chamber recently, and M. Spaak strongly reiterated in a public meeting which he addressed in London, British participation is essential to the success of a European Union. It is impossible to say at the moment what form this union will ultimately take, but I am sure that the next immediate step is to develop and strengthen by every means in our power the new Council of Europe.[88]

In November 1949, Churchill had told a large public audience in London for a European Movement rally essentially the same thing: 'The French Foreign

Minister, M. Schuman, declared in the French Parliament this week that "Without Britain there can be no Europe". This is entirely true.' Britain and its Commonwealth of Nations would join Europe all the way and in fact seek to create a European union with common imperial ambitions. 'Our friends on the Continent need have no misgivings,' Churchill said. 'Britain is an integral part of Europe, and we mean to play our part in the revival of her prosperity and greatness.'

Of course, Churchill reminded his audience at Kingsway Hall, Britain was not a single state in isolation. She was the founder and heart of a global empire and Commonwealth, and he would never do anything to weaken Britain's ties with these countries. 'But nobody is asking us to make such a desertion,' he said, continuing:

> For Britain to enter a European Union from which the Empire and Commonwealth would be excluded would not only be impossible but would, in the eyes of Europe, enormously reduce the value of our participation.

Churchill referred to the Assembly's 1949 economic report in support of this claim: 'The Strasbourg recommendations urged the creation of an economic system which will embrace not only the European States, but all those other States and territories elsewhere which are associated with them.' It would therefore be easy to convince the British Dominions, Churchill argued, that 'their interests as well as ours lie in a United Europe.'[89]

* * *

'Could you please see that there is sufficient Pol Roger champagne (1928 vintage if possible) and cognac for Mr. Churchill's use for about ten days, including a selection of other wines for entertaining guests,' a private secretary cabled to Strasbourg ahead of Churchill's return for the second session of the Assembly.

He left for Strasbourg at 12 noon on Sunday 6 August 1950 in a chartered Silver Cities Dakota aeroplane, packing all the necessities of life: a dinner jacket and light painting equipment. At 3 p.m. Churchill arrived at Villa Merckel, situated right next to last year's villa and adjoining the sprawling Parc de l'Orangerie. Villa Merckel would provide him with the peace and quiet he needed to focus on the preparations for a major Assembly speech.

The house itself, though considerably smaller than Villa Levy, was perfectly amenable to Churchill's personal and entertaining needs. It housed a grand Alsatian dining room, salon, wine cellar, bar, music room, library, massage room, a leafy, secluded garden and several comfortable sitting rooms.

In terms of Strasbourgeois staff, he was met in all his immediate needs by a butler, a parlour maid, housemaids and a chef he admired as 'an artist in his profession'.[90] Belonging to a local lawyer, the house was expensively furnished, though, according to an organising secretary at the European Movement, to somewhat doubtful taste.[91]

It bothered Churchill little. A selection of British papers were delivered daily; he had a direct telephone line to the new, specially constructed Assembly headquarters in Place Lenôtre; and his private secretaries made sure to bring a carload full of whisky, gin and cigars to Strasbourg.[92] To top it all off an astounding quantity of Pol Roger 1928 arrived at the villa just in time for his stay. The woman supervising the running of the house was so surprised that she wrote to one of Churchill's secretaries in palpable disbelief: 'We have seventy-two (72) bottles of Paul [sic] Roger. I think it will be enough for 10 days?'.[93]

When the Churchills went abroad on holiday in the late 1940s and early 1950s their expenses were usually paid by *Time* and *Life*, the magazines that funded Churchill's escapes from Britain for him to focus on writing his war memoirs.[94] As his political aspirations in Strasbourg had little to do with the war memoirs, Churchill felt it only right that he himself should pay for his expenses and that of his staff. This was not a decision necessarily taken lightly. With the many luncheons, dinners and drinks receptions at the villa providing the key to Churchill's influence and policy-making in Strasbourg, his arrival was a windfall for the butchers, grocers and liquor stores of the city.

For the ten days that Churchill stayed at Strasbourg in 1950, as far as the surviving bills indicate, he spent more than 60,000 francs on wine and champagne, nearly 20,000 on fresh fruit and vegetables and approximately 40,000 on the full range of exquisite meats, lobster and truffles coming in at £125, or nearly £4,000 today.[95] This merely covered local purchases. Even though the costs of unlimited supplies of beer and ice, and a chauffeur-driven car on standby were waived, Churchill still spent approximately £350 of his personal fortune on his visit to Strasbourg that year, or, almost £11,000 in today's prices.[96]

Harold Macmillan, who was again to lead the delegation of Strasbourg Tories after Churchill's departure, took up residence in the suite originally meant for Ernie Bevin in the grand Maison Rouge hotel on Place Kléber. Bevin was unable to come to Strasbourg for his duties on the Committee of Ministers because he had fallen seriously ill that week. This time, the general election of February 1950 having reduced Labour's majority to six seats, eight Conservative MPs were able to go to Strasbourg. The larger delegation size allowed Churchill to appoint Duncan Sandys, who resigned his chairmanship of the European Movement after regaining his seat in the elections.

Churchill invited Sandys, Maxwell Fyfe and Macmillan for dinner at Villa Merckel that Sunday night to prepare for the upcoming session and to discuss the one major speech Churchill was scheduled to give, on Friday 11 August. They hoped that the second session – against the grain of the restrictive Statute of the Council of Europe, which still generally forbade detailed Assembly discussions on defence – would focus principally on Churchill's radical and as yet unpublished idea to create with immediate effect a unified European army. The other main topics under discussion were the revolutionary Schuman Plan for a European Coal and Steel Community and the draft text for the European Convention on Human Rights.

On Monday 7 August 1950, the opening day of the Consultative Assembly's second session, mass crowds assembled outside the House of Europe to see the likes of Reynaud, Schuman and Churchill reunited in Strasbourg. Churchill gladly accepted a small box of fine 'Schimmelpenninck' cigars from representatives of a group of Dutch federalists just before setting foot in the new headquarters of the Assembly at 3 p.m. Once inside he took his place on the benches closest to the seats of the president and was joined by Mr Cingolani of Italy on his left. At his back he found the familiar face of the Dutch senator Pieter Kerstens.

The first order of business was the election of a president. Churchill addressed the Assembly 'shortly but decisively' to persuade them of last year's leader Paul-Henri Spaak's continued viability. It clinched his narrow re-election. Spaak later remembered that 'it was thanks to a speech by Churchill that I was spared a humiliating defeat'.[97]

It soon became obvious that the entire Assembly was focused on the issue of defence. Just over a month before the opening session, war had broken out in Korea when Soviet-sponsored Communist forces from the North invaded the US-backed Republic of Korea in the South. It broke the fragile postwar peace in the Far East and was the first active conflict in the Cold War between the two remaining world superpowers. The United Nations quickly intervened with American help and, as a result of the growing realisation that continental Europe might well be the next target for the Soviets, the Americans began to echo Churchill's idea of German rearmament as a much-needed contribution to the defence of Europe.

The disadvantage of the Russians, Churchill once told a friend over dinner in December 1946, was that 'one is not sure of their reactions. One strokes the nose of the alligator and the ensuing gurgle may be a purr of affection, a grunt of stimulated appetite, or a snarl of enraged animosity. One cannot tell.'[98] If the crocodile did choose to strike with enraged animosity, the pain would be measureless. Churchill grew convinced after the war that the Communists were 'not quite as wicked but much more formidable than Hitler' and were presently held back in their European ambitions only by the atomic deterrent.[99]

More so than many of his contemporaries Churchill understood the acute feeling of anxiety that gripped most of continental Europe in the late 1940s. His travels around the continent for the European Movement allowed him to experience this up close. Speaking in New York on a trip to solicit funds for the European Movement in March 1949 he vividly recounted what he felt when he addressed a rally in Brussels a month earlier. 'There were these 30,000 people in this great square at Brussels, and I could feel their anxiety. I could feel, as I spoke, their anxiety – their fear [...] In ten days – in ten days perhaps the Soviet armour might be in Brussels.'

How would the Strasbourg Assembly, the only real platform of European political opinion, respond to what looked increasingly like the real possibility of a Soviet-US clash on the European continent? Would it stroke the alligator's nose and await a reaction? Would it prepare itself for the worst?

Churchill's solution for the defence of Europe, which he developed even before the outbreak of the Korean War, was as bold as it was simple. On 28 March 1950 he told the House of Commons that German rearmament was the key to success and argued that Britain, France and Germany should combine to 'make the core or the nucleus upon which all other civilized democracies of Europe, bound or free, can one day rally and combine'.[100] Two months later, on 24 May, Churchill wrote privately to Prime Minister Attlee about the deteriorating international situation and the necessity of asking Germany to play a full role in the defence of the West. He estimated western Europe needed at least 70 divisions to resist 'a Russian attack on the Western front'. Without a German contribution, 'beginning with five and running up, as American, British and French armies grew, perhaps to twenty divisions', the West would be left unguarded in defence.[101]

The problem with the idea of German rearmament so soon after the war was that most Europeans were afraid of its long-term consequences. The French feared that a revived German national army would ultimately turn on Europe.

The Germans themselves were petrified that a revived German army might provoke the Soviets to launch their assault on Europe and at the same time would be too weak to fight them off. The solution was to create an integrated defence force in western Europe. In creating a European army Churchill and the French would have it both ways: Germany would rearm to help fight off the Russians for western Europe and Germany would be tightly contained in a larger European structure so as to avoid a repetition of the past.

On Tuesday 8 August, the first debate of the second session was underway. André Philip, a French federalist whom Churchill remembered serving de Gaulle in North Africa during the war, took the opportunity to build on Churchill's ideas for a German contribution to European defence and launch his plan for a European army inclusive of Germany. 'It is strange how, abroad as well as at home, what Churchill puts forward one year as a daring paradox, becomes an accepted truism a year later,' Macmillan wrote in his diary that day.[102] Following the morning session Churchill called the three leading Frenchmen in the Assembly to luncheon at Villa Merckel: Georges Bidault, who had been prime minister of France the previous year; Paul Reynaud, the federalist ex-prime minister who had wanted to accept Churchill's offer of Franco-British Union in 1940, and Pierre-Henri Teitgen, a brilliant legal mind and a leading French Christian democrat.[103] No record of the conversation exists, but, in light of what was to come, it is fair to surmise that the luncheon was meant as a platform for private talks about Churchill's plan to craft a resolution in the Assembly for a European army. If he proved able to persuade the leading Frenchmen of the validity of his ideas, there was a much greater chance that the Assembly would adopt his resolution.

That night, Churchill enlisted the help of Duncan Sandys to entertain a delegation of eight Germans, led by Dr Punder of Chancellor Adenauer's Christian Democrat Party, for a black tie dinner at the villa.[104] Macmillan and Maxwell Fyfe arrived for drinks after 10 p.m. to a moving scene. Just five years after the end of the war, Churchill was discussing enthusiastically with men and women from all West German parties how to structure a European army in which the Federal Republic of Germany could join. Maxwell Fyfe later wrote that he had 'seldom seen people so moved as [Churchill's] guests'.[105]

Churchill kept his party up well past midnight about the different options and possibilities for the new military structure, giving him a unique opportunity to sound out German views before his own major address at the end of the week. In Macmillan's account, Churchill ended the night on a darkly cautionary note, practically telling the Germans that if they refused to mount a defence against Soviet Russia they would find themselves in no-man's land, meaning they would inevitably be 'atom-bombed' in World War III.[106]

The next morning, Wednesday 9 August, Churchill was in similar form to that on the eve of the Zurich speech. He spent the morning in bed at Villa Merckel, taking his breakfast there and dictating draft after draft for Friday's speech surrounded by private secretaries, typists and family members. Macmillan wrote that night:

> I went round in the morning [to Churchill's villa]. He was in bed and working on a speech. He will speak tomorrow, Thursday; Spaak should be so informed. The truth is that he is in one of those moods, preparatory to some creative effort, when the artist is anxious, nervous, dissatisfied with himself, and everyone else – a good sign on the whole.[107]

In the House of Europe, meanwhile, Bidault started the morning proceedings of the Assembly just as suited Churchill's aims: with a speech in support of the European army. Boothby followed him, urging the establishment of a Supreme Command for the Western democracies and 'the appointment of a single Commander-in-Chief for Western Europe'.[108] In the afternoon it was Reynaud's turn. He began by presenting to the Assembly the figures he was using to estimate Russian military strength in Europe. As it stood, the NATO member countries in Europe were able to bring together a meagre 12 divisions against, at the very least, more than 80 Soviet divisions. Faced with this imbalance and the imminent danger of heated conflict on the continent, Reynaud said he wanted to create the position of minister of war for Europe. He pointed to Churchill as the ideal man for the task: 'If you want one you will not have to look beyond this hall to find one,' Reynaud said to warm applause as he looked at Churchill. It was not quite the job of president of the United States of Europe which Churchill thought in 1945 he might have been able to take up if he were ten years younger, but he saw no reason to dismiss the suggestion out of hand and smiled kindly in Reynaud's direction when the translation came through on his headset.[109] Yet, Boothby later recalled that Churchill 'had himself in mind as the Minister'.[110]

That afternoon, the first German ever to address the Assembly was a Christian Democrat close to Chancellor Adenauer called Eugen Gerstenmaier. Along with all moderate and right-wing parties in West Germany, he believed that the Germans, rather than building up their own army, should contribute to a single European force. The British socialists and the left-wing German Social Democrats were now the only groupings still opposed to any form of German rearmament.

That Wednesday night, Churchill resolved to end his speech on Friday 11 August by moving an emergency resolution calling for a European army with contributions from all member states of the Council of Europe – including West Germany.

Churchill called on Sandys, Maxwell Fyfe and Macmillan to help word a resolution on the European army over drinks at his villa that night after 10 p.m. Knowing that discussions of defence were strictly forbidden to the Assembly, there was considerable anxiety that the resolution would be ruled 'out of order' by President Spaak. But Spaak, much to the horror of the Assembly's obsessive–compulsive British clerk, was prone to making the rules as he went along. Though Spaak was a Socialist, Churchill saw eye to eye with him on most European issues and recognised in him a co-leader of the European movement. After a grand United Europe rally in the Royal Albert Hall on 21 July 1950, Churchill had invited Spaak, along with Ramadier and Reynaud, to what he called a 'Stag Supper' at his home at 28 Hyde Park Gate.[111] What the bibulous company discussed that night remains unknown but it may have solidified friendships that would come in handy in Strasbourg. No doubt Churchill further courted Spaak when he came over to Villa Merckel for luncheon earlier on Wednesday 9 August.[112]

Churchill began his 25-minute address at 11.30 in the morning on Friday 11 August, speaking as passionately and gravely as the year before while taking in his stride the fact that many in the Assembly had to cope with a rather flat translation through their headset. German representatives were in attendance to hear yet another historic call to action which took their nation for its subject. Churchill began by emphasising that he was glad that the Germans 'have come here to share our perils and augment our strength. They ought to have been here a year ago. A year has been wasted, but still it is not too late.' He quickly moved on to the core theme of his speech, telling the Assembly:

> Courage and unity must inspire us and direct the mighty energies at the disposal of our Governments to solid and adequate measures of defence. Those who serve supreme causes must not consider what they can get but what they can give. Let that be our rivalry in these years that lie before us.

A watertight system of European defence would keep out a Communist invasion and give the West the best chance of a postwar settlement with the Soviets on the basis of strength rather than weakness. Certainly the Assembly of parliamentarians before him had no power to act as did executive national governments, but what it could do was

make a gesture of practical and constructive guidance by declaring ourselves in
favour of the immediate creation of a European Army under a unified Command,
and in which we should *all* bear a worthy and honourable part.

Churchill then read to the Assembly the motion he had just placed upon the
order paper, stating his call for 'the immediate creation of a unified European
Army subject to proper European democratic control and acting in full cooperation with the United States and Canada'. It was, in Churchill's words, the
'greatest contribution that it is in our power to make to the safety and peace of
the world'.[113]

The resolution for the direct creation of a European army sent the Assembly
into a wild frenzy. Debate that day lasted deep into the night, interspersed with
the usual lobbying in restaurants and smoke-filled backrooms outside the
plenary chamber.[114] Churchill's speech immediately caused a stir in
Westminster, too. Within hours Prime Minister Attlee cabled to warn him
that the government was issuing a statement after midnight announcing an
emergency debate on the European defence situation at the end of the
Assembly's second session.[115]

At the end of the day, with overwhelming French and German support, the
resolution to recommend the creation of a unified European army subject to
proper democratic control was carried with 89 votes for, 5 against, and
27 abstentions. It was, as Spaak later put it, 'the most important decision yet
taken by the Consultative Assembly'.[116] Churchill dined with Macmillan that
night, bubbling over with happiness about the vote, which he felt proved that
the Franco-German reconciliation he first proposed at Zurich was near. 'No one
but he in Europe could have brought about this result,' Macmillan wrote before
bed that night. 'Without his immense personal prestige, which he has thrown
quite recklessly into this campaign, it could not have been achieved.'[117]

Churchill was not content to let things rest after the speech and the success
of the resolution. On returning to London that weekend, he started working
impatiently through diverse channels to promote his idea. After his request for
a special session in the Commons to debate the Strasbourg resolution for a
European army was denied, he cabled US President Truman an urgent letter,
hoping to win the approval and active support of the White House.[118] 'Your
speech was superb! Excellent! No fooling!' Lew Douglas, the American
ambassador in London, had said.[119] Churchill was fairly confident that
Truman would want to extend full American cooperation to Europe's own
defence. He started by telling the President that the speech and resolution on
the European army were in a sense the fruition of all that he had laboured for

since Zurich. 'The ending of the quarrel between France and Germany', Churchill wrote, 'by what is really a sublime act on the part of the French leaders, and a fine manifestation of the confidence which Western Germany have in our and your good faith and goodwill, is I feel an immense step forward towards the kind of world for which you and I are striving.'

Churchill warned Truman that the only alternative to a European army was a kind of neutrality arrangement between some major continental states and the Soviets. This was exactly what the Communists were after. It would allow them to gobble up many more countries in the heart of Europe in the sly manner in which they took over Czechoslovakia in February 1948. The countries that Churchill thought the Communists were after were 'in a sort of no-man's-land between Britain, with its American air-bombing base, and the Soviet armies'. He feared the Soviets might use the rest of Europe as bases for the bombardment of Britain. Rather than merely holding on to the Channel and the Pyrenees, Churchill hoped to persuade Truman to join him in saving as much of Europe as possible in the unfolding Cold War.

Specifically, he wanted to know from Truman whether the US could commit to helping the European army protect West Germany and the rest of western Europe, in case of Soviet incursion, by atomic means. The Soviets, he predicted, might choose to respond to the threat of a unified European army by invading West Germany. In that case, would the United States defend West Germany as it would France, the Benelux or Britain? 'Or should we let the German people,' he asked, 'whom we have disarmed and for whose safety we have accepted responsibility, be attacked without the shield of the atomic deterrent?' He hoped Truman would publicly express an American guarantee to extend atomic protection to all countries represented in the European army. 'I do not see how this [atomic guarantee] would risk or cost any more than what is now morally guaranteed by the United States,' Churchill wrote.

He ended with a written sigh of relief about the German position on the European army in the Assembly. Churchill and the Strasbourg Tories had feared that the Germans would demand a national army be built up, and then a contingent given to the European army. Instead, they agreed to just build up enough for a European contingent of about five or six divisions. This made all the difference to the French. It also made Churchill exceedingly happy: 'They and we can have it both ways.'[120]

Truman's initial reply was understandably neutral. Though he and Churchill had got along well when they first met at the end of the war in Potsdam, Truman's loyalties in Britain now lay inevitably with Prime Minister

Attlee. Churchill spoke in no official capacity for the British government, and all Truman could tell him was that he was 'sincerely hoping that the right decisions may be made by our Government to create a condition that will lead to general world peace'.[121]

Churchill's second and more direct method of pushing his idea along was through his bulldog in Strasbourg, Duncan Sandys, who had had been appointed one of the leading members of a new sub-committee on defence. Sandys was tireless in helping Churchill craft his European agenda and was, as Macmillan once put it, 'as full of 'projets' as old [Jean] Monnet himself. He pulls them out of his pocket, written on the backs of envelopes, one after another.'[122] On Churchill's instructions Sandys introduced a concrete outline for a European army for consideration by his sub-committee on 16 August. The day before, Churchill had telephoned a crucial message to Sandys for his guidance and eyes only. Churchill said he was wary of 'our getting involved in detail, for we have not the military knowledge or any kind of authority to make a plan.' He preferred a more general outline than a cut and dried plan:

> Each country would of course supply divisional units, tactically interchangeable, and the military organization would follow the model of SHAEF [the Allied forces from 1943 onwards]. It would seem that about sixty divisions should be formed at once and stationed in Europe with another forty ear-marked as reinforcements for the ninetieth day after general mobilization.

Churchill hoped that there would be a broadly unified military command where a civilian defence chief was ultimately responsible to national governments.[123]

Sandys's controversial final report, which he deliberately did not discuss with the other Strasbourg Tories for fear it would slow him down, did its most important work in explicating some of the terms and ideas used in Churchill's original resolution. The resolution had called for 'the immediate creation of a unified European Army, under the Authority of a Minister of Defence, subject to proper European democratic control and acting in full co-operation with the United States and Canada'. The word 'Army', Sandys clarified, in this context meant a well-balanced operational land army containing all the elements you would expect in a large military force in a foreign country. National governments would be allowed keep some forces for different purposes but were expected to deliver large contingents. The general purpose of the European army was to defend the territory of participating countries.

'Unified' signified that this would be more than a regular military alliance – a fully integrated European staff and command would direct the forces made available to it. Meanwhile, 'proper democratic control' meant that a European minister of defence would be accountable to a European authority directly or indirectly representing the peoples of Europe. This was most likely to resemble a strengthened version of the Council of Europe. Further, Sandys explained, it was Churchill's intention that the European army would supersede and replace the military clauses of Bevin's 1948 Brussels Pact, though its relationship to the collective security offered by NATO was left undefined.[124] In a defence debate in the Commons in September 1950, Churchill reiterated his support for the immediate creation of a European army consisting of at least 60 or 70 divisions to protect western Europe against 'a Russian-Communist onrush to the sea'. For this purpose, he said, every eligible parliamentary democracy 'must dedicate their quota of divisions'.[125] Two days later, again speaking on international affairs in the Commons, Churchill re-emphasised the import-ance of German participation in a European defence force. He was growing severely impatient with the government's lack of initiative. 'It is more than nine months since I pointed out that no effective defence of Europe was possible without the armed strength of Germany,' he said. Churchill continued angrily: 'No agreement has been reached, and meanwhile Germany lies even more undefended than other European countries under the menace of Communist and Russian aggression.'[126]

The Assembly adjourned its second session until November 1950 without a full plenary debate on Sandys's outline for a European army. Churchill, after taking into account the moderating views of Eden in London,[127] accepted this outcome without qualms. After all, he told Sandys in August, they could not 'possibly do better than by our Resolution'. The Assembly was there to 'point the way and give inspiration'; executive governments would have to sit down and work out the details of the plan.[128]

The French government did this almost immediately. On 24 October 1950, in the week China officially entered the Korean War with 260,000 soldiers,[129] Prime Minister René Pleven, whom we first encountered in the Franco-British Union episode as the assistant to Jean Monnet, announced his radical 'Pleven Plan' for what became known as the European Defence Community, or EDC.

The immediate problem was that the French envisaged something entirely different for the structure of the European army than did Churchill. First, Pleven did not allow for national contingents larger than battalions (about 800 soldiers). The basic thinking was: the first German soldiers to be recruited after the war would be Europeans, wear European uniforms and serve under European command.[130] This was unacceptable to the Americans and the

British, who understood that an effective army could not afford to have tiny German combat forces integrated into much larger non-German divisions. At the lowest level of the army pyramid the language barrier would make for a messy spectacle at best. It was for this reason that Churchill, who wanted to retain the morale-boosting power of national spirit up to the level of divisions (about 15,000 soldiers), famously and frequently characterised the French idea of a European army as 'a sludgy amalgam'.[131] In another iteration of colourful language, Churchill said he wanted 'a faggot of staves bound by a ring of steel and not a soft, putty affair such as is now contemplated'.[132]

Second, and politically even more problematic, Prime Minister Pleven cloaked his Plan in a far-reaching proposal for the creation of a political federation with an all-powerful 'High Authority' with a minister of defence, an independent budget and a new, directly elected European Parliament. Insisting on an altogether new and tightly integrated organisation to dilute German military might in a European system, the Pleven Plan blatantly bypassed Churchill's beloved Council of Europe. It was one solution to the problem of German rearmament in the West, but also a rather cruel distortion of what Churchill and Sandys originally proposed to the Strasbourg Assembly.

The first chance for Churchill and the Strasbourg Tories to officially respond to the Pleven developments came when the Assembly regrouped in mid-November to debate Sandys's original outline. While Churchill stayed in Westminster to lead the Conservative Party, Macmillan and Sandys went to Strasbourg to fight their corner. On 13 November, the Commons debate on the work of the Council of Europe demonstrated why Churchill was needed at home to fight back against the government's growing impatience and hostility. Bevin made an unusually acidic speech that day attacking the European movement for sabotaging his foreign policy, to which Churchill, growing angrier with every sentence, finally snarled back, 'you are the arch saboteur!'[133]

Macmillan reported to Churchill, just before returning to Strasbourg for the November leg of the second session, that the reactions in other countries to the Pleven Plan showed 'that any proposal to set up a supra-national Minister and parliamentary authority of this kind would, in present circumstances, be rejected by at least one-third of the Member States, including Great Britain'.[134] The clear danger was, however, that if Britain refused to join France in creating the European army as a founder partner, France itself might have to back out and the whole plan would collapse. Britain was still the geopolitical lubricant and a balancing force between France and Germany. Without Britain at its side, France would eventually wither in comparison to Germany's military might.

A federal Europe without Britain, Macmillan feared, 'hands Europe on a plate to Germany, and destroys in a day the fruits of our hard-won victory in two wars'.[135]

What Churchill and the Strasbourg Tories set out to do, therefore, was to look for a way to participate and, in order to be able to do so, find a method of securing ministerial control 'without raising the constitutional issues involved in the original [Pleven] proposal'. In other words, they aimed to bring the European army and a European defence minister under the control of the Council of Europe. It was a straightforward way of thinking and an attempt to keep Britain fully involved. In the absence of any new supranational parliamentary body, the Consultative Assembly would continue to provide the possibility for reviewing the problem of European defence. In a clear-cut summary of the Tory position Macmillan concluded that 'Great Britain will not take part in any system of European Defence involving the creation of a supranational parliamentary body or the appointment of a supranational Minister of Defence as proposed in the Pleven Plan. A compromise between the French and British standpoint might possibly be found in the appointment of a Commissioner for European Defence responsible to a Committee of European Defence Ministers.'[136]

On 22 November, after a long phone call to Strasbourg, Churchill sent Sandys his private thoughts ahead of the debate on the European army. Describing in some detail what he thought its structure should look like and expressing his wish for Britain to join, the note read in full:

The European Army should consist of the Brussels Treaty Powers [France, Britain and the Benelux] and other free nations who have joined them and should be an enclave in, or core of, the Atlantic Pact Powers [NATO], and under the Supreme Commander appointed by them. All countries concerned should dedicate from their National Armies the approved and agreed quota. Whether this should be expressed in 'Divisions' or in 'Combat Groups' of the three arms (infantry, armoured vehicles and artillery) should be no obstacle as long as numbers are sufficient and proportions right. The Germans who have no National Army and do not seek one, should be invited to make their due contribution. All troops of every country in the European Army, as in the Atlantic Pact Super-Army, should have equal status, and be equipped with equal weapons. Their supplies and munitions should be drawn from the common pool. At present this would be an Atlantic Pact pool, and later a European pool may develop subject of course to the great importance of uniformity or at least similarity of weapons. The question remains whether the British should dedicate their contribution to the European Army or to the Atlantic Pact Army. I am in favour of the former, namely the European Army, but the issue is not fundamental or final, and should not prevent general agreement.[137]

That was all to say that Churchill hoped to see a European army emerge under the umbrella of a NATO force so as to secure continued American involvement in the defence of Europe against the Soviets. He did not address the specifics of the Pleven Plan directly, but it was clear that he had no intention of going along with the French plan to use the European army to immediately build a federal union. Instead, he preferred what he first set out in his *Daily Telegraph* article of 31 December 1946, 'The High Road of the Future': a common European system of defence *within* the framework of the Council of Europe.

Sandys and Macmillan went into the debate on 24 November knowing that French Foreign Minister Robert Schuman would come to the Assembly to elaborate on the Pleven proposals. Schuman explained that, indeed, the EDC would come with a whole new set of political organs. As the Frenchman André Philip put it: 'Once we have a unified army this will be swiftly followed by a unification of our foreign policy and a genuine and speedy organisation of our European federation.'[138] As such the Pleven Plan was geared far more towards political union as an end in itself than it was to Churchill's immediate concern of defending Europe against the Soviet Union. For Britain to come into the European army it would from the outset have to be a system, without the federal controls proposed by the French government.

On Churchill's instructions Macmillan delivered an impassioned speech in the Assembly on the European destiny of West Germany ending with the reassurance that 'if the Germans joined a European Army they would be received as comrades with equally honourable military status.'[139] Knowing this, even the German Social Democrats, who had been outright hostile just a few months before, came around and pledged their support for the creation of a European army. That the Assembly adopted Churchill's resolution with an overwhelming majority ultimately contributed little to immediate diplomatic advances.

The all-powerful Committee of Ministers looked at the Assembly's recommendation and simply replied that defence matters were not within its competence. What the European army resolution did do was inspire the French government to propose the creation of a European Defence Community. While it was a perversion of the proposal outlined by Churchill and Sandys, it is still seen as the most ambitious project in the history of European integration. Churchill told the Commons on 15 February 1951, the day the negotiations on the EDC started in Paris, that the Labour government had been 'doing what they can, behind the scenes, to discourage the French from their plan of a

European Army'. On doing no more than sending a British observer to Paris, he warned Prime Minister Attlee to 'beware how you continue this halfhearted policy.'[140]

Later, when the EDC negotiations had been underway for nearly seven months, Churchill, the French assistant minister of defence, the British ambassador in Paris, Jean Monnet and former prime minister Paul Reynaud discussed the state of affairs over a dinner held in Churchill's honour. It was just another month until the general election in Britain and this was a golden opportunity both for the French to sound out Churchill's views and for Churchill to consider more fully French thinking behind the community proposals. As we know from the British Ambassador's account, Churchill stated bluntly that the Pleven Plan was fundamentally different than what he had in mind when he first proposed a European army at Strasbourg. He criticised the French plans sharply, hammering home some of his favourite themes: 'An army needed spirit and tradition. The European Army, as at present planned, could only be "a sludgy Amalgam". After years it might develop an *esprit de corps* but time was lacking and we should only have an inefficient and ineffective force.'[141]

Monnet, the Ambassador wrote, rebuked Churchill and said that the key difference in context was that the Germans 'were now insistent on equal treatment'. If the French were to avoid German calls for a revived national army, they had to be prepared to sacrifice theirs. The French, Monnet estimated, were ready for this: 'they no longer hankered after national glory, nor did they trust their national army, unassisted, to guard their frontiers. Materially they wanted a larger force to defend them. Spiritually, they were in search of new ideas.' Monnet argued that this was a sentiment felt more widely in continental Europe and argued that the French, in taking Germany by the hand, were doing exactly what Churchill had asked of them. Churchill was impressed with Monnet's case and, though deeply sceptical about the practicability of the Pleven Plan, promised to do 'nothing to obstruct its fulfilment'.[142]

The Defence Community would finally collapse in the ratification process in the French National Assembly in 1954, just as the Strasbourg Tories expected, because successive British governments rejected the constitutional elements of the final plan and refused to come in as a full member. In order to ratify, French deputies in the National Assembly needed more British guarantees than the British were willing to offer. Without Britain there could be no European army in the Pleven mould.

THE SCHUMAN PLAN

The Economist could not have been more damning in its assessment of the government's rejection of the Schuman Plan invitation in June 1950. 'The broad idea of the Schuman plan is of immense importance [...] to whittle it down, to throw shadows across the gleams of hope which flicker around it [...] is to incur the responsibility of producing some better idea. And there is no sign that Mr Bevin has a better one.'[143]

On 9 May 1950, without prior warning, the French government announced a practical plan for European economic integration that would change the dynamic of European unification for good. It deliberately wrestled the leadership and initiative for the closer union of European states out of British hands and into those of the continentals. The Schuman Plan, named for the French foreign minister who drew it up with the help of Jean Monnet, proposed that 'Franco-German production of coal and steel as a whole be placed under a common High Authority, within the framework of an organization open to the participation of the other countries of Europe.' Italy, Belgium, the Netherlands and Luxembourg joined France and Germany in the resulting European Coal and Steel Community (ECSC), which came about in the Treaty of Paris on 18 April 1951. Britain did not.

After the original bombshell announcement, three weeks of intense discussions were held between the governments and officials of France and Britain on the Schuman proposals and the terms of entrance into the international negotiations that began in mid-June 1950. There could have been little more at stake. The French government proposed to set up the 'common foundations for economic development as a first step in the federation of Europe'.[144] The sectorial integration of coal and steel markets and resources in western Europe held the promise of making war materially impossible, modernising production, expanding exports, and raising the living standards and wages of workers. The countries invited to participate were therefore asked to consider the economic idea of integrating Europe's basic industries, but, first and foremost, they were asked to consider the political idea of merging some national sovereignty into an independent and 'supranational' High Authority.

Bevin's furious reaction to the rather unexpected nature of the French invitation, if genuine, quickly turned out to be misplaced.[145] Having learned that both Chancellor Adenauer of West Germany and US Secretary of State Dean Acheson were informed of Schuman's intentions a day earlier, Bevin suspected that the French wanted to exclude Britain from the negotiations.

That was patently false. The French would always seek full British participation in a scheme of this nature while understanding that the British were hesitant to commit politically to Europe while it looked outwards to the United States and the Commonwealth. On 27 April 1950, Oliver Harvey, British ambassador in Paris, had written to Bevin saying that a 'European system based on France and Germany is unacceptable to France [...] the essential feature of a European system is the participation of the UK.'[146]

When, on 11 May 1950, Bevin asked for clarification straight from the horse's mouth, Schuman duly explained that he had been afraid of leakage, which would have reduced the effect of the announcement, and that the plan should be seen as 'merely a proposal, not a fait accompli'.[147] He further clarified that in order to achieve the 'requisite change in the psychological atmosphere', the French government had to act first and without delay or modification.[148]

In the formal Franco-British diplomatic exchanges about the Schuman Plan invitation, which commenced by telegram on 25 May, the French government did everything within reasonable boundaries to accommodate British protestations. The very basic difference between the governments was that the British Labour government did not feel ready to agree to the principle of ceding some sovereignty in a limited area. As this attitude became clear the French government stopped hoping for British participation in the negotiations and focused on saving the integrity of the plan.

Confident in the knowledge that all the other governments approached had agreed to negotiate a final agreement on the principles of the Schuman Plan, the French government issued an ultimatum for the British to reply to by 8 p.m. on 2 June 1950. The ultimatum came as a shock to the few officials and ministers left in Whitehall over the Whitsun break. But the draft communiqué for which the French government required approval was designed, quite unsuccessfully, to assuage British fears. In a revised communiqué the French had changed the language: instead of being 'resolved' to establish the much-feared High Authority, participants in the negotiations would now see this as an 'immediate objective'.[149] That concession was either misunderstood or wilfully ignored at the British end of the line.

Two senior Foreign Office officials went to find Deputy Prime Minister Herbert Morrison in a fancy London restaurant on the night of the ultimatum. Morrison, in charge of the government while Prime Minister Attlee vacationed in France and Ernie Bevin was taken ill, briskly refused participation. 'It's no good,' he said. 'We can't do it: the Durham miners wouldn't like it.'[150]

That final decision was confirmed the next day in a brief Cabinet meeting in the absence of three of the four most senior ministers, though with approval *in absentia* from a hospitalised and dazed Bevin.[151] The French government expressed deep regret at the British refusal to work out the details of the Schuman Plan.[152] Bevin just hoped for understanding from the world that his government refused, as he put it to the Americans, to buy 'a pig in a poke'.[153] *The Economist* showed no mercy: 'at the bar of world opinion, the Schuman proposal has become a test. And the British Government have failed it.'[154]

Churchill, as leader of the Opposition, was naturally not privy to behind-the-scenes manoeuvring in the Cabinet or the Foreign Office. Though wholly unlikely to embrace the idea that the coal and steel pool would lead to the short-term federation of western Europe, circumventing the Council of Europe and a more organic process of unity, Churchill was sure of one thing: the British needed to go to Paris to negotiate a deal that would make the plan more palatable to their particular concerns. He was convinced that if Britain took the lead in Paris by presenting a less politically radical alternative, the European coal and steel pool could usefully serve as another decisive step towards European union. Churchill's personal prestige and continental connections might then be valuable assets in ironing out a compromise structure in which Britain would take part.

Bidault and Adenauer may well have been open to going to some length to meet British demands. In an interview with the *Manchester Guardian* on 9 September 1949, Adenauer argued: 'I would be glad if the British government and British public opinion would accept the fact that England is a European power, that her history is bound up with that of Western Europe, and that she is bound in duty to play her part in European development.'[155] Adenauer had a vested interest in involving Britain in European integration. As he told Harold Macmillan as late as 1957, 'I don't want us to get strong again too quickly [...] that is why I yearn so for European Unity (and in view of France's weakness) for British participation.'[156] Adenauer's official biographer has even argued that he preferred Britain as principal partner in European integration to France.[157]

To the majority of the Strasbourg Tories, the basic idea of coordinating the European coal and steel industries was nowhere near as revolutionary or unexpected as it had seemed to Bevin. Germany's military potential, as was demonstrated in both world wars, was rooted in the rich sources of coal of the Ruhr valley, one of the largest industrial regions of Europe. Since the French steel industry was dependent on Ruhr coal, coal being central to the process of making iron usable for steel production, the French were keenly interested in having some control over the future of Germany's mighty coal industry.

Without Churchill's personal involvement, ideas about the pooling of European coal and steel industries as a path to peace had circulated even before World War II. Konrad Adenauer first entertained the idea in 1923, while Boothby discussed a version of the idea during a visit to continental industrialists in 1928.[158] After 1945 it was those involved in the transnational movement towards European unity who turned to the internationalisation of coal and steel as one of the areas of cooperation that could point the way to a European union. In May 1948, the economic committee of the Hague Congress at length debated the possibility of integrating Europe's coal and steel industries.[159] The Hague's Economic and Social Report concluded that the 'integration of European industry' was 'as indispensable as the modernization of production methods'. The immediate aim would be to 'lay down a common programme of development for the basic industries of the whole area, and especially for the production and distribution of the coal resources of Western Europe'.[160]

On 23 March 1949, Macmillan heralded the Schuman Plan when he told the House of Commons that the only way to prevent renewed German militarism was to control German heavy industry in a pooling arrangement that implied the 'internationalised control' of the coal, iron and steel industries of Britain and western Europe.[161] The idea was so commanding – and so economically necessary for the French – that it was inevitably going to recur until there was a final settlement for the Ruhr.

The major economic conference of the European Movement at Westminster in April 1949, loosely presided over by Churchill and actively organised by Macmillan, adopted a main resolution calling for the establishment of a European common market and customs union with a coal and steel community. It proposed three types of political organisation for coal, iron and steel: a European governmental body for general policy, a consultative body, and employer organisations for policy implementation.[162] Those 'common institutions' would seek to increase productivity, modernise production and raise the standard of living across Europe – all central aims that returned nearly verbatim in the Schuman Plan.

In the first session of the Consultative Assembly of the Council of Europe, the future of European coal and steel yet again appeared as a central theme. This was to be expected. Many considered the Assembly deliberations a smooth continuation of the policy concerns of the European Movement.

About two-thirds of the members of the Assembly were also members of the European Movement.[163] Harold Macmillan adopted a triumphant tone in reminding the Assembly of the work done by the European Movement. 'The "conclave of chatterboxes"', he said proudly, 'has turned into the first Parliament of Europe.'[164] At the end of the first session, the Economic Committee presented a report suggesting European governments should show the 'courage and vision to unite their markets [...] [and seek] the co-ordination of investments, of basic industries and of agriculture'.[165] As Tory leader in Churchill's absence, Macmillan agreed in the debate on this report that the problem of the Ruhr could only be solved 'if some degree of strategic guidance is accepted for basic industries'.[166]

In one of his daily reports on the progress of the Assembly, Macmillan notified Churchill that some of the leading Frenchmen were 'insisting on international planning of at least basic industries'. They asked that such industries as iron and steel be cartelised under public guidance and insisted this was the only way to solve the problem of the Ruhr. 'Germany would only accept a permanent control of the Ruhr industries if this control was European,' Macmillan wrote, 'and applied to other countries as well as herself.'[167]

That autumn, a committee of Tory MPs specifically designed to discuss the progress of the Council of Europe, the minutes of which were marked for and read by Churchill, had its first meeting. David Eccles, a frustratingly arrogant but undeniably gifted industrialist-turned-MP who represented the Conservatives on the Assembly's Economic Committee – he was known as 'Smartyboots' in Westminster – said that it seemed inevitable that Strasbourg would produce something on the Ruhr.[168] It was widely held, he reported, that 'the basic industries must come under a European Authority.' The solution, he expected, would be a kind of beneficent cartel which would be presented 'as necessary for the prevention of a German military revival'.[169]

As with the Pleven Plan later that year, the Schuman Plan also invited acceptance of the idea of what came to be known as 'supranational' governance on a European scale. This was the basic feature of the method of unification proposed by the French that defied any insistence on mere intergovernmental cooperation and the very structure of the Council of Europe in which the Committee of Ministers ignored most of the more far-reaching suggestions made in the Assembly. In the French method, High Authorities would require the abrogation of national sovereignty in defined spheres – coal and steel or defence, for instance – and would rapidly lead to fully fledged political federation.

Though certainly not as keen as some continental Europeans on the principle of supranationality, the Strasbourg Tories accepted early on the necessity of pooling sovereignty to a certain extent. As such, Churchill had said about his idea of political union in 1948: 'It is said with truth that this involves some sacrifice or merger of national sovereignty.'[170] In 1949, in much the same parlance, Boothby declared himself in favour of the 'merging or pooling of sovereignty – not so much the surrender as the joint exercise by common agreement of certain defined sovereign powers'. The structure Boothby had in mind to achieve a 'union or federation of free States' was one which developed 'functional authorities'. He hoped those functional authorities would be brought under the umbrella of a strengthened Council of Europe.[171]

Correspondingly, in a September 1949 memorandum, Sandys first proposed to create a European Political Authority out of the Council of Europe which would oversee the 'functional authorities' Boothby mentioned. Maxwell Fyfe, discussing the proposed Convention on Human Rights, argued that the supranational principle was a benign and familiar one, already inherent in the United Nations.[172] And Macmillan wrote of British goals in Strasbourg: 'While nearly all of us were averse to the federal concept which a few extremists enthusiastically promoted, we accepted that sincere partnership in the common task of rebuilding Europe must involve some surrender of sovereignty and the creation of some form of political organisation.'[173] None of that amounted to the unquestioned acceptance of supranationality, nor, clearly, to support for membership of a rigid federal union. The statements on merging sovereignty do point in the direction of a general commitment to pooling power in a European structure where it served British interests and where proper safeguards were in place. Churchill's disciples seemed to have a better grasp of how this might work than Churchill himself, offering more detailed plans than their leader.

When Schuman announced his Plan for a coal and steel pool, Churchill was in a difficult position. To maintain his leadership of the European campaign, he needed to both insist on British participation in the negotiations and warn that an organisation like the one Schuman proposed should be brought under control in the Council of Europe.

On 15 May, after a meeting chaired by Churchill, his United Europe Movement issued a statement to the press welcoming the Schuman Plan. Rather than warmly embrace all the particularities of the plan, however, it urged the government more generally to immediately announce that it was prepared to 'play its full part with the Governments of other European countries in working out methods for the practical implementation of the proposals formulated by M. Schuman'.[174] There were clear drawbacks for Britain to joining the Schuman Plan: it would involve a partial surrender of national sovereignty and have an unknown effect on the British economy. The British steel industry was still the most powerful in Europe, producing cheaper steel than any other country. Additionally, a loss of sovereignty in these defined areas would likely undermine imperial commitments and responsibilities. Then again, the reshuffling of European heavy industries without Britain even present at the negotiating table was a clear and present danger to Britain's interests in Europe and at home.

Three days later Churchill spoke to a large meeting of Scottish Unionists at Edinburgh's Usher Hall. In view of the momentous proposals coming from France, Churchill spent the last part of his speech considering the Schuman Plan. He called the plan 'an important and effective step in preventing another war between France and Germany' and thought it was 'right in principle'. He was proud and happy that the French, whom he had been encouraging to take the lead in Europe since touring Metz with Robert Schuman in 1946, finally rose to the occasion. But, he said, 'that by itself would not be enough.' Churchill suggested Britain had to find a way to come in side-by-side with the French: 'In order to make France able to deal on proper terms with Germany, we must be with France,' he said. United Europe had to be built on a Franco-British–German nucleus:

> The prime condition for the recovery of Europe is Britain and France standing together with all their strength and with all their wounds; and then these two nations offering their hands to Germany on honourable terms and with a great and merciful desire to look forward rather than back. For centuries France and England, and latterly Germany and France, have rent the world by their struggles. They have only to be united together to constitute the dominant force in the Old World and to become the centre of United Europe around which all other countries could rally.

So how could Great Britain participate most effectively in a grouping of European industry? Churchill had two clear requirements. One, there could be no 'lowering of British wages and standards of life and labour'. And two, the proud British steel industry would have to remain as competitive as ever. He saw no reason why this would not be the case in the new situation. 'We must be reassured on these and other points,' he said, 'while welcoming cordially the whole principle and spirit of what is proposed.'[175]

On 13 June 1950 Prime Minister Attlee, returning from his Whitsun holiday in the south of France, formally announced that the British government refused to participate in the Schuman Plan negotiations. A week after Attlee's announcement, Macmillan sent Churchill an urgent minute, passionately arguing that Britain should be 'in from the start'. Only that way, he said, could it 'mould the plan to our pattern' and prevent collapse, or even worse, ultimate German control of the coal and steel pool. Macmillan called on Churchill to keep pressuring the government to enter the negotiations and to 'give the lead for which Britain, the Empire, Europe and the world have been waiting'. He concluded: 'You started United Europe. Without you, there would be no Council of Europe, no Committee of Ministers, no Consultative Assembly, no Strasbourg. This is the first and supreme test. You cannot let down all Europe.'[176] Clearly Macmillan was afraid Churchill might back out at this critical juncture.

Responding to Macmillan's call, Churchill used his power as leader of the Opposition to put down a motion in the Commons to force the government into going to Paris to negotiate on the Netherlands reservation.[177] It was the first time since 1945 that Churchill had led his party into a 'division' on foreign policy, meaning the members of the House were free to literally 'divide' and walk into lobbies on either side of the Chamber to be counted.[178] The Netherlands government, though just as sceptical of the High Authority as the British, found Schuman ready to accept its participation in the negotiations while reserving the freedom to withdraw if the practicalities of the plan turned out to be unworkable. A two-day debate on the Schuman Plan was scheduled for 26 and 27 June 1950, a week into the Paris negotiations.

Although Labour complained Churchill was using the Schuman Plan controversy for party political benefit by slamming the government for fumbling a diplomatic opportunity, Churchill was acting in good faith. There was little to gain politically: neither the press nor the British public actively demanded a pro-Schuman Plan intervention from the Conservatives.[179] In fact, despite cautious approval of the plan from most of the mainstream press, Churchill's good friend the Canadian-British newspaper tycoon Lord Beaverbrook led a fiery opposition in his *Daily Express*, which wrote that the Schuman Plan would 'end British independence' and was 'part of a deliberate and concerted attempt to force Britain in a United Europe'.[180] Moreover, there were legitimate economic grounds to support British entry into the negotiations. The plan presented an alternative to Labour's nationalisation drive and proposed the type of international cooperation the Conservatives thought necessary to achieve full employment, a policy goal Labour thought would be frustrated rather than achieved by the coal and steel pool. The Empire and Commonwealth, too, stood to benefit from the expansion of European markets, especially if Britain would be able to ensure preferential treatment in the talks. The key was not to confine Britain to a European market: half of all its exports still went to the Commonwealth while just a quarter went to the countries of western Europe.[181] Perhaps most importantly, the Americans were openly in favour of Britain entering the talks and becoming a full member of the proposed organisation.[182]

Three days after the negotiations started, on 23 June, Anthony Eden received a telephone call from René Massigli, the French ambassador in London. Massigli, a modest, Anglophile diplomat who keenly understood British doubts and wanted nothing more than for Britain to join the plan, told Eden that the French government was now seriously considering making the High Authority responsible to another international body – most likely the Council of Europe. 'This justifies the view we have taken,' Eden told Churchill, reporting on his call, 'that had we come into the discussions we could have moulded events the way we wished.'[183]

Three days later, on 26 June, the House of Commons started its two-day debate. The first day, especially, was overshadowed by the international crisis developing after communist North Korean forces invaded South Korea. As Kenneth Younger, a junior minister in the Labour government, put it in his diary: 'The Korean situation has now knocked Schuman right into the background of public consciousness.'[184]

Nevertheless, the broad question emerging was about the implications of 'foreign' control of British coal and steel, the first of which was not long nationalised by Labour: how could Britain give over the direction of these industries to a High Authority of bureaucrats? The narrower question was whether the government should seek to participate in the negotiations while they were still in their early stages. If Massigli was right to inform Eden of the French openness to compromise, participation in the negotiations might still be useful. As the debate drew to a close on 26 June, Churchill moved it in the direction of the underlying, fundamental question of what could be Britain's place in a 'supranational' European union.

Agitated by some of the major Labour speeches on the topic, Churchill went on the offensive. There was 'no excuse for the British Government piling their own prejudices on the top of French pedantry', he said. Schuman's sudden announcement was problematic for the British position. Churchill admitted he was 'nettled by it', but went on to explain French procedural behaviour by pointing to the British government's long-standing hostility to the European movement and to its recent decision to suddenly and without warning devalue the pound sterling from \$4.03 to \$2.80, upsetting the whole financial and economic position of Britain's neighbours in continental Europe. Indeed, the French were displeased as it transpired that the Americans had known about plans for devaluation of the pound for weeks, and were further aggravated when the West German government followed suit and devalued its newly established Mark by 25 per cent.[185]

Churchill made a point of mocking the new jargon employed by the Labour frontbenchers who spoke in the debate – 'the infra-structure of a supra-national authority'. A band of intellectual highbrows, he said, they were perhaps overly keen to impress Attlee's Cabinet with the fact they had learned Latin at Westminster (a prestigious boarding school which had educated two senior Cabinet members). Churchill was astounded that the British government was busy 'finding excuses, elaborate excuses, to keep out of the conference altogether and thus perhaps spoil the hopes of a general settlement. The French have a saying: 'Les absents ont toujours tort' [he who is absent does not get the vote]. I do not know whether they learn French at Winchester.'

The absence of Britain from the negotiations, he said, 'deranged the balance of Europe'. Churchill therefore stressed his underlying principle that he was 'all for a reconciliation between France and Germany, and for receiving Germany back into the European family, but this implies, as I have always insisted, that Britain and France should in the main act together so as to be able to deal on even terms with Germany, which is so much stronger than France alone.' Britain's absence might also lead to continental Europe becoming a neutral geographical bloc, or 'Third Force', between America and Russia – a horror scenario for Churchill. Neutrality was 'a disaster second only to actual war'. He could see the Soviets taking over the continental states 'one by one and bit by bit exactly as we have seen Czechoslovakia devoured before our eyes'.[186]

On the merits of Schuman's proposals, of which few details were known, Churchill went back to explore the economic preconditions of British participation he had talked about nearly two weeks earlier in Edinburgh. To the point of the competitiveness of the British steel industry, he argued that under the Schuman Plan private ownership, as opposed to state ownership, remained unaffected. 'We cannot see any objection in principle', Churchill said, 'to a wider measure of international co-ordination if that proves practicable and in accordance with our essential interests.' On the second point of the protection of British wages, Churchill again leaned on the importance of having a seat at the table, arguing: 'Whereas our influence at the table might well have been sufficient to turn the balance in favour of the British standard [which was higher than the continental standard], it seems to me contrary to the interests of the British coal-miners and steel workers that they should never have been allowed to put their case for a levelling-up on the Continent instead of a levelling-down.'

As the debate moved to the broader idea of his United Europe campaign, Churchill justified the grounds on which he supported the creation of a European union. A constant criticism from the Labour benches and most of the press had been that Churchill was only pursuing the policy to outmanoeuvre Stalin in the early stages of the Cold War. Addressing the question directly, he said:

> It would be quite fair to ask me whether I should have welcomed [the Schuman Plan] even if there were no such thing as this Russian menace, or the Soviet government or the Communist movement in many lands. I should say, 'Yes, certainly.'

The threat of Russian invasion certainly did add to the value and urgency of the French proposals – it was by far the most important driver of Churchill's wish to involve Britain in the defence of western Europe – but the broader idea of European unification meant much more to him than a calculated geopolitical response to an international threat.

Churchill put the question before the Commons in language easy to follow for any of the members who might have tuned out during some of the more technical discussions on European steel production: 'Every Member should ask himself two simple practical questions: "Do I wish to see the unity of Western Europe advanced?" and anyhow, apart from that, "Had we not better take part in the conference subject to the reservation which the Dutch have made?" These are the issues before us tonight.'

On the first general matter, Churchill turned specifically to a question that was put to him the day before from the Labour benches. Would the Conservative Party be in favour of a federal union of western Europe? He was able to answer quite simply that, though he worked with the federalists in the European Movement, the party was 'not committed to their conclusions'. Churchill did not wish to become involved 'at this stage in all the tangles and intricacies of rigid constitution-making'. He could not conceive of Britain as 'an ordinary member of a Federal Union limited to Europe in any period which can at present be foreseen'. Britain could not accept 'full membership of a federal system of Europe' because of its ties to the Commonwealth and America.

If the continental Europeans did insist on building a federal union, Britain might seek ways to become intimately associated with it. Britain had its role to play in the three larger Western groupings – the English-speaking world, the British Commonwealth, and Europe – and, Churchill hoped, it would grow with Europe in a union that allowed fulfilment of its global responsibilities. Federation was impossible for Britain; membership of a looser union was preferable. In this connection there was reason for British optimism, Churchill argued: 'I am told that the difficulties of European federation are increasingly realized upon the Continent, and that it is one of the reasons why what I call "functional" associations, like this proposed merger of the heavy industries, are being sought.'

In a passage closer to poetry than prose, Churchill closed the debate by considering the difficult issue of surrendering national sovereignty for the sake of political organisation in a larger synthesis. The occasion justified emotion: Churchill was, he told the Commons in the debate, 'deeply moved' by the French attempt to make future European wars materially impossible. He urged the government one last time to accept the invitation for the negotiations – though not to blindly follow French wishes for a federal union – and agree to the principle of merging national sovereignty. It stands as one of the most moving contributions to parliamentary debate Churchill made since entering the House of Commons in 1901:

> We fought alone against tyranny for a whole year, not purely from national motives. It is true that our lives depended upon our doing so, but we fought the better because we felt with conviction that it was not only our own cause but a world cause for which the Union Jack was kept flying in 1940 and 1941. The soldier who laid down his life, the mother who wept for her son, and the wife who lost her husband, got inspiration or comfort, and felt a sense of being linked with the universal and the eternal by the fact that we fought for what was precious not only for ourselves but for mankind. The Conservative and Liberal Parties declare that national sovereignty is not inviolable, and that it may be resolutely diminished for the sake of all the men in all the lands finding their way home together.[187]

As so often with Churchill's best parliamentary speeches, it was a mixed marvel of vision, wit and – according to Harold Wilson, then a junior member of Attlee's Cabinet and later a Labour prime minister himself – 'forensic quality'.[188] Churchill handily outmanoeuvred all the Labour speakers in the debate and was, in Wilson's words, 'devastating on the question of "Why not be there"'.[189] Whatever the intensity of the argument and the emotion of its last passage, Churchill's motion to send the government to Paris was defeated by 309 votes to 296, reflecting the balance of parliamentary power at the time. Prime Minister Attlee was content with the outcome and wrote to his brother: 'I think WSC [Churchill] made a fool of himself over the Schuman Plan. He is apt to plunge in without considering the consequences. It is generally thought that we had the better of the debate.'[190]

The final vote was a tough verdict for Churchill and his inner circle of Europeanist Tories to accept. Before the Council of Europe had even had a chance to develop into something more meaningful than the relatively powerless organ of European opinion it was in 1950, the Schuman Plan clouded its chances of long-term success. Here was a new track, another course of European integration from which the British government deliberately decided to stay detached. Unless, perhaps, Churchill and the Strasbourg Tories could persuade the continentals during the second session of the European Assembly in August 1950 to bring the Schuman Plan into the existing structure of the Council of Europe.

Assembled on a hot summer's night in the dining room of Villa Merckel in Strasbourg, Churchill and the Tory delegation dived into a long discussion about the Schuman Plan and the role the British might play in it. It was Sunday 6 August, a day before the opening of the session, and a little over a month after the Schuman Plan debate in the Commons.

Most of the Assembly's returning members still shared Churchill's frustration over Labour's refusal to accept the French invitation to attend the Paris negotiations. They were disappointed that it looked like the coal and steel pool would remain outside the institutional structure of the Council of Europe. As Macmillan put it in his diary: 'Of what use then is all this machinery – Committee of Ministers, Consultative Assembly and so forth – if it is by-passed.'[191] The radical federalists felt equally disappointed that the British government, even now that the Schuman Plan proposed the kind of functionalist approach they thought would be welcomed in London, refused to at least negotiate about the terms of participation.

Churchill told the men at his villa that he was 'fairly satisfied' with the Conservative alternative to the Schuman Plan prepared by Harold Macmillan and David Eccles. He said he planned to give the Macmillan–Eccles plan, as it became known in Strasbourg, the broadest possible endorsement in his major speech on Friday 11 August and hoped Monnet and the French would come around to their point of view. It was decided, however, that the Macmillan–Eccles alternative – like any of the other major British proposals in the Assembly – would not carry Churchill's name, because, as Macmillan explained in his diary: 'First, as leader of the Conservative party, he ought not to be committed to detail; secondly, in this assembly he sh[oul]d keep himself a little aloof from detailed controversy.'[192]

The Macmillan–Eccles alternative proposed the Assembly come together and find 'a basis which will enable all the principal coal and steel producing countries of Europe to participate fully in the [Schuman Plan]'.[193] This was to say, the alternative sought the integration of heavy industry without committing to the explicit political aim of the Schuman Plan for short-term federation. As Macmillan explained it to Churchill, he and Eccles decided to put down an amendment to the resolution of the Economic Committee proposing 'a complete new scheme which we think may serve as a compromise acceptable to all parties'. Macmillan went around discussing his plans with the Conservative Party elders, the British Iron and Steel Federation, the trade union leaders and even some of his French connections who gave him reason to believe that they too were seeking some compromise.[194] A week earlier, at a meeting of the Tory Strasbourg representatives, it was decided to 'act urgently to influence the Six Power draft in our direction. The effect of Britain's absence was to encourage a revival of the third force idea, both in France and Germany'.[195]

On the afternoon of 10 August Robert Schuman himself came before the Assembly in Strasbourg to explain his plan. The plan, Schuman argued, would set free forces which would 'promote rapid and complete economic and political unification of Europe'. Macmillan was still desperate for some type of compromise. He continued in his diary on 10 August, rather optimistically:

> I cannot help feeling that there is a great possibility that one or both of two things may happen. When the Governments (especially Holland and Belgium) get the Monnet proposals, which are still up before the experts only, they will shrink from some aspects of the plan. Secondly, when the French Parliament and people realise that it means going in *without* Britain, they may shrink from handing over their rather weak and largely obsolescent industry to German control. For, in a few years, that is what it will mean.[196]

It was a somewhat arrogant view to take of British superiority in Europe and perhaps underestimated the determination with which the French sought to secure control over German industry and establish a federal union. After hearing Schuman's speech, Eden cabled Strasbourg strongly urging Churchill not to push the Tory alternative any further. 'In view of reports of Schuman's speech received here,' he said, 'suggest it is inadvisable Party should be committed to further initiative which can only court a rebuff.'[197]

Nevertheless, the Strasbourg Tories held on to the Macmillan–Eccles plan, for which Eccles best summarised the rationale in the European Assembly: 'most of us here are not frightened of a considerable surrender of sovereignty, but I believe we all want it to be done democratically [...] M. Schuman himself envisages a Committee of Ministers to sit alongside the Authority [...] that is what I believe would have been the contribution of the British had we entered the talks.'"[198] The single most important element of the Macmillan–Eccles alternative was its suggestion to make a Committee of Ministers, preferably within the Council of Europe, the final authority responsible for the coal and steel pool.[199]

Towards the end of the session in late August, the Macmillan–Eccles alternative passed as an amendment to the Economic Report in the Assembly, largely because of backroom manoeuvring. 'It took 20 minutes, in the bar, to do the deal,' Macmillan recounted in his diary. Sandys had grabbed the French leaders and his friends from the European movement Paul Reynaud, André Philip, and Maurice Schumann, an influential Christian democrat who had broadcast daily on BBC radio during the war as the 'Voice of France'. Macmillan went on: 'R[eynaud] (who is not a good fellow or friend) was very stiff at first and very hostile; Philip (after a lot of bombast) came round; M. Schumann (a really good and loyal friend) arrived at the right moment.' Schumann reminded those present that Macmillan could ask for this attempt to keep Britain involved in Europe as he had done even more for France than Churchill.[200]

However impressive the feat of persuading a group of dedicated federalists of the merits of the amendment, in the grand scheme of things it was a largely meaningless victory. It mattered little to the Labour government at home that the Assembly in Strasbourg advised altering the structure of the Schuman Plan to allow British participation. Unbound by the recommendations of the Council of Europe, the Labour government ignored them and refused to turn back on its rejection of the Schuman Plan invitation.

A friendly but discouraging letter Macmillan had received from Jean Monnet, his close wartime friend, neatly underlined the relative irrelevance of the Tory victory in Strasbourg. Macmillan had first met Monnet, the architect of the Schuman Plan and one of the prime movers in the plan for Franco-British Union, in April 1940. 'Monnet was already a whole-hearted European,' he later recalled, '[and] has remained a devoted friend of Britain.'[201] In 1942

Macmillan was appointed as minister resident of the Mediterranean and was based in Algiers as the British government representative to the Allies. Monnet arrived in Algiers in February 1943 to discuss French rearmament on behalf of the British Supply Council in Washington. He quickly won the trust of every major player from Churchill and Macmillan to Giraud, the French general in charge of the troops in North Africa, and de Gaulle, the leader of Free France. Macmillan and Monnet had successfully worked together to devise a solution to the opposing views of French governance between Giraud and de Gaulle. With an eye to shared aspirations for postwar European unity, Macmillan felt blessed to count Monnet among his friends. 'In his long and brilliantly effective labours for the European movement, he has never deviated into a narrow or particularist view, either of France's position in Western Europe, or of Britain's place as a European power,' Macmillan wrote.[202]

Monnet and Macmillan became intimately acquainted in North Africa. The two men often talked until deep into the night, scheming about their immediate and long-term challenges. They shared almost every meal together.[203] If an opportunity for relaxation presented itself, they preferred to visit the beaches and ancient ruins of Tipasa. On 8 May 1943, Macmillan noted in his diary: 'Monnet and I motored off to Tipasa along the coast. We had a delicious bathe in a little cove which we found. The sea was quite clear and not too cold. We bathed naked, but it was a deserted spot; and we sunbathed afterwards. Then we had a picnic lunch.'[204] The men would stay in touch, exchanging thoughts about the future of Europe, until Monnet's death in 1978.

With regard to the Schuman Plan, Monnet berated Macmillan for underestimating its political essence. 'The Schuman Proposals are revolutionary or they are nothing,' he began in his letter in response to the Macmillan–Eccles alternative. 'The indispensable first principle of the proposals is the abnegation of sovereignty in a limited but decisive field [...] any plan which does not involve this indispensable first principle can make no useful contribution to the solution of the grave problems which face us.' The Tory alternative, insisting on the control of a Committee of Ministers, seemed to undermine this first principle. Nonetheless, Monnet wrote that he would never 'cease to hope for the ultimate association of Great Britain in the carrying out of the Schuman proposal.'[205]

Ultimate association, it seems, was not what Churchill was looking for as a first choice, but it was certainly on the table as a viable alternative to full membership of a more elastic European union now that the Labour government had kept Britain squarely out of the tighter French community plans. Churchill, Macmillan and the rest of the inner circle initially held higher hopes for Britain, wanting it to 'take the lead to create a Europe which will work' rather than let the French create one without Britain.[206] In establishing British membership of the Council of Europe and supporting its attempts at a democratically accountable type of further unification, Churchill showed himself ready to go cautiously beyond intergovernmental cooperation. Whether the Council of Europe would establish or grow into a European union and what that union would look like in the future was a theoretical problem.

The Schuman Plan had the outright ambition of bringing about complete federal union in the shortest possible space of time. Hence Schuman's speech in the Assembly in which he made this goal explicit and the announcement of the Pleven Plan for a federally controlled European Defence Community in October 1950. The Tories, Churchill included, did not accept this as a viable idea for Britain. Britain could not be purely limited to Europe in a federal structure when it still held great responsibility in the world. Just as it seemed that Churchill had found a way for Britain to lead and grow with continental Europe, the Schuman and Pleven plans fundamentally undermined the notion that the continental states were willing to unite at the pace allowed by the structure of the Council of Europe.

It is likely that Churchill sincerely believed Britain could and should have negotiated either a more hybrid structure for the Schuman Plan in which it could take the lead or customize British conditions of membership. On 23 July 1951, the day Marshal Pétain died at the age of 95, Churchill once more expressed his regret that the government did not join the negotiations on the Schuman Plan. 'I believe', he said at the Mansion House in London, 'that if a British representative had been there, we might very likely have secured further modification which would have made it possible for Britain to join in this scheme, either on the same footing as the others or as some kind of associate member. From the Continental standpoint the Schuman Plan is greatly weakened by the absence of Britain – the largest steel and coal-producing nation in Europe.'[207]

We will never know what would have happened if instead of Attlee, Churchill had been in a position to respond to the Schuman Plan. But there is good reason to believe Churchill could have been successful in mending back together the fragile coalition of radical federalists, gradualists and inter-governmentalists which he and Sandys had forged in the aftermath of the

Zurich speech. Though Monnet was an ingenious, insistent and influential behind-the-scenes power broker, he would not have been able to talk his political bosses into pressing on with a rigidly federal structure if Churchill had been there to personally hammer home the necessity and conditions of British participation. On the German side, Adenauer, too, would have gone a long way in accommodating British needs. Even with Churchill absent from the negotiating table, Schuman ultimately accepted a deal for the European coal and steel pool by which a Committee of Ministers would oversee some of the work of the High Authority – a watered down version of the central demand of the Churchill-backed Macmillan–Eccles alternative.

In 1951, the third session of the Assembly raised nowhere near the level of excitement of the previous two. That, of course, was not according to any plan on the British side. Churchill had hoped to organise a public display of Commonwealth support for European unity and invited the Commonwealth prime ministers to come to Strasbourg. It was key to 'British leadership in Europe', he wrote in his invitation to the prime ministers, to ensure that 'developments towards European unity should be in fullest harmony with broad Commonwealth interests'.[208] As it turned out, the Commonwealth leaders, though generally sympathetic to the European campaign, were not as interested in being drawn into plans for a European union as Churchill and those involved with the European Movement in Britain might have hoped. The prime ministers of Canada, New Zealand and Australia, even after follow-up pleas from Churchill's disciples, all rejected the idea of attending Strasbourg. This put into question the feasibility of Churchill's thinking on Britain's dual role in Europe and the Commonwealth.[209]

In the end, rather than travelling to Strasbourg for the third session, Churchill spent his summer focusing on his parliamentary duties and the upcoming general election in the autumn. With Churchill away and the background tension of coming general elections in Britain and France, confidence in the achievability of European unity was in the balance amid frustrations over the slow working methods of the Council of Europe.

The Conservative MP Lady Tweedsmuir, Churchill's substitute at Strasbourg that year, reported back to Churchill on the May 1951 session: 'if the Council of Europe is not to drift into oblivion, discredited by its critics and undermined by the cynicism of its supporters, each Government must carry the ideas of Europe into their own Parliaments, and on to their own peoples.' Not at all discouraged by the current state of affairs, however, Lady Tweedsmuir said she remained 'convinced that with a Conservative Government in Britain taking the lead in Europe again, that the disillusioned elements on the Continent would rally once more, for they want and expect Britain to run Europe'.[210] She and many others would be deeply disappointed in the European travails of the first postwar Conservative government. Prime Minister Churchill, despite Macmillan's passionate exhortations on the eve on the Schuman Plan debate, was about to 'let down all Europe'.

CHAPTER 11

'A SAD DISILLUSIONMENT'
PEACETIME GOVERNMENT, 1951–1952

The Strasbourg Tories brimmed with ambition and enthusiasm after Churchill, aged 76, finally wrestled back No. 10 Downing Street from Attlee in the general election of 25 October 1951. The Conservatives, while receiving fewer votes than Labour, won a slim majority of 17 seats in the House of Commons. Six months after the signing of the Treaty of Paris for the European Coal and Steel Community, it fell to Churchill's new peacetime government to consider fighting to re-establish British leadership in Europe.

'Churchill's return', Julian Amery wrote to Harold Macmillan on 12 November 1951, 'has, certainly, created the psychological background for us to take up the leadership of Europe, and the present state of the Schuman and Pleven Plans seems to offer a practical opportunity to take the initiative.'[1] By the autumn of 1951, the Schuman proceedings had slowed down somewhat with dim prospects for a smooth parliamentary ratification process. The Pleven negotiations for a European Defence Community, of which Churchill was deeply sceptical, had not yet produced a final treaty. The leaders of France, Germany and the Benelux countries were still not altogether hostile to the idea of some type of British leadership.[2] Julian Amery was confident Churchill and the Tories could save the proposals. 'It is a question of going in and making them work,' he told Macmillan.[3]

What followed was deep disappointment and protracted frustration for those who wanted Britain to lead Europe. Never did Churchill's government aggressively pursue the kind of non-federal alternatives to the French community plans that the Strasbourg Tories preferred. Never did it bring itself to cast Europe in a mould acceptable to British public opinion and compatible with British global responsibilities. Never did Churchill regain for the Council of Europe the position of prominence he hoped it would hold until long after his death. Harold Macmillan, when he came to write his memoirs, thought of the early 1950s as 'a sad disillusionment, almost a betrayal'.[4]

How and why did things play out that way? In one part, Churchill adapted to the constitutional reality in the autumn of 1951: he was more apprehensive than Julian Amery about uprooting treaty negotiations, ratification processes and government continuity. It was broadly accepted in British politics at the time that there was such a thing as a constitutional gentleman's agreement by which a new government was unlikely to undertake the undoing of the core decisions of its predecessor.[5] The Labour government had already decided to go no further than association with Europe and that came close to settling the matter for Churchill. Roy Jenkins, one of the more successful Churchill biographers, concluded that his second administration 'fulminated at the fringes of the legacy of the Labour government of 1945–51 but left the core of its work inviolate'.[6] What is more, it could have been seen as 'sabotage' – in Europe as well in America, where support for a European federal union was near universal – if Britain turned around to block the continental states on their path to federation. This went for both major continental initiatives designed to move in that direction.

The Schuman Plan had not yet been ratified, but the Attlee government did not sign the April 1951 Treaty of Paris based on it. It would take until 27 May 1952 for a treaty to be signed for the European Defence Community, but the EDC conference produced its final report just a month after Churchill took office. The British government had already declined participation and was officially committed 'to establish the closest possible association with the European continental community'.[7] In his last year as Opposition leader, Churchill himself mooted the idea of constitutionally less disruptive 'association' as an alternative to membership. Churchill regretted, as he put it in a memorandum shortly after returning to office, that 'as year by year the project advanced, the Federal Movement in many European countries who participated became prominent'.[8]

In another part, Churchill was content that even without active British participation the French made meaningful strides towards tying Germany to the West – always one of his major priorities. As early as 1925, he told the Commons that he hoped it would one day be possible to 'weave Gaul and Teuton together so closely economically, socially and morally as to prevent the occasion of new quarrels and make old antagonism die in the realization of mutual prosperity and interdependence.'[9] And in the first volume of his own history of World War I, published in 1923, he asked: 'Could we in England, perhaps by some effort, by some compulsive gesture, at once of friendship and command, have reconciled France and Germany in time and forced that grand association on which alone the peace and glory of Europe would be safe? I cannot tell.'[10] Variations on the theme of Franco-German reconciliation he repeated over and over again in the years after World War II. The Zurich speech, arguably, was more about marrying Germany's Siegfried to France's Marianne than about Britain's role as master of ceremony.

In a third part, Churchill's foreign policy was still heavily focused on defending what was left of the Empire and strengthening relations with old British partners in the Commonwealth. Urgent threats to British interests in the far corners of the globe commanded his attention above plans for European unity. Continuing violent insurgency in Malaya and nationalist movements in Africa plagued his administration. Perhaps Churchill's peak performances of the second ministry, though light on detailed policy-making, were his set-piece contributions to the two meetings of Commonwealth prime ministers in London.[11] In the hierarchy of foreign policy objectives, it turned out that Europe ranked too low on Churchill's agenda to receive sustained attention when he became prime minister. Writing about Europe, his last private secretary remembered that 'there just wasn't time for an active Minister to pursue a "hobby enterprise"'.[12] Fittingly Churchill spent the best part of his last Cabinet meeting as prime minister on 5 April 1955 emphasising the importance of Commonwealth and Empire unity.[13]

In a fourth part, Churchill wanted to avoid any chance of the Americans returning to their traditional policy of isolationism – the way they had done after World War I – after Britain integrated too far into Europe.[14] Western Europe still needed the active involvement and military might of the United States to deter the Soviet army from marching to the North Sea. With the establishment of the transatlantic mutual defence pact NATO in 1949, Bevin had already gone a long way towards meeting this central goal of British foreign policy. General Hastings 'Pug' Ismay, a Churchill confidante, was right to point out that the new security structure in Europe 'kept the Americans in, the Russians out and the Germans down'.[15] Churchill himself saw in NATO a prime example of what the world needed to settle down, telling a German audience in 1956: 'NATO is a striking product and expression of a world wearied of war determined to build its own organisation in such strength and power that there will be peace henceforward.'[16] The realpolitik of the European project was that a US-backed Western grouping was a necessary preventative measure against World War III. Churchill hoped Britain could serve as a bridge between continental Europe and the United States.

In this dynamic, Churchill cared more urgently about what came to be known as the 'special relationship' with the United States than he did about Britain's part in a European union. When he invited Jock Colville to become his principal private secretary at No. 10, Churchill said he wanted to be in office for only just a year, which would give him enough time to 're-establish the intimate relationship with the United States'.[17] Rather than visit Strasbourg right after his election, he travelled to the United States to meet with Truman in January 1952, only paying a courtesy visit to Paris on his way there.[18] Rather than frequently consult European leaders and ambassadors, the US ambassador was the only one among his peers to have direct access to the Prime Minister.[19] Truman's successor, Eisenhower, even thought Churchill developed a 'childlike faith' in the Anglo-American relationship.[20] Revealingly, in his last address in the Commons on foreign affairs as prime minister, Churchill looked back with the greatest possible delight on his efforts to keep America close. 'One thing stands out in my mind above all others,' he said, 'that is the increase of our friendship and our understanding with our ally the United States.'[21] He bypassed the fact that the Americans had in fact been deeply opposed to British colonial policy and remained irritated by Britain's perceived unwillingness to lead Europe in its unification.[22]

In a fifth part, Churchill would become nearly obsessed with the idea that the only way to relieve Cold War tension and avoid nuclear catastrophe was to organise a major summit of the wartime Big Three powers and, potentially, France.[23] Boothby's explanation of Churchill's lack of European initiative in the second administration was simple: 'He was tired and his one big idea was a summit with Russia.'[24] The campaign for a summit had already become apparent in the last pronouncements of the 1951 general election campaign. Privately, speaking to French friends in Paris in September 1951, Churchill promised that if he were again prime minister he would seek a personal meeting with Stalin to iron out a settlement in much the same way he had gone to Moscow in 1944. 'You can't argue with Communists but you can bargain with them,' he declared.[25] Publicly, in his last stump speech of the 1951 campaign, Churchill said he wanted 'a friendly talk with the leaders of the free world [to] see if something could not be arranged which enabled us all to live together'. A lasting peace settlement was, he said, 'the last prize I seek to win'.[26] Just two weeks after winning back No. 10 he came back to his theme:

'Our great hope in foreign affairs is, of course, to bring about an abatement of what is called the 'cold war' by negotiation at the highest level from strength and not from weakness.'[27] For this to be successful, he hoped to persuade primarily the Americans and the Soviets, particularly after the death of Stalin in March 1953, to come together in a conference akin to the wartime gatherings at Yalta and Potsdam.

Churchill was highly unlikely to be able to bring in the Soviets if he was seen to keep pushing for his conception of a British-led union of all European states, including ultimately those in eastern Europe. Even the EDC, which the Soviets knew would not include Britain as an integral member, was viewed in Moscow as a grave threat and a way 'to include West Germany in the aggressive North Atlantic bloc'.[28] Here was one of the central ambiguities of Churchill's foreign policy after returning to office: he simultaneously advocated a defensive bloc *against* and a thawing of the cold war *with* the Soviet Union. It was what he called a 'double-dealing' policy of 'strength towards the Soviet Union combined with holding out the hand of friendship'.[29]

Alternatively, 'Peace through strength' is how Churchill described what he was after: a negotiated world settlement between the West and the Soviet Union.[30] Having been the first to warn about the geopolitical ambitions of the postwar Soviet Union, Churchill became the strongest voice advocating for détente. On the merits of the proposed summit, he told the Commons on 11 May 1953: 'It might well be that no hard-faced agreements would be reached, but there might be a general feeling among those gathered together that they might do something better than tear the human race, including themselves, into bits.'[31] Churchill expended almost all of his energy in the middle and latter parts of his second administration in pursuit of a summit, but to no avail. Amid Cabinet disagreements at home and facing pushback from the US government, he never succeeded in orchestrating a personal summit with Stalin's successor.

In a final part, Churchill was forced to engross himself in domestic politics, intent as he was on delivering the Tory election pledge of 'Work, Homes and Food', remedying a great housing shortage, getting rid of the embarrassment of rationing, ensuring industrial peace, courting the trade unions and spurring the denationalisation of road transport.[32] 'My policy is simple,' he told Jock Colville on returning to No. 10, 'it's houses, and meat, and not getting scuppered!'[33] The Cold War was putting an enormous strain on British public finances as the country lengthened national service to two years, sent troops to Korea, developed the atom bomb and stationed troops in Europe to deter the

Soviet Union. Defence spending had bulged to about 12 per cent of gross national product, and the British army was bigger than it had been at the height of its imperial power.[34]

Not for nothing did Churchill tell the Commons in his first speech upon his return to No. 10 that he was looking for 'several years of quiet, steady administration'.[35] His efforts paid off. By the end of his tenure in April 1955 the government proved successful in bringing an end to rationing, expanding the welfare state, maintaining good labour relations, largely denationalising transport and steel, and building almost 300,000 houses.[36]

All these political constraints contributed meaningfully to Churchill's reluctance to pursue British participation in a European union the way he had advocated in the years after the Zurich speech. No less importantly, the formulation of European policy in the first postwar Conservative administration was the product of a clash between different ideas about European unity and Britain's role in it.

On the one hand, Churchill and the Strasbourg Tories believed in principle in Britain's place as a European power as long as this did not preclude its having a role in its other spheres of influence. They still believed Britain could take the lead in an organic union of European states. On the other hand, the new foreign secretary, Anthony Eden, several other senior Cabinet ministers and the professionals at the Foreign Office believed Britain should stay away from genuine involvement in European integration, leaving the Continental powers to form a more integrated unit.

Eden, who had remained outside Churchill's European circles and shared little of his enthusiasm, was still a natural, desirable and almost inescapable appointment to lead the Foreign Office. He had already served as foreign secretary between 1935 and 1938 and from 1940 until 1945, was then Churchill's shadow foreign secretary and had been kept up to date on the intricacies of foreign policy by his friend Ernie Bevin.[37] Eden proved able to win the Prime Minister around to his point of view on Europe. He brought out the elements of Churchill's pre-war thinking, envisaging a role for Britain as a benevolent, slightly aloof neighbour to a federal continental Europe. Such thinking had all but disappeared on Churchill's part in the European campaign and the adventure of the Council of Europe.

Eden had always shown a certain disdain for the unofficial pressure groups that Churchill founded, chaired and attended, tending to believe, as Maxwell Fyfe put it, that 'it was all a "party stunt" of Winston's.'[38] While Churchill assumed the role of international statesman after the war, Eden tried to resuscitate the Conservative Party in the domestic arena.[39] Despite receiving repeated invitations from Churchill to join the campaign, he took little interest in the United Europe Movement and did not participate in the work of the European movement. At home, he did launch an assault on the Labour government in the Schuman Plan debate, which was the closest he came to outward sympathy for the European movement. Eden generally disregarded the proceedings of the Consultative Assembly in Strasbourg, leaving him largely clueless about the strength of European opinion in favour of integration. He resented the fact that Churchill, as leader of the Opposition, was running a powerful unofficial foreign policy in Europe while he, the shadow foreign secretary, was left to deal with the domestic consequences of Churchill's romantic enthusiasm for a revived Europe.[40]

Maxwell Fyfe lamented the consequences of Eden's self-exclusion from the European movement. 'The most conspicuous absentee from our party was Eden,' he wrote. 'I do not know why he did not participate [...] his exclusion was at least partly responsible for his subsequent hostility to the European Movement.'[41] With Eden there were other heavyweight Conservatives, some in senior Cabinet positions, who were far from convinced of the European cause. 'Salisbury [Lord Privy Seal] and – to my deep regret – Oliver Stanley, shared his prejudices to the full,' Maxwell Fyfe wrote.[42]

Looking at the surviving records we can see that within a month of Churchill's election, someone scribbled on a Foreign Office memorandum: 'Strasbourg was always a misfortune; it is now nearly a calamity.'[43] That was a shattering assessment of Churchill's proudest European achievement. Tragically, it was penned by Eden, Churchill's heir apparent and foreign policy guru – the very man he would now rely on to craft European policy. Eden's scepticism towards Strasbourg and a British role in European unification increased from there. In May 1952, against Churchill's wishes, Eden urged the Cabinet not to give any Parliamentary time at home to the Strasbourg Assembly's resolutions – a sign of antagonism that went far beyond the previous Labour government's refusal to take the Council of Europe seriously.[44] And in 1954, when Eden was asked to travel to the next meeting at Strasbourg, he shot a note back to the Foreign Office saying: 'I am astonished that I should be given this advice. Strasbourg is of no importance whatsoever.'[45]

In the first month of the new administration it emerged that Eden planned to pursue his line of European policy even where it was unclear the Cabinet fully supported him. On 21 November 1951, Churchill's choice to lead the UK delegation to the upcoming regular session of the Council of Europe, Home

Secretary Maxwell Fyfe, called a meeting to discuss how the new government would define and present its general attitude towards United Europe in Strasbourg. Parliamentary under-secretaries from almost every relevant department sat alongside a large contingent of officials from the Foreign Office that afternoon in his room in the Commons. Maxwell Fyfe steered the meeting towards a general agreement that the statement 'should be as positive as possible'.[46]

He recognised that the Schuman community and Pleven's European army were now in very different stages of development and could not quite be treated in the same way. The only feasible course of action for Britain with regard to the former seemed some type of association, not full membership, while the European army was still a far more sensitive, open-ended affair. Maxwell Fyfe thought there would have to be some sort of positive statement about Britain's intention to keep open the option of full participation in a scheme less restrictive than what Pleven had originally proposed.[47] It was clear early on that Churchill and his government would not support British entry into Pleven's EDC if the Community was to remain intent on combining with the Coal and Steel Community as the basis for short-term federation.

A day later, on 22 November, Maxwell Fyfe took his proposals to the first Cabinet meeting in which the subject of Europe arose under the new administration. With Housing Minister Macmillan and Maxwell Fyfe pitted against Foreign Secretary Eden for the first time, a compromise emerged in which Maxwell Fyfe would tell the Strasbourg Assembly that Britain could not accept complete federation but was still committed to finding other ways of full participation in Europe.[48] Though Maxwell Fyfe's speech was carefully calibrated not to commit the government to anything specific, it also adopted an encouragingly positive tone about what the new government would do to involve itself in Europe. 'No genuine method shall fail for lack of thorough examination,' he came to say in Strasbourg.[49] In a press conference after his speech, the Home Secretary further argued that Britain was 'not closing the door' on the European army: 'I made it plain that there is no refusal on the part of Britain.'[50]

On 28 November 1951, the day of Maxwell Fyfe's speech to the Assembly, Eden caused a real crisis by announcing at a press conference in Rome that under no circumstances would Britain contribute forces to the European army. Without the blessing of the Cabinet, Eden made his announcement in the full knowledge of what Maxwell Fyfe had said earlier that day.[51] Macmillan thought Eden 'unhelpful' and 'even contemptuous' in going brazenly against

Maxwell Fyfe just when the continentals were looking to the Conservatives to breathe new life into British leadership of Europe. Maxwell Fyfe remembered it, bitterly, as a 'personal humiliation' and a disastrous point of departure from which it would be difficult to recover.[52]

After Eden's statement, some of the British press seemed as disappointed with the direction of the government's European policy as the Strasbourg Tories. The *Manchester Guardian* reported after the Rome–Strasbourg incident: 'The European policy of the continental states is facing serious difficulties. Their solution depends to an almost frightening extent on this country. The United Kingdom seems unaware of it, though the Europeans and Americans are not.' The more conservative *Daily Express* wrote: 'The British government should stop acting as if it were plucking daisy petal to the tune of 'I love Europe – I love her not.'' It should state once and for all exactly where Great Britain stands on European union.'[53] Partly in response to this disappointment, Eden suggested privately to the Americans – NATO supreme commander Dwight Eisenhower and Secretary of State Dean Acheson – that Britain should seek 'institutional association' with the EDC. They agreed in principle that such a course might move the French deputies to ratify the treaty, but dissuaded Eden on the grounds that negotiations on association would take too long and thereby slow down German rearmament.[54] Eden later wrote that he had expected the disillusion on the Continent and among British Europeanists, but 'thought it better to make plain at once what we could not do'.[55]

Eisenhower noted in his diary after Eden's statements in Rome that from every side in Europe he was getting 'complaints reference Britain's attitude towards a European army'.[56] Some Europeans took those complaints directly to Churchill. On 29 November, the French ex-premier Paul Reynaud, still a prominent member of the Strasbourg Assembly, took up his pen to ask Churchill directly about the vague British position on the European army. 'I owe it to my old friendship for England [...] to tell you of the anxiety and trouble provoked by the attitude of your Government on the subject of European Army,' he began. He pointed out that British aloofness would strengthen pockets of French opinion against merging military forces in western Europe and that Eden's statement at Rome contradicted both Maxwell Fyfe's at Strasbourg and Churchill's own 1950 resolution for a European army with British participation. Reynaud believed a decision from Churchill not to partake in a European army would disagree 'with what Europe and the world expects from one of the big figures of history'.[57] In response,

Churchill simply and rightly pointed out that he never advocated a full integration of armies at the lowest levels: 'we must not lose sight of the military realities.'[58]

The Strasbourg Tories reacted to Eden's statement in Rome with a fervent letter demanding 'positive action' on European unification from Prime Minister Churchill 'to show that His Majesty's Government mean to play their part in the military defence and economic development of a united Europe'.[59] Julian Amery and Bob Boothby, amongst others, pointed to the incomprehensible gap between what Maxwell Fyfe and Eden had said in different European cities on the same day and described it as 'a shattering blow' to the European cause. They hoped Churchill would realise the degree of hope generated by his return to office and act accordingly.[60]

Ten days later they received a nondescript reply in a letter drafted by the Foreign Office, after Eden countered their arguments and told Churchill the Strasbourg letter was 'inaccurate both in detail and in emphasis'.[61] While Eden was in fact right to argue that both he and Maxwell Fyfe rejected the federal path to unity, it was also true that the Cabinet approved Maxwell Fyfe's more positive view of the possibility of British membership in an amended structure; it did not approve of an actively hostile approach.

By this time, however, Churchill had publicly given his own views on the EDC and Britain's attitude towards it. He was persuaded of Eden's preference for allowing the continental six to develop a geographically limited federation – a policy he had previously opposed. On 6 December 1951, Churchill told the Commons that 'most of us agreed that there should be a European Army and that Germany must take an honourable place in it.' He recalled his own contributions in Strasbourg on the matter and expressed his satisfaction with the progress made since then. He was happy to report that Adenauer reassured him a few days earlier that the German preference was still 'no national army'. Deeply sceptical of Pleven's specific design for the EDC, however, he ridiculed it thus:

> Should it be an amalgam of the European nations divested of all national characteristics and traditions, or should it be composed of elements essentially national but woven together by alliance, common organisation and unified command? On this point the discussions have at times assumed an almost metaphysical character, and the logic of continental minds has produced a scheme for what is called the European Defence Community. That is, at least, an enlightened if not an inspiring title.

As with the Schuman Plan, Churchill also still regretted Labour's decision not to negotiate on the EDC treaty with Britain's continental partners and that

Britain 'had no voice or share in the long argument'. As far as Britain was concerned, and here was the key, Churchill said he did not 'propose to merge in the European Army but we are already joined to it'. The 'metaphysical character' of the continental structure under discussion was not feasible for his own country. He was waiting for the Paris conference to produce a final settlement and until that time he argued Britain could do no more than wait and promise its own contribution alongside the European army in the defence of European democracy.[62]

The Rome–Strasbourg incident had two further consequences. First, desperate and frustrated about Britain's refusal to lead the way, Paul-Henri Spaak was moved to resign as president of the Strasbourg Assembly, heralding Belgium's wholehearted turn to the more radical federalist ambitions of the French. Second, the Cabinet Office was moved to circulate a short paper written by Churchill that week entitled 'United Europe'. It set out his thinking, contrasting with the French proposals for short-term federation, and catering to the sensitivities of some of his more Euro-agnostic or even openly hostile ministers. 'I never thought Britain or the British Commonwealth should,' he wrote, 'either individually or collectively, become an integral part of a European Federation.' That much was by now becoming obvious to the Cabinet and to the rest of Europe. As he had made clear many times before, Churchill held the middle ground between the do-nothings and the federalists. In Europe as at home he was a 'Unionist' – the difference being that the European union did not yet exist: he hoped it would be brought about organically.

Churchill also repeated in the memo his view that the European union he envisaged was one which made allowances for Britain's ambition to play a role of importance in the great intersecting circles of the West: the Empire and Commonwealth, the 'English-speaking world' and United Europe. How exactly this would work was unclear to him. Most likely he either wanted Britain to become an 'extraordinary' member of whatever political structure emerged in Europe with a special position and special exemptions, or the entire union to be formed on foundations acceptable to Britain. As such, Churchill explained to his Cabinet that he steadfastly resisted the American propensity to treat Britain 'on the same footing as the European states, none of whom have the advantages of the Channel and who were consequently conquered'. In his view, Britain took an exceptional place in the world and was far more than just the leading European power.

On the European Coal and Steel Community, he returned to his argument that the Labour government should have entered the negotiations for the

Schuman Plan. He welcomed it as 'probably rendering another Franco-German war impossible' but 'never contemplated Britain joining in this plan on the same terms as Continental partners'. A British presence at the negotiating table in June 1950, however, would have ensured that 'a better plan would have emerged'.

On the European army, Churchill offered another clear-cut piece of analysis. Based on the assumption that there could be no effective defence of western Europe without the Germans, he wrote: 'As things developed my idea has always been as follows: There is the N.A.T.O. Army. Inside the N.A.T.O. Army there is the European Army, and inside the European Army there is the Germany Army.' Britain and all the rest, including Germany, would contribute divisions from their national armies to fight in the European army. Rather than accepting Pleven's federalist idea of merging forces at the lowest levels, sinking national fighting forces into a non-existent European identity, Churchill wanted to use the benign effects of national spirit for an international force. 'The national characteristics should be preserved up to the divisional level,' he wrote. '[O]n this basis and within these limits national pride may be made to promote and serve international strength.'[63]

Eden and Churchill thus agreed that Britain was in no position to join a federal union. As Eden put it to an American audience in January 1952: 'This is something which we know, in our bones, we cannot do.'[64] In the same speech he declared that Britain would instead 'merge wholeheartedly in associations for common purposes among the European Governments, when control remains in the hands of Governments'.[65]

On their first trip to the United States in Churchill's peacetime administration, Eden and the Prime Minister arrived by boat in Brooklyn on the morning of 5 January 1952. US President Truman had his personal plane pick up the British and fly them to Washington, where on the first night of the visit he planned to entertain Churchill on his yacht the *Williamsburg*. The Prime Minister felt right at home cruising the river Potomac and brought out one of his favourite party tricks. He asked for the dimensions of the dining saloon and ordered the Prof, still in Churchill's inner circle, to calculate how high it would be filled with all the liquid alcohol he had ever consumed – a quart, on average, a day. The result, of course, was then a vast disappointment. Rather than submerging everyone in champagne, the Prof reported the guests would only be wet up to the knees.[66]

In the spirit of convivial absurdity, the Prime Minister later that evening painted a devastating picture of EDC functioning with 'a bewildered French drill sergeant sweating over a platoon made up of a few Greeks, Italians, Germans, Turks and Dutchmen, all in utter confusion over the simplest orders'.[67] US Secretary of State Acheson wrote that while Churchill was off the mark in his military assessment – EDC would also create national units in the form of divisions – Churchill could still be persuaded to help the French ratify even though 'at heart he did not approve of it.'[68]

In discussions with President Truman three days later, Churchill reiterated more seriously the broader point that Britain would not participate in a European federation. He also affirmed his general support for a European army. The American minutes of the meeting read in part:

> He [Churchill] saw no reasons why the British divisions could not serve temporarily in the midst of the European forces. That, he considered, was only a tactical matter. Whether or not these divisions are organically a part of the EDC is immaterial. Mr Churchill reaffirmed that the UK would do everything within its power to encourage the European army even though he personally still thought that the 'national spirit element' was most important.[69]

Two days later, meeting with American journalists in New York over luncheon, Churchill came back to his reticence about the Pleven plans for a multinational army. Moran was there to record the conversation in his diary. 'I have been doubtful about a European army only because I was concerned with its fighting power,' Churchill said. 'It will not fight if you remove all traces of nationalism. I love France and Belgium, but we cannot be reduced to that level.'[70] On 14 January, having travelled to Ottawa for a banquet given by the Canadian government, Churchill took away any Canadian fears that Britain might 'become a unit in a federated Europe' or that the British army would 'be merged in such a way as to lose its identity'.[71]

Churchill was concerned with building up 'deterrents against a World War Three' and wanted to focus on bolstering combined military might on the European front rather than haggle over the precise methods of 'fusion, or melding'. In fact, as he put it in his third address to a joint session of the United States Congress at the end of his visit to America: 'I cannot accept the slightest reproach from any quarter that we are not doing our full duty because the British Commonwealth of Nations, spread all over the world, is not prepared to become a state or a group of states in any Continental federal system on either side of the Atlantic.'[72]

The United States government then actively sought to push Britain towards bringing about the tight-knit integration of the continental six, even if it meant Britain itself would not be able to participate. After realising that a

British offer of membership would delay and complicate the mounting of a European army, the Americans, especially Acheson, pressed on Churchill the commitments entered into under Labour in the September 1951 Washington Declaration, which stated Britain's dedication to developing 'the closest possible association with the European Continental Community at all stages of its development.'[73] The result was an Anglo-American communiqué pledging Britain's full support and assistance in making a success of the Paris Treaty on the European Defence Community. 'Let the communiqué sing we are all in favour of a European Army,' Churchill had uttered, still unconvinced that EDC would have the necessary fighting spirit.[74]

The French idea of creating rigidly supranational communities for defence and the heavy industries was incompatible with Churchill's broad brushstrokes of organic union; of a concerted, democratic act of goodwill; of reconciliation as a condition for constitution-making rather than vice versa. Churchill therefore told Leo Amery that he was 'uncommitted to any immediate form of federation' but generally agreed with Amery's phrase '"if we cannot become full members we might be co-operative neighbours"'.[75] This was the policy ultimately followed in Churchill's peacetime administration, copying Attlee's before it. But judging by the many private and public statements Churchill and several of his Cabinet ministers made in favour of British participation in a European union in the late 1940s it was not the preferred option. Unilateral association was only pursued after the continental states invited Britain into the sort of federal structure that was unacceptable to Britain's global interests.

The key difference between Churchill and the sceptics was that the latter were unenthusiastic about the prospect of ceding *any* sovereignty, now or in the future, to the kind of looser British-led, confederal union that Churchill's Europeanists envisaged emerging. Primarily Atlanticist in outlook, Eden and many others first looked to America's broad shoulders for British power and security. As Eden put it to Boothby: 'The difference between us is that you are a European animal, whereas I am an Atlantic animal.'[76] A similar thing could have been said of Churchill, half-American by birth and wholly convinced of the importance of the relationship with the United States. Equally, however, he was as passionate a European as anyone else in the movement towards unity he helped build after the war.

Peter Thorneycroft, the president of the Board of Trade under Churchill and one of the younger supporters of a move forward into Europe, drew a sharp distinction between the Prime Minister and his Foreign Secretary in an interview with the BBC:

> Churchill was a European. He had it in his mind – in his heart, at any rate – that he would have liked to bring a great group of nations together [...] I was at the Hague Conference after the war, and the reception he got! He was a god-like figure in Europe. Here was the man who, at that time, really was the saviour of Europe, and the Europeans would have gone almost anywhere he asked them to go. This was the Churchill attitude. Anthony Eden did not feel *any* of that at all. He was really opposed to it. He and the Foreign Office believed that we should maintain a special relationship with the United States.[77]

Jock Colville, himself not a committed 'European' in any way, perhaps put it best when he said understatedly that Churchill 'thought that close union with Europe was very important, but I do not think he ever saw within, shall we say, living experience the end of the nation state'.[78] Churchill had on several occasions expounded the general idea that sovereignty could be diminished for the sake of union in Europe, but federation remained a clear no-go area for a nation straddling three great circles of power. Churchill failed to reconcile intellectually or confront practically the implications of increasingly closer union in Europe. On top of that, he gave the matter little serious thought at the end of his life. Duncan Sandys told Lady Violet in 1959, when at a party she asked what happened to European policy in Churchill's second administration, that his father-in-law never really understood it all. 'He didn't understand it & Anthony was strongly against it.' Lady Violet agreed in her diary: 'W[inston] was too old to grasp the *practical* implication of his own idea, & the F.O. – which hates *all* new ideas, led by Anthony – who never liked this one, sabotaged it. A real tragedy.'[79]

Partly Churchill did little to shape Europe in a mould acceptable to him because he had now lost much of his zest and determination to old age. He battled back from his stroke in France after the 1949 Assembly session and a spasm in February 1950 but was unable turn back time itself.[80] To many, not least his wife, it had been a foolish proposition in the first place to return to Downing Street. Even in the very early days of his administration, Churchill's friends and political allies were worried his age began to have a disconcerting effect on his statesmanship. On 15 November 1951 Bob Boothby told a friend after seeing Churchill that he was getting 'very, very old; tragically old.'[81]

Around the same time, Ian Jacob, who had been in Turkey with Churchill when he dictated his 'Morning Thoughts' and was now back working under Churchill, reflected in a private note: 'He no longer read and mastered papers or sent out his scintillating minutes [...] He could still muster his recourse for a big occasion but the humdrum slog of daily business bored him.'[82] West German Chancellor Adenauer and his trusted aide Blankenhorn, too, found Churchill worryingly fragile. Blankenhorn wrote in December 1951 after a visit to London: 'his manner of speaking is jerky, sometimes stuttering, hesitating, undecided, then suddenly four or five sentences come together in an impressive construction.'[83] In the same month, the French president, Vincent Auriol, was disheartened to see in Churchill 'a man whose hearing is poor and who often repeats himself'.[84]

Churchill's depleted energy diminished his ability to work out the specifics of the issues he cared about. Anthony Montague Browne, Churchill's last private secretary, thought his boss was 'too old to undertake a crusade of such major proportions as United Europe, with his Foreign Secretary and heir apparent opposed to him'.[85] Similarly, Sandys thought the Prime Minister 'dazed and unable to realise the degree of the disillusionment throughout Europe'.[86]

By April 1952, Churchill admitted to being 'extremely tired' and told Eden that it would not be long before he gave up.[87] Then, in June 1953, Churchill suffered a major stroke after giving a post-dinner speech for the Italian prime minister and co-patron of the European movement, Alcide De Gasperi. The details were deliberately and successfully covered up and heralded a period in which Churchill first held on for dear life and then was seriously diminished in his capacities until the end of his premiership – a stretch in which Anthony Eden at one point remarked that the Prime Minister was 'gaga'.[88]

Eden stepped in where Churchill failed to take a serious initiative on British alternatives to French federalist plans. On 11 December 1951, perhaps responding to the Strasbourg demands for positive action, Churchill proposed for the first and only time to the Cabinet to attempt to amend the Schuman and Pleven proposals along non-federalist lines. This was the opportunity the two pro-European Cabinet ministers in Churchill's government, Macmillan and Maxwell Fyfe, had been waiting for.

Churchill said he wanted to turn EDC into a permanently integrated European force akin in structure to the one that fought the Germans in World War II. He read out a letter from Field Marshal Montgomery in which the author explained his opposition to the European army as it was emerging in EDC – a viewpoint with which Churchill naturally declared himself 'in general agreement'.[89] Churchill's idea of a SHAEF-like alliance would include Britain. But before the ministers in favour of British interference in the

Defence Community could embolden Churchill to give a lead, Eden squashed the idea.

The Foreign Secretary argued forcefully in Cabinet that the British would be accused of 'sabotage' and any attempt at changing continental plans for short-term federation would endanger the stability of Europe.[90] He touted the Foreign Office line that the British could only step in with other plans if and when the Pleven Plan failed. Eden defeated Churchill and the pro-European ministers, and successfully avoided a merger between them.[91]

A day later, on 12 December, Churchill received what he characterised as a 'very good and sober letter' from Boothby asking him to step up and lead an organic union of Europe while it was still possible to intervene in continental developments. Boothby described the view of a European union arising out of the Council of Europe that Churchill had advocated in previous years. He wrote:

> In the early days of our movement you told me that the idea would either catch on, or it would not; and that, if it caught on, nothing – in the long run – could stop it. I believe this to be profoundly true. There can no longer be any doubt that, in continental Europe it has caught on; and that, in the course of time, the Committee of Ministers will become the executive authority for the conduct of purely European affairs, and the Consultative Assembly an effective forum of European opinion – with powers of suggestion, criticism and stimulation over the whole field.[92]

Churchill felt a pang of embarrassment about his diminished engagement with Strasbourg on reading the letter and decided to approach Eden. As prime minister, Churchill felt 'distressed at the way things have gone a Strasbourg' and took the blame: 'I did not feel able either to go there myself or to send a message.' A more damning condemnation of the current government's policy could not have been written by anyone else than Churchill himself: 'We seem in fact to have succumbed to the Socialist Party hostility to United Europe.'[93]

Eden was unimpressed and responded with a memorandum drawn up by the Foreign Office explaining his policy of committing to the purely collaborative NATO (defence) and the OEEC (economics) – essentially what Bevin had done in the late 1940s.[94] The Foreign Secretary was also openly combative about Boothby's letter. 'I am afraid that I do not agree with your estimate of Boothby's letter,' he told the Prime Minister. 'He mentions, and by implication supports, the "creation of an organic union of European under British leadership." This sounds all right but what does it mean?'[95]

Eden thought it could only mean entering into a federation in the short term. For Churchill it meant advocating the idea of gradualist growth and a dynamism lacking in the purely cooperative ventures set up under Labour as well as the supranational communities emerging on the continent. In either case, the Prime Minister decided against pushing the point. On the narrower issue at stake he repeated that he was 'in general agreement' with Eden that British defences could not be merged into a European federal system.[96]

The crux was that Churchill wanted Britain to contribute to a European army constituted on the lines he and Sandys proposed at Strasbourg in 1950. But in the early days of Churchill's administration, his Cabinet was largely hostile to the idea of fighting for anything like that. John Young, in his seminal article on Churchill's European policy in the peacetime administration, argued that by mid-December 1951 'Eden had defeated both the pro-Europeans and Churchill's desires to intervene in E.D.C.'[97]

Then, during a meeting with Robert Schuman and his aides in Paris on 17 December 1951, it also came to light that Churchill had given up on the idea of full British participation in a reformed Schuman community for heavy industries. The Prime Minister opened by reminding Schuman of his efforts to press Bevin into participating in the negotiations on the coal and steel pool and that he still wished Britain had joined under more favourable conditions. But there was no offer of a reversal of Labour's policy, no new ideas to break the impasse, only the general 'desire to co-operate to the fullest possible extent'.[98]

Further, Churchill told the Cabinet on 19 December that the communiqué issued after his visit to Paris made it clear that 'the United Kingdom Government favoured the creation of a European Defence Community, though they could not join it, and that they were ready to associate themselves with it as closely as possible in all stages of its political and military development'. That encouraging attitude, Churchill anticipated, would 'forestall any further suggestion that the delay in securing agreement to the creation of a European Army was due to the unhelpful attitude of the United Kingdom Government'.[99]

The French accepted the British position and were content with the statement. Certainly Churchill also pleased the American general Dwight D. Eisenhower, who was stationed just outside of Paris in his capacity as NATO commander. The General saw EDC as an essential prop to NATO and thought the communiqué was a 'very fine statement' of British support. But Eisenhower, who met with Churchill while in Paris, privately was unprepared to believe that the Prime Minister's heart was in the constitutional, federal approach to mounting a European army.[100]

A meaningful strain of resistance to British non-participation in Europe came from Macmillan in the early months of 1952. The European Coal and Steel Community was now nearly an established fact – it formally went into force in August 1952 – but EDC was still in difficulties as the French were looking for more Anglo-American guarantees. On 16 January, when Churchill was travelling in the United States, Macmillan sought to win Cabinet for a different approach to Europe. Pointing out that federation was not the only form of integration between states, he advocated for a kind of European Commonwealth. 'Britain, with the full support of the Commonwealth,' he wrote, 'might join with a European Union or Confederation organised on similar lines.' He saw Britain emerging as a leader of that confederation, allowing it to even out the relationship with the United States and face the Soviet Union on equal terms. The British government, he declared, should announce a policy embracing 'the kind of European Union which we should be prepared to join'. It would then be for the continental nations to choose between federation without Britain or union with Britain.[101]

Macmillan rebelled in Cabinet again when Eden announced he would travel to Strasbourg for the first time to present what became known as the 'Eden Plan'. On 29 February Macmillan submitted a memorandum to Eden and the Cabinet proposing the third way approach: 'confederal' alternatives to the French schemes for defence and heavy industries which allowed British membership from the start. Macmillan recognised that Britain could not join a federation but argued correctly that it had been Churchill's goal since the war to create a 'European *Community*' with Britain as a founding member and asked Eden to propose such a course to his colleagues on the Continent.[102] The Foreign Secretary ignored the request.

A few weeks later, Macmillan expressed his hope that the Council of Europe would be able to incorporate the continental plans for federation, allowing all member states represented in the Assembly to discuss and vote on their policies. The Eden Plan – nominally designed to involve Britain more closely in Europe through the Council of Europe – was far less ambitious. Eden wanted to give the emerging Schuman and Pleven communities the option of using the facilities of the Council of Europe without actually allowing the remaining members to discuss or vote on anything relating to their business. In other words, he wanted the organs of the Council of Europe to become institutions of the Schuman and Pleven communities.[103] Peter Thorneycroft called the plan mere 'window dressing'.[104]

Macmillan thought it was a counterproductive proposition. He told the Cabinet as much in a counter-piece in the first week of March. But Eden ultimately triumphed in the Cabinet discussions of the rival plans on 12 and 13 March and won authorisation to present the Eden Plan on behalf of the British government in Strasbourg.[105] It was Salisbury who, on the second day of the discussions, did most to make the argument that Britain could never enter a European union of states.[106] Maxwell Fyfe did little to put his weight in the balance for Macmillan. Prime Minister Churchill was a silent observer in all this, noting at the end as if he were a neutral presiding officer that Macmillan's resistance would be on record.[107] Macmillan took his defeat heavily. He seriously considered resigning, sounding out the views of senior officials in the Treasury and the Foreign Office about such a course, but eventually stayed on, he later claimed, out of loyalty to Churchill.[108]

On 17 March, Macmillan tried once more to fire Churchill's imagination, this time bypassing Eden and the Cabinet and pleading directly with the Prime Minister. 'As I see it,' Macmillan wrote in a note, 'it is only by adding the leadership of Europe to our natural leadership of the Empire that we can bring to bear [...] the influence on world affairs which should be ours.'[109] The Prime Minister had neither the energy nor the will to take the argument to Eden. He replied to Macmillan that he had referred the matter to the Foreign Secretary but doubted 'we can do any more than he is now planning.'[110] Churchill, at this point at least, was content to leave European policy to Eden.

As Churchill expected, Eden stuck to his line, arguing that Britain would have to let continental Europe pursue its constitutional adventures in peace. He wanted the Schuman and Pleven plans to succeed without Britain, telling Churchill what was the essence of his policy: 'On balance I had rather see France and Germany in confused but close embrace than at arm's length even though we think can better influence events that way.'[111] Churchill lost much of his interest in the argument and scribbled on Eden's letter a summary of what the Foreign Secretary proposed and what Salisbury said in Cabinet: '"with" not "in"'.[112] Macmillan never received a further reply, and on the afternoon of 27 May 1952 the EDC was signed in Paris without Britain. Churchill, focused only on the broad policy of getting an effective defence contribution from West Germany, sent Eden a telegram on behalf of the Cabinet to congratulate him.[113]

Even if Churchill had become weaker in old age, he was still the untouchable statesman standing miles above any of his Cabinet ministers in terms of national popularity. If he had willed it passionately, surely he could have bulldozed the Cabinet. But there were limits to his interest, influence and what he could ask of Eden, who had even by 1951 been waiting for a long time in Churchill's shadow to take over. 'He had a bit of a conscience,' said Churchill's parliamentary private secretary, Christopher Soames, 'that he perhaps should not have taken the Premiership in 1951.'[114] Similarly, Eden's principal private secretary said that one of his own main concerns during his tenure had been Eden's 'constant anxiety about the premiership' and 'impatience with the Prime Minister for staying on'.[115]

To be fair to his designated successor, Churchill had to give him the leeway to shape some of the decisions on Britain's future place in the world, including its role in Europe, which did not feature at the top of the agenda of things they disagreed about. Churchill's 'inherent constitutionalism', Eden's main political protégé Anthony Nutting argued, informed his wish not to 'saddle his chosen successor with a policy of which Eden disapproved'.[116] Nutting remembered tackling Churchill on the issue of Europe and the Prime Minister saying that he could not carry Britain to a greater extent into Europe for fear of 'embarrassing Anthony when he succeeds me as Prime Minister'. Nutting said Churchill told him: 'I hoped that by the time we got into office there would be some British participation in a European community [...] and that it would have developed before Anthony actually took office as Prime Minister.'[117] Anthony Montague Browne wrote about Churchill, Eden and Europe: 'WSC said that he had quite enough over which to fall out with Anthony Eden, without adding an issue that was not of urgent importance, and he was unwilling to receive delegations on the subject.'[118]

Still, even then, Churchill might have expected to rely on the energy of the Strasbourg Tories to shape the Cabinet's policy on Europe. Macmillan and Maxwell Fyfe, however, did not have the unity of purpose to be successful, while Sandys, Eccles and Boothby, holding junior positions, were far removed from the heart of power. Maxwell Fyfe recalled that the pro-Europeans in the Cabinet were simply 'powerless in the face of the enormous authority of Eden and Churchill', but offered no further explanation.[119] Macmillan, who was most determined in his resistance, justified his own failure with his need for 'an active alliance with No. 10 and at least the benevolent neutrality of the Foreign Office' to accomplish his ambitious task of building 300,000 houses.[120]

It was also helpful to Eden's cause that he succeeded in largely avoiding Churchill and the Cabinet in the making of foreign policy. A month into the administration, Eden had attended just one Cabinet meeting to discuss his plans.[121] When the Cabinet did discuss foreign affairs, often issues were discussed that required more urgent attention, such as the uprising in Malaya, the surge of African nationalism, the Korean ceasefire, war in Indochina, and the Persian oil dispute.[122] In the first month of his administration, when perhaps the more enthusiastic Europeans had hoped for some sort of positive action, Churchill proved especially prone to focus his attention on the armistice negotiations for the ongoing Korean War.[123] A little bit later, in the early months of 1952, Churchill's main concern in foreign policy was Egypt, quarrelling with Eden about the Foreign Secretary's argument that withdrawal of British troops from Suez was necessary to secure a peaceful settlement.[124]

Eden seems to have had few qualms about being left to his own devices. Once, after dinner with the British ambassador in Moscow when the Tories were still in opposition, Eden said the one thing he wanted to do was help advance Bevin's foreign policy agenda. He made no bones about being relieved Churchill was not there to disagree: 'Fortunately,' he told his Moscow hosts, 'Winston is away.'[125] Presumably it was for similar reasons that Eden resisted any attempt on Churchill's part to give him a Europe minister. Right when the new government was formed, Churchill sat Eden down and said: 'I want you to have a Minister of European Affairs, and I suggest this should be Duncan [Sandys].' Knowing what it would have meant to have Churchill's European bulldog barking at his heels at his every turn, Eden refused to accept the arrangement, saying there was no need to have such a minister and that he wanted his own Foreign Office adjutants to serve him in European affairs.[126]

This had been the second major blow to Sandys in the early days of the new administration, and a hugely significant setback for the Europeanists. Churchill had originally wanted to appoint Sandys as his secretary of state for war, working directly under the Prime Minister in his own dual capacity of minister of defence. That would have given Sandys a greater platform to push for the kind of European army he envisaged at Strasbourg. But Clemmie dissuaded Churchill from appointing his son-in-law for fear of upsetting familial peace. 'If anything were to go wrong,' she wrote, 'it would be delicate and tricky – first of all having to defend your son-in-law and later if by chance he made a mistake having to dismiss him.'[127] In his eventual non-Cabinet post of minister of supply, Sandys was much further removed from the heart of power.

Significantly, the Foreign Office and its most senior officials were sceptical of British participation in a European union. Eden got on well, both personally and ideologically, with Pierson Dixon, an influential deputy under-secretary who had served Eden as one of his principal aides during the war. Dixon was responsible for formulating the Foreign Office's policy ahead of talks on European integration with the French in December 1951. In his summary, he wrote that Britain would support federation 'short of actual membership', for it simply could not cede 'control of policy to any European supranational authority'.[128] The government, following its foreign policy officials in a continuation of Labour's European policy, would not put forth alternative forms of union allowing for British membership. On the eve of the visit to Paris, Eden drafted a memorandum clarifying British policy. He wrote that once plans for uniting Europe took a federal form, 'we cannot ourselves take part'. Rather, the government would 'continue to play our full part in plans for uniting national efforts on an intergovernmental basis'. He promised also to consider British association with plans for European integration.[129]

Then there was Roger Makins, the most powerful deputy under-secretary, who had an outspoken preference for strengthening Anglo-American relations and the Commonwealth, and actively encouraged Eden to neglect Europe.[130] Makins argued in a memorandum on British foreign policy that Britain would support the countries of western Europe 'short of entering into an organic relationship with all or any of them'.[131] Geoffrey McDermott, who was then at the Foreign Office, later accused his colleagues of handling European integration not only with traditional reserve but with a lack of seriousness. 'The attitude was that we were still the impregnable island centre of a great Empire, enjoying our special relationship with the United States,' he wrote, 'and the curious new bodies in Europe must wait.'[132]

The pro-European ministers and backbenchers who lost out in the equation ended up with few good things to say about the man in charge at the Foreign Office. Macmillan wrote in his diary in December 1951: 'Eden is a queer man [...] he is almost childishly jealous – hence his dislike for me, for David Fyfe, for Sandys and for all of us who have dared to show an interest in foreign affairs.'[133] Maxwell Fyfe later wrote in a biting assessment: 'his absence from the meetings of the Council of Europe in those exciting and very moving months of its existence was a great misfortune for himself, Europe, the Conservative Party, and the cause of world peace.'[134] Boothby concluded even more harshly: 'In the end, the combination of vanity with stupidity proved to be invincible.'[135]

These, of course, were the bitter views of defeated politicians. It is a dangerous oversimplification of history to cast Eden as a villain. In reality, he was a spectacularly intelligent, skilful diplomat and a fundamentally decent politician who cared deeply about the future of his country and the world. His second tenure at the Foreign Office under Churchill was widely perceived to be a success, presiding over what *The Times* at the time understood to be 'one of its [British foreign policy] most successful periods in modern history'.[136] What is more, Eden himself broadly shared Churchill's emphasis on the 'three circles' of British power. As he put it at the Conservative Party conference in 1948: 'Our foreign policy should pursue three immediate objectives, which we can call the three unities. First, unity within the British Commonwealth and Empire. Second, unity within Western Europe. Third, unity across the Atlantic.'[137]

On matters European, too, Eden had initially perhaps not been as indifferent as some of the Strasbourg Tories later claimed. His main political protégé, Anthony Nutting, remembered in his memoirs that Eden was deeply disturbed by the Labour government's decision to stay away from the Schuman Plan. 'As we paced up and down the garden,' Nutting wrote, 'he [Eden] kept repeating, "This folly will divide us deeply from our friends. Twice before in my lifetime we turned our backs on Europe and look what happened – two world wars. I hoped we had learnt our lesson"'.[138] Eden also shared with Churchill what he later, in his memoirs, called 'our English preference for taking our changes in doses rather than at a gulp'.[139] This was the attitude that partly determined their shared rejection of British participation in a federal union.

The problem for Churchill was, as Eden's parliamentary private secretary said about the difference in views towards Europe: 'there was an element of distaste, in Eden, for this whole *emotional* approach towards it.'[140] Eden, who had been upstaged in opposition by the idealistic views of his boss and other party notables, did not buy into the spiritual, romantic idea of Europe – the backbone of Churchill's postwar European campaign.[141] Returning to the Foreign Office, Eden's more pragmatic ideas, sceptical of the feasibility of British leadership in European integration, prevailed. Rather than pursue his wish to compromise the continental community's federal solutions, Churchill ceded to the view that perhaps Britain could maintain influence in western Europe through some form of association. For this to happen, the Schuman and Pleven communities would have to succeed.

CHAPTER 12

'EXACTLY WHAT I SUGGESTED AT STRASBOURG'
EUROPEAN DEFENCE, 1952–1955

Churchill showed little to no interest in European unification after it became clear to the world that his administration was unlikely to alter existing British policy on European integration. As before, European policy-making was left almost entirely to Eden, who announced on 5 February 1952 the government's intention to set up a permanent delegation at the seat of Schuman's coal and steel pool and to associate as closely as possible with Pleven's EDC.[1] This meant no participation in Europe but support for integration on the continent.

After preliminary talks between British representatives and Jean Monnet, who became the president of Schuman's High Authority, and further discussions in 1954, the British government and the European Coal and Steel Community established a Council of Association. This became a conduit for consultation and, where appropriate, coordination between the continental six and Britain. Churchill never devoted any real attention to the negotiations.

In matters of defence, which after the outbreak of the Korean War dominated discussions of European unity, Churchill's government and Churchill personally took a far more active interest. Intent on achieving German rearmament, Foreign Secretary Eden went to great lengths to help bring the treaty negotiations on EDC to a conclusion. This was both welcome and necessary for the French, whose general attitude was 'if you British want us to get into bed with the Germans, then you British must be the bolster!'[2]

Initially, the British association Eden sought with the defence community was too weak in the eyes of French Foreign Secretary Robert Schuman. According to Eden, Schuman 'was always coming back to get a little more of what wanted, and he usually did'.[3] As such, in March 1952, the EDC countries asked Britain to enter into an Anglo-EDC Treaty, which would obligate Britain to come to the defence of any member under attack. Eden, unsure whether this would lead Britain into a federation through the back door, brought the question to Cabinet, which accepted the principle of a mutual defence clause.[4] The British government thus offered association to EDC until 1969 – the year NATO nominally expired – involving itself not in a federation but committing to meaningful defence guarantees. This, Eden told Schuman, 'was the absolute limit to which my country could go'.[5]

Prime Minister Churchill still suspected that the defence community, in its quest to constrain Germany and dilute the national armies of western Europe, would lack the chutzpah necessary to fight a war. He needed European armies in good shape in order to achieve what became his central foreign policy objective of achieving some kind of easement with the Soviet Union from a position of strength. For a prime minister intent on strength through unity in Europe, however, Churchill was often rash about the possible consequences of pursuing German rearmament. On 6 May 1952, over dinner with the French ambassador, René Massigli, who was close to General de Gaulle, Churchill said: 'Germany must be given fair play: if France would not co-operate we, America and Germany must go forward without her.' Without France integrated into a Western system of defence, surely, the position of the Soviet Union in the Cold War would be greatly enhanced. Churchill, Colville reported in his diary after dinner, wanted to see 'British, American, German and French contingents march past him at Strasbourg, each to their own national songs: in creating international unity, national marching songs could play a great part.'[6] That, by now, was a familiar theme.

Shortly thereafter, it seemed the Prime Minister had little reason to worry about French willingness to give Germany fair play. France was still disappointed that Britain would not come in as a full member, but started practical talks with British military staff to associate British forces with those of the Community.[7] On 26 May 1952, after a weekend of difficult talks in the West German capital of Bonn, the Allies concluded what became known as the Bonn Conventions, ending the postwar occupation statute and restoring West German control over internal affairs and foreign policy. 'I found it a strange experience,' Eden later wrote. 'After two world wars which had filled my life, I was signing with a German in Germany a document which gave the greater part of the country a control of its affairs once again.'[8] The Bonn Conventions made possible the official signing of the treaty for the most ambitious project in the history of European integration. On 27 May, the foreign ministers of West Germany, Italy, Belgium, Luxembourg, the Netherlands and France gathered in the Salon de l'Horloge of the Quai d'Orsay to sign the EDC Treaty.

Not everyone in Britain was happy or confident about EDC's prospects for implementation. Harold Macmillan wrote in his diary on 30 May:

> The E.D.C. and the German agreements [Bonn Conventions] and the whole complex of undertakings and guarantees have been successfully negotiated – a great triumph for Eden. But I do not think they will be ratified by the French or German parliaments. Will this be a disaster, or does it give Britain another chance?[9]

Equally, Churchill did almost nothing to apply himself to the complex continental negotiations and continued to harbour intuitive suspicions. The Prime Minister would often warn bluntly in subsequent years that if France did not end up ratifying the agreement, the West would proceed without France. In December 1952 he told the Cabinet that he did not care if EDC collapsed altogether.[10]

Nevertheless, from the signing of the EDC treaty in May 1952 onwards, official British policy was to help its signatories ratify it in domestic parliaments as quickly as possible. The Americans, with a clear preference for the federal approach taken by the continentals, continued moving Churchill to accept, at least publicly, the position of outside encouragement. This was especially true after General Eisenhower, a Republican with deep European experience, won the presidency in a landslide in November 1952. Eisenhower had said at the Guildhall in 1951 that Churchill's role in the unification of Europe might 'prove to be the crowning achievement in a career crowned by achievement'.[11]

The new US president brought a number of important pro-Europeans to senior positions in his cabinet. Most significantly, John Foster Dulles became Eden's counterpart as secretary of state. He was an ardent supporter of the emerging supranational community, convinced that 'the prevention of war between neighbouring nations which have a long record of fighting cannot be dependably achieved merely by national promises or threats, but only by merging certain functions of their government into supranational institutions.'[12] Old Jean Monnet himself could not have put it better.

Travelling through Europe in February 1953, when still none of the EDC signatories had ratified the treaty, Dulles announced the United States might reconsider its commitment to western Europe if ratification ended up failing. In Washington, the chairman of the US Senate Foreign Relations Committee also warned that the new administration was 'unlikely to tolerate indefinite delay'.[13] This was a nightmare scenario for Churchill, who grew increasingly frustrated with the slow pace of ratification and feared the consequences it might have for American involvement in European defence.

The problems on the continent in the early months of 1953 were manifold. Germany's Social Democrats argued the EDC might be in violation of German Basic Law, while in France new leaders were asking for more than was agreed in Paris. French Gaullists feared the end of military independence, while Communists feared alienating Moscow. Colonial war in Indochina reduced the French military presence in Europe and bolstered existing anxieties that West Germany would dominate EDC. Still, it was widely agreed in the West that Pleven's European army was the only way to rearm Germany in a way that was satisfactory to all parties' sensitivities. It was, so to speak, the only game in town. The Americans wanted German rearmament within the Atlantic alliance, the West Germans wanted political equality, and the French wanted at least some control over the Germans.[14] In France, however, the newly appointed Socialist prime minister, René Mayer, also wanted additional protocols on closer British association and specific language on the status of the disputed Saar region, simultaneously upsetting Adenauer and the British with new delays.

Churchill's patience quickly evaporated. In mid-February 1953 he met with Georges Bidault, who had replaced Schuman at the French Foreign Ministry, and, completely torpedoing the idea of outside encouragement of integration, expounded to him the merits of staying away from integrating a proud national army in a federal structure. Bidault found Churchill to be 'rambling, obsessed with the past, and unable to understand vital details about his allies' military predicament'. Churchill then informed Cabinet on 26 February of his preference for developing a 'looser arrangement with a German national Army, as an alternative to the E.D.C. scheme'. Bidault, who was less focused on federal union than his predecessor, was especially keen to get more concessions from Britain before ratification. This led Eden, eager to avoid any suspicion of British intransigence, to open conversations about specific British troop contributions.[15]

Right when things came to a head in the spring of 1953, Eden, after botched bladder removal surgery, was forced to spend about six months in and out of nursing homes and hospitals in Britain and the United States. For the time being, Churchill took over the leadership of the Foreign Office. Stalin passed away on 5 March 1953, leading Churchill to hatch a plan in the early days of

May to coordinate a one-on-one summit with Stalin's successor in Moscow. When Churchill first told senior civil servants at the Foreign Office that he was seeking permission from Eisenhower to go to Moscow alone, their protestations included a consideration of its potential effect on EDC.

Would not the suggestion, the faint possibility, of an end to the Cold War compromise what was left of Franco-German resolve to ratify the Paris Treaty? And was that in the long-term British interest? The French would have less of a rationale to support West German rearmament if there was no real threat of war with the Soviet Union. Faced with this dilemma, Churchill had to admit to the officials that he did not truly care for EDC, especially not in the grand scheme of détente with the Soviets. He still thought the Germans might as well be brought straight into NATO and ruthlessly regarded the almost inevitably resulting isolation of France as a risk worth taking.[16]

Against this background, on 11 May 1953, Churchill gave a highly controversial, wide-ranging set-piece speech in the Commons on foreign affairs. It was designed primarily to help jump-start his campaign to get a high-level summit with the Soviet Union, without forewarning calling for one directly in the last passages of the address. Churchill also addressed the British position in relation to EDC and 'a European Federal system'. With federal union now developing in earnest on the continent, he reverted to his rhetoric from 1930: 'we are with them, but not of them. We have our own Commonwealth and Empire.'[17] The speech had a considerably negative effect on French and German opinion about EDC.[18] The prospect of some kind of reconciliation with the Soviets blunted the raw desire and necessity to integrate in the face of an external threat. A year and a half after the fact, Eden reflected in his diary that Churchill's daring speech 'probably cost us E.D.C. in France'.[19]

In Bonn, where elections were coming up in September 1953, Adenauer was forced to face the ambiguity of the address. Churchill made a point of committing Britain to West Germany and praising Adenauer for his leadership, but the fundamental idea of a friendly settlement with the Soviet Union raised serious questions for Adenauer's foreign policy. Would Germany indefinitely be divided between West and East? And would German rearmament within EDC still be achievable in the midst of speculation about détente? Adenauer, worried about the implications of Churchill's speech, travelled to London on 15 May 1953. Churchill reassured him that West Germany would not be sacrificed to the USSR and admitted that he did not think German reunification would happen on any short timeline. Also, to illustrate where he thought Britain stood in relation to Europe and the world, he literally drew out for Adenauer over dinner a sketch on a menu card of his three circles theory with Britain at the intersection of all three.[20]

In Paris, the foreign policy establishment was predictably up in arms. Fearing talks with the Soviet Union might produce an unwanted solution to the problem of German sovereignty and reunification, the Quai d'Orsay had decided even before the speech that it wanted to leave any kind of summit until after ratification of EDC. French Socialists, however, warmly welcomed Churchill's speech. It took just two days for the French Chamber to pass a motion calling for four-power talks with France, the UK, the US and the USSR – even though Churchill deliberately maintained silence on whether France would be invited. Foreign Minister Bidault, however, who was furious with Churchill for dividing French opinion, had no intention of agreeing to talks before EDC ratification.

To nip the crisis in the bud, French prime minister Mayer proposed three-power talks between himself, Eisenhower and Churchill. Both leaders were glad to accept a summit of Western powers and it was agreed they would meet in British-ruled Bermuda in June. Churchill arranged for accommodation in the posh Mid-Ocean Club, which allowed President Eisenhower to golf with a view. One thing that was not managed in any precise manner was expectations. While Churchill hoped to use Bermuda as a stepping-stone to a summit with Stalin's successor, Eisenhower and the French wanted above all to emphasise Western unity and support for EDC.[21]

On the night of 23 June 1953, just as HMS *Vanguard* was ready to transport Churchill from Southampton to Bermuda the following week, Churchill held a dinner in honour of the Italian premier, Alcide De Gasperi. After his speech, the Prime Minister suddenly collapsed in his chair and, according to Colville, was unable to move.[22] His doctor diagnosed the patient next morning. Churchill had succumbed to a major stroke. With Eden undergoing yet more surgery in Boston, Churchill had little choice but to stay on, cover up his incapacity, and leave the government largely rudderless while spending the summer recuperating at Chartwell and Chequers. Right after the stroke he was paralysed down the left side of his body and it looked as if he might die at Chartwell. Churchill's press baron friends 'gagged' Fleet Street, allowing the Prime Minister to say nothing in public about his stroke until he mentioned it in passing in the Commons a year later. With President Eisenhower's immediate blessing, the Bermuda conference was temporarily deferred.

Churchill, slowly recovering, told his ever-scribbling doctor in the first week of July that the French 'must sign E.D.C. or we must adopt punitive measures'.[23] His impatience was largely based on the knowledge that the Americans wanted the Defence Community to succeed in order to justify their own presence on the continent. It was unthinkable to the American public that their soldiers would continue to protect Europe while the Europeans, particularly the Germans, looked on from the sidelines. Eisenhower wrote to Churchill that failure of the Defence Community could possibly mean an American return to what Churchill had been hoping to prevent all along: 'a policy of almost complete isolationism, or at the very least, to a 'Western hemisphere only' philosophy of security and interest'.[24]

When the British Cabinet subsequently met to discuss EDC, Churchill showed Moran a memorandum he had just dictated for Lord Salisbury and the British ambassador in Washington. Churchill portrayed EDC as an instrument in his 'peace through strength' campaign to get the Soviet Union to agree to a summit:

> If we'd got E.D.C., then we could have spoken to Russia from strength, because German rearmament is the only thing they are afraid of. I want to use Germany and E.D.C. to keep Russia in the mood to be reasonable – to make her play. And I would use Russia to prevent Germany getting out of hand.[25]

Eden briefly returned to London in August 1953, spending the first weekend of the month at Chequers with the Prime Minister. At the end of the weekend, most which was devoted to Eden resisting asking Churchill when he could finally take over the premiership, Eden penned a memorandum of reflections in which he still viewed EDC as the best available instrument to secure a German contribution to European defence, though ratification seemed unlikely to materialise any time soon.[26] Churchill demurred, from the comfort of his bed in Kent, and found Eden's conclusions depressing. Macmillan still feared German domination of the looming continental federation and expressed his wish for EDC to fail so that Britain could seize the opportunity to regain leadership in Europe.[27]

That autumn, due to the cooling down of the conflict in Korea and the possibility of an end to the Cold War after Stalin's death, there seemed to be less urgency to the ratification of EDC than before. Nonetheless, Churchill still thought ratification of EDC, or at the very least the creation of a German army, necessary. And things were looking up. At the end of a recovery vacation in the south of France, Churchill told Clemmie in a letter written in his own paw that the French government 'feels stronger now that Guy Mollet, & the Socialists have rallied to E.D.C.'[28] His host in France was Lord Beaverbrook, a notorious critic of German rearmament, who lent his villa at Cap d'Ail to Churchill's party. Churchill reminded his friend in a letter on 26 September that having a German army on the side of the West might in fact help 'friendly relations with the bear'.[29]

On the problem of European defence Churchill once again advocated an alternative solution for German rearmament at the Conservative Party conference at Margate on 10 October 1953. The address, his first since the stroke in June, was a major personal trial for the Prime Minister, who sought to demonstrate his fitness to continue at No. 10 Downing Street. Despite some hesitation in his speech he made it through 50 minutes of standing at the lectern. That night a tired Churchill and Clemmie dined at No. 10 with Duncan and Diana Sandys to celebrate his success.[30]

'If the European Defence Community should not be adopted by the French,' Churchill had suggested at one point in the party conference speech, 'we shall have no choice in prudence but to fall in with some new arrangement which will join the strength of Germany to the Western allies through some re-arrangement of what is called NATO.'[31] Eden, still pale and thin but sufficiently recovered to return to public life, continued to argue the merits of continued outside British support for EDC. If the government were to revert to Churchill's original conception of a 'Grand Alliance', Eden warned in a letter, that would only have the effect of further delaying German rearmament: 'we should have to start all over again and open new negotiations to obtain Germany as an ally and a German army.'[32]

In the early days of December 1953, the French, British and Americans finally met on the island of Bermuda for Cold War talks. Their aim, in Churchill's words, was to show that the world was not gaping at a void and to 'brace the French up on E.D.C.'.[33] With the Soviet Union having developed the hydrogen bomb the year before and asserting itself in a flurry of written diplomacy about the future of Germany, both Churchill's proposed summit with Malenkov and European defence were key issues for the Western allies.

Eden wanted to avoid all mention of alternatives to the Defence Community, which he thought would lead to trouble in Paris and Bonn alike and give the false impression that there was a fallback plan.[34] His counterpart in Paris, Bidault, and the new prime minister, Joseph Laniel, hoped to gain more concessions from Britain before ratification. In fact, on 24 November 1953, Laniel told the French National Assembly outright that his policy for Bermuda was to demand more British military guarantees for EDC.[35] Here were the makings of a tense Franco-British stand-off.

Prime Minister Churchill and his closest advisers arrived in Bermuda in the same aircraft that had taken the Queen there the week before. The governor of Bermuda and an honorary guard of the Royal Welch Fusiliers with their mascot, a goat, welcomed the party at the airfield. Bermuda's temperate climate, white sands, and crystalline blue sea were welcome diversions. But amid the pleasures of swimming and diving – Churchill himself went no further than getting his feet wet – there were serious political setbacks during the conference, which met officially between 4 and 7 December. Most importantly, President Eisenhower balked at Churchill's idea of meeting with the Soviet Union in another summit. He thought the Soviets were setting a trap for the Western allies in order to endlessly delay EDC coming into force. The British and the French, the President thought, were naively falling into it. Eisenhower likened the Soviet Union to 'a woman of the streets' who could not be trusted. She might be wearing a new dress, Eisenhower said, but under it was likely 'the same old girl'. With that, Eisenhower closed the first plenary session and left.[36]

It was during the meetings of 5 December, Eden's private secretary Evelyn Shuckburgh reported in his diary, that Churchill first accosted French Foreign Minister Georges Bidault. It certainly did not help that Bidault outright blamed Churchill's scheme of détente for delays to ratification in the French Chamber, while telling the Americans that the French had done everything to meet their requirements.[37] 'Winston went into emotional attack on the French for not ratifying E.D.C.,' Shuckburgh wrote, 'during which he said that if it is not through in six to eight weeks there would have to be a German army.' Eisenhower, instead, wanted Britain to aid ratification through far-reaching association and asked Bidault what the Americans could do to help, further pressuring the British to do more than they were doing.[38] The Americans had in mind Britain satisfying French demands by 'guaranteeing to leave their troops on the continent for a defined number of years or even by joining the E. D.C.'.[39] Jock Colville, almost constantly by Churchill's side during the conference thought the answer to this should be obvious:

(i) we will keep our troops on the continent as long as the Americans agree to do so
(ii) we could not possibly get our parliament and people, or the Commonwealth, to accept our actual membership of E.D.C.[40]

It is difficult to judge to what extent Churchill grasped all of the diplomatic subtleties at play. He telegraphed Clemmie to say after the first session that

Bermuda was 'very heavy work'.[41] The Prime Minister was wearing a bulky hearing aid and gave Shuckburgh the distinct impression that 'he heard little of what was going on'.[42] Shuckburgh was frustrated that Churchill seemed 'confused and wrong on almost every issue'. Churchill, he wrote, was 'raring to be crude to the French, to ask the Americans to join us with trips in the Canal Zone, to bring Germans straight into NATO without conditions, and so on. He hardly listens to argument and constantly reverts to wartime and post-war analogies.'[43]

From the American minutes of the plenary session of 5 December, we know that Bidault admitted to having difficulties keeping his parliament in line. Hoping to encourage the French, Churchill intervened in discussions of European defence to reflect on the motivations behind the project. He told the sickly, ultimately short-lived Laniel, and Eisenhower, that when he first started propagating the idea he envisaged 'a grand alliance with all nations standing in line together under a unified command'. The problem was that 'all sorts of questions arose in connection with an army of a federation of Europe. Three years had been lost on complicated details and the only thing that had come out of it was the E.D.C. Treaty.'[44]

The EDC treaty now under discussion actually included improvements on Pleven's earlier plans in Churchill's eyes, as it also created national military units with their own uniforms, marching songs and identities. Nevertheless, he went on the defence for his original conception, purged of 'metaphysical' elements. The minutes read:

> Personally, he [Churchill] preferred a national presentation of armies bound by a grand alliance. The present army would be the best that could be obtained with a unified command. We would be prepared to take our part with our troops [...]. We would be prepared to take our part and submit to the Supreme Commander.[45]

Churchill pledged Britain to support EDC and promised that if someone not in the know were looking at the forces of the West in action, 'he could not tell whether they were operating as E.D.C. or as a grand alliance.' It made 'no difference' to the muscle of EDC, Churchill claimed, 'if the British were called partners – with E.D.C. but not in it. The greater part of British armed forces were there. Some countries had comfortable armed forces at home. The British had not a single brigade in the United Kingdom.' Churchill was not going to 'advise his fellow countrymen to undertake more'. The Prime Minister brought to mind his decades of fighting alongside his French friends and, quite suddenly, his voice choked and tears fell onto his cheeks. He remembered the enormous French losses sustained in two world wars and the valiant part

Bidault and Laniel played in the French Resistance. He begged for their understanding at this difficult moment in history and to go on with EDC in order to achieve German rearmament. But, indeed, if the French were not quick enough to ratify, Churchill would support establishing at least 12 battle-worthy German divisions in a new version of NATO, no matter whether the French agreed to it or not. The Soviets needed to know that the West was serious about its defences in Europe.[46]

The next day of the summit, 6 December 1953, Churchill again attacked Bidault, who made a speech about France's precarious situation. Churchill was unimpressed with Bidault's references to the Saar region on France's eastern frontier, which he condescendingly called 'a few fields'.[47] France and Germany were struggling to come to an agreement on the Saar, which was occupied by France but legally a part of Germany. Churchill said to his doctor after the day's plenary session: 'Bidault talked for an hour and a half about four villages in the Saar. I went for him, telling him plainly that if American troops were withdrawn from Europe British troops would leave too.'[48] Whatever Churchill's depreciation of French problems, the Americans remained rigid in support of ratification rather than alternative plans. They did not agree that Germany could be brought straight into NATO, and would, if EDC collapsed, probably pursue the alternative strategy of peripheral defence from American bases on the edges of Europe. Churchill said in that case he 'would view the future more sombrely than at any time in World War II'.[49] Still, before going to bed that night, Churchill told Colville that he and Eisenhower agreed 'to treat forcing through the ratification of E.D.C. as a combined military operation'.[50]

When it came time to discuss the Bermuda communiqué, on 7 December, the French were needlessly, inexplicably difficult in demanding the inclusion of a sentence that suggested the Allies were in a position to help France ratify the Paris Treaty. President Eisenhower was outraged and deeply disappointed in the conference and told Foreign Secretary Dulles that he would never again come to a summit unless everything had already been negotiated in advance. Churchill was just as furious, seeing no genuine desire for easement with the Soviet Union on the part of the Western allies, and said ominously: 'E.D.C. is dead. We want a German army.'[51]

It took until 1.30 a.m. to reach agreement on the text, everyone exhausted and agitated. Churchill muttered gloomily the next morning: 'The communiqué is a flop. In refusing E.D.C. the French may have thrown away the last chance of saving France.'[52] But he perked up when he said his goodbyes to Bidault after lunch, telling him his harshness came merely from his desire for France to save itself. Churchill did not think the French government 'was 'bitching' it all but the French parliamentary system.'[53] Bidault was in profound agreement. At least now everyone knew how seriously the Americans took ratification of EDC and how difficult it would be to strong-arm the French into accepting it.

The Bermuda conference struggled to demonstrate Western unity and to achieve any meaningful conclusions. Churchill himself was most disappointed that he was unable to convince his allies of the wisdom of personal diplomacy and détente with the Soviets. A week after the conference closed, NATO's Atlantic Council met for further discussions in Paris. Dulles now publicly threatened 'an agonizing reappraisal' of US commitment to mainland Europe unless EDC was implemented soon.[54] Churchill backed Dulles's harsh words and suggested to Eisenhower, in a letter of 19 December, preparing 'some variant of NATO' as an alternative to EDC. Eisenhower was not interested.[55] At least there was the good news of a new French president. René Coty, Churchill told Eisenhower, 'has for long been a keen supporter of European movements and has frequently spoken in favour of the European Defence Community. I think we might easily have got someone worse.'[56]

A few days after Dulles's warning, Churchill gave a speech on foreign affairs in the House of Commons. His address focused mostly on warnings to the French of the consequences of rejecting EDC. When his doctor told him the next day that the French were unlikely to change their policy towards EDC, Churchill shot back: 'impotence is not a policy.'[57]

By April 1954 every EDC country but Italy and France had ratified the treaty. Italy dealt with minor procedural objections, while the French still harboured serious nationalistic reservations about merging its proud army in a system including Germany. Gaullist electoral success challenged the Europeanist opinions of Robert Schuman, and as a result the French started to seek closer British association and a special French position within EDC.[58]

On the occasion of the 50th anniversary of the Entente Cordiale, the British government offered more far-reaching guarantees to the EDC powers. Macmillan later wrote that Britain was then proposing 'almost everything but marriage'.[59] On 13 April 1954 Churchill's government officially pledged in a treaty with EDC to add British army forces to the European army, to consult EDC on every mutual concern, and to embark on common development of technical improvements in training and equipment.

In the last week of June 1954, worried by gloom in Germany about French resistance to EDC, Churchill and Eisenhower held extensive talks. Churchill arrived in Washington on Friday the 25th after nine hours' sleep in a

Stratocruiser aircraft. John Foster Dulles and Vice-President Richard M. Nixon met Churchill at the airport before he set off in a car to the White House. The political talk started at once. Churchill suggested again that German rearmament might be achieved through direct membership of NATO. Eisenhower was now fed up with the French, calling them 'a hopeless, helpless mass of protoplasm' over dinner with Churchill.[60] The joint press statement eventually read in more civilised terms: 'The German Federal Republic should take its place as an equal partner in the community of Western nations, where it can make its proper contribution to the defence of the free world. We are determined to achieve this goal, convinced that the Bonn and Paris Treaties provide the best way.'[61] Importantly and surprisingly, Churchill also returned home with unenthusiastic consent from Eisenhower to attempt a bilateral meeting with Malenkov.[62]

After returning to Britain, Churchill personally took more of an acute interest in European unity again. On 4 July 1954, he read that Adenauer was demanding that the French get on with ratification. 'I am glad he has spoken out,' he told his doctor. 'The French are a disgrace. When they gave up in 1940 they wanted us to surrender too. We picked them out of the gutter, and now they think of nothing but themselves all the time; living in a welter of intrigue, they never seem to think of their country.'[63]

On 14 July Churchill, irritated with long delays in ratification of EDC, again asked Europe to focus on building up defensive capacity rather than get lost in 'metaphysical argument'. He told the Commons: 'What counts in matters of defence are the physical facts [...] By the combined working of the EDC scheme with NATO the British, Canadian and United States forces would be brought into the Continental line of defence together with all their European comrades. All will stand together on the same front [...] Surely, this giant fact should not be overlooked for the sake of complicated and almost metaphysical argument, however intricate or exciting it may be.'[64]

In the same speech he regretted once more Attlee's decision not to partake in negotiations over EDC at the start: 'If they had it might have been possible to obtain an agreement on a scheme of a less federalistic nature in which Britain could have played a fuller part.'[65] At the end of July, Churchill suffered a major blow in Cabinet. In the face of Soviet proposals to meet with all European governments, he failed to convince a majority of his ministers of the wisdom of organising personal high-level talks with Malenkov. That meant the Prime Minister's overarching foreign policy aim of the second administration failed and ended.[66] As Churchill's hopes for a summit settlement faded he was able and willing to focus more on EDC.

After a month spent resting while Parliament was in recess, Churchill hosted the French prime minister, Pierre Mendès-France, at Chartwell. He was most anxious to meet him, Churchill told his wife, for Mendès-France was a new fact in French politics.[67] Ahead of the meeting, Churchill told his doctor that he anticipated saying 'terrible things' to him. Wrapped in flattery, he would tell him that 'the world is not going to be ruled by the French Chamber' and that if the Chamber rejected EDC 'France would be alone in the world.'[68] With Eden in attendance, Churchill indeed hammered home the 'grave dangers' of not going ahead with EDC.[69] Mendès-France, just as the Prime Minister intended, left Kent under the impression that Churchill was a firm supporter of EDC.[70]

That same month, August 1954, saw the French government demanding still more amendments to make ratification possible. Churchill wrote to Eden about his concern at the endless delays and demands from the French, saying he grieved for 'the much maltreated famous Benelux as well as for the faithful Adenauer' and insinuating that some alternative solution for common European defence would have to be ready in case the French kept up their impossible recalcitrance. He did not actually expect the French to ratify, especially after Mendès-France had told him personally that he did not have a majority for it in the French Assembly.[71]

Eden indicated that he was now in general agreement, even with the possibility of bringing West Germany directly into NATO, and proposed going on a tour of European capitals to lay the groundwork for an alternative to EDC.[72] On 29 August Churchill dictated a letter to the American financier and European Movement enthusiast 'Bernie' Baruch. As a general update on his political life, Churchill wrote that he was 'on pretty strong ground about E.D.C., etc.'. Ten months had passed since he addressed the topic at Margate and he was consistent in his despair about the French: 'The French Chamber with its extraordinary constitution has enabled an indefinite stalemate to be maintained, greatly to the injury of our vital interests in the attitude of Germany.'[73]

As it turned out, Churchill's government would have almost no time at all to quietly prepare and build consensus around alternatives. On 30 August 1954 Mendès-France finally put the EDC treaty before the French National Assembly. He did so without enthusiasm, proclaiming the French government neutral on the issue. Before the treaty came to a vote, the National Assembly accepted a motion to keep it from being voted on in the first place. French deputies officially defeated the EDC treaty. 'Nothing like it had ever been witnessed before,' Paul-Henri Spaak later wrote, 'and it is difficult to see what Mendès-France hoped to achieve by these tactics.'[74] The Americans, most of the Europeans and many Britons, intent on making a success of the defence community, were devastated. The Atlantic alliance was in a state of utter disarray – exactly what the Soviet Union hoped for in the Cold War.

Churchill worried deeply about the state of the world: 'the throwing out of E.D.C. is a great score for the Russians,' he told Moran.[75] In the afternoon Cabinet of 1 September the Prime Minister also foresaw possible advantages for West Germany of this outcome, giving Adenauer 'a rare opportunity to restore Germany's moral standing and expose the failure of France to rise to the needs of the hour'.[76] Once more he was full of derision for the French after waking from an afternoon nap on 2 September. He thought their behaviour was 'execrable' and showed both ingratitude and conceit. 'I cannot feel the same about them in future,' he said full of grief. He was disappointed about the time and opportunity lost for European defence. With more excited anger, he told Moran:

> Look at the swine. Wasting three vital years. It was their own invention. They made us do it. My very pleasant relations with Anthony [Eden] make things more difficult. I would have liked to control this business, but if I did I would be taking the bread out of Anthony's mouth after denying him the square meal he so much wanted.[77]

That is to say, if Churchill had taken control of European policy, he would not have been able to justify taking and then holding onto the premiership. In this time of crisis, however, the Cabinet could not dissuade him from personally reaching out to Chancellor Adenauer. On 3 September, he telegraphed to Bonn: 'It seems to me that at this critical juncture a great opportunity has come to Germany to take her position among the leaders of free Europe.' The Prime Minister wanted Adenauer to consider a 'voluntary act of self-abnegation' by not asking for more troops in 'any new arrangement as a substitute for E.D.C.' than were originally provided for in the treaty. 'I beg you to think this over,' Churchill pleaded, 'as coming from one who after so many years of strife has few stronger wishes than to see the German nation take her true place in the worldwide family of free nations.'[78] Adenauer replied that he shared Churchill's view that 'the solution must consist in a voluntary act of self-limitation, if it is to give Germany moral dignity and respect.'[79]

Whatever Adenauer was thinking, the collapse of EDC in the French National Assembly completely changed the political landscape in Europe.

Churchill and others in Cabinet in favour of British leadership in Europe were now handed the opportunity to come up with an alternative structure for European defence. Europe and the West needed a solution and needed it fast. Macmillan, who had long advocated abandoning EDC in favour of looser, confederal arrangements, was encouraged by Churchill's renewed interest in European unity. He generally found the Foreign Office, in its active encouragement of a purely continental union, to demonstrate 'a degree of myopia which a mole would envy'. Macmillan feared both German domination of a continental federal union and the bloc's neutrality in case of World War III – both possible outcomes deeply adverse to British interests.[80]

Thus, when the opportunity arose to re-establish British leadership, Macmillan wrote to Eden with a practical idea. He saw in the collapse a golden opportunity. The postwar era had produced two major defence pacts: Bevin's 1948 Brussels Pact, also known as Western Union, and NATO. 'Would it be possible', Macmillan asked, 'to revive Western Union instead of EDC? Germany could join it, as a sort of solemn declaration against the wrong Germany. Italy could join it. So could Norway etc. It would be *European*, and not an *Atlantic* organisation.' Simultaneously, the Strasbourg Assembly would be linked to the Schuman Coal and Steel Community and oversee the non-defence elements of the revived Brussels Pact. This, Macmillan argued, might appeal equally to the French and the Germans now that the federal option had failed.[81] It was also certain to appeal to Churchill, restoring British leadership and avoiding federation all at once.

Macmillan put a report he prepared with Julian Amery before Cabinet, arguing their view that the Brussels Treaty Organisation should be extended, deepened and incorporated into NATO. This would allow for equal British membership and the possibility of keeping West Germany under control with limited defence contributions. Macmillan's proposal was clearly based on the Strasbourg plan which had been withdrawn at Eden's urging in 1950.[82] As foreign secretary, the task fell to Eden of selling the plan in Europe. He saw no other real options and agreed to use the Brussels Pact as a way out. It was not the case, as Eden claimed in his memoirs, that while taking a bath on the weekend of 5 September 'it suddenly occurred to me that I might use the Brussels Treaty to do the job.'[83] Around the same time Macmillan experienced his eureka moment there were also civil servants aiding Eden's diplomatic improvisations, hastily digging up plans out of the 'pigeon-holes' of the Foreign Office to permanently commit British forces to the continent.[84]

The supranational method had collapsed spectacularly in the realm of defence, and British leadership was required to keep the dream of European unity alive. By 9 September Churchill was able to report to Eisenhower that the Cabinet were 'all agreed that an 8-power meeting of allies, plus Canada, would be the right move now [...] and we should like very much to have it in London which is a big and well known place and has stood by the Thames for quite a long time without having a conference of this kind.' At the desire of the Cabinet, therefore, Eden was 'to start on a flying circuit of Brussels, Bonn, Rome and Paris to see what he can do'.[85]

Eden was successful first in interesting the Benelux countries in Macmillan's proposal of modifying the Brussels Treaty. The plan was kept a secret, Churchill informed Eisenhower on 12 September, until the British government was able to put it to the French. Six days later, after an agreeable lunch with Dulles and Eden in London, Churchill telegraphed Eisenhower again to update him on the situation. He gave a particularly lucid summary of all that he had wanted from European defence since 1950:

> As you know, E.D.C. was very different from the grand alliance theme I opened at Strasbourg in August, 1950. I disliked on military grounds the Pleven European army which began with mixing races in companies if not platoons. At that time when I saw you in Paris I was talking of it as a 'sludgy amalgam'.
>
> However, when I came to power again I swallowed my prejudices because I was led to believe that it was the only way in which the French could be persuaded to accept the limited Germany army which was my desire. I do not blame the French for rejecting E.D.C. but only for inventing it. Their harshness to Adenauer in wasting three years of his life and much of his power is a tragedy. Also I accepted the American wish to show all possible patience and not to compromise the chances of E.D.C. by running NATO as a confusing rival.
>
> All this time I kept one aim above all others in my view, namely a German contribution to the defence of an already uniting Europe. This, I felt, was your aim too, and I am sure we both liked the plan better when the intermingling was excluded from all units lower than a division.[86]

On 28 September 1954, with the foreign ministers and other representatives of the continental six, the UK, Canada and the US in attendance in London, Eden recommended reinstating full West German sovereignty and giving the country permission to rearm with light restrictions as a full member of NATO. He asked West Germany and Italy to join a deepened Brussels Pact, restyled as the Western European Union, which included Britain as one of its founding members. The carrot was a transformative, unprecedented British commitment to keeping at least four divisions and tactical air force on the continent for as long as was deemed necessary by the majority of Western Union powers.[87]

The stick was the threat of isolation from a Western defence pact and American departure from Europe. The Western European Union would operate militarily within NATO, be based in London, and have its assembly of parliamentarians meet simultaneously and cooperate actively with the Strasbourg Assembly.

In the midst of severe distress about failure of EDC, most European leaders, notwithstanding tough negotiations on the details, were eager to accept the British proposals. Churchill's government was offering something meaningful. It was surrendering partial sovereignty over British forces. 'My colleagues will realize', Eden said in the speech that made conference, 'that what I have announced is for us a very formidable step to take. You all know that ours is above all an island story. We are still an island people in thought and tradition [...] And it has not been without considerable reflection that the Government which I represent here has decided that this statement could be made to you this afternoon.'[88] René Massigli, the French ambassador to Britain, was in tears, for he knew that by accepting majority rule over British troops on the continent the British government had just given what France had long desired: a British guarantee against internal and external disruption.[89] Spaak turned to Mendès-France and said: 'You've won.'[90]

The October 1954 meeting of NATO's Atlantic Council in Paris confirmed the London agreements, which were subsequently known as the Paris Accords.[91] Where Bevin's Brussels Treaty Organisation had been humble in its ambitions for the future, the revised treaty on Western European Union expressed the desire to 'promote the unity and to encourage the progressive integration of Europe'.[92] The purpose of Western European Union, then, was in part to bring about the closer union of European states in the gradualist way first envisioned by Churchill. As Churchill put it to Eisenhower, the new defence organisation 'may lead as time passes to United Europe and also gain for us both what we have tried for so hard, namely, the German comradeship.'[93]

While Eden justifiably received praise for his role in saving the Atlantic alliance, Churchill also recognised Macmillan's part in crafting the idea and promoted him to the Ministry of Defence.[94] Julian Amery was typical of British Europeanists in applauding the outcome in *The Times*, arguing the new treaty 'allowed for organic growth'.[95] Churchill told his doctor the morning after the success of the London conference with a broad smile: 'Now they are going to do exactly what I suggested at Strasbourg in August 1950.'[96]

The House of Commons, with the Opposition abstaining, ratified the treaty by an overwhelming majority of 264 votes to 4. It was too early, however, to raise the flag of victory. At 5 a.m. on Christmas Eve 1954, the French Assembly, still anxious about German power in the newly proposed structure, defeated Western European Union narrowly.[97] The vote and subsequent French delays brought Churchill to a level of anger some around him had never seen before.[98] In the week that Britain officially joined the European Coal and Steel Community as an associated member, Eden publicly declared that Britain would retract all its forces from the continent if the French Assembly did not turn around and ratify the Paris Accords.[99] The warning had the desired effect.

* * *

Just a week later, on 30 December 1954, the French deputies voted to ratify the Paris Accords.

Churchill was not quite satisfied with the result, seeing new detractors on the horizon. The French Senate still needed to approve the Paris Accords. He shared his concerns with Eisenhower, in a letter of 12 January 1955, that 'French obstructers' in the Senate would spread the whole process out for four or five months. In a letter to Mendès-France of the same day he said more delicately that he was aware of 'the many opportunities for uncertainty and delay which still remain'.[100] Time was not a luxury Churchill thought Europe could afford. No matter how old and tired, the Prime Minister still embraced the fierce urgency of now. The Soviet Union would soon reach a nuclear saturation point, he estimated, whereby it could 'inflict mortal injury upon the civilized structure of the free world'.[101] Western Europe needed to pull together and be ready before that time.

The ratification procedure did indeed drag on for months. Churchill was so anxious to see the French ratify that he asked the Commons in a speech delivered on 14 March 1955 to await a decision from Paris before pushing on with his own key initiative of a high-level meeting with the Soviet Union. 'Earnestly as I desire to get a peaceful arrangement for co-existence brought with Russia,' he said, 'I regard it as an act of insanity to drive the German people into the hands of the Kremlin and thus tilt into Communist tyranny the destiny of mankind.'[102] Without Western unity, without strength, and without Adenauer's Germany tied to the West, easement with the Soviet Union would be worthless and probably impossible. Churchill was also supremely cheerful about the American renewal of its pledge to keep forces in Europe as long as there was a threat to NATO. 'The United States will work closely with the Western European Union,' Churchill told the Commons, and characterised that assurance as being 'of the highest value not only for Western European Union but for NATO and for the free world as a whole'.[103]

Two weeks later the French Senate finally approved the treaty. The day after, relieved to have seen the episode to a satisfactory end, Churchill told his most senior Cabinet ministers at 6.30 p.m. that he had made his final decision to retire. The young Queen Elizabeth II was notified on the 31st and visited Churchill for a dinner party a few days later at No. 10 Downing Street. Churchill left believing his successor, Eden, would fail.[104]

Now, late at night on 4 April 1955, Churchill silently sat on his bed at the prime minister's residence, still wearing his decorations after a first-class, dignified farewell. Colville entered the room and dared not speak first. Then, suddenly, Churchill turned, stared at his private secretary intently, and said forcefully: 'I don't believe Anthony can do it.' The next morning Churchill went to Buckingham Palace to offer his resignation. He passed up the dukedom offered by the Queen and remained in the House of Commons for the rest of his life.[105]

CHAPTER 13

'MY PARTY WAS TOO STRONG FOR ME'
LAST THOUGHTS, 1955–1965

Long after his retirement, in the midst of the political desperation about British isolation from the European Economic Community, a continuation of the Schuman Plan's economic approach to integration more commonly known as the Common Market, Eden started worrying about his European legacy. Boothby, Maxwell Fyfe and Macmillan all wrote memoirs making serious, personal accusations about the defects of his European policy. In vain, Eden asked one of his most trusted aides to produce material that could prove his critics wrong.[1] Evelyn Shuckburgh simply reassured Eden that he had been right and that 'the British were not ready to put their forces into anything like the EDC in 1951.'[2] While an accurate reflection of the British political and public moods, this misunderstood the essence of the critiques launched against Eden and Churchill, which held not that Britain should have become a member of a federal union but that its leaders had not done enough to shape the new Europe in Britain's mould when the iron was still hot.

Churchill became all too familiar with this self-doubt regarding his legacy on European unity. After all, he had done little to fight Eden, the party and the Cabinet when he returned to office. Two years after his resignation, he started to express his regret that Britain had not yet been able to join Europe in some way. 'If the European trade community were to be permanently restricted to the six nations,' he said at a United Europe rally in Westminster, 'the result would be worse than if nothing was done at all – worse for them as well as for us. It would tend not to unite Europe but to divide it – and not only in the economic field.'[3]

In January 1963, Churchill started composing a letter to Paul-Henri Spaak. It was never actually sent but it read in its first lines: 'The future of Europe if Britain were to be excluded is black indeed.'[4] Around that time, he told a former colleague in the United Europe Movement that he had wanted to take Britain into Europe and explained why he had failed to do so: 'My party was too strong for me.'[5] The uncomfortable truth was that Churchill had done very little himself to steer his party on Europe when he returned to office. The collapse of EDC gave Churchill's second administration a chance to offer a British-led alternative for European defence cooperation, but he did not grasp the larger hopes of Europeans by truly leading the way to European unification.

However Churchill might be judged for failing to translate his romantic idealism into policy after his return as prime minister, his spirit permeated the whole of the European project. The climate of opinion he created from the Zurich speech onwards allowed and directly inspired the continental federalists to launch their proposals in the first place. His short-term focus on the reconciliation of France and Germany and long-term vision of a revived and united Europe created hope for a postwar future where there had been none.

In the early 1960s Harold Macmillan, of whom we have heard more than any other Churchillian protégé, succeeded Anthony Eden as prime minister. According to one active political diarist, Churchill and the Queen had together decided that Macmillan was the best man available after Eden ended a short-lived tenure at No. 10, marred by illness and the Suez crisis, in 1957.[6] In the summer of 1960 Macmillan first decided that it was in Britain's interests to seek membership of the Common Market. It was as much an ideologically and geopolitically driven decision as it was an economic one: between 1954 and 1961 average growth rates on the European Continent were so much higher than in the United Kingdom that Macmillan was left with little choice but to look across the Channel for a new foundation for British prosperity: Germany's GDP grew at an average annual rate of 6.6 per cent, France's by 4.2 per cent, and Italy's by 5.7 per cent, while the UK struggled with a meagre 2.3 per cent.[7] To make matters worse, the United States was no longer susceptible to British influence in any meaningful manner and the Commonwealth had dropped its pretences of political cohesion.

For Macmillan personally his decision to apply to join the Common Market was the logical outcome of a career-long commitment to internationalism and European integration in particular. In Churchill's European campaign and even before that, Macmillan had befriended some of the most important European politicians of the time and become increasingly wedded to the idea that Britain should lead Europe. In large measure, Macmillan's application was also the realisation of a principle he knew his mentor Churchill to endorse. He believed that 'Britain could in his [Churchill's] view play a full role in Europe without loss or disloyalty to the tradition of her Empire and Commonwealth.'[8]

In 1962, when the nation looked to Churchill to pronounce an opinion on Macmillan's controversial course, Churchill was hospitalised after breaking his hip in Monte Carlo and unable to comment. Field Marshal Montgomery, however, after visiting the patient at Middlesex Hospital, boldly stated to the press that Churchill opposed Macmillan's application. This was a deliberate misrepresentation of an old and sick man's views. Churchill told his granddaughter Edwina Sandys who also came to visit him in hospital that week that 'Monty's behaviour was monstrous.'[9] In response to Montgomery, Churchill's secretary, Anthony Montague Browne, without consulting anyone, 'released to the press a statement of WSC's views on the subject that he had embodied in a private and unpublished letter to his Constituency Chairman, Mrs Moss, in August 1961'. While rightly sceptical of the chances of success and careful to stress that no damage should be done to Commonwealth interests, the statement read: 'I think that the Government are right to apply to join the European Economic Community, not because I am yet convinced that we shall be able to join, but because there appears to be no other way by which we can find out exactly whether the conditions of membership are acceptable.'[10] Churchill's letter was not an outright statement of support for accession whatever the terms – that would have been absurd – but it was a significant public rebuke of the principled negativity claimed by Montgomery. In his old age, according to his private secretary, Churchill did not have 'any very decided view on the Common Market question'.[11]

Macmillan unleashed the old driving force of the European movement, Duncan Sandys, then minister for Commonwealth relations, to persuade the governments of New Zealand, Canada and Australia of the wisdom of Britain's accession. As Churchill had urged in his letter in support of the application: 'In the negotiations [...] the six countries should recognise that the Commonwealth is one of the most valuable assets that we could bring, for them as well as for ourselves, and should be ready to work out arrangements to prevent any damage to Commonwealth interests.'[12] This was completely consistent with Churchill's long-held idea that European and Commonwealth unity were compatible and with a worldview that went far beyond Europe alone.

All of it mattered little to General de Gaulle, who by this time had found his way back to power and was deeply suspicious of Britain's challenge to French leadership in Europe. The General ensured Macmillan's efforts collapsed in humiliation by vetoing British membership of the Common Market twice in a decade – in 1963 and 1967. Churchill had withdrawn from the public eye, but held little regard for de Gaulle's rejection of British accession in 1963. He told his private secretary, who remarked at the time that de Gaulle seemed to be proving the old adage that no country can afford to show gratitude: 'It would indeed be sad if so melancholy and so historically disprovable a maxim should be the epitaph on so great a man.'[13] Shortly thereafter, Churchill left the minister at the French Embassy during an informal luncheon in no doubt of 'his anger and disappointment at her [France's] present stance'.[14]

In December 1967, nearly three years after Churchill's passing and a month after the second time de Gaulle humiliated Britain, one of Churchill's oldest friends conjured up the old man's ghost to criticise French policy and stir up support for British accession. Lady Violet Bonham Carter went on French television on 13 December 1967 intent on 'insult[ing] de Gaulle in his own capital'. In what should have been a historical discussion of the Entente Cordiale with a set of mumbling French professors, Lady Violet seized her moment to talk about de Gaulle's second veto and link it to the moment in history when Britain and France almost became one nation. She described de Gaulle's arrival in London in 1940, when he found friends and a platform from which to speak to the French public. She then turned to Churchill's offer of indissoluble union: 'Churchill did not ask,' she said, now in full swing, "And how is your franc? Is he in good shape? And your reserves? [...] Churchill said: "Let us unite. Let us share everything. What is ours is yours. Our destiny is inseparable."' The broadcast made a great impact on both sides of the Channel, with Lady Violet receiving fan mail from all over France and even from Churchill's son Randolph.[15]

In the first failed attempt at accession Macmillan appointed a somewhat reserved, self-disciplined and serious 44-year-old to serve as his chief negotiator. Edward Heath became Lord Privy Seal with responsibility for the Foreign Office in July 1960 – the same year he was elected to The Other Club at Churchill's urging. He was a new breed of Tory for a new world. Heath was the first working-class man to rise to the top of the Conservative Party, and a proven Europeanist. After the fall of Czechoslovakia in February 1948, he publicly praised the 'amazing truth and clarity' of Churchill's warnings about the Soviets, and in June 1950 he gave his maiden speech in the Schuman Plan debate.[16] Before seeing and hearing Churchill say at the conclusion of the debate that 'national sovereignty may be resolutely diminished', Heath impressed a fully packed Commons with his own, 14-minute long, passionate call for Britain to enter Europe. In the final sentences of his address, he argued: 'It was said long ago in the House that magnanimity in politics is not seldom the truest wisdom. I appeal tonight to the government to follow that dictum, and to go into the Schuman Plan to develop Europe and to coordinate it in the way suggested.'[17] Afterwards, Churchill promoted him to the Whips' Office.

Heath worked breathtakingly hard for Macmillan's first attempt at accession, covering over 50,000 miles in 27 trips to Brussels, 11 to Paris and 22 to other countries.[18] Churchill was the undisputed inspiring force for his travels. At one point in the early 1960s, the BBC asked Heath if he wanted to hear a tape of Churchill's Zurich speech which they had found and previously had not known existed. Heath convened the British negotiation delegations from Brussels and London in his room at the Foreign Office and played the tape. 'I shall never forget the feelings of exhilaration,' he later wrote, 'with which I heard that powerful voice come back over the years, unmistakable in its resonance, and I shall always prize the intense feeling of purpose which it gave us.'[19]

In 1962, deeply impressed with Heath's endeavours, Churchill invited him to spend Boxing Day at Chartwell and asked him to speak to his constituency at Woodford on United Europe.[20] He gave Heath permission to use the record of his Zurich speech. On 10 April 1963, shortly after de Gaulle's first shattering 'Non', Churchill wrote to congratulate Heath on winning the Charlemagne Prize awarded by the German city of Aachen, the highest honour for services to European unity. Churchill himself had been awarded the prize in 1956, had gone to Aachen to accept it and had given a speech advocating détente with the Soviet Union. 'Certainly your efforts for the unity of Europe', Churchill told Heath in his letter, 'have been on the highest scale, and I cannot think of anyone who deserves it more.'[21] Seven years later, when Heath was elected prime minister, one of the first things he noticed at Chequers was that it did not yet possess a painting by Churchill. Heath thought it would be appropriate to hang one on the wall of the White Parlour. He decided on one of Churchill's portraits of Lake Geneva, painted on the lawn of Villa Choisi in September 1946.[22]

Ultimately, de Gaulle's intransigence was quickly forgotten after Heath's successful attempt as prime minister to fulfil Britain's European destiny. In 1973, eight years after Churchill had died at the age of 90, Britain officially entered the European Economic Community, which set out in its founding treaty a determination to lay the foundations of an ever-closer union. Heath and the living generation of Churchillians who helped build the European movement understood full well the historic importance of that decision. In a gesture of special symbolism, Prime Minister Heath took Macmillan with him for the official signing of the Accession Treaty in Brussels.

In June 1975, after the people endorsed Britain's accession in the first 'European' referendum, Macmillan telephoned Sandys to share his joy. Sandys wrote to him afterwards: 'It was a great thrill for me to hear your voice at this historic moment, which means so much to us both. The way is now open for Britain to play a leading part in shaping the future of Europe.' He then looked ahead to what Britain could contribute specifically: 'With our unique parliamentary tradition, we should be second to none in pressing for the introduction of direct elections to the European Parliament, which must of course be given real powers.'[23] Britain was lunging into a future contemplated long before by its most celebrated statesman.

* * *

On 31 October 1959, in the closing words of the last speech Churchill was able to work on himself, he pondered the balance between progress and ruin in the preceding 35 years. The occasion was the unveiling of a statue of himself in his constituency. He was 84 years old. 'In Western Europe,' he told his audience,

> many of the age-old enmities are at last dispersing and the outlook for a closer unity of those who share the common fruit of Western civilization, both here and overseas, is full of promise. There is no reason why these developments should conflict with our ever closer association with the countries of the Commonwealth and the United States [...] In all this we in Britain have a great part to play, a leading part. By our courage, our endurance, and our brains we have made our way in the world to the lasting benefit of mankind. Let us not lose heart. Our future is one of high hope.

NOTES

1 'SOMETHING THAT WILL ASTONISH YOU': ZURICH, 19 SEPTEMBER 1946

1. J. Colville, *The Fringes of Power: Downing Street Diaries, 1939–1955* (London, 1985), p. 611.
2. A. Eden, *The Reckoning* (Cambridge, 1965), p. 639.
3. M. Soames, *Clementine Churchill* (London, 2003), p. 388.
4. Lord Moran, *Churchill: The Struggle for Survival 1945–1960* (New York, 2006), pp. 5–6.
5. M. Gilbert, *Winston S. Churchill,*, vol. VIII (London, 1988), p. 138.
6. Origins of the 'Iron Curtain' phrase: V. Sebestyen, *1946* (London, 2014), p. 163; P. White, *Churchill's Cold War: How the Iron Curtain Speech Shaped the Post War World* (London, 2013).
7. Cited in N. Ashford, 'The Conservative Party and European Integration 1945–75', Ph.D. thesis, University of Warwick, 1983, p. 43; C. Moran, *Winston Churchill: The Struggle for Survival 1940–1965* (London, 1966).
8. Churchill Archives Centre (CAC), Churchill Papers (CHUR), 1/42, Sandys to WSC, 15 September 1946.
9. The National Archives (TNA), Foreign Office (FO) 371/60490, 313/59/46, T.M Snow to E. Bevin, 25 September 1946.
10. W. Vogt, *Winston Churchill und die Schweiz* (Zurich, 2015), p. 134.
11. Db.dodis.ch (Swiss Diplomatic Archives online), 'Bericht von Oberstleutnant Bracher', Nr. 2184, 18 October 1946, p. 29.
12. Db.dodis.ch, 'Très Confidentiel: Notice pour monsieur le Conseiller fédéral Petitpierre sur mes entretiens avec M. Churchill et M. Montag', 22 September 1946, Nr. 1659, p. 5.
13. CHUR 2/247, 'Visite de M. Winston Churchill à Zurich', 19 September 1946.
14. CHUR 5/8A–C, Press Cutting: *Daily Express*, 20 September 1946.
15. CHUR 2/248, Press cutting: *Daily Telegraph*, 'London Day by Day', 20 September 1946.
16. Text of the Zurich speech: WSC, *The Sinews of Peace*, pp. 198–202.
17. CHUR 2/247, Press Cutting: *Neue Zürcher Zeitung*, 'Die Feier in der Universität', 19 September 1946.

18. WSC, *The Sinews of Peace*, p. 198.
19. Ibid., p. 198.
20. Ibid., pp. 198–9.
21. Ibid., p. 199. The word 'Gentlemen' was omitted in the edited and published text of the speech but is clearly audible in the existing live recording.
22. Ibid.
23. Ibid.
24. Ibid., p. 200.
25. Ibid.
26. Ibid.
27. Ibid.
28. Ibid., p. 201.
29. CHUR 2/21A-B, 'Sitting of the National Assembly – 1st March 1871', copy of text undated.
30. WSC, *The Sinews of Peace*, p. 201.
31. H.J. Küsters and H.P. Mensing, 'Konrad Adenauer zur Politischen Lage, 1946–1949, Aus den Berichten des schweizerischen Generalkonsuls in Köln Franz Rudolf v. Weiss', *Vierteljahrshefte für Zeitgeschichte*, xxxii (1984), p. 295.
32. Churchill set out his intentions and role as general inspiring force in personal letters after the Zurich speech. See, for instance, his letter to the Archbishop of Canterbury in which he proposed to 'rouse the fervour of a crusade': CHUR 2/22A-B, WSC to the Archbishop of Canterbury, 17 November 1946.
33. WSC, *The Sinews of Peace*, p. 201.
34. Ibid., pp. 201–2.
35. Ibid., p. 202.
36. Ibid.
37. Martin Gilbert, in his essay 'Churchill and the European Idea', in R.A.C. Parker (ed.), *Winston Churchill, Studies in Statesmanship* (London, 1995), pp. 201–16, argues that it would have moved Churchill deeply to see the ancient states and capitals of eastern Europe finally join the European Union after the collapse of the Soviet Union in the 1990s. Churchill predicted to Jock Colville in 1953 that he would 'assuredly see Eastern Europe free of Communism' within his life span. Colville died in 1987. Colville, *Fringes*, p. 658.
38. Text of the Zurich speech: WSC, *The Sinews of Peace*, pp. 198–202.
39. Db.dodis.ch, 'Très Confidentiel: Notice pour monsieur le Conseiller fédéral Petitpierre sur mes entretiens avec M. Churchill et M. Montag', 22 September 1946, Nr. 1659, p. 7.
40. Db.dodis.ch., Petitpierre to WSC, 19 September 1946, Nr. 298.
41. Db.dodis.ch., 'Après le discours de Zurich de M. Winston Churchill', P. Ruegger to Petitpierre, 24 September 1946, Nr. 2176, p. 9.

2 'VAGUE AND PUZZLING IDEALISM': 1930–1940

1. R. Coudenhove-Kalergi, *An Idea Conquers the World* (London, 1953), p. 155.
2. Ibid., p. 124.
3. Ibid., p. 95.

4. Ibid., p. 127.
5. F.B. Czarnomski (ed.), *The Wisdom of Winston Churchill* (London, 1956), p. 212.
6. *New York Times*, 6 September 1929.
7. B. Dexter, 'Locarno Again', *Foreign Affairs*, October 1953.
8. For a detailed analysis of Churchill's finances, see D. Lough, *No More Champagne: Churchill and His Money* (London, 2015).
9. Possibly the first time Churchill was confronted about ideas for a kind of United States of Europe was in 1904 when he was sent a seven-page paper – titled 'The United States of Europe' and written by a German army officer – arguing that 'the economic well being of Europe was being sapped by the huge proliferation of military expenditure on separate armies and navies, and suggesting a defensive alliance of Britain and France that would see the former supply the bulk of the navy and the latter the main army.' A. Packwood, 'Winston Churchill and the United States of Europe, 1904–1948', *Comillas Journal of International Relations*, iii/vii (Sept.–Dec. 2016), p. 2; CAC, CHAR 2/18/36, Mr Jameson of Leadenhall House to WSC, 12 October 1904.
10. WSC, 'The United States of Europe', *Saturday Evening Post*, 15 February 1930.
11. Ibid., p. 48.
12. Ibid.
13. M. Gilbert, *Winston S. Churchill*, vol. V (London, 1976), pp. 359–66, 371–3.
14. WSC, 'The United States of Europe', *Saturday Evening Post*, 15 February 1930, p. 48.
15. WSC, *London to Ladysmith via Pretoria* (London, 1900), p. 292.
16. Cited in M. Gilbert, 'Churchill and the European Idea', in R.A.C. Parker, *Winston Churchill: Studies in Statesmanship* (London, 1995), p. 205.
17. Ibid.
18. WSC, 'The Days Ahead in Europe', *Weekly Despatch*, 15 June 1924.
19. Packwood, 'Winston Churchill and the United States of Europe, p. 3.
20. *The Times*, 12 April 1919.
21. Gilbert, 'Churchill and the European Idea', p. 208.
22. R. Toye, *Churchill's Empire* (London, 2010), p. 137.
23. WSC, 'The United States of Europe'. *Saturday Evening Post*, 15 February 1930.
24. CAC, CHAR 2/328, Coudenhove-Kalergi to WSC, 2 February 1938.
25. WSC, 'The United States of Europe'. *Saturday Evening Post*, 15 February 1930
26. Ibid.
27. Ibid.
28. Toye, *Churchill's Empire*, p. 168.
29. R. Boyce, 'Britain First "No" to Europe: Britain and the Briand Plan, 1929–30', *European Studies Review*, x (1980), p. 26.
30. Boyce, 'Britain's First "No" to Europe', pp. 24–5.
31. Coudenhove-Kalergi, *An Idea Conquers the World*, p. 164.
32. 'The Full Text of Briand's Plan for a Union of European Nations', *New York Times*, 18 May 1930.
33. E.L Woodward and R. Butler (eds), *Documents on British Foreign Policy, 1919–1939* (London, 1947), p. 326; Boyce, 'Britain's First "No" to Europe', p. 43.
34. L.S. Amery, *My Political Life, Volume Two: War and Peace, 1914–1929* (London, 1953), p. 510.

35. Amery made a splash in Berlin. He spoke perfect German and warned the continental leaders of the Union that England would not feel able at that time to participate in a federation. See John Barnes and David Nicolson (eds), *The Empire at Bay: The Leo Amery Diaries 1929–1945* (London, 1988), p. 70.
36. CAC, Chartwell Papers (CHAR), 2/238, L.S. Amery to WSC, 11 February 1938; Coudenhove to WSC, 22 February 1938; WSC to Coudenhove, 25 February 1938.
37. Coudenhove-Kalergi, *An Idea Conquers the World*, p. 214.
38. WSC, 'Nations on the Loose', *Collier's*, 4 May 1935.
39. Coudenhove-Kalergi, *An Idea Conquers the World*, pp. 213–14.
40. CHAR 8/615, Press Cutting: WSC, 'Why Not a United States of Europe?', *News of the World*, 29 May 1938.
41. Ibid.
42. Ibid.

3   THREE DAYS IN JUNE: INDISSOLUBLE UNION, 1940

1. WSC, *The Second World War*, vol. I (London: The Reprint Society, 1950), p. 532.
2. WSC, *The Second World War*, vol. II (London: The Reprint Society, 1951), p. 190.
3. I am grateful to Avi Shlaim for his seminal article on the Franco-British Union episode. The narrative of this chapter, though not as complete and more specifically focused on Churchill's involvement, is inevitably based on his work: A. Shlaim, 'Prelude to Downfall: The British Offer of Union to France', *Journal of Contemporary History*, July 1974, 9.
4. A. Shlaim, 'Prelude to Downfall: The British Offer of Union to France', *Journal of Contemporary History*, ix (July 1974), p. 32.
5. Colville, *Fringes*, p. 152.
6. Shlaim, 'Prelude to Downfall, p. 35.
7. Ibid., p. 38.
8. TNA, Prime Minister's Papers (PREM) 3/176, 'Anglo-French Unity', attachment to letter from Leo Amery.
9. J. Monnet, *Memoirs* (London, 1978), p. 22.
10. WSC, *Second World War*, vol. II, p. 162.
11. 'Lord Duncan-Sandys, 79, Dead', *New York Times*, 27 November 1987.
12. Colville, *Fringes*, p. 156.
13. Ibid., p. 156.
14. A. Shlaim, 'Prelude to Downfall', p. 40.
15. Ibid., p. 41.
16. Ibid., p. 42.
17. WSC, *Second World War*, vol. II, p. 176.
18. Ibid., pp. 176–7.
19. Colville, *Fringes*, p. 157. The account of the night as it developed comes from Colville's diary.
20. Ibid.
21. Ibid.
22. Ibid.
23. Ibid., p. 158.

24. Ibid., pp. 157–8.
25. Ibid.
26. C. de Gaulle, *L'Appel* (Paris, 1954), p. 59.
27. WSC, *Second World War*, vol. II, p. 178.
28. P. Reynaud, *In the Thick of the Fight* (London, 1955), p. 540.
29. Cited in P. Kersaudy, *Churchill and de Gaulle* (London, 1981), p. 70.
30. Monnet, *Memoirs*, p. 28.
31. Colville, *Fringes*, p. 160.
32. WSC, *Second World War*, vol. II, p. 184.
33. Reynaud, *Thick of the Fight*, p. 540.
34. WSC, *Second World War*, vol. II, p. 181.
35. Shlaim, 'Prelude to Downfall', p. 51.
36. Monnet, *Memoirs*, p. 29.
37. WSC, *Second World War*, vol. II, p. 181.
38. Full text provided in WSC, *Second World War*, vol. II, p. 179.
39. Reynaud, *Thick of the Fight*, p. 536.
40. Ibid.
41. Shlaim, 'Prelude to Downfall', p. 53.
42. WSC, *Second World War*, vol. II, p. 181.
43. F. Williams, *A Prime Minister Remembers* (London, 1951), pp. 43–4.
44. WSC, *Second World War*, vol. II, p. 183.
45. M. Gilbert, *Winston S. Churchill*, vol. VI (London, 1983), p. 561.
46. Monnet, *Memoirs*, pp. 31–2.
47. This is Avi Shlaim's central argument in 'Prelude to Downfall'.
48. WSC, *Second World War*, Vol. II, p. 181.
49. Reynaud, *Thick of the Fight*, p. 541.
50. Colville, *Fringes*, p. 159.
51. WSC, *Second World War*, vol. II, p. 189.
52. Monnet, *Memoirs*, p. 34.
53. W. Meurs et al., *Europa in Alle Staten – Zestig Jaar Gescheidenis van de Europese Integratie* (Nijmegen, 2013), p. 77.
54. This is the assessment of F. Duchène, *Jean Monnet* (New York, 1994), p. 80.
55. Ibid., p. 81.
56. CHAR 20/127/4, 'Most Secret Message: 52. Strategem No. 30', Prime Minister to Foreign Secretary, 16 January 1943.
57. CHAR 20/94B/208–212, WSC to Duff Cooper, 19 October 1943.
58. PREM 3/176, P. Reynaud to WSC from Bordeaux, 17 June 1940.
59. Reynaud, *Thick of the Fight*, p. 541.
60. Coudenhove-Kalergi, *An Idea Conquers the World*, p. 226.
61. Colville, *Fringes*, p. 161.
62. Colville, *Fringes*, p. 159. Arthur Salter, a civil servant whose ties to Jean Monnet went back to World War I, evidently attached no great importance to his involvement. He makes no mention of it in either of his published books of memoirs.
63. M. Charlton, *The Price of Victory* (London, 1983), p. 38.
64. WSC, *Second World War*, vol. II, pp. 188–90.
65. W. Hayter , *A Double Life* (London, 1974), p. 87.

66. Hansard, HC deb vol. 413 c89, 16 August 1945.
67. Ibid., c101, 16 August 1945.
68. Gilbert, *Winston S. Churchill*, vol. VIII, p. 141.
69. CHUR, 5/18A-D, 'Hague Congress: Notes for Mr. Churchill's Speech', not dated.
70. WSC, *Europe Unite* (London, 1950), p. 320.

4 'A GOOD EUROPEAN': FROM ADANA TO POTSDAM, 1940–1945

1. Colville, *The Fringes of Power: Downing Street Diaries*, pp. 312–13.
2. For a close analysis of Churchill's wartime regionalist thinking (and American and British Foreign Office opposition to it), see R.V. Harrison, 'Winston Churchill and European Integration', unpublished Ph.D. thesis, University of Aberdeen, 1985, ch. 2, pp. 75–113.
3. H. Macmillan, *Tides of Fortune* (London, 1969), Appendix One.
4. Ibid.
5. John Harvey (ed.), *The War Diaries of Oliver Harvey* (London, 1978), pp. 175–6.
6. WSC, *The Second World War*, vol. IV (London: The Reprint Society, 1954), p. 568.
7. For an excellent overview and analysis of Churchill's views on Turkey and its role in Europe, see W. Dockter, 'Churchill, Europe and Turkey', *Comillas Journal of International Relations*, iii/7 (Sept.–Dec. 2016), pp. 57–67.
8. WSC, *The Second World War*, vol. IV, p. 569.
9. D. Dilks (ed.), *The Diaries of Alexander Cadogan* (London, 2010), p. 511.
10. G. Jebb, *The Memoirs of Lord Gladwyn* (London, 1972), pp. 121–3.
11. Charlton, *Price of Victory*, p. 22.
12. WSC, *The Second World War*, Vol. IV, p. 569.
13. Charlton, *Price of Victory*, p. 18.
14. 'Mr. Churchill on Britain After Victory', *Manchester Guardian*, 22 March 1943, p. 5.
15. WSC, 'A Four Years' Plan', 21 March 1943, in C. Eade (ed.), *Onwards to Victory* (London, 1944), p. 36.
16. Ibid.
17. Ibid.
18. Ibid., p. 37.
19. Ibid., pp. 32–45.
20. Charlton, *Price of Victory*, p. 12.
21. WSC, *Second World War*, vol. IV, p. 645.
22. Harrison, 'Winston Churchill and European Integration', pp. 99–110.
23. Eden, *The Reckoning*, p. 424.
24. Harrison, 'Winston Churchill and European Integration', p. 106.
25. WSC, *The Second World War*, vol. VI (London: The Reprint Society, 1956), pp. 194–5.
26. Ibid., p. 289.
27. Churchill underplays de Gaulle's influence in his own account of the Yalta conference: ibid., p. 291.
28. Cited in Kersaudy, *Churchill and de Gaulle*, p. 392.
29. Ibid., p. 394. Kersaudy gives an account of the Yalta conference from the perspective of Churchill's relationship with de Gaulle and argues that it was both British self-interest and Francophilia that moved Churchill to fight France's corner.

30. M. Gilbert, *Winston S. Churchill*, vol. VII (London, 1986), p. 1230. Gilbert describes Churchill's perceived success in the preceding pages.
31. Charlton, *Price of Victory*, p. 25.
32. Colville, *Fringes*, p. 565.
33. Ibid., p. 566.
34. WSC, *Second World War*, vol. VI, p. 440.
35. Charlton, *Price of Victory*, p. 38.
36. D. Reynolds, *In Command of History* (London, 2005), p. 481.
37. Gilbert, *Winston S. Churchill*, vol. VIII, p. 61.
38. Reynolds, *In Command of History*, p. 2.
39. WSC, *Second World War*, vol. VI, p. 502.
40. Ibid., p. 503.
41. Ibid., p. 507.
42. Ibid., p. 532.
43. Ibid., p. 536.
44. Ibid., p. 536.
45. Eden, *The Reckoning*, p. 639.
46. Gilbert, *Winston S. Churchill*, vol. VIII, p. 126.

5 'LET EUROPE ARISE!': SWITZERLAND, SEPTEMBER 1946

1. See: C. Bell, *Churchill and the Dardanelles* (Oxford, 2017).
2. WSC, *Painting as a Pastime*, pp. 36–7.
3. Ibid., pp. 40–1. Churchill often painted in John Lavery's London studio in the years after 1915. Lavery once said: 'Mr Churchill has been called a pupil of mine, which is highly flattering, for I know few amateur wielders of the brush with a keener sense of light and colour, or a surer grasp of essentials.' D. Coombs with M. Churchill, *Sir Winston Churchill: His Life and His Paintings* (London, 2015), p. 26.
4. W. Vogt, *Winston Churchill und die Schweiz* (Zürich, 2015), pp. 118–19.
5. Gilbert, *Winston S. Churchill*, vol. IV (London, 1975), p. 792.
6. Without mentioning him by name, and perhaps forgetting he was actually a Swiss citizen living in Paris, I believe Churchill is talking about Montag when he writes: 'My French friend, for instance, after looking at some of my daubs, took me round the galleries of Paris, pausing here and there.' WSC, *Painting as a Pastime*, p. 73. For a closer look at Churchill's use of his pseudonym, Charles Morin, and the 1921 Parisian exhibition, see D. Coombs, 'Charles Morin and the Search for Churchill's Nom De Palette', http://www.winstonchurchill. org/support?catid=0&id = 2639. See also: Coombs and Churchill, *Sir Winston Churchill*, p. 34.
7. Moran, *The Struggle for Survival 1945–1960*, pp. 5–6.
8. Gilbert, *Winston S. Churchill*, vol. VIII, p. 149.
9. Moran, *The Struggle for Survival 1945–1960*, p. 19.
10. Gilbert, *Winston S. Churchill*, vol. VIII, p. 149
11. Ibid.
12. Ibid.
13. Ibid., p. 138.

14. Cited in W. Vogt, *Winston Churchill: Mahnung, Hoffnung und Vision 1938–1946, Das Churchill-Bild in der Berichterstattung under Kommentierung der Neuen Zürcher Zeitung* (Zurich, 1996), p. 374.

15. Cited ibid.

16. Db.dodis.ch, Vogel to A. Bon, 23 May 1946, Nr. 781. In this letter, Vogel lists the companies that were definitely sponsoring the visit: Zurich Allgemeine Unfall- und Haftplicht-Versicherungs A.G., Schweizerisches Rückversicherungs-Gesellschaft, Firmer Gebr, Sulzer A.G., Firma Gebrüder Volkar, A.G. der Eisen- und Stahlwerke vorm. Georg Fischer, Schaffhausen, Dr. A. Wander A.G., Bern, Nestlé & Anglo-Swiss Holding Co., C.F. Bally A.G. and the various Basle chemical works.

17. CHUR 2/238, T.M. Snow to WSC, 15 June 1946. It has since become clear, through the work of an independent experts committee led by Swiss historian Jean François Bergier, that Swiss industry did benefit significantly from the Nazi regime. Nestlé and others, for instance, were well aware that their German subsidiaries used forced labour. The full report is available online: https://www.uek.ch/en/schlussbericht/synthesis/ueke.pdf.

18. CHUR 2/238, WSC to Montag, 12 May 1946.

19. db.dodis.ch, Burckhardt to Petitpierre, 27 July 1946, Nr. 146, p. 3.

20. 'Mr. Churchill in Switzerland', *The Times*, 24 August 1946.

21. WSC, *The Second World War: Abridged Edition With an Epilogue on the Years 1945 to 1957* (London, 2013), p. 956.

22. TNA, FO 371/60490, 313/59/46, T.M. Snow (Legate in Bern) to E. Bevin, 25 September 1946.

23. Vogt, *Winston Churchill und die Schweiz*, p. 125.

24. Ibid. In July 1946, however, Montag told Ambassador Burckhardt in Paris that the consortium had gathered 60,000 Swiss francs altogether for Churchill's vacation. See db.dodis.ch, Burckhardt to Petitpierre, 27 July 1946, Nr. 146, pp. 1–2.

25. This was £1,000 in 1946. See CHUR 2/238, WSC to Private Secretary, 17 June 1946; db.dodis.ch, 'Bericht von Oberstleutnant Bracher über den Besuch von Winston Churchill in der Schweiz 23. August – 20. September 1946', Nr. 2184, 21 October 1946.

26. db.dodis.ch, Burckhardt to Petitpierre, 27 July 1946, Nr. 146, p. 2.

27. Origins of the 'Iron Curtain' phrase: Sebestyen, *1946*, p. 163.

28. Db.dodis.ch, 'Très Confidentiel: Notice pour monsieur le Conseiller fédéral Petitpierre sur mes entretiens avec M. Churchill et M. Montag', 22 September 1946, Nr. 1659, p. 3.

29. Vogt, *Winston Churchill und die Schweiz*, p. 141.

30. W. Graebner, *Dear Mister Churchill* (London, 1965), p. 66.

31. See WSC, *Second World War and Epilogue*, p. 954; Harrison, 'Winston Churchill and European Integration', pp. 151–2.

32. WSC, *The Sinews of Peace*, pp. 128–34.

33. Ibid.

34. CHUR 2/19, Coudenhove-Kalergi to WSC, 21 May 1946.

35. CHUR 2/19, WSC to Coudenhove-Kalergi, 4 January 1946; Coudenhove-Kalergi to WSC, 15 December 1945.

36. Cited in Gilbert, *Winston S. Churchill*, vol. VIII, pp. 242–3.

37. CHUR 2/19, Viscount Cecil ('Bob') to WSC, 19 June 1946; WSC to Viscount Cecil, 25 June 1946; CHUR 2/23, WSC to Duncan Sandys, 29 June 1946.

38. WSC, *Sinews*, p. 166.
39. Ibid., pp. 167–8.
40. Ibid., p. 171.
41. Moran, *Churchill*, p. 23.
42. WSC, *Sinews*, p. 171.
43. Ibid., p. 174.
44. Ibid., p. 175.
45. 'Churchill for United Europe As Basis for U.N. Success', *New York Times*, 15 July 1946.
46. Bodleian Library, Harold Macmillan Papers (Ms. Macmillan), 'Strasbourg Letters: August–September 1949', 24 August 1929.
47. P. Catterall, *The Macmillan Diaries: The Cabinet Years, 1950–1957* (London, 2003), November 1950, pp. 22–24.
48. Db.dodis.ch, 'Très Confidentiel: Notice pour monsieur le Conseiller fédéral Petitpierre sur mes entretiens avec M. Churchill et M. Montag', 22 September 1946, Nr. 1659, p. 1.
49. Db.dodis.ch, 'Bericht von Oberstleutnant Bracher', Nr. 2184, 18 October 1946.
50. 'Strictly Guarded', *Manchester Guardian*, 26 August 1946, p. 5.
51. In 1967, David Coombs compiled a comprehensive catalogue of Churchill's paintings which lists four painted in Switzerland in the autumn of 1946. Three of them were then in Churchill's studio at Chartwell, one in Lord Moran's collection. See numbers 397, 398, 399 and 444 in D. Coombs, *Churchill: His Paintings* (London, 1967).
52. 'Mr. Churchill Sketching By Lakeside', *The Times*, 29 August 1946.
53. Gilbert, *Winston S. Churchill*, vol. VIII, p. 262.
54. In the early days of September Churchill also received a letter enclosing a recent speech given by Reynaud, a well-known supporter of European federalism. There were also invitations to attend a federalist congress of the Swiss Europa-Union and an invitation to answer a questionnaire from the group L'Action Fédéraliste Européenne. CHUR 2/238, 'List: Despatched by Air Mail on 28 August', undated.
55. Gilbert, *Winston S. Churchill*, vol. VIII, p. 262.
56. Ibid., p. 140.
57. Db.dodis.ch: 'Bericht von Oberstleutnant Bracher', Nr. 2184, 18 October 1946.
58. J. Smuts, *Memoirs of the Boer War* (London, 1994), p. 19.
59. N. Nicolson (ed.), *Harold Nicolson, Diaries & Letters, 1945–62* (London, 1968), pp. 59–60.
60. Speech by J.F. Byrnes, United States Secretary of State Restatement of Policy on Germany, Stuttgart, 6 September 1946, https://usa.usembassy.de/etexts/ga4-460906.htm.
61. CHUR 2/18, WSC to Amery, 25 July 1946.
62. This conversation was recounted by Sandys in 1971 to Prime Minister Edward Heath, who was then on the eve of taking Britain into the Common Market. E. Heath, *The Course of My Life: My Autobiography* (London, 1998), p. 146.
63. S. Onslow, *Backbench Debate within the Conservative Party and its Influence on British Foreign Policy, 1948–57* (London, 1997), p. 17.
64. CHUR 2/19, Coudenhove-Kalergi to WSC, 4 September 1946.
65. Coudenhove-Kalergi, *An Idea Conquers the World*, p. 268.
66. CHUR 2/18, WSC to Amery, 25 July 1946.
67. CAC, Leo Amery Papers (AMEL), 2/2/4, L.S. Amery to WSC, 24 July 1946.

68. AMEL 7/40, typescript diary, 22 August 1946.
69. Db.dodis.ch, 'Très Confidentiel: Notice pour monsieur le Conseiller fédéral Petitpierre sur mes entretiens avec M. Churchill et M. Montag', 22 September 1946, Nr. 1659, p. 3.
70. Coudenhove-Kalergi, *An Idea Conquers the World*, pp. 267–71.
71. WSC, *The Second World War: Abridged Edition With an Epilogue*, pp. 956–7.
72. CHUR 2/40, Bauer-Anders to WSC, 10 September 1946.
73. 'Accident to Mrs. Churchill', *The Times*, 16 September 1946.
76. Petitpierre penned his memory of the encounter in February 1947 on 17 September 1946: 'Il m'a parlé discours qu'il devait prononcer à Zurich le surlendemain, en me demandant si cela me gênait qu'il le prononçât. Je lui ai répondu négativement.' See db.dodis.ch, 'Entretien avec M. Winston Churchill 18 Septembre 1946', February 1947, Nr. 2185, p. 4.
77. Db.dodis.ch, 'Très Confidentiel: Notice pour monsieur le Conseiller fédéral Petitpierre sur mes entretiens avec M. Churchill et M. Montag', 22 September 1946, Nr. 1659, p. 5.

6 'THE BIG THING IN A BIG WAY': ZURICH, SEPTEMBER 1946

1. Db.dodis.ch, 'Très Confidentiel: Notice pour monsieur le Conseiller fédéral Petitpierre sur mes entretiens avec M. Churchill et M. Montag', 22 September 1946, Nr. 1659, p. 5.
2. 'Bericht von Oberstleutnant Bracher', p. 32.
3. CHUR 2/247, Miss Gilliat to Miss Sturdee (private secretaries), 9 September 1946.
4. Db.dodis.ch, 'Très Confidentiel: Notice pour monsieur le Conseiller fédéral Petitpierre sur mes entretiens avec M. Churchill et M. Montag', 22 September 1946, Nr. 1659, p. 6.
5. Ibid.
6. '"Weighty" Speech By Mr Churchill Today', *Manchester Guardian*, 19 September 1946, p. 5.
7. Bericht von Oberstleutnant Bracher', Nr. 2184, 18 October 1946, p. 33.
8. R.A. Butler, 'Churchill's personality and Europe: first Winston Churchill Memorial Lecture, given in the University of Zürich, 24th January 1967', in *Schweizer Monatshefte: Zeitschrift für Politik, Wirtschaft, Kultur*, 47 (1967–8).
9. CHUR 2/4, WSC to Attlee, 6 October 1946.
10. Cited in Sebestyen, *1946*, pp. 72–3.
11. TNA, Lord Keynes Papers, T: 247/40, Reel 6.
12. Hansard, HC deb vol. 417 c. 469, 12 December 1946; R. Boothby, *Recollections of a Rebel* (London, 1978), p. 207.
13. 'U.S. Loan Assailed by British M.P.'s', *New York Times*, 13 December 1945.
14. Cited in Sebestyen, *1946*, p. 76.
15. CHUR 2/158, Truman to WSC, 14 October 1947.
16. CHUR 2/20A-B, 'Attachment: Personal and Confidential, From Professor W. Stewart', Duff Cooper to WSC, 25 September 1946. Professor Stewart worked at the Foreign Office before the war and was Professor of Foreign Policy at Bristol University, of which Churchill was honorary chancellor. He had 'sound views' in the eyes of Cooper and Churchill.

17. 5/8A-C, Press Cutting: *Daily Express*, 20 September 1946.
18. Db.dodis.ch., 'Après le discours de Zurich de M. Winston Churchill', P. Ruegger to Petitpierre, 24 September 1946, Nr. 2176, p. 7.
19. Diplomatic Correspondent, 'An Ill-Timed Speech?', *Manchester Guardian*, 20 September 1946, p. 5.
20. D. Weaver, 'Churchill Speech Perturbs Paris', *News Chronicle*, 20 September 1946.
21. CHUR 5/8A-C, Press Cutting: *The Observer*, 22 September 1946.
22. CHUR 2/248, Press Cutting: *The Weekly Review*, 26 September 1946.
23. *The Times*, 20 September 1946.
24. Ibid.
25. Ibid.
26. CHUR 5/18A-C, Zurich Speech Notes, 19 September 1946.
27. Cited in Vogt, *Winston Churchill: Mahnung, Hoffnung und Vision*, p. 390.
28. Cited in W. Lipgens, *A History of European Integration*, vol. 1. *1945–1947: The Formation of the European Unity Movement* (Oxford, 1982), p. 479.
29. CHUR 2/23, Telegram on American Press Reactions, undated.
30. 'Today and Tomorrow: The Great Churchill', *Washington Post*, 21 September 1946, p. 7.
31. Vogt, *Winston Churchill: Mahnung, Hoffnung und Vision*, pp. 388–9.
32. 'Russians in Berlin Upbraid Churchill', *New York Times*, 20 September 1946.
33. Cited in Lipgens, *A History*, p. 386.
34. Ibid.
35. *Le Monde*, 21 September 1946.
36. CHUR 5/8A-C: Press Cutting, *Daily Express*, 20 September 1946.
37. P. Courtade, 'Le coup des grands sentiments', *L'Humanité*, 20 September 1946. Translation: M. Duranti, *The Conservative Human Rights Revolution: European Identity, Transnational Politics, and the Origins of the European Convention* (Oxford, 2017), p. 110.
38. TNA, FO 371/60490, file 428, 'Mr. Churchill's Speech', 20 September 1946.
39. Db.dodis.ch., 'Après le discours de Zurich de M. Winston Churchill', P. Ruegger to Petitpierre, 24 September 1946, Nr. 2176, p. 7.
40. CHUR 5/18A-C, Zurich speech notes, 18–19 September 1946.
41. CHUR 2/18, Amery to WSC, 20 September 1946.
42. CHUR 2/18, Amery to Sandys, 20 September 1946.
43. AMEL 7/40, typescript diary, 19 September 1946.
44. CHUR 2/19, Coudenhove-Kalergi to WSC, 23 September 1946.
45. See Boothby, *Recollections*, p. 217.
46. These frank and critical words only appeared in the German version of his memoirs: R. Coudenhove-Kalergi, *Eine Idee erobert Europa* (Basel, 1958), p. 292.
47. 'Mr. Churchill at Zurich', *The Times*, 24 September 1946.
48. H.J. Küsters and H.P. Mensing, 'Konrad Adenauer zur Politischen Lage, 1946–1949', pp. 302–3.
49. Adenauer to Adolf Sonnenschein, 12 October 1946, in K. Adenauer, *Briefe 1945–1947* (Berlin, 1983), p. 337.
50. Cited in Vogt, *Winston Churchill: Mahnung, Hoffnung und Vision*, p. 385.
51. Vogt, *Winston Churchill und die Schweiz*, p. 121.

7 'THE IDEAL SHOULD BE EUROPE': CAMPAIGNING IN BRITAIN I, 1946–1947

1. CHUR 2/18, L.S. Amery to Duncan Sandys, 20 September 1946.
2. Churchill soon asked Sandys to take care of almost all his correspondence relating to United Europe. He offered to come to a different arrangement if it became too much of a burden, but Sandys and his secretary, Miss Freda Smith, never wavered in their duty. See CHUR 2/23, WSC to Sandys, 20 October 1946. Sandys enjoyed unparalleled trust and affection from Churchill. In a telegram from Marrakech, Churchill signed off with 'LOVE', normally reserved for his wife and daughters. See CHUR 2/23, WSC to Sandys, 18 December 1947.
3. CHUR 2/18, L.S. Amery to WSC, 20 September 1946.
4. CHUR 2/19, WSC to Coudenhove-Kalergi, 23 September 1946.
5. Onslow, *Backbench Debate*, p. 19.
6. Hansard, HC deb vol. 419 cc1251–2, 20 February 1946.
7. CHUR 5/8A-C, Press Cutting: *News of the World*, 22 September 1946.
8. CHUR 2/22A-B, WSC to the Archbishop of Canterbury, 17 November 1946.
9. CHUR 2/23, Archibald Sinclair to WSC, 18 November 1946.
10. E. Spier, *Focus: A Footnote to the History of the Thirties* (London, 1963).
11. Cited ibid., p. 14. Churchill names his old adversary Walter Citrine and Sir Archibald Sinclair as examples of cross-party support at the Albert Hall. He would later approach both of them to become leading figures in the United Europe Movement.
12. CHUR 2/23, Archibald Sinclair to WSC, 18 November 1946.
13. CHUR 2/23, Duncan Sandys to WSC, 11 October 1946; CHUR 2/23, WSC to Duncan Sandys, 14 October 1946.
14. M. Gilbert, *Churchill and The Jews: A Lifelong Friendship* (London, 2008), p. 135; Spier, *Focus*, p. 152.
15. CHUR 2/23, Sandys to WSC, 1 May 1947.
16. TNA, FO 371/60490, 'Press Notice', 14 September 1946.
17. CAC, Julian Amery Papers (AMEJ), 4/1/1, typescript diary, 24–25 September 1946.
18. AMEJ, 4/1/1, typescript diary, 26 September 1946.
19. CHUR 2/19, Julian Amery to WSC, 27 September 1946.
20. It is possible Randolph secretly hoped to be drawn into his father's nucleus as well. On the eve of the luncheon he sent him a pamphlet on European unity written by Dr Joseph Retinger. See CHUR 2/19, 'My dearest Papa', Randolph Churchill to WSC, 27 September 1946. Randolph is not necessarily a reliable source on his father's opinions and he had a long-standing feud with Eden.
21. Account of the luncheon takes citations from and paraphrases: CAC, AMEJ, 4/1/1, typescript diary, 30 September 1946; AMEL, 7/40, typescript diary, 30 September 1946.
22. Cited in N. Forman, 'The European Movement in Great Britain, 1945–54', unpublished M.Phil. thesis, University of Sussex, p. 128; CAC, AMEL 2/2/4, L.S. Amery to WSC, 28 October 1946.
23. *The Times*, 5 October 1946.
24. CHUR 2/18, L.S. Amery to WSC, 9 October 1946.
25. CAC, AMEL, 7/40, typescript diary, 10 October 1946.
26. P. Stokes, 'Unpublished letters give insight into "fat boy" Goering at Nuremberg Trials', *Daily* Telegraph, 20 March 2009.

27. F. Cockburn, 'Maxwell Fyfe: The Atlas of Nuremberg', *Daily Sketch*, 30 August 1946; M. Duranti, *The Conservative Human Rights Revolution: European Identity, Transnational Politics, and the Origins of the European Convention* (Oxford, 2017), p. 140.

28. Nicolson, *Harold Nicolson Diaries & Letters*, p. 178.

29. Onslow, *Backbench Debate*, p. 21.

30. CAC, AMEL, 7/40, typescript diary, 17 October 1946.

31. CHUR 2/23, WSC to Cranborne (nicknamed 'Bobbety'), 19 October 1946.

32. CHUR 2/23, Phone Transcript Sandys to WSC, 24 October 1946.

33. Ibid.

34. Coudenhove-Kalergi, *An Idea Conquers the World*, p. 271.

35. AMEL 2/2/4, L.S. Amery to WSC, 28 October 1946.

36. CHUR 2/19, 'Statement of Aims', attachment in letter from WSC to Lord Citrine, 20 October 1946.

37. Onslow, *Backbench Debate*, p. 18.

38. CHUR 2/20A-B, Freda Smith (Sandys's private secretary) to Miss Gilliat (WSC's private secretary), 26 November 1946.

39. CHUR 2/30, WSC to de Gaulle, 1 November 1946.

40. A. Beevor and A. Cooper, *Paris after the Liberation: 1944–1949* (London, 1995), p. 340.

41. CHUR 2/30, WSC to de Gaulle, 26 November 1946.

42. This paraphrases Churchill from a story he wrote that would become known as 'The Dream', in which he imagines telling his late father about the horrors of the twentieth century. M. Gilbert, *Winston S. Churchill*, vol. VIII, pp. 364–72.

43. CHUR 2/20A-B, 'Visit to General de Gaulle – November 29th, 1946', 13 December 1946.

44. Ibid.

45. CHUR 2/18, WSC to Attlee, 27 November 1946.

46. CHUR 20A-B, 'Draft Statement of Policy by Stephen King-Hall', 3 December 1946.

47. CAC, AMEL, 7/40, typescript diary, 3 December 1946; CHUR 2/20A-B, 'Chairman's Notes', 3 December 1946.

48. CHUR 2/22A-B, 'Confidential', Private Secretary to Mr. Churchill to Boothby, 28 December 1946. Churchill was hesitant to include Russell at first, for he thought he was 'a notorious agnostic'. Boothby and Gollancz talked him out of the idea. See CHUR 2/20A-B, Gollancz to WSC, 23 December 1946.

49. CHUR 2/18, Attlee to WSC, 4 December 1946.

50. CHUR 2/20A-B, WSC to Dr Ballard, 28 December 1946.

51. AMEL 7/40, typescript diary, 18 December 1946.

52. WSC, 'The Scaffolding of Rhetoric', unpublished essay, November 1897.

8 'WE SHALL HAVE DONE OUR BEST': CAMPAIGNING IN BRITAIN II, 1947–1948

1. WSC, 'One Way to Stop a New War', 30 December 1946, in W. Dockter (ed.), *Winston Churchill at The Telegraph* (London, 2015), pp. 184–90.

2. After the tribute, Mr Sewell was immediately offered a leader writer appointment at the *Daily Express*. A few months later, Churchill seriously considered writing the foreword to Mr Sewell's book *Europe's Fate*, then being published by Victor Gollancz. Before it came to that, Randolph found a few passages with which his father might not want to be associated. Churchill's only criticism was: 'one must not try to be too clever. No one comprehends the world.' See CHUR 2/23, WSC to Sewell, 20 May 1947; Sewell to WSC, 17 May 1947; CHUR 2/20A-B, WSC to Gollancz, undated.

3. 'The Grand Design of a United Europe', 31 December 1946, in Dockter, *Winston Churchill at The Telegraph* pp. 191–6.

4. The full membership of the Committee was as follows: Robert Boothby, David Maxwell Fyfe, Oliver Stanley (Conservative MPs), L.S. Amery, Ernest Brown, Duncan Sandys (leading Conservatives without a seat), Evelyn King, the Rev. Gordon Lang, Lord Lindsay of Berker (Labour MPs), George Gibson, Victor Gollancz, Commander Stephen King-Hall (leading Labourites without a seat), Frances Josephy, Sir Walter Layton, Lady Rhys Williams (leading Liberals), Dr J. J. Mallon, Prof. Gilbert Murray, Earl Bertrand Russell (scientists), W.R. Matthews, S.E. Ellis, Dr S. Berry (Church leaders) and the well-known federalist Lionel Curtis. Earl Russell and Dr Mallon were members of the Labour Party. Evelyn King, Gordon Lang and Miss Josephy were also known as ardent federalists.

5. This is also the assessment of Walter Lipgens in *A History of European Integration* (1982), p. 325.

6. CHUR 2/20A-B, 'Statement of Aims: Revised Draft "E"', 16 January 1947.

7. Cited in Lipgens, *A History*, p. 325.

8. CHUR 2/18, 'General News Talks (as broadcast): "United Europe" by Commander King-Hall', 17 January 1947.

9. CHUR 2/18. 'Private: WSC to DS', 7 April 1947.

10. TNA, FO 371/67578, Circular No. 064, UN 2041/842/78, Ernest Bevin, 10 April 1947.

11. TNA, FO 371/67578, Foreign Office to Paris and Washington, 3 February 1948.

12. TNA, FO 371/67578, NEC to all Labour Party Members, 22 January 1947.

13. CHUR 2/20A-B, 'Mr. Dalton on European Union (collection of citations)', undated.

14. Layton Papers, Box 132/2&3, Richards to Layton, 27 August & 20 November 1947.

15. CHUR 2/22A-B, Private Secretary to WSC, 10 June 1947.

16. CHUR 2/22A-B, Sandys to WSC, 9 September 1948.

17. List of donations cited in Forman, 'The European Movement in Great Britain, 1945–1954', Appendix I, pp. 419–20.

18. CHUR 2/22A-B, Harry McGowan to WSC, 10 November 1948.

19. CHUR 2/27, WSC to Harry McGowan, 6 July 1949.

20. CHUR 2/18, Sandys to WSC, 11 June 1948.

21. CHUR 2/18, Beddington-Behrens to Churchill, 14 July 1948.

22. R.J. Aldrich, 'OSS, CIA and European unity: The American committee on United Europe, 1948–60', *Diplomacy & Statecraft*, viii/1 (1997), pp. 184–227.

23. Churchill wrote to thank Bill Donovan, the leader of the committee, for the money: 'I am most grateful to your Committee for voting $25,000 to support our campaign for European unity, and for the indication contained in your letter of the further assistance which we may hope to retain during the course of the year.' He had already told Donovan that he wanted the money for immediate use by the

European Movement. Donovan promised there would be at least $50,000 more in the upcoming months. CHUR 2/26A-B, WSC to Donovan, 24 July 1949; Donovan to WSC, 15 July 1949; WSC to Donovan, 4 June 1949.

24. Ibid., p. 28.
25. B. Simms, *Britain's Europe: A Thousand Years of Conflict and Cooperation* (London, 2016), p. 175.
26. CHUR 2/20A-B, 'United Europe Committee: Minutes of a luncheon meeting held on Tuesday, March 18th at the Savoy Hotel'.
27. M. Pottle, *Daring to Hope: The Diaries and Letters of Violet Bonham Carter 1946–1969* (London, 2000), pp. 25–6.
28. Study cited in B. Grob-Fitzgibbon, *Continental Drift: Britain and Europe from the End of Empire to the Rise of Euroscepticism* (Cambridge, 2016), pp. 74–5. Original source: CAC, Mark Abrams Papers (ABMS) 3/8, 'Public Opinion Survey: Marshall Plan: J.112', March 1948.
29. CHUR 2/18, Sandys to WSC, 31 March 1947.
30. CHUR 2/22, Sandys to WSC, 17 April 1947; WSC, *Europe Unite*, p. 65.
31. CHUR 2/18, 'Speeches at Albert Hall Meeting', 29 April 1947.
32. Story from Julian Amery's memory in Onslow, *Backbench Debate*, p. 18.
33. CHUR 2/19, Pamphlet sent to WSC ('Europe Seek Unity', p. 59), 18 January 1949.
34. 'Churchill Opens Europe Union Drive', *New York Times*, 15 May 1947.
35. Gilbert, *Winston S. Churchill*, vol. VIII, p. 398. The 16 nations were: Austria, Belgium, Denmark, France, Greece, Iceland, Ireland, Italy, Luxembourg, The Netherlands, Norway, Portugal, Sweden, Switzerland, Turkey and the United Kingdom.
36. Benjamin Grob-Fitzgibbon, in his close study of Britain, Empire and Europe since 1945, writes of the Albert Hall address: 'Gone was the earlier ambivalence of Churchill's pre-war speeches and articles. The United Kingdom was 'profoundly blended' with Europe – was, indeed, European – and it would be a 'prime mover' in the cause of a United Europe.' Grob-Fitzgibbon, *Continental Drift*, p. 52.
37. WSC, *The Second World War: Abridged Edition With an Epilogue*, p. 968.
38. Text of the full Albert Hall speech in: WSC, *Europe Unite*, pp. 77–85.
39. Lipgens, *A History*, p. 329.
40. CHUR 2/22 B, Rhys Williams to WSC, 15 May 1947.
41. 'Mr Churchill's Challenge', *The Economist*, 17 May 1947.
42. CHUR 2/18, Boggs to WSC, 21 May 1947.
43. CHUR 2/20A-B, WSC to Eden, 19 April 1947; WSC to Eden, 15 June 1947; Eden to WSC, 19 June 1947.
44. All information on UEM development in 1948 from: CAC, Duncan Sandys Papers (DSND), 9/1/7, GP/P/11, 'United Europe Movement – The Campaign in Britain (Paper submitted by the Organising Secretary)', undated.
45. WSC, *Europe Unite*, p. 465.

9 'HERE I AM AT HOME': THE CONGRESS OF EUROPE, MAY 1948

1. 'The Walrus and the Carpenter' appeared as a narrative poem in Lewis Carroll's *Through the Looking Glass* (1871).
2. Cited in Charlton, *Price of Victory*, p. 78.

3. J. Pomian (ed.), *Joseph Retinger: Memoirs of an Eminence Grise* (London, 1972), p. 215.

4. Pottle, *Daring to Hope*, p. 50; K. Larres, *Churchill's Cold War* (New Haven, CT, 2002), p. 147.

5. CHUR 2/20A-B, United Europe Movement: Minutes of a meeting of the General Purposes Committee at the House of Commons', 23 October 1947. The Committee also approved in principle of the idea of holding a European Conference at The Hague next Easter.

6. Lipgens, *A History*, p. 674.

7. Ibid., p. 682.

8. European Movement, *The European Movement and the Council of Europe* (London, 1949), p. 33.

9. Duncan Sandys Papers (DSND), 9/1/7, Sandys to Boothby, 16 January 1948.

10. Hansard, HC deb, vol 446 cc529–622, 23 January 1948.

11. CHUR 2/21A-B: WSC to Attlee, 1 February 1948; Attlee to WSC, 4 February 1948; Shinwell to WSC, 10 February 1948; WSC to Attlee 12 February 1948.

12. Pottle, *Daring to Hope*, p. 41.

13. CHUR 2/21A-B, WSC to Attlee, 1 February 1948; Attlee to WSC, 4 February 1948; Shinwell to WSC, 10 February 1948; WSC to Attlee 12 February 1948; Press Cuttings: *The Times*, 13 February 1948; *Manchester Guardian*, 13 February; *Daily Telegraph*, 15 February.

14. CHUR 2/21A-B, WSC to Attlee 12 February 1948.

15. WSC, *Europe Unite*, pp. 239–40.

16. Pottle, *Daring to Hope*, p. 43; Gilbert, *Winston S. Churchill*, vol. VIII, p. 399.

17. DSND, 9/1/7, Retinger to Morgan Phillips, 10 March 1948.

18. CAC, John Hynd Papers (HYND), 4/9, Morgan Phillips (NEC) to John Hynd, 21 April 1948.

19. CHUR 2/21A-B, Boothby to WSC, 23 March 1948.

20. DSND, 9/1/7, 'United Europe News No. I', January 1948.

21. DSND 9/1/7, Document IC/P/18, 'Arrangements for the Hague Congress: Note by Chairman of Executive', not dated but can only have been circulated after 30 March 1948.

22. Marco Duranti argues that it was the fall of Czechoslovakia and the hapless response of the United Nations that informed Churchill's support for a supranational human rights regime in Europe. See Duranti, *The Conservative Human Rights Revolution*, pp. 153–5.

23. CHUR 2/18, WSC to Blum, 7 April 1948.

24. Ibid.

25. Ibid.

26. DSND, 9/1/7, Mackay to Sandys, 14 May 1948.

27. CHUR 2/20A-B, 'Agenda: United Europe Movement, Luncheon Meeting of the Executive', 3 March 1948; 'R. Boothby, Memorandum on United Europe', 3 March 1948.

28. Packwood, 'Winston Churchill and the United States of Europe', p. 8; CAC, CHUR 2/19, 'Draft political report', Joint International Committee of the Movements for European Unity, 12 March 1948.

29. Dutch National Archives (NL-HaNA), Collection 378, P.A. Kerstens, 2.21.183.43, inv.nr. 53. All information on finances is in this file.

30. Macmillan, *Tides of Fortune*, p. 161.
31. NL-HaNA, Collection 378, P.A. Kerstens, 2.21.183.43, 53.
32. Cited in M. Beers, 'Hosting Europe: Local Organisation of the Congress of Europe', in *Congrès de l'Europe à la Haye, 1948–2008* (Brussels, 2009), p. 142.
33. DSND, 9/1/6, Claire Haremaker to Duncan Sandys, 23 April 1948.
34. CHUR 2/20A-B, 'United Europe Movement: Minutes of a meeting of the General Purposes Committee at the House of Commons', 17 March 1948. During the same meeting Churchill directed the General Purpose Committee of the United Europe Movement to start looking into a statement on human rights on the lines of those enumerated by the United Nations.
35. Onslow, *Backbench Debate*, pp. 34–8.
36. NL-HaNa, Council of Ministers 1823–1977, 2.02.05.02, inv. No. 390.
37. Konrad-Adenauer Stiftung (ed.), *Konrad Adenauer und die CDU der britischen Besatzungszone 1946–1949, Dokumente zur Gründungsgeschichte der CDU Deutschlands* (Bonn, 1975), p. 882.
38. CHUR 2/17. Churchill and Adenauer needed an interpreter to communicate. Churchill's quote on Adenauer is from WSC, *The Unwritten Alliance: Speeches 1953 to 1959 by Winston Churchill* (London, 1961), pp. 45–54.
39. CHUR 6/6, WSC to Adenauer, 1 December 1954; Gilbert, *Winston S. Churchill*, vol. VIII, p. 1075.
40. CHUR 2/80. Churchill responded: 'I particularly appreciated your message after our pleasant talk about United Europe at the Hague two years ago.' Ibid., 7 December 1949.
41. CHUR 2/261.
42. 'Letter from The Hague', *New Yorker*, 22 May 1948.
43. DSND, 9/1/1, UEM Minutes, 17 March 1948.
44. London School of Economics (LSE), Juliet Rhys Williams Archives, 6/6/1, Rhys Williams to Kerstens, 18 March 1948.
45. NL-HaNa, Kerstens, 2.21.183.43, inv. No. 55.
46. DSND, 9/1/6, Sandys to Mackay, 9 March 1948.
47. DSND, 9/1/6, L.S. Amery to Sandys, 20 April 1948.
48. DSND, 9/1/6, Sandys to Coudenhove-Kalergi, 21 April 1948.
49. AMEJ 4/1/3. Typescript Diary, 8 May 1948.
50. 'Letter From The Hague', *New* Yorker, 22 May 1948.
51. TNA, FO 371/73271, File 2735, 537/8/48, No. 313, Philip Nichols (Ambassador in The Hague) to Ernest Bevin, 13 May 1948.
52. *Leeuwarder Courant*, 9 May 1948.
53. CHUR 2/23, Christopher Soames paper: 'A European Democratic Union', 1944 (not more specifically dated in the accompanying minute). Churchill revisited this paper in 1947.
54. 'Letter From The Hague', *New* Yorker, 22 May 1948.
55. CHUR, 5/18A, 'Hague Congress: Notes for Mr. Churchill's Speech', not dated.
56. CHUR 2/18, VBC to WSC, 30 April 1948.
57. Churchill and HRH Prince Bernhard of the Netherlands got along like a house on fire. After the Congress, Churchill got in touch with Bernhard about the Cuban cigars he brought to The Hague. Bernhard had seemed to take a liking to them, prompting Churchill to arrange with the manufacturer to make similar ones for the

Dutch Prince. CHUR 2/174, WSC to His Royal Highness Prince Bernhard of the Netherlands, 5 July 1948.

58. *The Times*, 8 May 1948.
59. CHUR, 5/18A, 'Hague Congress: Notes for Mr. Churchill's Speech', not dated.
60. WSC, *Europe Unite*, pp. 312–13.
61. Cited in Grob-Fitzgibbon, *Continental Drift*, pp. 54–5.
62. Cited in ibid., p. 55.
63. CHUR, 5/18A-D, Copy of L.S. Amery speech, Leeds, 4 March 1948.
64. WSC, *Europe Unite*, p. 316.
65. CAC, AMEJ 4/1/3, Typescript Diary, 8 May 1948.
66. 'Winston Op 't Loo', *De Tijd*, 10 May 1948.
67. 'I want to have a nice cool drink', *De Locomotief*, 9 May 1948.
68. Pottle, *Daring to Hope*, p. 50.
69. Ibid., p. 51.
70. 'Het Bezoek van Winston Churchill', *Nieuwsblad Van Friesland*, 7 May 1948.
71. European Movement, *European Movement and the Council of Europe*, pp. 47–8.
72. For different accounts of the storm, its timing and Churchill's reaction to it: Pottle, *Daring to Hope*, p. 51; Macmillan, *Tides of Fortune*, p. 162; Lord Kilmuir, *Political Adventure: The Memoirs of the Earl of Kilmuir* (London, 1964), p. 175; CAC, AMEJ 4/1/3, Typescript Diary, 10 May 1948.
73. TNA, FO 371/73271, File 2735, 537/8/48, No. 313, Philip Nichols (Ambassador in The Hague) to Ernest Bevin, 13 May 1948.
74. CAC, CHUR 2/22A, WSC to Lord Layton, 25 May 1948.
75. P. Spaak, 'The European Tragedy', 15 March 1951, *Vital Speeches*, xvii/11, p. 325.
76. 'Lessons of The Hague', *The Economist*, 15 May 1948.
77. D. de Rougemont, *The Meaning of Europe* (London, 1965), pp. 82–3.
78. Coudenhove-Kalergi, *An Idea Conquers the World*, pp. 287–8.
79. For an account of the 'March on Downing Street' of 17 June 1948 see Macmillan, *Tides of Fortune*, pp. 163–4. Lord Layton, Mr R.W.G. Mackay and Mr Kenneth Lindsay also spoke in the Prime Minister's office on the proceedings at The Hague. The rest of the deputation of 20 consisted of: Sir Peter Macdonald, Alderman H. Hynd, Commander King-Hall, Sir Harold Butler, Mr Kenneth Lindsay, Lady Violet Bonham Carter, Mr Duncan Sandys, Mr Churchill, Mr Delargy, Mr Boothby, Mr Christopher Shawcross, Mr Harold Macmillan, Lady Rhys-Williams, Mr Clement Davies, Mr Henry Hopkinson, Miss Josephy, Mr Beddington-Behrens and Sir Arthur Salter.
80. Czarnomski, *The Wisdom of Winston Churchill* (London, 1956), p. 36.
81. C. Attlee, *As It Happened* (London, 1954), 169.

10 'WHERE ARE THE GERMANS?': THE COUNCIL OF EUROPE, AUGUST 1949–1951

1. Cited in Gilbert, *Winston S. Churchill*, vol. VIII, p. 598.
2. CAC, CHUR 2/22A, King-Hall to WSC, June 1948.
3. WSC, *The Second World War: Abridged Edition With an Epilogue*, p. 959.
4. Charlton, *Price of Victory*, p. 75.

5. TNA, CAB 21/14/31/205, 'Western Union: Note on The Hague Deputation', 17 June 1948.

6. Ibid.

7. Account of meeting in Attlee's room and Bevin's arguments in CHUR 2/18, Violet Bonham Carter to WSC, 24 June 1948.

8. CAC, CHUR 2/18, WSC to Attlee, 27 July 1948.

9. CAC, CHUR 2/18, Attlee to WSC, 30 July 1948.

10. Cited in Gilbert, *Winston S. Churchill*, vol. VIII, p. 425.

11. H. Spaak, *The Continuing Battle: Memoirs of a European, 1936–1966* (London, 1971), p. 202.

12. CHUR 2/22A-B, 'Press Cutting: United Europeans, Manchester Guardian', undated.

13. CHUR 2/68A-B, WSC to Anthony Eden, 12 September 1948 (writing from a holiday in Aix-en-Provence, Hôtel du Roy René).

14. WSC, *The Second World War: Abridged Edition With an Epilogue*, p. 962.

15. Grob-Fitzgibbon, *Continental Drift*, p. 99; Cadbury Research Library, AP 19/1/33B, *Daily Express*, 8 September 1948.

16. Ibid.

17. Charlton, *Price of Victory*, p. 77.

18. TNA, CAB 21/14/31/205, 'The Second Session of the Consultative Assembly of the Council of Europe' by Denis Healey, undated.

19. In December 1952, after dinner at Chartwell, Boothby wrote to thank Churchill for his rehabilitation: 'I do hope I am not now the cause of any embarrassment to you. I have had a long and hard struggle for survival, but I see the light at the end of the tunnel; and, thanks to you, I have been able to do some work at Strasbourg which may one day bear fruit. I have no grievances.' CAC, CHUR 2/181, Boothby to WSC, 14 December 1952.

20. DSND, 9/1/7, Bob Boothby to Duncan Sandys, 6 May 1949.

21. For Boothby's assessment of Churchill and his relationship with him: Boothby, *Recollections*, pp. 54–7.

22. CHUR 2/75A-B, 'Mr. Churchill: Telephone Message', Sandys to WSC, 16 May 1949.

23. Boothby, *Recollections*, p. 217.

24. Ibid.

25. Ms. Macmillan, 'Strasbourg Letters', dep. c. 11/2, Number 1, 22 August 1949.

26. Macmillan, *Tides of Fortune*, p. 168.

27. Ibid., p. 165.

28. Bodleian Library (Oxford), Macmillan Papers (Ms. Macmillan), 'Letters from Harold Macmillan to Lady Dorothy Written at Strasbourg 1949', dep. c. 11/2, Number 1, 22 August 1949.

29. Ibid.

30. Ibid.

31. Edouard Herriot cited in Harrison, 'Winston Churchill and European Integration', p. 232.

32. TNA, PREM 8/1431, 4, handwritten note by Attlee, 16 August 1949. Cited in A. Deighton, 'The British in Strasbourg: Negotiating the European Convention on Human Rights, 1950', in R. Mariager, K. Molin & K. Brathagen (eds), *Human Rights Europe during the Cold War* (London, 2014), p. 29. Deighton confirms in the same

chapter that 'the ECHR idea came from the European Movement, led by the leader of the Conservative Party, Churchill.' Ibid., p. 38.

33. Ms. Macmillan, 'Strasbourg Letters', dep. c. 11/2, Number 1, 22 August 1949.
34. Ibid.
35. Macmillan, *Tides of Fortune*, p. 172.
36. Ms. Macmillan, 'Strasbourg Letters', dep. c. 11/2, Number 2, 22 August 1949.
37. Ibid.
38. Macmillan, *Tides of Fortune*, p. 173.
39. Ms. Macmillan, 'Strasbourg Letters', dep. c. 11/2, Number 2, 22 August 1949.
40. Ibid.
41. E. Shuckburgh, *Descent to Suez, Diaries 1951–1956* (London, 1986), p. 11.
42. Ms. Macmillan, 'Strasbourg Letters', dep. c. 11/2, Number 2, 22 August 1949.
43. Cited in Grob-Fitzgibbon, *Continental Drift*, p. 114; TNA, FO 371/80024, Minute from F.D.W. Brown, 6 October 1949.
44. Churchill may have been encouraged to take up West German membership as his main focus by a letter from Henry Hopkinson, a Conservative MP and declared federalist who wrote in July 1949 that German inclusion in European union was the only way to counter the feelings of German nationalism which were on the upsurge in the lead-up to the elections. See CHUR 2/26A-B, Henry Hopkinson to WSC, 13 July 1949.
45. Simms, *Britain's Europe*, p. 175.
46. Macmillan, *Tides of Fortune*, p. 176.
47. Despite the disappointment about the festivities, Churchill gifted 200,000 francs of his personal fortune to the mayor of Strasbourg to use as he saw fit. The Mayor decided to allocate the money to the poor Strasbourgeois elderly. Archives de la Ville et de l'Eurométropole de Strasbourg, 235MW 135 89/968, item 44, internal record taking note of gift, 6 September 1950.
48. Macmillan, *Tides of Fortune*, p. 175.
49. Ms. Macmillan, dep. c. 896, Press Cutting: 'Verdict on Strasbourg', *The Spectator*, 16 September 1949.
50. Ms. Macmillan, dep. c. 896, Press Cutting: 'Verdict on Strasbourg', *The Spectator*, 16 September 1949.
51. All in all there were 24 reports which confirm the general narrative presented in the letters to Lady Dorothy and later recounted in Macmillan's memoirs. The only major difference is that Macmillan does make reference in the reports to Bob Boothby, who was still sexually involved with his wife. He does so in a remarkably balanced way, complimenting him at times and at other times offering critique. For an example of this, see Ms. Macmillan, dep. c. 896, Report No. 17, 3 September 1949.
52. Ms. Macmillan, dep. c. 896, 'Resolution: Proposed Addition to the Agenda'.
53. Moran, *The Struggle for Survival 1945–60*, p. 39.
54. Ibid. p. 40.
55. Ibid.
56. Ms. Macmillan, dep. c. 896, 'Report: No. 15', 30 August 1949.
57. Macmillan, *Tides of Fortune*, p. 181.
58. Ms. Macmillan, 'Strasbourg Letters', dep. c. 11/2, Number 7, 7 September 1949.
59. Ibid.

60. Ms. Macmillan, dep. c. 896, 'Extract from Minute from Winston S. Churchill to Anthony Eden, 21 October 1942,' 5 September 1949. Macmillan and Churchill left out some passages and sentences that were either of minor importance or did not correspond with Churchill's beliefs anymore. For example, they decided to remove the part where Churchill included in the Council of Europe 'several confederations – Scandinavian, Danubian, Balkan, etc. – which would possess an international police and be charged with keeping Prussia disarmed'. And after 'Europe is our prime care,' it originally read: 'and we certainly do not wish to be shut up with the Russians and the Chinese.' Churchill at the time was already wary of Russian intentions and did not recognise China as a great power, while Eden wanted to build a system of world security with the four 'great powers' – the USA, the USSR, Great Britain and China.

61. Eden was seemingly not as impressed: he never mentioned the minute in his memoirs.

62. It is true that there were undeniable partisan advantages to the Conservatives. The Strasbourg Tories were acutely aware of this. Maxwell Fyfe wrote to Macmillan upon his departure: 'Probably the [Conservative] Party will fail to grasp what a masterstroke for their interest was played at Strasbourg. But the intelligent people in Europe know. Reynaud said our Socialists were caught on a metro staircase which suddenly began to move downwards. They puffed and panted but all the time lost ground.' Ms. Macmillan, dep. c. 896, David Maxwell Fyfe to Harold Macmillan, 6 September 1946.

63. Ben Pimlott (ed.), *The Political Diary of Hugh Dalton 1918–40, 1945–60* (London, 1986), p. 425.

64. CHUR 2/25A-B, 'United Europe Movement: Meeting of the Council of Management Held in the House of Commons', 26 April 1950.

65. R. Churchill, *In The Balance* (London, 1951), Speech in the House of Commons, 28 March 1950, p. 250.

66. See Boothby, *Recollections*, p. 218. Churchill, though it is unlikely he was intimately involved in drawing up specific plans, generally approved of Boothby's original call for the political authority.

67. CHUR 2/25A-B, 'Creation of a European Political Authority and Functional Institutions: States approved by the International Executive Committee of the European Movement and submitted to the General Affairs Committee of the European Assembly,' 21 January 1950.

68. For a complication of this narrative, see M. Duranti, 'From Vichy to Strasbourg: The French Far Right, National Reconciliation and Supranational Human Rights Law', in Birgit Schwelling (ed.), *Reconciliation, Civil Society and the Politics of Memory: Transnational Initiatives in the 20th Century* (Bielefeld, 2012). Duranti confirms that Teitgen, Maxwell Fyfe and Churchill are the three most important names associated with the postwar European human rights revolution but argues that the charter was a right-wing ploy to reassert illiberal Catholic communitarianism after the war.

69. 'Ministers Disagree on Human Rights', *The Scotsman*, 10 August 1949.

70. CHUR 2/25A-B, Lord Cherwell to WSC, 4 August 1949.

71. CAC, DSND, 9/1/2, GP/M/9: 'Minutes of a meeting of the General Purposes Committee, 17 March 1948'; Duranti, *The Conservative Human Rights Revolution* (Oxford, 2017), p. 155.

72. WSC, *Europe Unite*, p. 312.

73. European Movement, *The European Movement and the Council of Europe*, p. 38.

74. WSC, *In the Balance*, pp. 26–30.

75. CHUR 2/75A-B, 'Confidential (Stras. 49, 1): Minutes of the Meeting of the United Kingdom Delegation to the Consultative Assembly of the Council of Europe On Wednesday July 20th, at 5 P.M., The Lord President of the Council in the Chair', undated.

76. Kilmuir, *Political Adventure*, p. 175.

77. Ibid., p. 176.

78. Deighton, 'The British in Strasbourg', p. 38.

79. CHUR 2/26A-B, 'Translation: Robert Schuman to Paul Ramadier', 3 February 1951.

80. See Kilmuir, *Political Adventure*, p. 180. And for a largely British perspective: A. W. Brian Simpson, *Human Rights and the End of Empire* (Oxford, 2001), pp. 597–807.

81. Ms. Macmillan, dep. c. 896, Macmillan to Churchill, 15 August 1949.

82. CHUR 2/25A-B, 'Strasbourg Report, Annex D: Extracts From Speeches of Conservative Representatives', 26 September 1949.

83. Packwood, 'Winston Churchill and the United States of Europe',, p. 9.

84. CHUR 2/25A, Coudenhove-Kalergi to WSC, 22 April 1949.

85. CHUR 2/25A, Duncan Sandys to WSC, 3 May 1949.

86. CHUR 2/25A-B, WSC to Coudenhove-Kalergi, 8 May 1949.

87. CHUR 2/25A, Coudenhove-Kalergi to WSC, 17 May 1949.

88. CHUR 2/25A, WSC to Coudenhove-Kalergi, December 1949.

89. WSC, *In The Balance*, pp. 151–4.

90. CHUR 2/275, 'WSC: Recommendation for Chef Camille Pichot', 22 August 1950.

91. CHUR 2/275, Duncan Sandys' private secretary to WSC, 25 May 1950.

92. CHUR 2/275, Private Secretary to Mr. Davies, 27 July 1950; 'Private Office: Strasbourg Arrangements', 13 July 1950.

93. CHUR 2/275, Madame Ehret to Lettice Marston (private secretary), 26 July 1950.

94. For Churchill's finances in the years 1948–50, see Lough, *No More Champagne*, pp. 348–64. Lough makes no mention of the Strasbourg trip and focuses on the memoirs instead.

95. All calculations based on the bills in the file for the Strasbourg visit in the Churchill papers: CHUR 2/275. The main beneficiaries were local stores like *FRICK* (meat), *Brucker* (fish), *Ungemach* (regular groceries), *P. Saillard* (fruit), *Boeckel* (50 liters of red wine) and *Charles Rauch Barr* (white wine). Conversion rates for 1950 from francs to pounds sterling are provided for Churchill in the papers, and inflation rates are calculated with the online historic inflation calculator of the Bank of England. David Lough provides the following figures: francs $1,250 = 1$ pound [1948], inflation multiples: UK × 30: Lough, *No More Champagne*, p. 348.

96. The car belonged to the mayor of Strasbourg, Charles Frey. See Archives de la Ville et de l'Eurométropole de Strasbourg, 235MW 135 89/965, Charles Frey to Miss Ford, 26 June 1950.

97. Spaak, *The Continuing Battle*, p. 73.

98. Nicolson, *Harold Nicolson Diaries & Letters, 1945–62*, p. 41

99. WSC, *In the Balance*, pp. 32–9.

100. Hansard, HC deb, vol. 463 cc931–2, 28 March 1950.

101. Cited in Gilbert, *Winston S. Churchill*, vol. VIII, pp. 530–1.

102. Catterall, *The Macmillan Diaries*, p. 6.
103. CHUR 2/76A-B, 'Luncheon & Dinner Guests', 8 August 1950.
104. As the luncheon and dinner planning lists for Strasbourg show, Sandys, functioning as Churchill's chief of staff, was in attendance at almost every important turn. He was there on Wednesday 9 August for luncheon with President Spaak and Count Coudenhove-Kalergi; that same day for dinner with André Philip and the Dutch federalist Piet Serrarens; and the next day for dinner with representatives from Italy, Norway and Greece. See CHUR 2/76A-B, 'Luncheon & Dinner Guests', 8, 9 & 10 August 1950.
105. Kilmuir, *Political Adventure*, p. 185.
106. Catterall, *Macmillan Diaries*, p. 7.
107. Macmillan, *Tides of Fortune*, p. 215.
108. CHUR 2/76A-B, 'IP/171/PL/YM: M. Boothby on European Army', 25 August 1950.
109. CHUR 2/76A-B, 'Reuters Frankfurt Summary of Strasbourg Debate', undated.
110. Boothby, *Recollections*, p. 219.
111. CHUR 2/27, Private Secretary to WSC, 14 June 1950.
112. CHUR 2/76A-B, 'Luncheon & Dinner Guests', 10 August 1950.
113. Ms. Macmillan, dep. c. 894, 'Assembly Statements on European Army: IP/171/PL/ SD', 25 October 1950.
114. Catterall, *Macmillan Diaries*, 11 August, pp. 8–10.
115. CHUR 2/76A-B, "Confidential: Emergency', Prime Minister Attlee to WSC, 11 August 1950.
116. Spaak, *The Continuing Battle*, p. 217.
117. Catterall, *Macmillan Diaries*, 11 August 1950, pp. 8–10.
118. Grob-Fitzgibbon, *Continental Drift*, p. 142.
119. CHUR 2/32 (whole file on European Army), Lew Douglas to WSC, 29 August 1950.
120. CHUR 2/32, WSC to President Truman, 13 August 1950.
121. CHUR 2/32, President Truman to WSC, 18 August 1950.
122. Catterall, *Macmillan Diaries*, 19 August 1950, p. 11.
123. CHUR 2/32, 'A Note', WSC to Sandys, 15 August 1950.
124. CHUR 2/32, 'European Army', by Duncan Sandys, undated.
125. Cited in Gilbert, *Winston S. Churchill*, vol. VIII, p. 556.
126. Cited in ibid., p. 574.
127. Macmillan deliberately copied Eden into a message to Churchill which was meant as a protest against his private instructions to Sandys. He knew Eden would be able to bring Churchill down to earth. See Catterall, *Macmillan Diaries*, 16 and 18 August 1950, pp. 10–11.
128. CHUR 2/32, 'Message to Mr. Macmillan', WSC to Macmillan, 17 August 1950.
129. Grob-Fitzgibbon, *Continental Drift*, p. 144.
130. Charlton, *Price of Victory*, p. 145.
131. TNA, CAB 129/48, C(51)32, memorandum by WSC, 29 November 1951.
132. Cited by J.W. Young, 'German Rearmament and the European Defence Community', in J.W. Young (ed.), *The Foreign Policy of Churchill's Peacetime Administration, 1951–1955* (Leicester, 1988), p. 83.
133. Hansard, HC Deb vol 480 cc1501–2, 13 November 1950.
134. Ms. Macmillan, dep. c. 894, 'Progress of European Defence, Part A: Summary and Conclusions', undated.

135. Catterall, *Macmillan Diaries*, 17 November 1950, p. 28.
136. Ms. Macmillan, dep. c. 894, 'Progress of European Defence, Part A: Summary and Conclusions', undated.
137. CHUR 2/32, 'Attachment: A Note', WSC to Sandys, 22 November 1950.
138. Cited in Harrison, 'Winston Churchill and European Integration', p. 270.
139. CHUR 2/32, WSC to Duncan Sandys, 23 November 1950.
140. Hansard, HC Deb vol 484 cc633–4, 15 February 1951.
141. CAC, CHUR 2/221, 'Dinner at the Embassy', 10 September 1951; Gilbert, *Winston S. Churchill*, vol. VIII, pp. 634–5.
142. Ibid.
143. *The Economist*, 3 June 1950.
144. 'The Schuman Declaration', printed in *Pour L'Europe* (Geneva, 2010).
145. R. Bullen and M.E. Pelly (eds), 'The London Conferences; Anglo-American Relations and Cold War Strategy: January–June 1950', in *Documents on British Policy Overseas* (henceforth *DBPO*), Series II, vol. II (London, 1986), p. xvii.
146. C. Lord, *Absent at the Creation: Britain and the Formation of the European Community, 1950–2* (Aldershot, 1995), p. 14.
147. R. Bullen and M.E. Pelly (eds), 'The Schuman Plan, the Council of Europe and Western European Integration: May 1950–December 1952', in *DBPO*, Series II, vol. I (London, 1986), no. 12.
148. *DBPO*, Series II, vol. II, no. 95.
149. Cmd 7970.
150. Plowden, p. 91. Morrison was mistaken. The President of the National Union of Mineworkers, Will Lawther, welcomed the negotiations on the Schuman Plan. See R.M. Douglas, *The Labour Party, Nationalism and Internationalism, 1939–51* (London, 2004), n. 127.
151. TNA, CAB 128/40; CM(50)129, 2 June 1950.
152. Cmd 7970.
153. P. Woodhouse, *British Policy towards France, 1945–51* (London, 1995), p. 106.
154. *The Economist*, 10 July 1950.
155. CAC, CHUR 2/139.
156. Catterall, *Macmillan Diaries*, 12 May 1957.
157. Schwarz, 'Adenauer and Churchill', p. 176.
158. Kaiser, *Christian Democracy and the Origins of European Union*, p. 224.
159. S. Skår, 'The British Conservative Party and Supranational European Integration, 1948–1955', Ph.D. thesis, Oxford University, 2000, pp. 93–117.
160. Ms. Macmillan dep. c. 389. fol. 100.
161. Hansard, 23 March 1949.
162. A. Loveday, 'The European Movement', *International Organization*, iii/4 (Nov. 1949), pp. 623–4.
163. Ms. Macmillan, 'Strasbourg Letters', dep. c. 11/2, Number 3, 24 August 1949.
164. CA, Reports, 11th Sitting, 24 August 1949.
165. CA, Documents, 13th Sitting, 2 September 1949.
166. CA, Reports, 11th Sitting, 24 August 1949.
167. Ms. Macmillan, dep. c. 896, 'Report: No. 10', 23 August 1949.
168. Onslow, *Backbench Debate*, p. 21.

169. CHUR 2/25A-B, 'Minutes of the Conservative Parliamentary Inter-Committee Group', autumn 1949, sent to Churchill in a larger batch on 3 April 1950.

170. WSC, *Europe Unite*, pp. 312–13.

171. CA, Reports, Sixth Sitting, 16 August 1949.

172. CA, 8th Sitting, 19 August 1949.

173. Macmillan, *Tides of Fortune*, p. 168.

174. CHUR 2/27, 'Press Notice: UEM on Schuman Plan', 15 May 1950.

175. Speech on 18 May 1950, in WSC, *In the Balance*, pp. 279–80.

176. Memorandum cited in Macmillan, *Tides of Fortune*, pp. 193–5.

177. The motion on the order paper read in full: 'That this House requests HMG, in the interests of peace and full employment, to accept the invitation to take part in the discussions on the Schuman Plan subject to the same condition as that made by the Netherlands Government namely, that if the discussions show the Plan not to be practicable, freedom of action is reserved.'

178. Harrison, 'Winston Churchill and European Integration', p. 259.

179. J. Moon, *European Integration in British Politics 1950–63, A Study of Issue Change* (Aldershot, 1985), pp.109–12.

180. Cited in E. Dell, *The Schuman Plan and the British Abdication of Leadership in Europe* (Oxford, 1995), p. 236.

181. Simms, *Britain's Europe*, p. 177.

182. Skar, *British Conservative Party*, pp. 151–5.

183. CHUR 2/112, 'Secret', Anthony Eden to WSC, 23 June 1950.

184. G. Warner (ed.), *In the Midst of Events: The Foreign Office Diaries and Papers of Kenneth Younger, February 1950–October 1951* (Abingdon, 2005), p. 25.

185. Grob-Fitzgibbon, *Continental Drift*, p. 113.

186. WSC, *In The Balance*, 'The Schuman Plan, 27 June 1950', p. 298.

187. Ibid., pp. 287–303.

188. Charlton, *Price of Victory*, pp. 109–10.

189. Ibid., p. 110.

190. Cited in E. Dell, *The Schuman Plan*, p. 283.

191. Catterall, *The Macmillan Diaries*, p. 5

192. Ibid., pp. 3–4.

193. CA, Documents, 10th Sitting, 24 August 1950.

194. CHUR 2/76A-B, Harold Macmillan to WSC, 2 August 1950.

195. CAC, DSND 9/3/2.

196. Catterall, *The Macmillan Diaries*, p. 3.

197. CHUR 2/112, Eden to WSC, 11 August 1950.

198. CA, Reports, 7th Sitting, 14 August 1950.

199. CHUR 2/76A-B, Harold Macmillan to WSC, 2 August 1950.

200. *Macmillan Diaries*, 26 August 1950.

201. H. Macmillan, *The Blast of War, 1939–1945* (London, 1967), p. 92.

202. Ibid., pp. 297–8.

203. H. Macmillan, *War Diaries: Politics and War in the Mediterranean, January 1943–May 1945* (London, 1984), 26 March–7 July 1943. Almost every other diary entry in this period features Monnet, who preferred seeing Macmillan 'for the same talk as usual' in his room after dinner.

204. Ibid., p. 82.

205. Ms. Macmillan dep.c.396, fols. 208–10. Monnet to Macmillan, 8 August 1950. Monnet forwarded this letter to his friends in Strasbourg at the time, including Schuman, Bidault, Philip and Schumann.
206. Ms. Macmillan dep.c.13/1, fol. 103. 29 November 1952.
207. WSC, *Stemming the Tide*, pp. 98–100.
208. Cited in Grob-Fitzgibbon, *Continental Drift*, pp. 148–9.
209. Grob-Fitzgibbon, *Continental Drift*, pp. 149–50.
210. CHUR 2/27, 'Report: The Council of Europe, Strasbourg, May 1951', Lady Tweedsmuir to WSC, 28 May 1951.

11 'A SAD DISILLUSIONMENT': PEACETIME GOVERNMENT, 1951–1952

1. Ibid.
2. Kaiser, *Christian Democracy and the Origins of European Union*, p. 228; Dell, *The Schuman Plan*, pp. 218–33. John Young thinks a Conservative alternative would not have been successful and that there was no missed opportunity: 'Churchill's "No" to Europe: The "Rejection" of European Union by Churchill's Post-War Government, 1951–1952', *The Historical Journal*, No. 4 (Dec. 1985), pp. 923–37.
3. R. Bullen and H. Pelly (eds), *DBPO*, Series II, vols I & II, no. 398. The letter was passed on to Eden.
4. Macmillan, *Tides of Fortune*, p. 214.
5. In seeking denationalisation of transport and steel, Churchill actually violated that silent agreement in domestic affairs. See Colville, *Fringes*, p. 649.
6. R. Jenkins, 'Churchill: The Government of 1951–1955', in R. Blake and W. R. Louis (eds), *Churchill* (Oxford, 1996), p. 499.
7. Cited in Young, 'German Rearmament and the European Defence Community', p. 82.
8. TNA, CAB 129/48, C(51)32, 'United Europe', 29 November 1951.
9. Cited in Simms, *Britain's Europe*, p. 155.
10. WSC, *The World Crisis* (London, 1923), p. 14.
11. A. Seldon, *Churchill's Indian Summer* (London, 1981), p. 30.
12. A. Montague Browne, *Long Sunset: Memoirs of Winston Churchill's Last Private Secretary* (London, 1995), p. 138.
13. TNA, CAB 128/28, CC (55) 28th, 5 April 1955.
14. Klaus Larres, in *Churchill's Cold War* (2002), argues that committing the USA to Europe was the overriding objective of European unity under both Attlee and Churchill. See also Harrison, 'Winston Churchill and European Integration', pp. 278–346.
15. Simms, *Britain's Europe*, p. 177.
16. WSC, *The Unwritten Alliance*, p. 290.
17. Colville, *Fringes*, p. 633.
18. Shuckburgh, *Descent to Suez*, p. 28.
19. Seldon, *Indian Summer*, p. 388.
20. L. Galambos (ed.), *The Papers of Dwight David Eisenhower* (Baltimore, 2001), pp. 1481–3.
21. Seldon, *Indian Summer*, p. 388.
22. Ibid., p. 393.

23. Ibid., pp. 30–1.
24. Onslow, *Backbench Debate*, p. 90.
25. CAC, CHUR 2/221, 'Dinner at the Embassy', 10 September 1951; Gilbert, *Winston S. Churchill*, vol. VIII, pp. 634–5.
26. Cited in Larres, *Churchill's Cold War*, p. 154.
27. Hansard, HC deb vol. 493 c79, 6 November 1951.
28. J.W. Young, *Winston Churchill's Last Campaign: Britain and the Cold War 1951–5* (Oxford, 1996), p. 99. Young's excellent study details Churchill's pursuit of a summit and inevitably explores the role of EDC.
29. Colville, *Fringes*, p. 683.
30. See WSC, *Second World War and Epilogue*, pp. 972–3.
31. Hansard, HC deb vol. 515 c897, 11 May 1953.
32. Seldon, *Indian Summer*, pp. 29–30.
33. Charlton, *Price of Victory*, p. 129.
34. Simms, *Britain's Europe*, pp. 179–80.
35. Gilbert, *Winston S. Churchill*, vol. VIII, p. 659.
36. Seldon, *Indian Summer*, pp. 416–18.
37. Ibid., p. 379.
38. Kilmuir, *Political Adventure*, p. 177.
39. N.J. Crowson, *The Conservative Party and European Integration since 1945: At the Heart of Europe?* (Abingdon, 2007), p. 14.
40. For an analysis of the internationalist romantic underpinnings of Churchill's European campaign, and specifically his advocacy for a European human rights court, see Duranti, *The Conservative Human Rights Revolution*, Part One, 3. Accessed online.
41. Kilmuir, *Political Adventure*, p. 177.
42. Ibid., p. 186.
43. *DBPO*, no. 402, n.10.
44. CAB 128/25 C.C (52) 3, 15 May 1952.
45. Onslow, *Backbench Debate*, p. 93.
46. TNA, FO 371/96344, 10712/32, 'Report of a Meeting Held in the Home Secretary's Room in the House of Commons', 21 November 1951.
47. Ibid.
48. CAB 128/23 C.C (51) 10, item 4, 22 November 1951.
49. Kilmuir, *Political Adventure*, p. 187.
50. 'The British View at Strasbourg', *The Times*, 29 November 1951; FO 371/96345, UK Delegation to the Council of Europe to Prime Minister, 3 December 1951.
51. *DBPO*, no. 401.
52. Kilmuir, *Political Adventure*, p. 187.
53. FO 371/96346, 'Clipping from *The Milwaukee Journal*', 1 December 1951.
54. Young, 'German Rearmament and the European Defence Community', p. 84.
55. A. Eden, *Full Circle* (London, 1960), p. 33.
56. R. Ferrell (ed.), *The Eisenhower Diaries* (New York, 1981), p. 207.
57. TNA, PREM 11/73, Reynaud to WSC, 29 November 1951.
58. PREM 11/73, WSC to Reynaud, 29 November 1951.
59. FO 371/96345, UK Delegation to the Council of Europe to Prime Minister, 3 December 1951.

60. Ibid.
61. *DBPO*, no. 408.
62. Hansard, HC Deb vol. 494 cc2595–6, 6 December 1951.
63. TNA, CAB 129/48/32, 'United Europe Memorandum', written on 25 November 1951 (PREM 11/373), circulated on 29 November 1951.
64. Eden, *Full Circle*, p. 36.
65. Cited in Grob-Fitzgibbon, *Continental Drift*, pp. 164–5.
66. D. Acheson, *Present at the Creation: My Years in the State Department* (New York, 1969), p. 596.
67. Ibid., p. 598.
68. Ibid., pp. 598–9.
69. Cited in Gilbert, *Winston S. Churchill*, vol. VIII, p. 682.
70. Moran, *The Struggle for Survival*, p. 360; Gilbert, *Winston S. Churchill*, vol. VIII, p. 684.
71. WSC, *Stemming the Tide*, p. 217.
72. Ibid., p. 226.
73. Eden, *Full Circle*, p. 32.
74. Young, *Winston Churchill's Last Campaign*, p. 81.
75. CHUR 2/25A-B, WSC to Leo Amery, 9 February 1949.
76. Boothby, *Recollections*, p. 211.
77. Charlton, *Price of Victory*, pp. 128–9.
78. Ibid., p. 132.
79. Pottle, *Daring to Hope*, p. 208.
80. Seldon, *Indian Summer*, p. 515.
81. Nicolson, *Harold Nicolson Diaries & Letters, 1945–62*, p. 196.
82. Cited in Seldon, *Indian Summer*, p. 515.
83. H.P. Schwarz, 'Churchill and Adenauer', p. 173.
84. M. Vaisse, 'Churchill and France, 1951–55', in Parker, *Studies in Statesmanship*, p. 164.
85. Montague Browne, *Long Sunset*, p. 272.
86. Macmillan, *Tides of Fortune*, p. 471. The disillusionment referred to Britain's apparent reticence to join plans for European unity.
87. Shuckburgh, *Descent to Suez*, p. 42.
88. Seldon, *Indian Summer*, p. 34. In his assessment of the Churchill government's foreign policy between 1951 and 1955, Seldon writes about the effect of Churchill's infirmity on European policy: 'His vision was conceived in abstract terms: by the time he became Prime Minister in October 1951 he was too old to undertake the translation of his general feelings into concrete policy.' Ibid., p. 413. For Eden on this period of WSC's life, see Shuckburgh, *Descent to Suez*, p. 157.
89. CAB 128/23; C.C.(51)16, 11 December 1951.
90. Eden, *Full Circle*, pp. 33–4. Eden devotes very little space to Europe in his memoirs. In the first three paragraphs of describing the European Movement, he places the Congress of Europe in The Hague in 1949, which should be 1948. Later on, when claiming he first thought to use the Brussels Treaty as a solution for European defence after the collapse of EDC, he misplaces the original signing date of the treaty. It was 1948, not 1946. See ibid., p. 151.
91. Young, 'Churchill's "No"', p. 929.
92. TNA, FO 371/96346, Boothby to WSC, 12 December 1951.

93. *DBPO*, no. 413.
94. *DBPO*, no. 417.
95. FO 371/96346, Eden to WSC, 15 December 1951.
96. PREM 11/153, Churchill to Eden, 16 December 1951.
97. Young, 'Churchill's "No"', p. 931. More generally, but in the same spirit, Anthony Seldon concludes in his painstakingly detailed account of Churchill's peacetime administration: 'With Europe, he [Churchill] had given a mighty clarion call for greater unity in Opposition. But once in office he lacked the energy to translate his thoughts into precise proposals and the determination which would have been needed to force them on Eden and the Foreign Office.' Seldon, *Indian Summer*, p. 38.
98. *DBPO*, no. 418.
99. CAB 128/23; C.C.(51)18, 19 December 1951; Young, *Winston Churchill's Last Campaign*, p. 61.
100. Young, *Winston Churchill's Last Campaign*, p. 61.
101. CAC, DSND 9/3/22, 'European integration: Note by Minister of Housing and Local Government', 16 January 1952.
102. PREM 11/153, 'Future of the Council of Europe: Memorandum by the Minister of Housing and Local Government', C (52) 56, 29 February 1952.
103. Shuckburgh, who travelled with Eden to present the plan, wrote in his diary: 'The idea is that it [the Council of Europe] should provide the political institutions for the EDC and the Schuman Plan. It was extremely well received, and for the first time at a meeting of the Council in my experience the United Kingdom was not "dragging its feet".' Shuckburgh, *Descent to Suez*, p. 38.
104. Onslow, *Backbench Debate*, p. 84.
105. CAB 128/24, C.C (52). 29–30. 12 & 13 March.
106. Ibid.
107. Macmillan, *Tides of Fortune*, pp. 471–2.
108. Ibid., p. 472.
109. PREM 11/153, Macmillan to Churchill, 17 March 1952.
110. Ms. Macmillan, dep. c. 900, 'Prime Minister Personal Minute', WSC to HM, 20 March 1952.
111. PREM 11/153, Eden to WSC, 18 March 1952.
112. Ibid.
113. Shuckburgh, *Descent to Suez*, p. 45.
114. Charlton, *Price of Victory*, p. 135.
115. Shuckburgh, *Descent to Suez*, p. 14.
116. Onslow, *Backbench Debate*, p. 90.
117. Charlton, *Price of Victory*, pp. 137–8.
118. Montague Browne, *Long Sunset*, p. 138.
119. Kilmuir, *Political Adventure*, p. 189.
120. Macmillan, *Tides of Fortune*, p. 465.
121. Catterall, *The Macmillan Diaries*, 29 November 1951.
122. Harrison, 'Winston Churchill and European Integration', p. 301.
123. H. Pelling, *Churchill's Peacetime Ministry, 1951–1955* (Basingstoke and London, 1997), pp. 45–63.
124. Young, *Winston Churchill's Last Campaign*, p. 90.
125. Nicolson, *Harold Nicolson Diaries & Letters*, p. 58.

126. Onslow, *Backbench Debate*, p. 91.
127. Gilbert, *Winston S. Churchill*, vol. VIII, p. 656.
128. TNA, FO 371/96345, 'Paris Talks: European integration', 31 October 1951.
129. TNA, FO 1009/67, FO Telegram to H.M. Ambassador Paris, UK Delegation OEEC Paris and UK Delegation UN General Assembly, 15 December 1951.
130. Seldon, *Indian Summer*, pp. 385–7.
131. TNA, FO 371/124968, No. 24/2, 11 August 1951.
132. G. McDermott, *The Eden Legacy* (London, 1969), p. 102.
133. Ms.Macmillan, dep.c.13/1, 4 December 1951.
134. Kilmuir, *Political Adventure*, p. 177.
135. Boothby, *Recollections*, p. 223.
136. Seldon, *Indian Summer*, p. 409.
137. A. Shlaim, *British Foreign Secretaries since 1945* (Newton Abbot, 1977), p. 91.
138. A. Nutting, *Europe Will Not Wait: A Warning and a Way Out* (London, 1960), p. 29.
139. Eden, *Full Circle*, p. 32.
140. Charlton, *Price of Victory*, p. 139.
141. Shuckburgh, *Descent to Suez*, p. 17.

12 'EXACTLY WHAT I SUGGESTED AT STRASBOURG': EUROPEAN DEFENCE, 1952–1955

1. Hansard HC deb vol 495 c819, 5 February 1952.
2. Charlton, *Price of Victory*, p. 148. Anthony Nutting remembered Hervé Alphand saying something along these lines at the Berlin conference in 1954.
3. Eden, *Full Circle*, p. 37.
4. S. Dockrill, *Britain's Policy for West German Rearmament, 1950–1955* (Cambridge, 1991), p. 99.
5. Eden, *Full Circle*, p. 44.
6. Colville, *Fringes*, p. 646.
7. TNA, CAB 128/25, C 52, 13 May 1952.
8. Eden, *Full Circle*, pp. 46–7.
9. Macmillan, *Tides of Fortune*, p. 473.
10. TNA, CAB. 128/25, C (52) 102, 4 December 1952.
11. Charlton, *Price of Victory*, p. 158.
12. *New York Times*, 1 September 1954.
13. Grob-Fitzgibbon, *Continental Drift*, p. 178.
14. Young, *Churchill's Last Campaign*, pp. 116–17.
15. Grob-Fitzgibbon, *Continental Drift*, pp. 182–3.
16. TNA, FO 800/821, 4 May 1953; Young, *Churchill's Last Campaign*, p. 157.
17. WSC, *The Unwritten Alliance*, p. 49.
18. Macmillan, *Tides of Fortune*, p. 478; Colville, *Fringes*, p. 667.
19. R.R. James, *Anthony Eden* (London: Weidenfeld & Nicolson, 1986), p. 365.
20. H-P. Schwarz, 'Churchill and Adenauer' in *Churchill: Studies in Statesmanship* (London, 1995), p. 177; Young, *Churchill's Last Campaign*, pp. 164–5.
21. Ibid., pp. 166–8.
22. Colville, *Fringes*, p. 668.

23. Moran, *Churchill* (2006), p. 136.
24. K. Ruane, *The Rise and Fall of the European Defence Community* (London, 2000), p. 47.
25. Moran, *Churchill* (2006), p. 143.
26. TNA, PREM 11/426, 4 August 1953.
27. Grob-Fitzgibbon, *Continental Drift*, pp. 185–6; Ms. Macmillan, dep. C. 392, 'EDC and European unity', summer 1953.
28. Gilbert, *Winston S. Churchill*, vol. VIII, p. 890.
29. CHUR 2/211, WSC to Max Beaverbrook, 26 September 1953.
30. Colville, *Fringes*, p. 680.
31. WSC, *The Unwritten Alliance*, p. 65.
32. Grob-Fitzgibbon, *Continental Drift*, p. 187.
33. P.G. Boyle (ed.), *The Churchill-Eisenhower Correspondence, 1953–1955* (Chapel Hill: University of North Carolina Press, 1990), pp. 93–8.
34. Grob-Fitzgibbon, *Continental Drift*, p. 188.
35. Young, *Churchill's Last Campaign*, p. 220.
36. Gilbert, *Winston S. Churchill*, vol. VIII, p. 923.
37. Young, *Churchill's Last Campaign*, p. 227.
38. Shuckburgh, *Descent to Suez*, pp. 113–14.
39. Colville, *Fringes*, p. 685.
40. Ibid., p. 685.
41. Gilbert, *Winston S. Churchill*, vol. VIII, p. 924.
42. Shuckburgh, *Descent to Suez*, pp. 113–14.
43. Ibid., p. 115.
44. Gilbert, *Winston S. Churchill*, vol. VIII, p. 925.
45. Ibid., pp. 925–6.
46. Ibid., pp. 926–8.
47. Shuckburgh, *Descent to Suez*, p. 115.
48. Moran, *Churchill*, p. 226.
49. Gilbert, *Winston S. Churchill*, vol. VIII, p. 932.
50. Colville, *Fringes*, p. 687.
51. Shuckburgh, *Descent to Suez*, p. 116.
52. Moran, *Churchill*, p. 229.
53. Colville, *Fringes*, p. 688.
54. TNA, PREM. 11/369, 15 December 1953.
55. P.G. Boyle, *Correspondence*, pp. 115–18; Gilbert, *Winston S. Churchill*, vol. VIII, p. 940.
56. Gilbert, *Winston S. Churchill*, vol VIII, p. 941.
57. Moran, *Churchill*, pp. 234–5.
58. Young, *Winston Churchill's Last Campaign*, p. 59.
59. Macmillan, *Tides of Fortune*, p. 478.
60. Colville, *Fringes*, p. 693.
61. Cited in Harrison, 'Winston Churchill and European Integration', p. 325.
62. Jenkins, 'Churchill: The Government of 1951–1955', p. 496.
63. Moran, *Churchill*, p. 292.
64. Hansard HC Deb vol 530 c499, 14 July 1954.
65. Ibid.

66. Jenkins, 'Churchill: The Government of 1951–1955', p. 496; W. Krieger, 'Churchill and the Defence of the West, 1951–55' in R.A.C. Parker, *Winston Churchill: Studies in Statesmanship* (London, 1995), p. 194.
67. Gilbert, *Winston S. Churchill*, vol. VIII, p. 1044.
68. Moran, *Churchill*, p. 310.
69. Eden, *Full Circle*, pp. 148–9.
70. TNA, PREM 11/672, 23 August 1954; P. Mendès-France, *Œuvres Complètes: gouverneur c'est choisir, 1954–5* (Paris, 1986), pp. 245–7.
71. TNA, PREM. 11/618, 29 Aug 1954; W. Krieger, 'Churchill and the Defence of the West', p. 196.
72. Grob-Fitzgibbon, *Continental Drift*, p. 194.
73. CHUR 2/210, WSC to Bernard Baruch, 29 August 1954; Gilbert, *Winston S. Churchill*, vol. VIII, p. 1054.
74. Spaak, *The Continuing Battle*, p. 175.
75. Moran, *Churchill*, p. 315.
76. TNA, CAB 128/27, C 58, 1 September 1954.
77. Moran, *Churchill*, p. 315.
78. Gilbert, *Winston S. Churchill*, vol. VIII, p. 1056.
79. H-P. Schwarz, 'Churchill and Adenauer', p. 178.
80. Macmillan, *Tides of Fortune*, p. 468.
81. Ms. Macmillan, dep. C. 387, Macmillan to Eden, 1 September 1954.
82. Ms. Macmillan, dep. C. 387, Cabinet Memorandum, September 1954.
83. Eden, *Full Circle*, p. 151.
84. Charlton, *Price of Victory*, pp. 163–4.
85. Gilbert, *Winston S. Churchill*, vol. VIII, p. 1056.
86. Ibid., p. 1057.
87. For Churchill's criticisms of specific troop contributions on the continent, see TNA, FO 800/795, 9 September 1954; TNA, PREM 11/843, 9 & 28 September 1954; TNA, FO 800/779, 27 September 1954. The British troop commitments were also subject to two exceptions: overseas emergencies or financial problems would allow Britain to ask to pull forces out of Europe. Churchill told Moran he did not get the fuss about the British pledge to keep troops in mainland Europe, because 'no one in their senses thought we could bring our troops home from the Continent [...] if there is war we are bound to fight.' Moran, *Churchill*, p. 321.
88. Eden, *Full Circle*, p. 168.
89. Spaak, *The Continuing Battle*, pp. 183–5.
90. Moran, *Churchill*, p. 320.
91. Young, *Winston Churchill's Last Campaign*, p. 291.
92. Cmd 9304., London: HMSO, 1954.
93. M. Gilbert, 'Churchill and the European Idea', p. 211.
94. Grob-Fitzgibbon, *Continental Drift*, pp. 196–7.
95. Onslow, *Backbench Debate*, p. 82.
96. Moran, *Churchill*, p. 321.
97. Eden, *Full Circle*, pp. 170–1.
98. Nutting, *Europe Will Not Wait*, p. 80.
99. TNA, PREM 11/891, 24 December 1954.
100. CHUR 6/6, WSC to Mendès-France, 12 January 1955.

101. CHUR 2/217, WSC to Eisenhower, 12 January 1955; Gilbert, *Winston S. Churchill*, vol. VIII, pp. 1090–1.
102. WSC, *The Unwritten Alliance*, p. 241.
103. Ibid., pp. 244–5.
104. Colville, *Fringes*, pp. 704–9.
105. Ibid.

13 'MY PARTY WAS TOO STRONG FOR ME': LAST THOUGHTS, 1955–1965

1. Shuckburgh, *Descent to Suez*, pp. 17–19.
2. Ibid., p. 18.
3. WSC, *The Unwritten Alliance*, p. 300 (7 July 1957).
4. Montague Browne, *Long Sunset*, p. 273.
5. J. Ramsden, *Man of the Century: Winston Churchill and His Legend since 1945* (London, 2002), p. 319.
6. Nicolson, *Harold Nicolson Diaries & Letters*, p. 301.
7. M.M. Postan, *An Economic History of Western Europe, 1945–64* (London, 1967).
8. Macmillan, *Tides of Fortune*, p. 156.
9. Gilbert, *Winston S. Churchill*, vol. VIII, p. 1337.
10. Montague Browne, *Long Sunset*, pp. 273–4.
11. Ibid., p. 276.
12. 'What Sir Winston Said: Text of Market Statement', *The Times*, 15 September 1962.
13. Montague Browne, *Long Sunset*, p. 269.
14. Ibid., p. 270.
15. Pottle, *Daring to Hope*, pp. 327–31.
16. J. Campbell, *Edward Heath* (London, 1994), p. 65.
17. Cited in Heath, *The Course of My Life*, p. 145.
18. M. Laing, *Edward Heath: Prime Minister* (London, 1972), p. 137.
19. E. Heath, *Old World, New Horizons: Britain, the Common Market, and the Atlantic Alliance* (London, 1970), p. 14.
20. Gilbert, *Winston S. Churchill*, vol. VIII, p. 1332.
21. CHUR 2/526A-B, WSC to Ted Heath, 10 April 1963.
22. The painting given to Chequers is listed in D. Coombs and M. Churchill, *Sir Winston Churchill*, p. 191. This update and expanded version of Coombs's earlier catalogue (1967) lists five paintings from Bursinel, Switzerland (Figures 391–395). The painting gifted to Lord Moran was exhibited at New York's World Fair in 1965.
23. Ms. Macmillan, dep. c. 387, Sandys to Macmillan, 7 June 1975.

BIBLIOGRAPHY

MANUSCRIPT AND ARCHIVAL SOURCES

Bodleian Library, Oxford, UK:
Harold Macmillan Papers (Ms. Macmillan).
Violet Bonham Carter Papers (Ms. Bonham Carter).
Clement Attlee Papers (Ms. Attlee).

Churchill Archive Centre (CAC), Cambridge, UK:
Chartwell Papers (CHAR) – digitally accessed in Cambridge and at the British Library in London.
Churchill Papers (CHUR) – digitally accessed in Cambridge and at the British Library in London.
Ernest Bevin Papers (BEVN).
Duncan Sandys Papers (DSND).
Lord Kilmuir Papers (KLMR).
Julian Amery Papers (AMEJ).
Leo Amery Papers (AMEL).

The National Archives (TNA), Kew, UK:
Cabinet Papers (CAB).
Foreign Office Papers (FO 371).
Prime Minister's Papers (PREM 3, 11 and 15).

Het Nationaal Archief (NA), The Hague, NL:
Collection 378 P.A. Kerstens (2.21.183.43, Nr. 51–55).

Staatsarchiv Zürich [STAZH], Zürich, CH:
Akten des Rektoratsarchivs der Universität Zürich zur Churchill-Feier (252/5, U 750).
Akten der Staatskanzlei – Besuche und Empfänge (M 17.17–521).
Grapische Sammlung 'Winston Churchill in Zurich' – 46 photos.

Universitätsarchiv Zürich [UAZ].
Akten zur Churchill-Feier (E.7.1.187 – Mappe Nr. 131.102).

Dodis.CH: Diplomatische Documente der Schweiz (online archive):
Swiss Federal Archives Papers (Bern) on Churchill's Visit in September 1946.

Archives de la Ville et de l'Eurométropole de Strasbourg:
BAMS: Magasin BRB 4451 and MS 144 (Churchill: dossier de presse).
235 89/965-68 (Mouvement Européen).
208 MW 126 (citoyen d'honneur).
1 FL 14-15 (photos).

PRINTED PRIMARY SOURCES

Adenauer, K. (ed.), *Konrad Adenauer und die CDU der britischen Besatzungszone 1946–1949, Dokumente zur Gründungsgeschichte der CDU Deutschlands*, Bonn, 1975.
Bullen. R. and Pelly, H. (eds), *Documents on British Policy Overseas*, Series II, vols I & II, London, 1986.
Catterall, P. (ed.), *The Macmillan Diaries: The Cabinet Years, 1950–57*, London, 2004.
Council of Europe, Consultative Assembly, *Official Reports, I–IV, 1st Session 1949.*
—— *Minutes, Documents, Texts Adopted, 1st Session 1949.*
—— *Official Reports, 2nd Session 1950.*
—— *Minutes, Documents, Texts Adopted, 2nd Session 1950.*
European Movement, *Statement of Policy issued on the formation of the British Committee of the United Europe Movement*, Winston Churchill Chairman, 1947.
—— *Minutes of the Meetings of the British Council of the European-Movement.*
—— *Minutes of the Meetings of the Executive Committee of the British Council of the European Movement.*
—— *Congress of Europe Resolutions*, Brussels, May 1948.
—— *European Movement and Council of Europe* by Sandys, D. (ed.), London, 1949.
—— *Creation of the Council of Europe: Account of the Successive Steps taken by the European Movement to Secure the establishment of the Council of Europe*, Brussels, 1949.
—— *The Schuman Plan: Nucleus of a European Community*, Brussels, June 1951.
Foreign Office, *Anglo-French Discussions Regarding French Proposals for the West European Coal, Iron and Steel Industries in May–June 1950*, Cmd 7970, London, 1950.
HMSO, *Documents on British Foreign Policy 1919–1939*, 1947.
James, R.R., *Winston S. Churchill His Complete Speeches, Volume VII: 1943–1949*, New York and London, 1974.
Labour Party, 'Feet on the Ground: A Study of Western Union', September 1948.
—— 'European Unity: A Statement by the National Executive Committee', May 1950.
Lipgens, W. and Loth, W. (eds), *Documents on the History of European Integration*, vol. 4: *Transnational Organizations of Political Parties and Pressure Groups in the Struggle for European Union, 1945–1950*, Berlin, 1991.
—— (eds) *Documents on the History of European Integration*, vol. 3: *The Struggle for European Union by Political Parties and Pressure Groups in Western European Countries, 1945–50*, Berlin, 1988.

Macmillan, H., *War Diaries: Politics and War in The Mediterranean, January 1943–May 1945*, London, 1984.

Parliamentary Debates (Hansard), House of Commons, Official Report, 5th Series, vols 474–487, London, 1950–1.

PRINTED SECONDARY WORKS

Acheson, D., *Present at the Creation*, London, 1970.

Adamthwaite, A., 'Britain and the World, 1945–9: The View from the Foreign Office', *International Affairs*, lxi/2 (Spring 1985), pp. 223–5.

Adenauer, K., *Briefe 1945–1947*, Berlin, 1983.

Amery, L.S., 'The British Commonwealth and European Unity', *National Review*, November 1948.

—— *My Political Life*, vol. III, London, 1955.

Attlee, C., *As It Happened*, London, 1954.

Barclay, R., *Ernest Bevin and the Foreign Office 1932–1969*, London, 1969.

Barnes, J. and Nicolson, D. (eds), *The Empire at Bay: The Leo Amery Diaries 1929–1945*, London, 1988.

Beers, M, 'Hosting Europe: Local Organisation of the Congress of Europe', in *Congrès de l'Europe à la Haye, 1948–2008*, Brussels, 2009.

Beevor, A. and Cooper, A., *Paris after the Liberation 1944–1949*, London, 1994.

Beloff, Max, 'The Anglo-French Union Proposal', *Mélanges Pierre Rénouvin: Etudes d'Histoire des Relations Internationales*, Paris, 1966.

Bidault, G., transl. Sinclair, M., *Resistance: The Political Autobiography of Georges Bidault*, London, 1967.

Bitsch, M. and Bossuat, G., *L'Europe Unie et L'Afrique: De l'Idée d'Eurafrique à la Convention de Lomé I*, Brussels, 2005.

Blake, R. and Louis, W.R. (eds), *Churchill*, Oxford, 1996.

Bonham Carter, Lady Violet, *Winston Churchill: As I Knew Him*, London, 1965.

Boothby, R., 'The Future of the Council of Europe', *International Affairs*, xxvii, July 1952.

—— *Recollections of a Rebel*, London, 1978.

Boyce, R., 'Britain First "No" to Europe: Britain and the Briand Plan, 1929–30', *European Studies Review*, x, 1980.

Boyle, P.G. (ed.), *The Churchill-Eisenhower Correspondence, 1953–1955*, Chapel Hill, 1990.

Brivati, B. and Jones, H. (eds), *From Reconstruction to Integration: Britain and Europe since 1945*, London, 1993.

Bullock, A., *Ernest Bevin: Foreign Secretary, 1945–51*, London, 1983.

Buruma, I., *Year Zero. A History of 1945*, London, 2013.

Butler, L.J., *Britain and Empire: Adjusting to a Post-Imperial World*, London, 2002.

Butler, R.A., *The Art of the Possible: The Memoirs of Lord Butler*, London, 1971.

Campbell, J. *Edward Heath: A Biography*, London, 1994.

Charlton, M., *The Price of Victory*, London, 1983.

Churchill, R., *Winston Churchill*, vols I and II, London, 1966 and 1967.

Churchill, W.S., *The World Crisis*, vol. V, *The Aftermath*, London, 1931.

—— *My Early Life*, London, 1979.

—— *The Second World War*, 6 vols, London, 1950–6.

———— *The Second World War: Abridged Edition With an Epilogue on the Years 1945 to 1957*, London, 2013.

———— 'A Great Big Idea', *John Bull*, 15 February 1930.

———— 'The United States of Europe', *Saturday Evening Post*, 15 February 1930.

———— 'Nations on the Loose', *Collier's*, 4 May 1935.

———— 'Why Not a United States of Europe?' *News of the World*, 29 May 1938.

———— 'The Grand Design for a United Europe', *Daily Telegraph*, 30–31 December 1946.

———— 'The Highroad of the Future', *Collier's*, 4 January 1947.

———— 'One Way to Stop a New War', United Europe Movement, 1947.

———— 'United Europe': Magazine of the United Europe Movement, 1 March 1948.

———— *Arms and the Covenant*, London, 1938.

———— *Step by Step*, London, 1949.

———— *Into Battle*, London, 1941.

———— *The Unrelenting Struggle*, London, 1942.

———— *The End of the Beginning*, London, 1943.

———— *Onwards to Victory*, London, 1944.

———— *The Dawn of Liberation*, London, 1945.

———— *Victory*, London, 1946.

———— *Secret Session Speeches*, London, 1946.

———— *The Sinews of Peace*, London, 1948.

———— *Great Contemporaries*, vols 1 and 2, London, 1949.

———— *Europe Unite*, London, 1950.

———— *In the Balance*, London, 1951.

———— *Stemming the Tide*, London, 1953.

———— *The Unwritten Alliance*, London, 1963.

———— Foreword in *Europe Unites – The Hague Conference and After*, London, 1948.

———— Foreword in Richard Coudenhove-Kalgeri, *An Idea Conquers the World*, London: European Movement, 1949.

———— Foreword in Duncan Sandys, *European Movement and Council*, London, 1966–76.

———— *Painting as a Pastime*, London, 2013.

Cini, M. and Borragán, N.P.-S., *European Union Politics*, Oxford, 2010.

Clarke, P., *Mr Churchill's Profession*, London, 2012.

Colville, J., *Footprints in Time*, London, 1976.

———— *Winston Churchill and his Inner Circle*, New York, 1981.

———— *The Fringes of Power; Downing Street Diaries 1939–1955*, London, 1985.

Coombs, D. with Churchill, M., *Sir Winston Churchill: His Life and His Paintings*, London, 2015.

Coudenhove-Kalergi, R., *An Idea Conquers the World*, London, 1953.

Crowson, N.J., *The Conservative Party and European Integration since 1945: At the Heart of Europe?*, Abingdon, 2007.

Czarnomski, F.B., *The Wisdom of Winston Churchill*, London, 1956.

Davenport-Hines, R., *Universal Man: The Seven Lives of John Maynard Keynes*, London, 2015.

de Gaulle, C., *L'Appel*, Paris, 1954.

———— *War Memoirs*, vol. I, London, 1955.

de Rougement, D., 'The Campaign of the European Congresses', *Government and Opposition*, 1967, 2.3.

—— *The Meaning of Europe*, London, 1965.

Dell, E., *The Schuman Plan and the British Abdication of Leadership in Europe*, Oxford, 1995.

Deighton, A., *The Impossible Peace: Britain, the Division of Germany, and the Origins of the Cold War*, Oxford, 1993.

—— *Building Postwar Europe: National Decision-Makers and European Institutions, 1948–63*, London, 1995.

—— 'Entente Néo-Coloniale?: Ernest Bevin and the Proposals for an Anglo-French Third World Power, 1945–1949', in Bitsch, M. and Bossuat, G., *L'Europe Unie et L'Afrique: De l'Idée d'Eurafrique à la Convention de Lomé* I, Brussels, 2005.

—— 'The British in Strasbourg: Negotiating the European Convention on Human Rights, 1950', in Mariager, R., Molin, K. and Brathagen, K. (eds), *Human Rights Europe during the Cold War*, London, 2014.

Dilks, D., *Churchill and Company*, London, 2015.

—— *The Diaries of Alexander Cadogan*, London, 2010.

Dixon, P., *Double Diploma*, London, 1968.

Dobbs, M., *Six Months in 1945. FDR, Stalin, Churchill, and Truman – From World War to Cold War*, New York, 2012.

Dockter, W., *Winston Churchill at The Telegraph*, London, 2015.

—— 'Churchill, Europe and Turkey', *Comillas Journal of International Relations*, iii/7, Sept.–Dec., 2016.

Dockrill, S., *Britain's Policy for West German Rearmament, 1950–1955*, Cambridge, 1991.

Douglas, R.M., *The Labour Party, Nationalism and Internationalism, 1939–51*, London, 2004.

Duchène, F., *Jean Monnet*, New York, 1994.

Dulles, J.F., *War and Peace*, New York, 1950.

Duranti, *The Conservative Human Rights Revolution: European Identity, Transnational Politics, and the Origins of the European Convention*, Oxford, 2017.

Eade, C., *Churchill by His Contemporaries*, London, 1953.

Eden, A., *Full Circle*, London, 1960.

—— *The Reckoning*, Cambridge, 1965.

Fieldhouse, D.K., 'The Labour Governments and the Empire-Commonwealth', in Ovendale, R. (ed.), *The Foreign Policy of the British Labour Governments, 1945–51*, Leicester, 1984.

Fursden, E., *The European Defence Community*, London, 1980.

Geddes, A., *Britain and the European Union*, London, 2013.

Gehler, M. and Kaiser, W., 'Transnationalism and Early European Integration: The Nouvelles Equipes Internationales and the Geneva Circle 1947–1957', *The Historical Journal*, xliv/3 (Sept. 2001), pp. 773–98.

George, S., *An Awkward Partner: Britain in the European Community*, Oxford, 1990.

Gilbert, M., *Winston S. Churchill, 1945–1965*, vols III–VIII, London, 1971–88.

—— *Churchill's Political Philosophy*, Oxford, 1981.

—— *The Wilderness Years*, London, 1981.

—— *In Search of Churchill*, London, 1985.

—— *Churchill – A Life*, London, 1991.

—— *Churchill and The Jews: A Lifelong Friendship*, London, 2008.

—— *Churchill – The Power of Words*, London, 2012.

Gildea, R., *France since 1945*, Oxford, 2002.

Gillingham, J., *Coal, Steel, and the Rebirth of Europe, 1945–1955: The Germans and the French from Ruhr Conflict to Economic Community*, Cambridge, 1991.

Gladwyn, Lord, *The European Idea*, London, 1966.

—— *Memoirs*, London, 1972.

Graebner, W., *Dear Mister Churchill*, London, 1965.

Grob-Fitzgibbon, B., *Continental Drift: Britain and Europe from the End of Empire to the Rise of Euroscepticism*, Cambridge, 2016.

Guerrieri, S., 'From the Hague Congress to the Council of Europe: Hopes, Achievements and Disappointments in the Parliamentary Way to European Integration (1948–51)', *Parliaments, Estates and Representation*, xxxiv/2 (2014), pp. 216–27.

Hansen, P. and Jonsson, S., *Eurafrica: The Untold History of European Integration and Colonialism*, London, 2014.

Harvey, J. (ed.), *The War Diaries of Oliver Harvey*, London, 1978.

Hastings, M., *Winston's War: Churchill 1940–1945*, New York, 2009.

Hayter, W., *A Double Life*, London, 1974.

Heath, E., *Old World New Horizons: Godkin Lecture at Harvard University, 1967*. London, 1970.

—— *The Course of My Life*, London, 1998.

Hennessy, J., *Britain and Europe since 1945: A Biographical Guide*, Brighton, 1973.

Hitchcock, W. and Gaddis, J., 'The Hard Road to Franco-German Rapprochement, 1948–1950', in *France Restored: Cold War Diplomacy and the Quest for Leadership in Europe, 1944–1954*, pp. 99–134, Chapel Hill, NC, 1998.

Horne, A., *Macmillan, The Official Biography*, London, 2008.

Horsfall Carter, W., *Speaking European*, London, 1966.

Howells, R., *Simply Churchill*, London, 1965.

James, L., *Churchill and Empire*, London, 2013.

Jenkins, R., *Churchill*, London, 2002.

Kaiser, W., *Using Europe, Abusing the Europeans. Britain and European Integration, 1945–63*, Basingstoke and London, 1996.

—— 'From State to Society? The Historiography of European Integration', in Cini, M. and Bourne, A.K. (eds), *Palgrave Advances in European Union Studies*, pp. 190–209, Basingstoke, 2006.

—— *Christian Democracy and the Origins of European Union*, Cambridge, 2007.

—— 'Bringing History Back In to the Study of Transnational Networks in European Integration', *Journal of Public Policy*, 29 (Aug. 2009), pp. 223–39.

Kaiser, W. and Leucht, B., 'Informal Politics of Integration: Christian Democratic and Transatlantic Networks in the Creation of ECSC Core Europe', *Journal of European Integration Historiography*, xiv/1 (2008), pp. 35–49.

Kersaudy, F., *Churchill and de Gaulle*, London, 1981.

Kilmuir, Lord, *Political Adventure: The Memoirs of the Earl of Kilmuir David Maxwell Fyfe*, London, 1962.

Kottos, L., 'A "European Commonwealth": Britain, the European League for Economic Co-Operation, and European Debates on Empire, 1947–1957', *Journal of Contemporary European Studies*, xx/4 (December 2012), pp. 497–515.

Küsters, H.J. and Mensing H.P., 'Konrad Adenauer zur Politischen Lage, 1946–1949, Aus den Berichten des schweizerischen Generalkonsuls in Köln Franz Rudolf v. Weiss', *Vierteljahrshefte für Zeitgeschichte*, xxxii, 1984.

Laing, M., *Edward Heath: Prime Minister*, London, 1972.

Larres, K., *Churchill's Cold War*, New Haven, 2002.

—— *A Companion to Europe since 1945*, Oxford, 2014.

Layton, Lord, 'Little Europe and Britain', *International Affairs*, xxix/3 (July 1953).

Leaming, B., *Churchill Defiant*, New York, 2010.

Leucht, B., Rasmussen, M. and Kaiser, W., *Transnational Networks in Regional Integration*, Basingstoke, 2010.

Liddle, R., *The Europe Dilemma: Britain and the Drama of EU Integration*, London, 2014.

Lipgens, W., *A History of European Integration*, vol. 1: *1945–1947. The Formation of the European Unity Movement*, Oxford, 1982.

Lord, C., *Absent at the Creation: Britain and the Formation of the European Community, 1950–52*. Aldershot, 1996.

Loth, W., *Europas Einigung – eine Unvollendete Geschichte*, Frankfurt, 2014.

Lough, D., *No More Champagne: Churchill and His Money*, London, 2015.

Loveday, A., 'The European Movement', *International Organisation*, iii/4 (1949).

Lukacs, J., *Churchill: Visionary. Statesman. Historian*, New Haven, CT, 2002.

Manchester, W., *The Last Lion*, London, 1984.

Mazower, M., *Dark Continent: Europe's Twentieth Century*, London, 1998.

McDermott, G., *The Eden Legacy*, London, 1969.

McGowan, N., *My Years with Churchill*, London, 1958.

Macmillan, H., 'Britain and Europe', *World Review*, September 1951.

—— *Winds of Change*, London, 1966.

—— *The Blast of War*, London, 1967.

—— *Tides of Fortune*, London, 1969.

—— *At the End of the Day*, London, 1973.

Meacham, J., *Franklin and Winston*, New York, 2004.

Mendès-France, Œuvres Complètes: *gouverneur c'est choisir, 1954–5*, Paris, 1986.

Meurs, Wim van with de Bruin, R., Hoetink, C., van Leeuwen, K., Rijnen, C. and van de Grift, L. (eds), *Europa in Alle Staten – Zestig Jaar Gescheidenis van de Europese Integratie*, Nijmegen, 2013.

Milward, A., *The Reconstruction of Western Europe, 1945–51*, London, 1984.

—— *The European Rescue of the Nation State*, Berkeley, CA, 1992.

Monnet, J., *Memoirs*, London, 1978.

Montague Browne, A., *Long Sunset: Memoirs of Winston Churchill's Last Private Secretary*, London, 1995.

Moon, J., *European Integration in British Politics 1950–63, A Study of Issue Change*, London, 1985.

Moran, C., *Churchill: The Struggle For Survival 1945–60*, New York, 2006.

Morgan, K., *Labour in Power 1945–51*, London, 1985.

Nicolson, N., *Harold Nicolson, Diaries & Letters 1945–62*, London, 1971.

Northedge, F.S., *Descent from Power*, London, 1974.

Nutting, A., *Europe Will Not Wait. A Warning and a Way Out*, London, 1960.

Onslow, S., *Backbench Debate within the Conservatieve Party and its Influence on British Foreign Policy, 1948–57*, London, 1997.

Ovendale, R., *The Foreign Policy of the British Labour Governments, 1945–51*, Leicester, 1984.

Packwood, A., 'Winston Churchill and the United States of Europe, 1904–1948', *Comillas Journal of International Relations*, iii/vii, Sept.–Dec., 2016.

Parker, R.A.C., *Churchill: Studies in Statesmanship*, London, 1995.

Pelling, H., *The Labour Government 1945–51*, London, 1992.

—— *Churchill's Peacetime Ministry, 1951–1955*, Basingstoke and London, 1997.

Pimlott, B. (ed.), *The Political Diary of Hugh Dalton 1918–40, 1945–60*, London, 1986.

Plowden, E., *An Industrialist in the Treasury: The Post-War Years*, London, 1989.

Pomian, J. (ed.), *Joseph Retinger: Memoirs of an Eminence Grise*, London, 1972.

Pottle, M. (ed.), *Daring to Hope: The Diaries and Letters of Violet Bonham Carter 1946–1969*, London, 2000.

Ramsden, J., *The Age of Churchill and Eden*, Harlow, 1995.

—— *Man of the Century: Winston Churchill and His Legend since 1945*, London, 2002.

Reynaud, P., *Unite or Perish*, London, 1951.

—— *In the Thick of the Fight*, London, 1955.

Reynolds, D., *In Command of History*, London, 2005.

Rhodes James, R., *Churchill: A Study in Failure*, London, 1973.

Roberts, A., *Eminent Churchillians*, London, 1995.

—— *Hitler and Cburchill*, London, 2004.

Roll, E., *Crowded Hours: An Autobiography*, London, 1995.

Rosengarten, M., *Grossbritannien und der Schuman-Plan*, Frankfurt am Main, 1997.

Ruane, K., *The Rise and Fall of the European Defence Community*, London, 2000.

Sahm, U. and Younger, K., 'Britain and Europe, 1950', *International Affairs*, xliii/1, (Jan. 1967), pp. 12–24.

Salter, A., *Slave of the Lamp*, London, 1967.

—— *Memoirs of a Public Servant*, London, 1961.

Schirman, S., Foreword to *Robert Schuman 1886–1963 and the Beginnings of Europe*, Milano, 2009.

Shlaim, A., 'Prelude to Downfall: The British Offer of Union to France', *Journal of Contemporary History*, ix (Jul. 1974).

——*Britain and the Origins of European Unity 1940–1951*, Reading, 1978.

Shlaim, A., Jones, P. and Sainsbury, K., *British Foreign Secretaries since 1945*, Newton Abbot, 1977.

Schlesinger, A., 'Origins of the Cold War', *Foreign Affairs*, xlvi (October 1967).

Schuman, R., *For Europe*, Geneva, 2010.

Schwarz, H.-P., *Adenauer, Band 1: Der Aufstieg 1876–1952*, Munich, 1994.

—— *Churchill and Adenauer*, Churchill Colloquium 1994, Cambridge: Churchill Archives Centre/Konrad Adenauer Foundation, 1994.

Sebestyen, V., *1946*, London, 2014.

Seldon, A., *Churchill's Indian Summer*, London, 1981.

Shuckburgh, E., *Descent to Suez, Diaries 1951–1956*, London, 1986.

Simms, B., *Britain's Europe: A Thousand Years of Conflict and Cooperation*, London, 2016.

Simpson, B.A.W., *Human Rights and the End of Empire*, Oxford, 2001.

Singer, B., *Churchill Style: The Art of Being Winston Churchill*, New York, 2012.

Soames, M., *Clementine Churchill*, London, 2003.

Spaak, P.-H., *The Continuing Battle*, London, 1971.

Spier, E., *Focus*, London, 1963.

Spierenburg, D. and Poidevin, R., *The History of the High Authority of the European Coal and Steel Community*, London, 1994.

Stansky, P. (ed.), *Churchill: A Profile*, New York, 1973.

Toye, R., *Churchill's Empire*, London, 2011.

Vaughan, R., *Documents of Modern History: Post-War Integration in Europe*, London, 1976.

Vogt, W., *Winston Churchill: Mahnung, Hoffnung und Vision, 1938–1946*, Zürich, 1996.

—— *Winston Churchill und die Schweiz*, Zürich, 2015.

Warner, G., 'The Labour Governments and the Unity of Western Europe', in Ovendale, R. (ed.), *The Foreign Policy of the British Labour Governments, 1945–51*, Leicester, 1984.

—— *In the Midst of Events: The Foreign Office Diaries and Papers of Kenneth Younger, February 1950–October 1951*, Abingdon, 2005.

White, P., *Churchill's Cold War*, London, 2013.

Williams, C., *Harold Macmillan*, London, 2009.

Williams, F., *A Prime Minister Remembers: The War and Post-War Memories of the Rt. Hon. Earl Attlee*, London, 1961.

Woodhouse, *British Policy towards France, 1945–51*, Basingstoke and London, 1995.

Wurm, C., 'Two Paths to Europe: Great Britain and France from a Comparative Perspective', in Wurm, C., *Western Europe and Germany: The Beginnings of European Integration 1945–60*, Oxford, 1995.

—— 'Britain and European Integration, 1945–63', *Contemporary European History*, vii/2, (July1998), pp. 249–61.

Young, H., *This Blessed Plot: Britain and Europe from Churchill to Blair*, London, 1998.

Young, J.W., *Britain, France and the Unity of Europe, 1945–51*, Leicester, 1984.

—— *The Foreign Policy of Churchill's Peacetime Administration 1951–5*, Leicester, 1988.

—— *Britain and European Unity, 1945–1992*, Basingstoke and London, 1993.

—— *Winston Churchill's Last Campaign: Britain and the Cold War 1951–5*, Oxford, 1996.

—— 'Churchill's "No" to Europe: The "Rejection" of European Union by Churchill's Post-War Government, 1951–1952', *The Historical Journal*, xxviii/4, Dec. 1985.

Younger, K., 'Comments on Sahm's Article', *International Affairs*, xliii (1967).

Zametica, J. (ed.), *British Officials and British Foreign Policy 1945–50*, Leicester, 1990.

Zurcher, A.J., *The Struggle to Unite Europe*, New York, 1958.

UNPUBLISHED THESES

Ashford, N., 'The Conservative Party and European Integration 1945–75', Ph.D. thesis, University of Warwick, 1983.

Forman, N., 'The European Movement in Great Britain, 1945–1954', M.Phil. thesis, University of Sussex, 1973.

Harrison, R.V., 'Winston Churchill and European Integration', D.Phil. thesis, University of Aberdeen, 1985.

Skår, S., 'The British Conservative Party and Supranational European Integration, 1948–1955', D.Phil. thesis, University of Oxford, 2000.

INDEX